Orality and the Scriptures
Composition, Translation, and Transmission

SIL International®
Publications in Translation and Textlinguistics
6

Publications in Translation and Textlinguistics is a peer-reviewed series published by SIL International®. The series is a venue for works concerned with all aspects of translation and textlinguistics, including translation theory, exegesis, pragmatics, and discourse analysis. While most volumes are authored by members of SIL, suitable works by others will also form part of the series.

Series Editors
Mike Cahill

Volume Editor
George Huttar

Production Staff
Bonnie Brown, Managing Editor
Judy Benjamin, Compositor
Barb Alber, Cover Design

Orality and the Scriptures
Composition, Translation, and Transmission

Ernst R. Wendland

SIL International®
Dallas, Texas

© 2013 by SIL International®
Library of Congress Catalog No: 2013944331
ISBN: 978-1-55671-298-2
ISSN: 1550-588X

Printed in the United States of America

All Rights Reserved.

No part of this publication may be reproduced, stored in a retrieval system, or transmitted in any form or by any means—electronic, mechanical, photocopy, recording, or otherwise—without the express permission of SIL International®. However, short passages, generally understood to be within the limits of fair use, may be quoted without permission.

Copies of this and other publications of SIL International® may be obtained from

SIL International Publications
7500 W. Camp Wisdom Road
Dallas, TX 75236-5629

Voice: 972-708-7404
Fax: 972-708-7363
publications_intl@sil.org
http://www.sil.org/resources/publications

Contents

Foreword ix
Introduction 1
I. ORIENTATION: Exploring the Dimensions of Orality in Relation to the Scriptures 9
1 Defining the Notion of "Orality" and Related Concepts 11
   1.1 On the essential orality of the Scriptures 11
   1.2 Overview 16
      1.2.1 Orality 18
      1.2.2 Scribality 21
      1.2.3 Literature 24
      1.2.4 Orature 26
      1.2.5 Performance 29
      1.2.6 Rhetoric 32
      1.2.7 Elocution 36
      1.2.8 Memory 38
      1.2.9 Tradition 45
      1.2.10 Multimodality 49
2 Methodologies for Investigating the Oral-Aural Analysis, Translation, and Transmission of Biblical Texts 53
   2.1 Overview 53
   2.2 Investigating orality 56
      2.2.1 Conversational analysis 57
      2.2.2 Relevance theory 58
      2.2.3 Speech act theory 60
      2.2.4 Argument-structure analysis 61

    2.2.5 Functionalist strategy..64
    2.2.6 Frames of reference..66
    2.2.7 Performance criticism...69
  2.3 Application of orality-oriented methodologies to Bible translation.......... 73
3 Two Models of Oral-Based Scripture Text Transmission................. 77
  3.1 Overview: A summary of the issue...77
  3.2 A more flexible model of text transmission 79
  3.3 A more restrained model of text transmission 91
  3.4 Some unresolved issues..103
  3.5 Text transmission in relation to Bible translation 106
II. DOCUMENTATION: Examining the Dimensions of Orality in Selected Texts of Scripture..113
4 "Hearing the Word of the LORD" (Isaiah 66:5): Amplifying the "Orality" of the Original Text in Translations of Scripture................. 115
  4.1 Overview...115
  4.2 Situating Isaiah 66:1–16 in its textual setting............................117
  4.3 A linguistic, literary-rhetorical analysis of Isaiah 66:1–16.......120
  4.4 Discourse display chart of Isaiah 66:1–16..................................124
  4.5 Summary of the strophic structure of Isaiah 66:1–16..............133
  4.6 The oral-aural basis and background of Isaiah 66:1–16 136
  4.7 Investigating the orality of the target language.......................142
  4.8 Re-oralizing the biblical text in translation................................145
  4.9 Testing the translation in public performance 156
  4.10 Conclusion: On the importance of orality for translation studies..... 160
5 Rhetorical Oral-Aural Dynamics of the Word: Revisiting John 17 ..165
  5.1 Overview...165
  5.2 Understanding John 17 from a "speech-act" perspective..................166
  5.3 Analysis: John 17 as a system of complementary textual structures...... 175
    5.3.1 Paradigmatic-topical analysis 176
    5.3.2 Syntagmatic-propositional analysis...178
    5.3.3 Poetic-architectonic analysis..181
  5.4 Rhetoric: The persuasive logic of the logotactic word in John 17 185
  5.5 Orality: Markers of a literary text's "rhythmic envelope"................188
  5.6 Display: The oral-elocutionary structure of John 17.........................192
  5.7 Implications: Seeking a rhetorical-poetic style for Bible translation....... 202
  5.8 Translation: An experiment in intertextual generic re-presentation....... 206
  5.9 Conclusion: Towards a more sight and sound sensitive translation 212
6 Modeling the Message: The Christological Core of Philippians (2:5–11) and Its Contemporary Communicative Implications......................217
  6.1 Overview...217
  6.2 Defining the epistolary epicenter of Philippians.......................218

Contents

- 6.3 Displaying the distinctive audio-visual structure of Philippians 2:5–11 .. 219
- 6.4 How does Philippians 2:5–11 relate to its cotext? 224
- 6.5 The epistolary-rhetorical organization of Philippians 228
- 6.6 The thematic composition of Philippians 233
- 6.7 A model of discourse: A literary-structural overview of Philippians 238
- 6.8 Modeling the message—another rhetorical perspective 250
- 6.9 Modeling the message in translation—An "oratorical" version of Philippians 2:5–11 258
- 6.10 Conclusion: Modeling the message in performance 263

III. APPLICATION: Discovering the Dimensions of Orality in Scripture Texts .. 265

7 Identifying and Displaying the Oral-Aural Dimension of Two Dramatic Biblical Texts 267
- 7.1 Introduction 267
- 7.2 Song of Songs 8 268
- 7.3 Revelation 5 277
- 7.4 Conclusion: Putting theory into practice 284

8 Notes on the "Sonic Structure" of Paul's Epistle to Philemon 287
- 8.1 Overview 287
- 8.2 Sonic structure display and commentary 288
- 8.3 Hearing and performing Paul for yourself 299

9 An Exercise in Poetic, Oral-Aural Analysis and Translation 301
- 9.1 Overview: The purpose of an applied study of 1 Corinthians 13 301
- 9.2 Analysis: Eight suggested steps for studying a biblical text 302
  - 9.2.1 Evaluate the text's "given" external boundaries plus any text-critical issues. 304
  - 9.2.2 Locate the chief "break points" within the text—its internal boundaries. 306
  - 9.2.3 Mark areas of key term/phrase repetition and parallelism. 307
  - 9.2.4 Determine places where important literary-rhetorical features converge. 308
  - 9.2.5 Do a lexical-semantic study of key terms and figurative expressions. 308
  - 9.2.6 Posit a structural-thematic outline for the entire text. 310
  - 9.2.7 Note the primary "speech acts" (illocutions) and "text act" (genre). 311
  - 9.2.8 Identify the major oral-aural characteristics of the text 312
- 9.3 Synthesis: Eight suggested steps for translating a biblical text 314
  - 9.3.1 Identify the intended audience for the translation 314
  - 9.3.2 Specify the primary purpose, medium, and principal setting of use. 315
  - 9.3.3 Determine the type of translation to be prepared. 316
  - 9.3.4 Outline a text-comparative translation methodology. 317

    9.3.5 Prepare an English draft translation on the basis of the prior analysis. 317
    9.3.6 Translate the same text in another language. 319
    9.3.7 Check the draft with added attention to its oral-aural dimension. 319
    9.3.8 Indicate how the translation will be tested after publication.... 321
  9.4 A final exercise—1 Cor 13:7 322
  9.5 Implications: Practicing what you preach.. 332

10 Giving "Voice" to the Ancient Orality of the Scriptures Today 335
  10.1 The challenge... 335
  10.2 Seven suggestions 336
    10.2.1 Analysis.. 337
    10.2.2 Testing 339
    10.2.3 Publishing.. 341
    10.2.4 Research... 342
    10.2.5 Scripting... 344
    10.2.6 Training 345
    10.2.7 Networking 346
  10.3 Orality—beyond the written Word 349
  10.4 Conclusion—a meditation: "in defense of listening".................... 354

References 357
Index 377

Foreword

Stories, songs, and speeches move us; instructions, reports, and histories do not. Yet not all stories, songs, or speeches are equally moving, and there are a host of reasons why this is so. A story's *manner of production* alone can make a critical difference.[1] Compare, for example, written narrative productions and oral narrative productions. Both production types typically share many common communicative properties, and so share many common communicative effects. Their distinctive manners of production, however, prompt distinctive effects in human experience. Our critique of the socio-cultural merits of these distinctives—consciously or unconsciously—varies according to the degree to which these distinctives effect our communicative purposes. And according to Ernie Wendland, as argued in this present volume, if contemporary practitioners of biblical "interpretation, translation, and transmission" would more fully effect the communicative purposes of biblical authors, more "serious consideration" should be devoted to "the crucial *soundscape* of biblical compositions." By "soundscape," Wendland means the "oral-aural" phenomena that have continually informed the historical record and performance of verbal discourse and composition. My own experience with such oral-aural phenomena profoundly resonates with Wendland's conviction, even and especially in wildly different socio-cultural contexts.

As an ethnomusicologist, I am, perhaps, more easily persuaded to Wendland's cause, for there are many parallels between the study of ancient "oral literature" and ancient oral music traditions. For musicologists, "serious consideration" of the sonic dimensions of human behavior and experience is

---

[1] The notion of a discourse's "manner of production" is taken from Chapters 1–4 in Robert A. Dooley and Stephen H. Levinsohn's *Analyzing Discourse: A Manual of Basic Concepts*. Dallas, Tex: SIL International, 2001.

assumed. Not all readers of this volume, however, need to be so predisposed. The strength of Wendland's argument is still amply persuasive, especially to those who will not only *read* Wendland's description *about* the "rich oral artistry" of biblical literature, but heed his advice, follow his "re-oralization" pedagogy, and so, reactivate and experience some of biblical orality's effects firsthand.

The importance of actually hearing certain communicative phenomena is nowhere more plain to me than when I teach introductory music history courses. No student would ever register for such a course, if word got around that all the prof was going to do was *talk* about music and song. For as someone once said, "talking about music is like dancing about architecture." For what can be uniquely known through musically organized sound is best, if not exclusively, known through the experience of listening to it, not reading or talking about it. Music history courses, then, are typically replete with audio-visual recordings, and when possible, live performances. Similarly, whenever I lecture on oral verbal arts—song, story, oratory, and the like—it is never adequate to lecture on these traditions by simply describing their socio-cultural contexts or by conducting a literary analysis of a transcribed lyrical, narrative, or rhetorical text. Again, audio-visual recordings, or even live oral performances, are central to every study. For just as a recipe is no substitute for a sauce, transcribed lyrics or printed texts are no substitutes for sung songs, or told tales.

That said, when it comes to gaining first-hand knowledge of the sonic nature of *ancient* oral traditions, students of the literature and music of antiquity are particularly disadvantaged. Living memory, electronic recordings and the music notation systems of post-antiquity provide no direct access to ancient soundscapes. Still, traces do exist. Researchers from a number of disciplines cumulatively infer and deduce sonic data from numerous artifacts, beginning with extant phonograms, phonetic alphabets, punctuation signs, and neumatic symbols from numerous verbal and musical writing systems. Other researchers also gather evidence from archeological sites of ancient performing arts; or ancient writings *about* music, singing, chanting, reciting, or orating; or iconographies depicting oratorical events, oratorical aids, and orators, musical events, musical instruments, and musicians; or physical specimens of ancient musical instruments, intact or fragmented.

In recent years, for example, in a region of caves in southwestern Germany, archeologists have excavated the remains of a number of ancient flutes. One such flute, a 35,000-year-old, bird-wing-bone flute, is said to be "the world's oldest musical instrument."[2] Researchers from a number of disciplines

---

[2] Robert Lee Hotz, "Magic Flute: Primal Find Sings of Music's Mystery" in *Wall Street Journal: Science Journal,* 2009. http://online.wsj.com/article/SB124656639970388165.html?mod=slideshow_overlay_mod (accessed 11 november 2011).

(archeology, anthropology, biology, neurobiology, etc.) have weighed in on this fascinating discovery. Some of the scientists, however, were not content to speculate exclusively on what they could *see*. As a result, on at least one occasion, music researchers painstakingly reconstructed a less fragile replica from the scattered remains of one of the ancient flutes, and then, played it. The ancient instrument's dormant sonic capacities *re-sounded*, and most importantly, its essential tones were *heard*. The sequence of tones that resulted from their experimental playing techniques could not, of course, begin to reveal the full melodic and rhythmic potential of the instrument. Nonetheless, in the semiotic "chain" of signifying forms that give rise to any sonic experience, knowledge of the basic physical form of that ancient instrument—its organic properties, its length and diameter, its beveled mouthpiece, and especially the fixed proportional distances of its five flint-carved fingerholes—went a long way toward understanding and experiencing both the limits and potential of its correlating sonic forms.

The communication of particular sonic forms and their experiential effects is contingent, however, upon many more correlating forms than merely those of the vibrating material forms that produce them. Indeed, had researchers in those German caves discovered song lyrics on ancient scrolls, instead of the remains of an ancient musical instrument, literary forms would have been analyzed instead of organological forms. And if the analytical approach advocated and modeled by Ernie Wendland in this present study had been applied to such literary forms, the fruit of that research would have been no less "resounding." For Wendland's treatment of ancient texts, artistic biblical texts in particular, does not just seek to preserve the past, or simply "learn from" the past, but to reinvigorate the latent oral performance properties lying dormant in those ancient written forms.

Throughout this book, Wendland progressively, and with increasing intensity, draws our attention to an enormous number of detailed examples of the manifold poetic and rhetorical phenomena encoded in biblical orature. The cumulative effect of these detailed examples builds a powerful case for the necessity of recognizing and exploiting the expressive nature and potential of biblical oral arts. Clearly, oral verbal arts communicate much more than "mere words." As Wendland puts it, they also "animate hearts." The reader, however, should not mistake Wendland's zeal for the expressive nature of the Sacred Scriptures as yet another postmodern fixation on subjective human experience. To be sure, the words of biblical stories, songs, and hortatory are *artistically* formulated words; that is, they do not simply employ the ordinary language and patterns of everyday speech, but rather, employ extra-ordinary patterns of speech and manners of speaking. These extra-ordinary formalizations, in turn, signal extra-ordinary effects, expressive effects: attitudes, feelings, sentiments, tone. But Wendland makes it clear that these special forms of discourse do not exclusively function expressively. These same artistic forms are also supremely well suited, even vital, for clarifying semantic meaning. This meaning-making function is most evident when particular words, phrases, actions, and themes are orally highlighted or brought into focus by extra-ordinary intonational patterns, rhythmic segmentations, contrastive dynamics, or inflected speech registers. Oral manners of production, then, do not simply intensify expression, they also clarify thought.[3] And as Wendland insists, "Where poetry is concerned, sound not only enhances, it also constitutes meaning!" Thus, semantic-oriented, "meaning-based" practitioners of biblical interpretation, translation, and transmission will find little comfort in this book for neglecting "serious consideration of the crucial soundscape of biblical compositions." They will, however, find considerable help in re-creating some of the same biblical soundscapes for contemporary audiences that generated so much of the vital artistic expression, "persuasive force," and clarity of meaning that audiences surely experienced through the Scriptures "when publicly proclaimed millennia ago."

Daniel Fitzgerald

---

[3] Fitzgerald, Dan, "Oral Verbal Arts," in Brian Schrag (ed.), *Researching and Creating Together*. Pasadena: William Carey Press, forthcoming.

Introduction: "Proclaiming the Word Fearlessly"

I am proposing "proclaiming the Word fearlessly" as a secondary title for this volume which discusses the oral-oriented analysis, translation, and transmission of Scripture. This expression derives from Philippians 1:14, with the key verb transposed from v. 15: ἀφόβως τὸν λόγον κηρύσσειν. My study—actually, a collection of them—focuses upon the manifold process of communicating the Word of God, that is, the Former (Hebrew) and Latter (Greek) Christian Scriptures in diverse contextual settings. "Proclaiming" suggests the use of an oral-aural text, and this *phonic* dimension will receive special attention throughout the book. Accordingly, the *orality* factor will be considered from several different perspectives, including analyses that highlight the influence of sound in the original composition of the biblical documents, and also its relevance today we seek to convey those same sacred texts in a correspondingly dynamic manner in other languages as well as via various media of message transmission.[1]

---

[1] The importance of "sound" in the ultimate creation and maintenance of the universe has been suggested in the theory of "cymatics" (Jenny 1967); thus, "we live in a universe influenced and kept in concert by sound frequencies" (Pretorius 2011:5). In this book I argue for the fundamentality of sound in the formation and

That leaves the adverb "fearlessly," which the Apostle Paul happens to emphasize in this passage, but how does that specific quality fit in with the subject matter of this book? In the given context, Paul obviously had the Christian Gospel in mind (Phil 1:12–14), with the implication that believers must not refrain or shirk from courageously sharing their faith despite the prevailing adverse social, political, and religious pressures that surrounded them, including persecution (1:29–30). Such apostolic encouragement is needed just as much nowadays for individuals as well as entire religious communities. But my subtitle applies the use of "fearlessly" in a figurative or transferred sense with reference to our contemporary manner or mode of communicating the Scriptures. Thus in keeping with what is most appropriate in the context, we must boldly, even daringly under certain circumstances, make use of all the media and message delivery systems that are available to convey the Word today, especially the many "non-traditional," non-print techniques and tools at our disposal— MP3 downloads, Bluetooth technology, satellite radio, enhanced interactive websites, electronic tablets, and cellphone "apps." Clearly, in the case of most of these resources, the factor of *audio* transmission and *aural* reception will feature very prominently.

This particular emphasis on the sense of sound is brought out in the book's primary title: *Orality and the Scriptures: Composition, translations, and transmission*. How then do these essential activities relate to each other? With "analysis" I am referring to a careful examination of the Bible's received canonical text, making use of several, possibly new methods of discourse study that seek to reveal more fully certain aspects of its orality-mediated structural, artistic, and rhetorical character. "Translation" then takes up the obvious (but often underestimated) necessity of re-presenting the primary sense, sentiment, and significance of the diverse documents of Scripture in other languages, sociocultural settings, and cognitive (worldview) environments. Finally, the process of "transmission" (a 'sending across') has a twofold focus—first of all, the methods and means whereby the biblical text, after its original expression, was preserved and transferred from one generation to the next (the early history of which we know very little about). Then, as already suggested, the activity of transmitting

---

transmission of Scripture, both in the original languages and in all subsequent languages of translation.

Introduction: "Proclaiming the Word Fearlessly"

the text also has a vital contemporary application. The term "Scriptures" refers to texts that have been written in some (semi) permanent form, but my study underscores the influence of orality in their initial creation as well as in their continued accurate and acceptable articulation today in a modern world where diversity is the norm and the whole concept of "meaning" is roundly debated.[2] In any case, the point is that the oral-aural medium of communication is becoming increasingly more important as a means of delivery to complement the purely visible words on pages of print.

The two major questions which the ten chapters in this volume therefore seek to address are these: What do we mean by the term "orality," and what does this notion have to do with analyzing, translating, and transmitting the written Scriptures? In other words, how does the oral/aural dimension of communication serve to give us a new, indeed, a sharper perception of, and appreciation for the various literary (artistic and rhetorical) features of the biblical writings and of their associated semantic and pragmatic (moral-spiritual) implications? I trust that the varied approaches to the text discussed in the following chapters will help to clarify and popularize some of the diverse facets of the broad field of *orality studies* as they impact upon our understanding and dissemination of the Hebrew Bible (Old Testament) as well as the Greek New Testament.

In the chapters that follow, the four interrelated facets of the biblical text outlined above are considered in both general and specific terms. There is thus a focus upon the original *composition*, on the one hand, as well as its

---

[2] Richard Horsley makes the following interesting observation on the notion of "text" in relation to (or, in suspended animation, as it were, between) the oral and written channels of communication: "Conceptually, once we back away from the modern print-cultural definition of scripture, it is more satisfactory and more historically accurate to say that the text of scripture functioned as much (or more) in scribal memory and oral recitation as in (but not independent of) writing on scrolls. Correspondingly the term 'text' then would refer to the contents that are learned and recited as well as written on scrolls (as in older usage; see OED; and compare the Latin textus, that which has been woven, texture, and even context; also the Greek verb rhaptô, 'to stitch,' behind the compound rhapsôdeô, 'to recite')" (2010:96). I might just add from my perspective that, while the text of Scripture may have "functioned" in this way during the process of communication, its authoritative foundation, or point of departure and normative source, once divinely delivered, was always the written word, from beginning (e.g., Exod 17:14) to end (e.g., Rev 21:5).

subsequent *analysis, translation, transmission,* and—adding an important fifth factor—the qualitative *testing* of the various products of translation. The individual books of the Bible were undoubtedly created and circulated within a pervasive ancient oral and aural sociocultural environment. This foundational fact must, first of all, influence the current manner and method whereby one studies these biblical texts in terms of their manifest form, content, and function. The worldwide task of translating the Scriptures is likewise affected by the new, enhanced perspectives on "meaning" that an orality-oriented study provides. So is the ongoing process of transmission since this, as in the original event, is carried out predominantly today by means of some audio (+/– visual) device. And finally, the manifold factor of orality also concerns the constant research and testing of printed as well as non-print Scripture versions that must be carried out to ensure that they are communicating effectively and acceptably—including aurally—with their intended audiences. A variety of important attributes of this complex interactional endeavor will be described and exemplified in this book with reference to a selection of key biblical texts, poetic as well as prosaic.

The individual chapters of this book fall into three general groups. In *Part One*, ORIENTATION, I offer an initial overview that aims to introduce readers to some of the principal aspects of the diverse domain of "orality studies," beginning with a survey of a selection of key terms and related fields in this multidisciplinary approach (ch. 1). This leads to a review of some helpful methodologies that are frequently employed in its scholarly exploration (ch. 2), and a discussion of several contrastive perspectives regarding the nature and effects of orality with regard to composing and transmitting the disparate source texts of Scripture (ch. 3).

This is followed in *Part Two*, DOCUMENTATION, by a set of three individual "case studies," which present full-text analyses that expound and illustrate an oral-oriented, structural-stylistic, literary-rhetorical approach to the biblical document at hand—that is, Isaiah 66 (ch. 4), John 17 (ch. 5), and the Philippian epistle (ch. 6).

In *Part Three*, APPLICATION, I encourage readers to engage more closely with my analysis of the biblical text by offering four additional passages to critically consider from an oral-aural "soundpoint"—first, a preliminary study of two vividly imagistic lyric pericopes (Song of Songs 8, Revelation 5) (ch. 7). Next, the detailed "sonic structure" of Paul's personal appeal to Philemon is set forth (ch. 8), with a special view towards revealing the letter's characteristic phonological features, an exercise which supports, in turn, a corresponding contemporary "oratorical" translation of the Apostle's persuasive petition. The ninth chapter challenges readers to put their own competence and creativity into practice with special reference to the sound-based elements of a biblical text in a directed exercise aimed at analyzing and translating the well-known theological lyric on Christian "love" (*agape*), 1 Corinthians 13.

The final chapter (10) concludes by offering a number of suggestions intended to stimulate and to encourage the application of an orality-based methodology, one which seeks to achieve a more precise understanding that results in an accurate, yet also artistic transmission of the Bible in today's media-rich world of communication. The overall intention is to "re-oralize" the practice of Scripture interpretation and translation, no matter what type of version is envisioned or the medium of transmission being used in the process. I end with some closing thoughts on the relevance of orality for studies of contemporary Scripture engagement and use, especially in public assembly as the Holy Word is read, recited, chanted, sung, and otherwise proclaimed aloud in the communal hearing of the "people of God."

A solid foundation for the various topics discussed in this volume, in particular the prominence of the sound dimension in Scripture analysis and translation, has been laid by the excellent presentation in James Maxey's (2009) recent book, *From Orality to Orality*. I have preceded the present study with several books in this same area of academic investigation, for example with reference to the OT prophets and the NT epistles (Wendland 2009, 2008b). The goal now is to broaden and in certain respects also to sharpen my earlier perspective on the basis of additional text analyses and readings in the ever expanding field of orality studies and, more specifically, "performance criticism" (Hearon and Ruge-Jones 2009; Wire 2011). The purpose of this volume then is to present the results of my recent research, which has clearly benefitted from the insights of others, to whom I am most grateful, even in cases where I do not always agree with their conclusions regarding the compositional history and character of the biblical writings that have come down to us. I have included a rather large number of footnotes, in order to cut down on the amount of technical information given in the main text and to streamline the various arguments presented there.

The footnotes also direct readers to additional topics, resources, and areas of study that pertain in particular to orality and related subjects.

My paramount objective is, as in prior publications, twofold: first of all, to draw attention to the rich verbal *artistry* and rhetorical *power* that is abundantly evident in the literature of Scripture. Second, I wish to encourage, whenever conditions and circumstances allow, a re-creation of the same beauty of *poetic* expression and *persuasive* force in our contemporary Bible translations. The distinctive contribution of the present volume is to advocate that such dynamic re-productions also take into serious consideration the crucial *soundscape* of biblical compositions so that they might similarly resound in the ears (and accordingly animate the hearts) of audiences today as they must have done when publicly proclaimed millennia ago. This book has as its primary readership those who are actually engaged in the practice of Scripture interpretation, translation, and transmission—so that "in every way...Christ is proclaimed" (καταγγέλλεται, Phil 1:17). But it is hoped that many aspects of this exploration will also be of interest to scholars, as well as a source of information for advanced students who are currently working in orality studies and related fields of intercultural, cross-media communication. The same principles apply to all literary texts, whether religious or secular in nature—wherever a specific high-value document must be conveyed audibly and meaningfully from one text and/or medium to another.[3] With these purposes in view, and to conclude my introduction, the following quotations from some recognized experts in the field of orality studies and secular literary translation respectively seem appropriate:

> Translators are potentially helped by the fact that much of the Bible was intended for oral reading and therefore has extensive oral features embedded in its text. The identification and retention of these features can enable a translation to be more accessible to listeners. The beauty of language, of course, requires the contribution of translators and their culture. (Thomas and Thomas 2006:72; see also Thomas 1990)

---

[3] The designation "high-value" may include what Carr terms "long-duration literature," which he defines as "texts—usually viewed in some way as particularly archaic/ancient, inspired/holy, and obscure/inaccessible—that are passed from generation to generation, transcending whatever their original time-bound contexts might be and being consumed by generation after generation" (2010:18).

> Any translation should—make that *must*—be read aloud for sonority. Sound is paramount to poets, and more that one translator has been told by the SL poet, 'When it's impossible to preserve both meaning and sound, go with the sound.' Although not all poems (both translations and originals) that sound good *are* good, it's a pretty safe bet that a translation that sounds bad is, well, bad. (Landers 2001:100)[4]

In closing, there are several important *acknowledgements* that I need to make: To *Dr. David Rhoads* (Emeritus Professor of New Testament at the Lutheran School of Theology at Chicago), Series Editor for the *Biblical Performance Criticism Series* (Cascade Books)—for his detailed critical comments and suggestions based on an initial draft of this text; to *Dr. Daniel Fitzgerald* (Ethnomusicologist, and Oral Strategies Consultant for The Seed Company, Arlington, TX) for his equally helpful critique, including many proposed suggestions for stylistic improvement, and indeed, for his insightful Foreword to this volume; to *Dr. George Huttar* for his excellent editing work; to *Dr. Mike Cahill*, Editor-in-chief of SIL Academic Publications, for his support of the present study; to *Lois Gourley* and other SIL International production staff for their invaluable help in bringing this volume to the light of print. None of the preceding individuals is responsible for any errors or infelicities that remain in the present text; that is solely my responsibility.

The Scripture quotations in chapters 4 and 5 are taken from *The Holy Bible, English Standard Version*, copyright © 2001 by Crossway Bibles, a division of Good News Publishers. Used by permission. All rights reserved.

As always, I very much appreciate any sort of feedback regarding the content of this book and the various issues discussed; please direct these to me at erwendland@hotmail.com or wendland@gmail.com.

Epiphany 2012

---

[4] Of course, when translating the Scriptures one cannot downplay the meaning of the text in preference to its sonority. However, the point is still valid that a poor-sounding translation probably has a number of things that need fixing in terms of form, if not content.

I. ORIENTATION

Exploring the Dimensions of Orality in Relation to the Scriptures

1

Defining the Notion of "Orality" and Related Concepts

1.1 On the essential orality of the Scriptures[1]

When one thinks of Scriptures—whether the Jewish *Tanakh*, the Muslim *Koran*, or the Christian *Bible*—a carefully printed sacred book normally comes to mind. Indeed, the word "Scripture" (Lat. *scriptura*) literally refers to a text that has been "written" down, originally by hand, but now by any available means that renders words visible—hence legible and readable—on some physical surface.[2] However, past and present research has revealed two very significant facts about these ancient "holy books":

---

[1] Chapters 1–3 and 7 are derived from a paper that I presented in part at the SBL Annual Meeting in Atlanta in November 2010. The original study was my attempt to supplement and further develop various ideas on the subject of orality, performance, and Bible translation that I expressed in a preliminary way in Wendland 2008a, and then more fully in Wendland 2008b.

[2] There are of course various types of sacred text (narratives about God/the gods, songs, dramas, prayers, etc.) which exist only in oral form, that is, within an ancient memory and performance tradition; see for example, the various essays in Wendland and Hachibamba 2007.

- In most cases their constituent texts were first generated orally in public performance and then written down, immediately on the spot or, more likely, at a later date, either by a designated scribe or by the original speaker. Alternatively, these texts were composed in private by an author, probably as he (less likely "she") actually spoke the words aloud, and always with some sort of an eventual oral-aural proclamation in mind.[3]

- After their creation, these sacred documents circulated in a textual environment and a social setting that were characterized by a dynamic orality which,[4] as will be shown, left its mark on their structure, style, and to a certain extent their content as well. And though they now exist in a more stable (unalterable), authoritative (i.e., canonical) written form, the texts are more frequently accessed and transmitted via some setting-determined sonic medium of communication—that is, by the human voice and/or through instrumental means, e.g., radio, TV, CD/DVD recording, cell phone, MP3 player.

One concludes from this research that although our primary point of reference may be a printed document, where the Scriptures are concerned, the *phonic* factor—the meaningful use of sound in discourse—cannot be ignored. On the contrary, the potential influence from phenomena involving orality must be duly considered. This is first applicable when analyzing any originally written composition for exegetical understanding—that is, to determine the source text's intended meaning, its formally inscribed hermeneutical "clues"—and second, when evaluating the best way of communicating its sense and significance to a contemporary audience or readership.

The term "orality" refers generally to the characteristic modes of thought[5] and verbal expression in societies that depend for communication

---

[3] For some background information and documentation regarding these assertions, see Wendland 2008b:1–56.

[4] To highlight this point, we may note that an alternative designation for the Hebrew Scriptures is *Miqra* (מקרא), "that which is read (recited, chanted, sung, etc.)."

[5] The mode of thinking in primarily oral-aural societies is arguably more fully attuned to receiving, processing, and responding to sensory information directly from the so-called physical "world of nature" than print- and/or electronics-oriented societies are.

essentially upon the spoken word, accompanied by various associated nonverbal techniques, such as gestures, facial features, and body movements. Thus, the skills derived from literacy (notably reading and writing) are perhaps unavailable, unfamiliar to, or unused by most of the population. Typical communication strategies in primarily oral-aural settings would thus capitalize on specific sense-based "memory technologies" and prominent verbal stylistic techniques, such as structured repetition, graphic imagery,[6] temporal or spatial sequencing, and standard formulas. These devices, and more, are all available in order to help recall and revitalize culturally critical texts with varying degrees of precision, depending on the nature of the composition and the social occasion at hand. Assorted "performance directions" might also be given in the case of "sensitive" or especially significant (e.g., religious) messages to coach speakers with regard to how to incorporate the various non-verbal elements mentioned earlier. Such variable, pragmatic traits of message transmission during a performance would include, for example, what sort of hand-arm motions to use to indicate special emphasis or specific feelings and attitudes, such as joy, anger, sorrow, shame, or sincerity.

It was once thought that strictly oral creations displayed a verbal style that was very different from written texts. For example, in addition to the features indicated above (repetition, graphic imagery, and conventional constituent ordering), oral texts manifested a variety of other mnemonic attributes that would promote memorability, memorizability, and effective recall, for example: a paratactic, rhythmic, additive style (e.g., Genesis 1); formulaic language in conventional thematic settings (e.g., "This is what the LORD says...//...declares the LORD" in Amos); much redundancy and structural reiteration (e.g., Numbers 1); highly polarized, agonistic and antithetical thought patterns (e.g., Deuteronomy 28); empathetic and participatory discourse, with a great deal of direct speech (e.g., Numbers 16); content that tends to be concrete and situational, rather than abstract or theoretical (e.g., Exodus 25).[7]

---

[6] In African languages, for example, the "ideophone" is a phonologically distinct and expressive, even dramatic "part of speech" that may be used as a complete predication to convey various attitudes, impressions, sensations, and emotions in addition to conceptually evoking virtually any of life's experiences or one's personal perceptions (cf. Noss 2001).

[7] These qualities are discussed in Ong 1982:33–57.

However, as has just been noted, these same typically "oral" properties are also abundantly exhibited throughout the literature of the Scriptures—and corresponding NT passages could be found to match those listed from the OT. Furthermore, my research in traditional African oral and published texts would indicate that most of these stylistic devices (excluding exact repetition) are found in great density and diversity also in popular, well-composed written literary genres (Wendland 1979:ch. 8). Why should this be the case? In societies today that are characterized by a vibrant, "persistent" orality,[8] that is, those which have been exposed to, but have not fully accepted, adapted to, or adopted writing and print, many functionally effective verbal modes and manners of expression commonly found in strictly oral discourse will find their way also into dynamic literary compositions of all types.[9] Furthermore, skilled authors might deliberately choose to include relatively more of these stylistic qualities as a means of creatively compensating for the loss of immediate, face-to-face contact with an audience and the ability to employ non-verbal means of communication. This would be especially important at certain critical places in the text, such as introductions and conclusions, sectional boundaries, thematic peak points, and areas where strong personal feelings, opinions, and attitudes are being expressed.

---

[8] I am using the term "persistent" in preference to "residual orality" (Ong ibid., 29), which seems to suggest something merely "left over" or remaining without much functionality. In addition, such usage appears to indicate some sort of clearly defined dichotomy and to privilege written communication over oral discourse as being the normal, unmarked, or "default," mode (I owe this observation to Dan Fitzgerald).

[9] With reference to the Hebrew narrative, Miller offers another possibility, namely, that such features may be identified as "folk motifs" or "orally derived bits" within the written text (2011:73, 78), for example, "'gobbets,' intentionally crafted *aides-mémoires* that are constitutive for narration, such as storylines, images of situations, cliché, numeric schemes, visual metaphors, and parallelism. Prominent linguistic devices include paronomasia, redundant pronominal and deictic usage, and archaisms (ibid., 79–80). Yet as Miller himself notes, one should be "very wary" of trying to identify (ibid., 78) such apparently obvious oralisms in any written text. These so-called "gobbets" are analogous to the general *gnomai*, or maxims, and *chreiai* of NT rhetoric (and its criticism). A chreia can be defined as a memorable "saying or action that is expressed concisely, attributed to a character, and regarded as useful for living" (Hock and O'Neill 1986:26)—and, we might add, for use in formal oral and written discourse.

1.1 On the essential orality of the Scriptures

The preceding introductory remarks apply to "Scripture," the Hebrew Bible as well as the Greek New Testament, also with respect to the influence of orality within another crucial dimension of the communication process, namely, the manner of textual *transmission*. A religious composition, whether oral or in written form, is one that normally needs to be accessed by, or conveyed to its adherents on a regular basis in various venues and formats. It is the word of God to humanity concerning his will and his ways, containing diverse didactic as well as hortatory (admonitory and encouraging), persuasive, consolatory, predictive, etc. messages, as the prevailing situation or occasion dictates. The problem in ANE (Ancient Near Eastern) times was that writing was an extremely difficult, time-consuming, and hence also expensive procedure. Therefore, everything was done to conserve space on the scarce writing material available; a typical scroll, for example, or later book-like codex or tablet reveals no word or sentence breaks and few, if any punctuation marks. As a result texts, especially the scrolls, were very difficult to read directly from the document itself, and accordingly it was often necessary for them to be initially internalized and proclaimed at least partially from memory before significant public gatherings such as for worship or religious instruction. The written text then served as the authoritative point of reference for both memorizing a certain passage and also for preserving the sacred tradition; it was this remembered "text on the heart" then that served as the generative source on most occasions of actual transmission. In summary, as David Carr has observed:[10]

> The written text [including various religious texts such as the developing Hebrew Scriptures], whether readable by many or not, provides both an emblem of continuity and a stable means for ensuring the stability of the cultural formation into the next generation...Most cultural usage of written traditions has involved significant elements of both oral performance and cognitive mastery...[Thus, there was a continual] interplay of the oral and the written in the performance and transmission of ancient literature, along with the achievement—at least among the chief tradents of the cultural tradition—of cognitive mastery of that tra-

---

[10] Carr 2005:285, 288, 300; material in brackets added; with specific reference to the memorization of literary-religious texts in ancient Israel, see Deut 6:6–9; 31:19, 22, 30; 32:44–46; Ps 40:7–8; Prov 3:3; 7:3; Isa 30:8–9; Ezek 2:9–3:3.

dition. The ideal, at least, was the writing of the tradition "on the tablet of the heart," whether or not many people in a given time achieved that ideal.... Certain types of long-duration texts found in written form—whether on tablet, papyrus, or parchment—were intended to be used primarily for writing on the mind and hearts of elite students, a memorization reinforced through poetry and musical modes and demonstrated and corrected through the use of written copies.

The preceding citation also stresses several key themes—for example, oral performance, writing, and textual transmission—that will be taken up from various analytical perspectives in the theoretical discussion and several detailed text studies that are presented in this book. These topics will be considered in particular from the point of view of Bible translation, that is, a multifaceted enterprise that is devoted to promoting a continuation of sacred tradition via diverse media in the multitude of languages and cultures in the world today.

1.2 Overview

The broadly based exploratory investigation embarked upon in this book focuses on the manifold subject of "orality" as it pertains to the contemporary analysis, translation, transmission, and popular engagement of the ancient texts of Scripture. A key question that arises throughout my study is this: Are the various texts of Scripture the *result* of the stimulus of orality (i.e., they were originally orally composed and later written down), the communicative *goal* within a contextual setting permeated by orality (i.e., texts written under the influence of orality), or a compositional mixture of both types of influence? It is advisable not to be dogmatic regarding this issue since the available evidence, normally scarce to begin with, may often be interpreted in one way or the other.[11]

---

[11] J. Verheyden gives a specific example to illustrate this point with regard to the alleged Gospel precursor "Q": "Draper (and Horsley) seem to accept only one mode, that of 'the scribal transcription of a performed event' that is 'frozen into' a text. They do not really take into account the possibility of an author 'composing in the oral traditional manner,' in view of the oral performance that he knew was the common mode of communicating his written message. In short, how can one tell for sure if the 'sound map' and aural elements that Horsley and Draper are keen to discover in the Q material in Matthew and in Luke are remnants of an originally oral composition and not the result of an author accommodating to the way his text

1.2 Overview

In order to orient readers to some of the key specifics of this subject, I present below a brief descriptive survey of several core concepts, noting along the way a selection of significant works in this rapidly developing, interdisciplinary field. This overview introduces some of the main topics in the area of orality studies, with special reference to the theory and practice of Bible translation. The subject of orality in general is a major area of current biblical research and writing, where this vital aspect of communication is becoming increasingly important and more overtly demonstrated,[12] especially with regard to the New Testament and to a somewhat lesser extent to the Old Testament.[13]

Earlier studies focused largely on the nature, interpretation, and transmission of the biblical text,[14] but in the past few years greater attention is also being devoted to the influence of orality in the translation and reception of vernacular Scriptures. First-rate expositions of these latter developments already exist in print,[15] so there is no need for me to reiterate this excellent material. In this chapter I will summarize my understanding of a selection of nine key concepts that pertain to the broad subject of "orality": scribality, literature, orature, performance, rhetoric, elocution, memory, tradition, and multimodality. These will hopefully provide an introductory "frame of reference" for some of the central issues which this book

---

will be used?" (Verheyden 2008:349). Thus, with reference to the Synoptic tradition, Dunn claims that "[s]pecialists are largely agreed that a common feature of oral tradition is 'the same yet different': retellings of the same story or teaching but with different details that the storyteller or teacher deemed appropriate in the delivery or performance" (2011:157). But how does such a theory jibe with what Luke himself writes about his methodology in the prologue to his gospel (Luke 1:1–4; cf. Acts 1:1)? According to the Evangelist, he was the sole person responsible for the composition of his gospel, whether he happened to make use of oral or written "sources."

[12] The inclusion of extensive pointing (both vowelization and marks of cantillation) in Masoretic Hebrew suggests that the "Old Testament" Scriptures include primarily oral/aural documents. Further evidence is given by the ancient tradition of public readings (or chantings) of the Torah and later also the Haftarah (from the Prophets, the Nǝbî'îm).

[13] For some prominent New Testament studies in the field of orality, see: Horsley, Draper, and Foley 2006; Kelber 2007, Hearon and Ruge-Jones 2009. Several influential Old Testament studies include: Doan and Giles 2005, Giles and Doan 2009; van der Toorn 2007.

[14] For example, Kelber 1983.

[15] For example, see Rhoads 2006a, b; Maxey 2009.

proposes to discuss and illustrate from a multidisciplinary and practice-oriented perspective.[16]

1.2.1 Orality

I have not as yet found a concise definition for the multifaceted concept of "orality," which is the focal point of the present study.[17] In any case, I view this term as referring to three primary sectors of scholarly research with respect to *performance style* in terms of the modes of communication (a) within a particular society, (b) within all oral texts in a certain language, and/or (c) reflected in the oral traits manifested in written documents. To explain:

> a. The notion of orality may be taken to refer in general to semiotic behavior and the various verbal and non-verbal attributes, including the exceptional sensory perceptiveness, memory capacity, and performance skills, of an entire society. Its members thus normally prefer in large measure to orally communicate texts of all types—formal and informal, religious and secular, artistic and mundane. This would include, for example, a typical "story-telling session" within a rural African community, including all the features that distinguish such a public event (who, when, where, why, how long, which order, etc.).[18]

---

[16] The different terms being considered in this section pertain to the so-called "*textual* frame of reference," which is conceptually linked in turn with a number of other macro-frames of reference (mental models) within the thought-world of a given ethnic or speech community, e.g., the *cognitive* (worldview related), *sociocultural* (pertaining to a people's traditions, customs, institutions, and way-of-life), *organizational* (having to do with social roles and responsibilities), and *conversational* (primary speech acts and events) conceptual constructs (see Wilt and Wendland 2008).

[17] The following is concise, but not particularly enlightening: "Orality refers to the experience of words (and speech) in the habitat of sound" (Botha 1990:40, cited in Maxey 2009:116).

[18] In this connection, we must keep in mind the fact that "cognitive anthropologists themselves have rejected universal dichotomies in which literate societies were contrasted with illiterate societies in oppositions like rational versus traditional and abstract versus concrete thinking" (de Vries 2008:300; cf. Ong 1982:36–77). Instead, global postulations such as this must be "replaced by more limited hypotheses about local, culture-specific cognitive effects of writing systems" (de Vries ibid., 300).

b. More specifically, orality refers to the distinctive oral-aural properties of language that characterize the diverse verbal genres of a given speech community (cf. point (a) above), which are originally composed and transmitted orally (spoken, recited, chanted, sung, etc.). An example would be the features which characterize the Chewa nthano ("folktale" with included choral refrains) tradition of eastern Zambia.[19]

c. Most specifically, orality refers to the prominent oral structural and stylistic features that remain in evidence ("voiceprints") when particular oral texts (cf. (b) above) are written down for dissemination and/or preservation.[20] The term may also designate those characteristics which are typically reproduced when written texts are composed with eventual oral utterance ("performance") in mind,[21] for

---

[19] Again, it is worth noting in this diagnostic effort the caution that "[t]he characteristics of primary orality as additive-paratactic, redundant, formulaic, bound to concrete contexts and so on…seem to result from universalistic projections on these societies of pictures from various academic debates such as the Homeric debate, the debate of written versus oral style in English and the anthropological debate on cognitive dichotomies in terms of literate versus illiterate societies" (de Vries 2008:303). Comparisons of oral versus written style in artistic compositions must normally be reported in terms of localized tendencies or degrees. In other words, there may be considerably more (or less) of a certain linguistic feature, for example, exact repetition, use of the present tense, ideophones, in oral as opposed to written texts within a particular corpus of oral and written literature (orature). But even then, the actual percentages in a given instance may vary outside the norms due to the influence of genre, communicative purpose, paralinguistic features, the medium or setting of use, and so forth.

[20] For example, "It is possible [*I would say highly likely*] that some works of the Hebrew Bible were composed in oral performance in accordance with certain conventions of composition, content, structure, and style" (Niditch 1996:117; material in brackets added). Doan and Giles term this factor of orality "a *performance mode of thought*, in which oral performances were conveyed and compositional characteristics of which still reside embedded in the written literature" (2005:5; original italics), for example, "in the prophetic literature of the Hebrew Bible" (ibid., 171).

[21] However, to move behind the specific forms of a text and speculate concerning the underlying motivating mentality of its generation is not very helpful. For example: "This is a [*performative*] way of thinking that engages both the cognitive and the imaginative aspects of thought to conceive of reality not in propositions but in actions and being" (Doan and Giles 2005:171). One wonders how the preceding assertion can be proved—or if it is even intuitively correct to begin with. Certainly, there are many *propositional utterances* in the prophets (i.e., ostensibly informative affirmations whose truth or falsity can be evaluated by means of logic) that

example, a transcribed nthano tale later reshaped and scripted for a subsequent radio broadcast.[22]

It is to be expected that, when texts initially composed and performed orally are eventually written down, many of their constituent linguistic elements, especially phonological features (volume, tempo, stress, etc.), are either rendered implicitly or left under-represented due to the inability or failure, whether scribal or orthographic, to accurately record them. Also lost are any *contextual* (e.g., physical, social, climatic, presuppositional, etc.)[23] and *non-verbal* accompaniments that may have contributed to the overall message (e.g., facial features, manual gestures, bodily postures). However, these virtual components of potential meaning are (or should be) important to Bible translators as well as to all interpreters of the text of Scripture, to the extent that they can be determined. Thus, the fact of point (a) above in a specific sociocultural setting will occasion the relevance of considerations relating to (b) and (c), as far as the communication dynamics and possibilities within the society are concerned.

Nowadays of course there are very few purely (primary) "oral" societies in the world. Most communities have been influenced to one degree or another by the practice of writing and the capacity to print and read texts—whether this involves composing a formal scholarly treatise for an academic journal or sending out a casual text message (SMS) to a friend on one's multifunctional cell phone. However, it is important to recognize that such intermedia influence goes both ways; thus, many of the oral characteristics of a certain traditional genre may be naturally reproduced when those texts are either recorded or recreated in writing, for example, discourse transitional markers, verbal signals of peak and climax, basic sentence and paragraph structure, various idiomatic expressions and figures of speech.

The term "orality," then, is a multifaceted concept. The nine terms discussed in the sections that follow (§§1.2.2–1.2.10) are necessary

---

naturally refer to certain human actions and beings, for example, in that most visionary of prophets, Ezekiel: "But you are a man and not a god, though you think you are as wise as a god" (28:2d—picked at random).

[22] As documented, for example, in Wendland 2004a:9–38.

[23] Contextual factors are much more important during acts of communication, typically oral, in so-called "high-context cultures," where interpersonal and social influences too tend to be much more critical in the formulation of texts (cf. Katan 2004:245–253).

1.2 Overview

complements to any discussion about "orality" in relation to the interpretation, translation, and transmission of Scripture.

1.2.2 Scribality

"Scribality" is a technical term (i.e., not found in a general dictionary) in the academic field of "orality-scribality studies" (Kelber 2007:2–3). It refers rather broadly to "anything from writing down something [by hand] from oral dictation to composition in writing" (Culley 2000:52).[24] Similarly, the term "scribe" (or its ancient equivalents, e.g., *sofer*, *grammateus*) may refer, depending on the context, to " a range of positions or professions in which literacy is a critical requirement, such as bureaucrats associated with official institutions, accountants, notaries, teachers of literacy skills, and finally, full-fledged transmitters and composers of legal, historical, or sapiential traditions" (Jaffee 2001:20). Furthermore, from the perspective of society as a whole:

> The principal aim of education was the internalization of texts in people's minds and hearts for the purpose of generating and/or reinforcing what today we might call the cultural identity of a people. Skilled scribes were expected to possess or acquire mastery of their core writings by way of memorization and recitation. (Kelber 2010:116)

Thus, in an ancient setting of text production, there was always a dynamic interaction between the principal media of literary composition:[25] Initially then, "the oral was converted to the written," while later during

---

[24] In normal usage, scribal activity is more or less limited to the function of *copying* texts, viz., "*historical* – a person who copied out documents" (Soanes and Stevenson 2006:1293). However, there is evidence that "[s]cribes in antiquity were not just secretaries copying documents; they were the scholars of their world" (Witherington 2009a:35), and thus, "[t]he role of the scribe in ancient Israel could and did take on components of creativity and composition" (Hess 2008:718). At issue here then is the degree to which such scribal "creativity" impacted upon the original "composition" of the books of the Hebrew Bible. We might also note in this connection that it is possible to "affirm that there were scribes in Israel as early as the tenth century [BCE], and perhaps even earlier" (Floyd 2000:134).

[25] Hermeneutical issues that concern the history of a biblical text's oral and written composition (traditionally termed "higher criticism") cannot be separated from those that involve questions of scribal activity in transmitting the text ("lower criticism").

normal textual transmission "in reading aloud the written was converted to the oral" (Gamble 1995:104).²⁶ Or, from a slightly different perspective, "literary authors in antiquity composed from both oral and written sources, interweaving them with their own contributions, always composing for oral/aural performance" (Miller 2011:121). The degree of scribal as distinct from oral influence within a given biblical text is probably reflected in its prominent stylistic features, both literary and syntactic. In a careful statistical study of Hebrew narrative, for example, Polak (1998) noted a greater use of discourse formulas, rhythmic speech, and parallelism, coupled with a less frequent occurrence of grammatical complexity in texts that are more oral-aurally based.²⁷

According to many scholars then, there would appear to have been a complex continuum of potential scribal activity in the production of Ancient Near Eastern (ANE) written texts,²⁸ ranging from "passive" scribes, those who simply copied as exactly as possible what a speaker uttered, or what

---

²⁶ Perhaps the first report of this oral-written-oral interaction in the Scriptures is recorded in Exod 17:14: "Then the LORD said to Moses, 'Write this as a reminder in a book and recite it in the hearing [lit. put it in the ears] of JoshuA!...'"—וַיֹּאמֶר יְהוָה אֶל־מֹשֶׁה כְּתֹב זֹאת זִכָּרוֹן בַּסֵּפֶר וְשִׂים בְּאָזְנֵי יְהוֹשֻׁעַ.

²⁷ To be specific: "[A] number of features in the prose style of Biblical Hebrew relate to the differences between oral and written language, namely (a) the use of subordinate clauses (hypotaxis), (b) the length of the noun string, (c) the number of explicit syntactic constituents in the clause, and (d) the frequency of reference by means of pronouns and deictic particles. Systematic analysis of these features shows that texts from the Persian era typically contain many subordinated clauses (hypotaxis), long noun strings and explicit syntactic constituents.... In contrast, most texts belonging to the tales of the Patriarchs, the rise of the monarchy (Samuel, Saul and David), the Omride dynasty and the northern prophets (Elijah and Elisha), and part of the Exodus narrative, consist of short clauses, containing only a small number of explicit syntactic constituents. In these texts hypotaxis and long noun strings are relatively rare, whereas reference by pronoun and deictic particles is frequent.... [T]he more a text is rooted in the scribal context, the more complicated its language, in terms of hypotaxis, length of the noun string, and the number of explicit sentence constituents. In contrast, the closer a text is to spoken language and oral literature, the simpler it is, in terms of syntactic structure, reference, and clause length" (Polak 1998:59).

²⁸ One recent study suggests that "the Old Hebrew epigraphic evidence demonstrates that there was a formal, standardized scribal education in ancient Israel," i.e., between the 8th and 6th century BCE (Rollston 2010:91). "Many will welcome Rollston's conclusion, countering views that deny Hebrew books were written before 700 B.C.: 'I am absolutely certain that a nation (Israel) that has a scribal apparatus that is capable of developing a national script and employing standardized orthographic conventions is certainly capable of producing literature'" (Millard 2012b).

1.2 Overview

was already written in a pre-existing document—to "proactive" scribes, those who were authorized to edit and update an extant document in terms of orthography, spelling, historical-geographical data, etc.[29]—and finally to "hyperactive" scribes, those who felt free not only to modify an existing text formally, but also to significantly change or to add content to the original, often under the name of the ascribed author/speaker.[30] In any case, it is important to recognize the importance of memory and performance (see below) in connection with normal scribal chirographic action. As Kelber has pointed out:

> The notion of scribes copying an extant text or juggling multiple texts that were physically present to them is, for the most part, not a fitting model for the communication dynamics in the ancient world. Undoubtedly, texts were written down, stored, consulted, and also copied. But the core tradition was not primarily carried forward by copying of texts. Rather, scribes who were literate in the core curriculum carried texts as mental templates, using them, recasting them, and/or repeating them. They had ingested the tradition consisting of one or more than one text so as to be able to rewrite the tradition without any need for physical texts. (Kelber 2007:8)[31]

---

[29] Thus, proactive "professional scribes were not merely slavish copyists of the material which they handled, but rather minor partners in the variegated aspects of the literary process" (Talmon 2010:84). Hence, "These manuscripts and fragments evidence a 'textual strategy' consisting of the interaction of the original authors and the transmitters of their work. Scribes and editors were minor partners of the authors. They did not refrain from occasionally changing wordings within a given range of 'poetic license,' often adapting literary techniques and patterns that had been used by the primary creators of the texts that they copied" (Review of Biblical Literature 2011, http://www.bookreviews.org). "Hyperactive" scribes, if granted, would be viewed as being "major partners" in transmitting the text.

[30] Persen also refers to three general categories of scribal action; however, his second category, corresponding to my "proactive" group, seems to be more rather liberal in character, with the result that "any text that has undergone multiple occasions of such copying could certainly diverge significantly, according to our modern perspective, from its earliest version..." (2010:67).

[31] The crucial question is this: *What does it mean to "rewrite the tradition"?* Furthermore, Kelber does not cite any evidence for his theory concerning the nature of scribal activity (repeated also in 2010:117).

Many scholars have come to the conclusion that the "liberated" redactor-scribe was really the norm for that age. In this view then, the question of authorship, an "original setting" of communication, or the notion of fidelity to an authoritative textual tradition would seem to be a moot point. With respect to the Hebrew Bible, for example, some would claim that "[w]hile the temple scribes in Israel were responsible for teaching the scribal craft, they were also the ones who created the bulk of the biblical literature…and composition being largely an oral art, scribes thus had to acquire rhetorical skills" (van der Toorn 2007:89, 100).[32] This perception of the literarily creative, but anonymously collective "scribal author" of Scripture cannot remain unchallenged, however, and I will offer some criticisms of, and alternatives to this perspective in chapter three (i.e., a "restrained" versus a more "flexible" mode of textual transmission in relation to an "original" author and text).[33]

1.2.3 Literature

According to one prestigious dictionary, "literature" refers to "written works, especially those regarded as having artistic merit."[34] In any "literary" work, "meaning" is "communicated *through form*…. The standard elements of artistic form include unity, theme-and-variation, pattern, design, progression, contrast, balance, recurrence, coherence, and symmetry" (Ryken 2012:37, 42).[35] Who then carries out the critical act of "regarding"—

---

[32] Van der Toorn makes the rather controversial claim that professional scribes "are the main figures behind biblical literature; we owe the Bible entirely to them" (ibid., 75). He must admit, however, that his evidence for this position is "both indirect and tailored to other needs than those of the historian" (ibid., 76). Thus his hypothesis is based largely on the unreliable foundation of alleged cross-cultural analogy, namely, the practice of "the scribes of Mesopotamia and Egypt" on account of "the scarcity of written artifacts from pre-Hellenistic Palestine" (ibid., 75). In contrast, Peter Williams argues on the basis of features such as the Hebrew alphabet, flexible writing materials, an honest historicity, relatively long interconnected narratives, and careful scribal practice, that: "There is thus the necessary evidence for us to be able legitimately to conclude that through a process involving copying over long periods of time we could have access to ancient Israelite literature" (Williams 2010).

[33] See also my studies: 2008b:32–48 and 2009:383–388.

[34] Soanes and Stevenson 2006:832; the oral equivalent will be discussed under the next term, "orature."

[35] The meaningful use of literary form for highlighting elements of the *content* of a text is *artistry*, while its use for highlighting aspects of *function* is *rhetoric*.

1.2 Overview

that is, who conducts the necessary comparative evaluation to determine degrees of aesthetic "merit" (presumably also "demerit")? Certainly, academic scholars and literary "experts" are thus engaged, but because literature, both factive and fictive, is normally an important sociocultural phenomenon, the general public is also involved (i.e., "popular opinion"). Therefore, the assessment of any given instance of composition concerns not only the appraisal of *artistic form* and quality of *content*, but also a consideration of contextually-determined text *function*. This would include general aims (e.g., social, educational, historical, religious, etc.) as well as more specific communicative goals (e.g., the functions of motivation, inspiration, commemoration, admonition, enlightenment, consolation, value-reinforcement, tradition-preservation, and so forth).

However, is it correct or appropriate to regard the diverse writings of the Scriptures (Hebrew and Greek) as being "literature"—individual works of appreciable artistic worth in fact? I endeavor to make the case for an affirmative response to this question in several recent studies,[36] so it is not

---

[36] My assumption, as argued in Wendland 2004b:2–12, for example, is that the prophetic writings along with the Scriptures generally, are instances of genuine "literature," which according to the *Concise Oxford Dictionary* refers to "written works, especially those regarded as having artistic merit." This point is contested by a recent study that claims that "there is no biblical literature" (Mazor 2009:21). Mazor reasons as follows: "The primary objectives of the Hebrew Bible—religious, philosophical, historical, moral—are not discrete…but intertwined, and they are all pragmatic, seeking to educate, teach, preach, and impart knowledge, values, and religious instruction. *Being devoid of aesthetic objectives,* the Bible cannot be considered a literary work but a collection of books with a defined pragmatic goal, making use of an astounding array of aesthetic patterns and devices. These patterns and devices are there only to serve the main purpose" (ibid., 21–22; italics added). Such reasoning is obviously flawed. In the first place, why must a particular composition serve only a single communicative function? As Mazor himself observes, the aesthetic-artistic is employed in the service of the "pragmatic" (I would say, rather, the combined "theological-moral" goal). One might even argue that artistry, or aesthetics, is itself a "pragmatic" goal. Good literature gives evidence of a complex of aims, which may vary in priority according to the particular section in view (e.g., Isaiah 40:1–5, prophetic/revelatory; 9–14, 28–31, theological; 19–20, moral). Second, according to common critical understanding, as reflected in the dictionary definition, a literary work is one that manifests clear "artistic merit," something that Mazor himself presumably grants with reference to the Hebrew Bible (and describes in great detail in his book). "Since Scripture is a text of literature, the bulk of interpretive [and translational!] work entails coming to grips with the various literary and linguistic aspects of the biblical material" (Köstenberger and Patterson 2011:66; cf. 237–238 and Vanhoozer 1986).

necessary to rehearse those arguments here.³⁷ Moreover, this positive literary-critical estimation will be supported later by a number of text-based practical illustrations (see the studies of parts II and III). My point is that the compositional excellence of Scripture, where demonstrated, in prose as well as in poetic texts, ought to be matched, to the degree possible under the prevailing circumstances, in translation—that is, in terms of form and function as well as content. This includes the essential orality of the received canonical text, for despite their current classification as "literature," the various books of the Bible also originated to one degree or another in oral form and they accordingly manifest this influence in various ways. Therefore, they need to be analyzed, interpreted, expressed, and ultimately crafted in the target language with this sonic dimension clearly in view—or better, for one's actual "hearing."³⁸ Thus, the following topic, "orature," may actually be more appropriate as a designation for the type of writing that we have generally represented in the Scriptures—that is, a *collection of sacred, religious texts orally composed for eventual oral articulation.*

1.2.4 Orature

Or, "Did you say 'oral literature'?" With this query Walter Ong introduces his discussion of the terminological problem that we face here (1982:10): What can we call the oral correspondent of "literature"—with reference to vocal genres such as traditional narratives, folk tales, proverbs, riddles, and songs of all types?³⁹ Ong suggests that this "monstrous concept" was coined

---

³⁷ "The Bible is an aesthetic as well as utilitarian book...in which theology and history are usually embedded in literary forms. These forms include genres, the incarnation of human experience in concrete form, stylistic and rhetorical techniques, and artistry" (Ryken 2012:42–43).

³⁸ The terms "target language" (TL), into which is translated a text originally composed in a different, a "source language" (SL), are admittedly not the best and open to possible misunderstanding (cf. Maxey 2009:73). However, since they are current in the literature of modern secular translation studies (e.g., Munday 2009a:127, 130; Pym 2010:1) as well as contemporary Bible translation (e.g., Wilt 2003:x; Naudé and van der Merwe 2002:3), I will continue to use them for convenience in this book. Possible alternatives are: producer/consumer, guest/host, or donor/client languages and texts.

³⁹ Memory is crucial also in the establishment of genre, for "we make sense of what is new by comparing it to what is not new. This classification of similar types of verbal discourse creates a 'genre'" (Sparks 2008:207).

and continues to be perpetuated by scholars who "assume, often without reflection, that oral verbalization was essentially the same as the written verbalization they normally dealt with, and that oral art forms were to all intents and purposes simply texts, except for the fact that they were not written down" (1982:10–11).[40]

However, before we dismiss the expression "oral literature" too quickly, we must consider the alternatives: Will Ong's "oral verbalization" do? Probably not. How about "oral art forms" then? This is too broad, for it would include non-verbal artistry—for instance, yodeling, humming a melody, or "skat singing" (i.e., nonsense syllables), while "verbal art" could conceivably encompass written compositions too. "Oral verbal art" becomes awkward again. So what are we left with? "Oratory" is a possibility, but perhaps too specific in meaning, as in certain dictionary entries like "1. the art or practice of formal public speaking; 2. rhetorical or eloquent language" (Webster). I have been using "orature" (Wendland: 2004b:4–6),[41] but this term may sound rather too esoteric for some critics.

As in the case of ancient scribality, nowadays there is in most world cultures a multiple interactive *interface* embracing purely spoken verbal art forms as well as written ones, i.e., orature and literature.[42] Thus, different amounts of a stylistic "mixing" of features may be manifested along a fluid

---

[40] Furthermore, "[t]hinking of oral tradition or a heritage of oral performance, genres and styles as 'oral literature' is rather like thinking of horses as automobiles without wheels" (ibid., 12). Ong goes on to develop a humorous exposition of the futility (perhaps also folly) of such an imaginative effort and concludes: "The same is true of those who deal in terms of 'oral literature', that is 'oral writing'. You cannot without serious and disabling distortion describe a primary phenomenon by starting with a subsequent secondary phenomenon and paring away the differences. Indeed, starting backwards in this way—putting the car before the horse—you can never become aware of the real differences at all" (ibid., 13).

[41] Strictly speaking, it should probably be "oralature" (Terry 2009a).

[42] "On the one hand, biblical texts and similar texts in other cultures were 'oral' in the sense that they were memorized, and—in certain cases—publicly performed. On the other hand, written copies of these texts were used in this process to help students accurately internalize the textual tradition, check their accuracy and correct it, and/or as an aid in the oral presentation of the text" (Carr 2010:18–19; the "reference manuscripts" of later Jewish tradition; ibid., 28). In this vital interaction of the oral with the written text, Carr suggests the analogy of "how written musical scores function in the training and performance of music" (ibid., 19). Dan Fitzgerald adds, "Only certain 'modernist' composers of the 20th century considered their musical notation as 'the music'. All others expected their compositions to be traditionally interpreted and aurally communicated" (personal correspondence, 2012).

oral-written continuum, engaging in a manifold manner one medium with another and one communication setting with the next. Any categorization of discourse types is further complicated by what Oesterreicher calls their "conceptual profiles," which "are, as a matter of principle, independent of the medium of discourse" and involve interpersonal variables, such as degrees of formality, familiarity, immediacy, spontaneity, privacy, and others, depending on the culture and society concerned (1997:191).[43]

In the end, no matter which designative terms are used, students of biblical "literature/orature" need to have their analytical and hermeneutical feet firmly fixed in the textual space of both disciplines. "[W]riting often supports oral tradition and vice versa" (Miller 2011:21). Thus, characteristics of both orature and literature influenced the oral-aural performance setting and compositional style in which most, if not all, of the books of Scripture originated in, as well as the written forms in which they were finally recorded and preserved in the OT and NT canon. As Shiner observes, "as a result of the dictation process [during literary composition], the author composes with an awareness of the aural effect, and writers often 'wrote' by speaking in a manner that would approximate the intended oral delivery" (2003:16). Biblical texts must therefore be actually heard, then conceptualized, interpreted, translated, and transmitted in an integrated manner from the joint perspective of each of these primary modes of verbal communication, utilizing ancient traditional as well as modern technological means.

---

[43] Doan and Giles attempt to categorize and display these features in terms of a "variable discourse grid" that offers a "conceptual profile" of a given text and context of transmission (2005:6–9). Their cumulative grid purporting to display the "pertinent characteristics of a performative mode of thought in a given piece of literature" [including "orature"?] plots the "conceptual mode of discourse" against the "linguistic medium of discourse" (ibid., 45–47; material in brackets added). The result is complicated, hence difficult to follow, and rather controversial (debatable) in many respects, but it does serve at least to indicate a number of important compositional and presentational variables that translators need to take into consideration as they analyze a source text, whether oral or written, on the one hand, and then seek to communicate that text meaningfully in a specific target language and sociocultural setting.

1.2 Overview 29

1.2.5 Performance

The term "performance" refers to a public communication event whereby one or more speakers present(s) a verbal text, whether originally oral or written, in dramatic or documentary (plain, unembellished) form and in the presence of a communal listening audience.[44] "Oral performance is a means of transforming silent texts into sounds and movements through the mediums of speech and gesture" (Ward 1994:95). Such a general definition allows for a number of options, for example:[45]

- the level of formality of the text and/or the social occasion;
- the style of delivery (plain/dramatic speech, recitation, chanting, cantillation, singing, etc.);
- the amount of non-verbal communication manifested during performance;
- whether the text is created on the spot, is read from a written script, has been memorized or recycled from oral tradition;
- the degree of overt interaction (if any) with the audience;
- the genre and subject field represented by the text;
- its relative artistic quality as "literature" or "orature";
- whether the speakers are professional or amateurs;
- the inclusion of intervening or accompanying music or song;
- the physical setting or venue of performance—and so forth.

---

[44] Doan and Giles cite (and seemingly leave readers with) the opaque definition of *performance* as "a consciousness of doubleness, through which the actual execution of an action is placed in mental comparison with a potential, an ideal, or a remembered model of that action" (2005:14). Much better is Richard Bauman's description: "performance usually suggests an aesthetically marked and heightened mode of communication, framed in a special way and put on display for an audience" (1992:41). See also Carlson 1984:5.

[45] The following listing may be complemented by Rhoads' description of a "performance event," which includes considerations such as the following: "the oral/written composition, the act of performing, the performer, the audience, the location, the cultural/historical circumstances, and the rhetorical impact on the audience. To construct such performance events, we need to investigate ancient art and literature for depictions and descriptions of ancient performances done by artists and rhetoricians and storytellers and dramatists" (2010:164).

So what difference does a "performance" make—is it not simply a cosmetic add-on, the finishing vocal, visual, and gestural touches that accompany the utterance of a given verbal text, which is always focal and central? By no means; in the case of many oral discourses, especially in a society that is characterized by a vibrant artistic orality, the public performance of the text is everything, the *sine qua non*. Without an audience, for example, the communal communication event could not occur in the first place. Furthermore, in these ancient communities virtually all significant discourse was orally performed, from texts involved in basic education to those presented in senate debates or for entertainment in the theatre. People took their oral performances seriously and carefully prepared and practiced them, whether formally or informally:

> Preparation for performance was central to every educational system in antiquity. And memory training was critical for performance. Hence, memory training was essential. Practice and rehearsal were integral to preparation for performance. Memory techniques were taught to enhance the natural memory. All oriented to performance. (Rhoads 2009)

Perhaps only someone who has experienced such an energetic oral performance can really appreciate the difference that stimulating the entire sensorium makes. As I wrote in an introduction to a collection of Chewa folktales that were recorded live in rural Zambia early in 1974:

> When reading a collection of traditional tales…, it is important to bear in mind a few of the chief characteristics of this popular performing art. What we are dealing with here is not simply a collection of text transcriptions and translations, but a corpus of dramatic performances, each of which represents a truly unique and unrepeatable communal event, one that involves both artist and audience in an experience that can never be repeated in exactly the same way again. A linguistic representation in the form of a printed text, no matter how detailed and accurate, is by no means sufficient to give one an adequate appreciation of this art form and its dynamic communicative potential in society. The written text of a tale, even in the original language, exists as a mere shadow of its full realization as an aesthetic and emotive

1.2 Overview

> experience for all participants. The permanence of print gives one an impression of rigidity that masks the flexible nature of these stories, both in composition and in performance. The bare printed word also eliminates a variety of non-verbal adjuncts of performance, such as the use of changes of voice to convey impressions of anger, fear, anxiety, etc.; facial expressions; gestures, especially of the hands and head; rhythmic and mimetic body movements; and also the specific external circumstances which form a background to the telling of the tale, e.g., the narrator having to cope with a crying baby; the intrusion of chickens, goats, cows and dogs, either physically or vocally; the onset of a sudden thunderstorm.[46] (Wendland 1976:1–2)

In addition, James Maxey points out that oral performance in traditional communities functions as a multi-sensory "social drama" that serves to shape "community identity."[47] The formal analysis and evaluation of any type of oral text presentation is termed "performance criticism" (Doan and Giles 2005:ix), a scholarly discipline that has, especially in the 21st century, also been rigorously applied to various facets of the study of biblical literature:[48]

> Conceived broadly, biblical performance criticism embraces many methods as a means to reframe the biblical materials in the context of traditional oral cultures, construct scenarios of ancient performances, learn from contemporary performances of these materials, and reinterpret biblical writings accordingly.

---

[46] The entire communal and interactive performance setting thus acts as a contextualizing sociocultural "frame of reference" that facilitates an interpretation of the verbal text: "Performance sets up, or represents, an interpretive frame within which the messages being communicated are to be understood..." (Bauman 1984:9).

[47] Maxey 2009:2. The diverse category of communications media termed "traditional performing arts" include oral-aural forms that span the perceptual range of the human sensorium, such as "song composition, drama, dance, story telling, chanting, visual and other locally thriving arts" (Schrag 2007:199)—one mode often being presented serially or in parallel along with one or more of the others, e.g., folk-tales with incorporated periodic communal songs (*nthano* in Chewa).

[48] The following quotation comes from David Rhoads in his general editorial preface to the Cascade Books Series "Biblical Performance Criticism" (which includes Maxey 2009:ii).

Considerations of orality and how it should be formally manifested ("performed") in a particular setting of transmission are obviously crucial in all phases of Scripture-centered communication, as will become more evident as we continue to explore the five remaining aspects of this manifold process below.

1.2.6 Rhetoric

In its narrow classical Aristotelian sense, "rhetoric" is the *art* and *technique* of verbal persuasion (*Ars rhetorica*).[49] In practice, this entails the application of a definite, clearly definable literary (oratorical) strategy that aims, through conventional, but skillfully utilized, means of argumentation,[50] to modify the current cognitive, emotive, and/or volitional stance of the intended audience. The author's aim may be to reinforce, to change, or to augment the thinking of his/her hearers with regard to a particular topic. The term "art" suggests a specific ability or personal proficiency that one is simply endowed with, while "technique" implies a compositional or technical skill that can be learned and perfected on the basis of concrete heuristic principles and procedures.

The discipline that attends then to a critical evaluation of this rhetorical component or characteristic of literary discourse (i.e., its "rhetoricity") is called "rhetorical criticism." In essence, rhetoricity constitutes *effective communication* ("the science of speaking well" *scientia bene dicendi*—Quintilian). Such rhetorical practice pertains primarily to an oral text (by extension, also to a written one) that accomplishes the principal goal of audience *persuasion* by effecting a discrete speech function (or a small set of them).[51] The different stylistic devices that contribute to the unity, diversity,

---

[49] I must admit at the outset that we are faced with a certain problem of definition with this category. As one critic noted a number of years ago: "The basic problem with rhetorical criticism is that English literary critics are by no means agreed as to what that well-worn term 'rhetoric' signifies or ought to signify. In the light of this it can hardly be deemed surprising if biblical critics wonder (as well)" (Kessler 1982:1). This problem presents itself because, as "rhetoric" has become more commonly used in the literary analysis of biblical discourse, so the term has been correspondingly employed with an increasingly wide, ill-defined referential scope.

[50] According to Ryken, rhetoric involves the "arrangement of content in patterns and use of conventional literary techniques or formulas" (2012:42) in order to accomplish strategic communicative goals.

[51] According to Peter Phillips, "Secondary rhetoric is *handbook* rhetoric—the conscious development of primary (oral) rhetoric into a practical (textual) skill, fully

1.2 Overview

beauty, structure, or any other literary quality simultaneously achieve one or more of these communicative aims in and through the text at hand, e.g., the expressive, directive, referential, ritual functions. While such notions may be useful in a general sense when analyzing a biblical passage, it is probably more helpful for analytical purposes to be more specific. To this end, the various concepts, categories, and procedures associated with "speech act theory," including its extension to "text acts" and "relevance theory" (see ch. 2) may be used profitably.[52]

There are several distinct types of "rhetorical criticism" that are being applied nowadays with respect to the varied literature of the Scriptures, but I will briefly summarize what is perhaps the most popular approach, the Greco-Roman model.[53] Ancient, and to a great extent also contemporary, promoters of the discipline of classical rhetoric decidedly emphasize the persuasive strategies and compositional techniques of the original *source* of communication, whether oral (that is, by an orator) or written (by an author). Great importance is also attached to a text's actual generative setting, the "rhetorical situation." This contextual setting, or motivational environment, encompasses all of the relevant factors, personal and impersonal, which together occasion some crisis or stimulus (*"exigency"*) that calls for an appropriate human response in the form of a verbal discourse. The next matter to deal with is the precise problem, question, or issue (*stasis*) under consideration along with the particular manner (*species*) of rhetoric that has been chosen to present it. There were three basic types of rhetorical argumentation: *judicial*, dealing with accusation and/or defense of justice or wrong—with a past temporal orientation; *deliberative*, concerning confirmation or refutation according to what is beneficial or expedient—having a future focus; and *epideictic*, involving a celebration or condemnation of seminal beliefs and values—generally with a present time setting.

The text itself is then normally analyzed on the basis of the so-called "rhetorical canons" of invention, arrangement, and style. Invention (*inventio*) documents the choice of assorted proofs and topics to best support the

---

conceptualized, with a developed theoretical framework, education system and supportive literature" (2008:235).

[52] For an overview, see Hatim and Mason 1990:78–79, 95–96.

[53] See, for example: Phillips 2008:226–227; Kennedy 1984:33–38; Wendland 2002a:171–186. A helpful recent survey of classical rhetorical criticism is found in DeSilva 2009:18–25.

case being argued, whether according to *ethos* (character), *pathos* (emotions), or *logos* (modes of reasoning). Arrangement (*dispositio*) involves the compositional structure of the discourse in terms of ordered constituents, such as the *exordium* (introduction), *narratio* (initial statement of the case), *probatio* (main body of the argument), and *peroratio* (conclusion) according to the principles of logical deduction or experiential induction. Matters of structure (*dispositio*) and style (*elocutio*) pertain to the linguistic specifics of how a particular speech is put together in a persuasive way through the use of devices such as artful arrangements, distinctive diction, repetition, syntax, and figures of speech or thought. Often ignored by modern rhetorical critics are two other "canons" studied in the classical approach, namely, *memoria*, which deals with the process of effectively committing a speech to memory, and *pronunciatio*, or elocution, which focuses on the procedures used to dramatically deliver a speech (see below).[54]

However, one cannot apply Greco-Roman rhetorical categories and standards indiscriminately to the New Testament literature, for two primary reasons: (a) the authors (scribes) of the NT were not professional Greek orators or rhetoricians, and so they were not bound in principle or practice to compose their historical, hortatory, evangelistic, and apologetic religious works according to classical norms; and (b) these writers were undoubtedly also influenced intertextually to a significant degree by OT (LXX) rhetorical

---

[54] For example, "Since we have only the texts themselves and not their performance, the material on memory and delivery plays almost no role in New Testament interpretation. It is not likely that the reader memorized the letter before sharing its contents, so memory would not apply" (DeSilva 2009:21). Another important aspect of the "style" of rhetoric not mentioned here concerns the study of various types of *chreiai* (sg. *chreia*), that is, characteristic and memorable sayings (less often actions) that were associated with a given illustrious personage in Greco-Roman as well as rabbinic oral and written literature. These sayings, which may be categorized into different types (e.g., wish, maxim, explanation, syllogism), were regarded as being instructive, affective, or beneficial in some notable way. Consequently, they were frequently strung together as either "statements" or "responses" and employed in the composition of the biographies of famous persons and in the exposition or argumentation involved in presenting a particular debatable issue or controversial case (cf. Watson 1992:104–106). Witherington argues that *chreiai* are the basis for the distinctive compositional style of Mark: "As a rhetorical term, it makes very good sense with regard to what we find in our earliest Gospel—short narratives that contain actions or sayings, or actions and sayings often climaxing with a pithy memorable remark" (Witherington 2009a:140).

1.2 Overview

texts and a Semitic mode of style and expression.[55] Thus, the varied works of the "evangelists and apostles" often manifest a mixed or localized manner of composition, each of which must be analyzed according to its intrinsic written as well as oral-aural characteristics. This may be accomplished by a method that is, at the same time, more general with regard to particular rhetorical schools or styles of influence and also more specific in terms of the various facets of discourse examined.[56]

Why devote so much space here to the topic of rhetoric? In the first place, it is clear (or at least arguable) that the diverse writings of Scripture were rhetorically as well as artistically conceived and constructed,[57] although the precise origin and nature of literary influence may not be as discernable as some scholars often suggest. Therefore, the knowledge of Hebrew and Greek rhetorical techniques (the former being more *inductive*, the latter more *deductive*) can provide many significant insights into the structure, style, and hence also the message of the biblical writers.[58] Furthermore, since rhetorical investigation is interested in getting at the heart of the interpersonal communicative dynamics of literature, or orature, it tends to take the intended audience very seriously. Accordingly, typical studies focus on revealing how the author fashioned his text and then presented it, whether orally or in writing, so as to have the appropriate impact on and appeal to a specific listening group.[59] The same structure-functional

---

[55] As Watson and Hauser note: "There is the question of the degree that rhetorical theory influenced the epistolary genre...and if it is rightly used in analyzing Jewish texts, particularly those from a specifically Palestinian context;.... Greco-Roman rhetorical analysis may leave peculiar features of early Christian rhetoric unappreciated or undiscovered;.... There is the danger of glossing over the changes rhetoric must undergo in the transition from oral to written form or from one written genre to another;...there is also the danger of a too rigid application of rhetorical categories to the biblical texts" (Watson and Hauser 1994:111). An example would be the attempt to interpret NT texts based on Hellenistic "typologies of literary style" (austere, elegant, plain, etc.), e.g., "By its lack of ornamentation, the plain literary style creates an unaffected tone. Luke's prohibition of anxiety provides an example" (i.e., in Luke 12:22b–26) (Lee and Scott 2009:186; cf. 111–122).

[56] For one such approach applied to several biblical books, see Wilt and Wendland 2008:chs. 8–10.

[57] For a discussion of this point, see Wendland 2004b:189–228.

[58] See for example, with regard to the OT: Gitay 1991; de Regt et al. 1996; NT: Porter and Olbricht 1993; Witherington 2009b.

[59] Vernon K. Robbins in fact defines "rhetoric" with a focus on the *oral* declamation of a literary text: "The field of study that specializes in analysis and interpretation

concerns are just as crucial today since Bible translators must not only analyze the original documents for understanding but must also formulate their vernacular text in a correspondingly *persuasive* oral-aural manner, whatever the medium. This should be as *effectively* as possible in keeping with a project's target audience, predetermined job commission (*brief*) and communicative goal(s) (*Skopos*).[60]

1.2.7 Elocution

As noted above, modern rhetorical critics have tended to downplay or simply disregard "elocution," which was the phonic dimension of the elaborate textual technique that was theorized and practiced by ancient orators and authors as well. However, it is a well-established fact that in those days of enhanced orality even written documents were typically composed aloud and simultaneously inscribed, either by the author himself or, more likely, by an attendant secretary (Witherington 2009b:1–5). Enunciation (technically, *pronunciatio*) was concerned with all facets of the public delivery of a speech, including timing, the use of pause, and the manipulation and control of a speaker's voice to create special audio effects, as well as the use of non-verbal communication through facial expressions, hand and body movements, and strategic spatial positioning.[61] Ensuring the correct pronunciation—and public performance—of the sacred biblical text also became an increasingly important consideration as "classical" Hebrew became less commonly spoken as a living vernacular in later second Temple times. This concern subsequently developed into the Masoretic tradition of inserting phonological markers for vowels and accents, including signs for cantillation or ritual chanting, in the traditional Hebrew consonantal text.

---

of 'the expressible,' i.e., expressive language in a concrete utterance, is rhetoric" (2009:9).

[60] "Rhetoric as the art of persuasion encompasses all forms of purposeful communication in the various media available for communication" (Phillips 2008:237). The project-related concepts of *brief* and *Skopos* derive from functionalist theory and practice (Wendland 2004b:26); this approach to translation will be more fully described in the next chapter.

[61] "Elocution" in English does not include reference to these paralinguistic supplements to speech but is more restricted to "the skill of clear and expressive speech, especially of distinct pronunciation and articulation" (Soanes and Stevenson 2006:464).

1.2 Overview

Unfortunately, this vital oral (and aural) articulatory activity is often a greatly neglected element of consideration also during the process of transmitting a translated text of Scripture. Thus, liturgical readers of biblical pericopes as well as many pulpit preachers do not always take the time or make the effort necessary either to practice their elocution beforehand or to delve into the orality of the printed version at hand sufficiently to see how different "readings" of the same passage may reflect distinct interpretations of the words on the page. In this respect, the "performance critics" have contributed a great deal to the overall hermeneutical procedure that is necessary both when analyzing a biblical text for its assumed "oral potential" in the original language and also when exploring the corresponding possibilities for oral and accompanying visual presentation in one's mother tongue (e.g., Rhoads 2009). David Rhoads draws our attention to what is so often a fundamental missing link in our contemporary approach to understanding and communicating the biblical text:

> When you think of the Second Testament writings as performance literature—either as transcriptions of prior oral compositions or as written compositions designed for oral performance—you wonder why Second Testament scholars do not function more like musicologists or dramatists. Interpretation of music and drama is done primarily by both performers and music/drama specialists. Can you imagine a musicologist who does nothing but sit in libraries and study the score of a composition without ever hearing a performance of it? Would it not seem strange for interpreters of drama, including ancient Greek drama, to analyze a play apart from interpretations of it in performance? Similarly, does it not seem odd that biblical critics interpret writings that were composed *in and for oral performance*—as gospels, letters, and apocalypses were—without ever experiencing performances of them and without giving some attention to the nature of the performance of these works in ancient and modern times? (Rhoads 2006a:2)

So what would help overcome this serious theoretical and practical deficiency? Rhoads suggests: "When we seek to imagine performances in oral cultures, we moderns need to shift our thinking from written to oral, from private to public, from 'public readers' to performers, from silent readers to hearers/audience, from individual to communal audience, and from manuscript transmission to oral transmission" (ibid., 6).[62] We will be devoting special attention to this important "performance factor," including the quality of *pronunciatio*, in sections II and III of this book. There we will consider a set of texts that have been selected for examination with a view towards first recognizing their underlying orality and then communicating them more dynamically (arguably, as in the initial event) via a vivid vocal vernacular translation today.

1.2.8 Memory

Rhoads summarizes the importance of "memory" studies and mnemonic techniques in the ancient world as follows:

> We cannot understand either orality or literacy without understanding the ways memory interfaced with them. What we need is to study orality, memory, and literacy, in that order—because ancient literacy served mainly to support memory and oral performance. (Rhoads 2009)

And further, given the rather awkward nature of using the scrolls of lengthy Hebrew biblical texts for reading, memorization became a very important practice for the literate religious elite. Thus, according to Martin Jaffee, "those best able to use the scroll for what we might call 'informational' purposes would be people who in a basic sense already knew its contents through approximate memorization. The text was as much a fact of their memory as it was a physical object" (2001:17).

The operation of "memory" (*memoria*) was also a crucial stage in the Greco-Roman rhetorical process, and ancient practitioners paid a great deal of attention to it.[63] This exercise naturally preceded the final oral "delivery"

---

[62] Although it is sometimes claimed that there was no "silent reading" in antiquity, several recent studies have shown that "both kinds of reading, silent and oral, were known and practiced," though the latter was undoubtedly the norm (Martin 2010:92, Bickle 2011:17).

[63] Memory, including its facilitation in texts (structural patterning) and practice (memorization), was a characteristic feature also of ancient Jewish education and religious instruction: "Learning involved a great deal of memorization. In the eyes of the rabbis, repetition was the key…. Many methods were used to assist the student in memorizing his lessons, and one passage in the Talmud [B. Shabbat 104a] even describes in

1.2 Overview

stage of *pronunciatio* and was concerned with the development of mnemonic tactics to assist the orator when preparing for public elocution, with respect to both content (what to say) and form (how and when to say it). In fact, the exercise of one's memory was probably engaged at the very beginning of the compositional process, as an author would first generate a text, or some portion of one, in his mind before "recording" it orally and in writing, either copying the text himself or, more commonly, using the services of an amanuensis (Brickle 2011:16). The skills and techniques associated with the perfection of memory in the transmission and reception of classical texts have been largely disregarded by modern scholars,[64] except again for those who have been seriously engaged in orality studies and performance criticism. Rhetorical analyses aside, recent biblical scholarship in general seems to have forgotten about memory technology: "In its own typographical captivity, modern western academe had forgotten that late antiquity and medieval Europe were cultures in which other strategies of memory prevailed beyond the written text" (Horsley 2006a:xi).[65]

Researchers in the field distinguish between several types of "memory." Thus, approaching the issue from a larger social perspective, "'cultural memory,' as distinguished from the 'communicative memory' of daily interaction, transcends the everyday and maintains itself through cultural forms such as texts, rites, festivals, monuments, or images" (Horsley 2006a:xii.).[66]

detail the mnemonic devices employed to teach small children the Hebrew alphabet" (Biven 2007:6; see also Safrai 1976:953). For an ideological-historical approach to "collective memory" in the prophetic literature, see Yehoshua Gitay 2009.

[64] Murphy, for example, after her summary of Quintilian's "five canons of rhetoric" concludes: "Memory and delivery will not concern us here"—but then adds in a footnote: "…knowledge of *memoria* is sometimes useful for biblical interpretation, since much of what we find in the Bible began as oral tradition. Recognition of mnemonic devices helps piece together the history of the text" (Murphy 1994:63). It is difficult, if not impossible, to determine which portions of Scripture, though initially composed orally, did actually develop into a free-standing oral "tradition" (as opposed to being inscribed relatively soon thereafter). As for "piecing together the history of the text" on the basis of putative "mnemonic devices" therein, that would seem to be a fool's errand. Such orality-oriented and performance-based features could only assist in determining the structure of a text, and they would probably tend to indicate that it is, in fact, a more holistic composition, rather than consisting of a patchwork of "sources" and "seams."

[65] See also Coleman 1992.

[66] "Such 'cultural memory' consists of a body of recollections transmitted in organized ways to participants in a given group, recollections of values and views that shape each individual into a member of the group" (Carr 2005:11). Gitay adds:

Both "cultural" and "communicative" memory would have been important, for example, in preserving the textual and historical traditions concerning Jesus the Messiah (cf. Allison 2010). The pragmatic everyday memory of individuals is developed by enculturation, education, socialization, and the use of various culturally based symbol systems into harmony with a dynamic communal cognitive core, which in turn forms a vital component of a group's unifying "worldview." The result is that "[o]ur memory enables us to orient ourselves in both the temporal and the social dimension, to 'belong' in the broadest sense, to form relations with others" (Assmann 2006:68).

So how does the rather abstract, generic notion of "collective memory" become transformed into something concrete, namely, in an oral-aural society? Jan Assmann explains:

> Only by acquiring certain additional distinctive features of form and genre is an utterance capable of staying in memory and remaining accessible to later recourse, repetition, elaboration, and commentary. A formalized utterance is a carrier of memory, a mnemonic mark in being both an element of tradition (which is in itself a form of memory) and memorable for future recourse. It employs memory and creates memory.... "Text," in everyday use, means "formalized utterance," formalized, that is, in view of being remembered, transmitted, and repeatedly taken up. Text is speech in the status of a mnemonic mark.[67] (Assmann 2006:72)

"The narratives that have been created as the collective memory function as [cognitive] frames which rhetorically serve as communicative vehicles that do not require elaboration, and function as an argumentative axiom that does not require further illustration" (2009:282–283). As for personal memory used for performance, Rhoads notes: "Placing something in memory must be distinguished from recollection. We are not talking about people who have good memories to recall names or events or experiences. Rather we are talking about intentional efforts to remember material to be performed in some public or private place before gathered audiences with the purpose of shaping the values, beliefs, and actions of that audience" (2009). Thus, one's individual memory and the communal memory of one's society were integrally intertwined.

[67] Assmann's seemingly restrictive definition of "text" should probably be understood in a technical sense, for there can of course also be *informal* "texts" and utterances, both oral and written. Furthermore, one cannot necessarily argue that ancient "compositions existed more authentically in memory than in writing" (Lee and Scott 2009:28). Thus, "authentically" in what sense—whose memory is "authentic"?

1.2 Overview

And what are some of these critical "distinctive features of form" that serve to cement the essential content of a certain "message" into a written text such that it can be more readily preserved and remembered—as well as more easily proclaimed orally and understood aurally? There are a variety of stylistic devices within such ancient written compositions that were utilized for macro-structural design purposes and also to orally shape the text; among them are these:

- the recycling of major, culturally-relevant themes, concepts, key terms, and images;
- cohesive and strategic (boundary-marking) repetition, restatement, and paraphrase;
- the use of standard opening and closing transitional formulas;
- much parallelism and patterning in doublets/triads, or in terraced and chiastic arrangements;
- a preference for graphic, "memorable" imagery, figures of speech, sayings, epithets, catch-words, familiar symbols, acrostic-alphabetic arrangements;
- citations of, and allusions to information that is already well-known;
- frequent dramatic, interactive discourse (real and rhetorical questions, interjections, imperatives, vocatives, etc.);
- periodic poetic or rhythmic, euphonic, sound-sensitive sequences of utterances;
- and, as a general rule, the inclusion of as much direct "character" speech as possible.

James Maxey highlights the importance of these verbal forms for preserving and presenting oral traditions in a memory-based society:

> The special features that key performance are often mnemonic in a double sense: they aid the performer in the remembrance of what to perform, but they are also the metonymic references that engage an audience in their tradition. These special features act (metonymically) as a gateway for the audience to access their traditions by hearing a few brief words or phrases in a performance.... Memory was integral to public presentation. As a result, documents were composed not only

for the aesthetic appreciation of the spoken word, but for retention. The compositions were structured to facilitate the retention for the oral performer as well as for the hearing audience. Written texts can be understood as memory aids.[68] (Maxey 2009:100, 112)

Thus, although the level of literacy was relatively low (estimates vary between 3 and 15%, mainly among the male socio-cultural elite), ancient Palestine, whether in OT or NT times, was not a completely (primary) oral culture.[69] Rather, as noted earlier, there was a complex exchange at the interface between speech and writing—between orality and scribality—a mutual influence that must have affected the communication process in different ways.[70] Furthermore, as Bickle points out, "[i]t is almost certain…that many,

---

[68] Memory was also necessary in the case of biblical documents, which were utilized to more or less "permanently" store the sacred text as a point of reference. However, this had to be done as efficiently and economically as possible, using techniques of condensation to save space on the page (scroll), which consequently made the text (all caps!) very difficult to read since it had, for example, little if any punctuation and no separation between words, sentences, and paragraphs. Carr adds: "The visual presentation of such texts presupposed that the reader already knew the given text and had probably memorized it to some extent.... Cultures interested in preserving the integrity of the tradition can use a variety of means to preserve it, including both different uses of writing and intense implementation of older means of aiding recall—formulae, rhyming, link of text to music and movement, use of overarching themes, memory techniques, and so on. Orality and writing technology are joint means for accomplishing a common goal: accurate recall of the treasured tradition" (2005:5, 7).

[69] For a discussion of some of the problems involved in determining the level of literacy in ancient Israel, see Miller 2011:43–47. Posited figures regarding the relative level of "literacy" in a given age and area are complicated by the differing definitions of what constitutes *literacy*: Does it include both reading and writing, or just the former, as a minimum? A given culture (or community) may be classified as being generally "literate" because it depends on the recording and reading of texts for most essential educational, economic, social, political, and religious activities—even though many people can only read, but not perform the more technical activity of writing texts, for which a professional scribe would be readily available. Reading—and memorizing—would obviously be important skills to cultivate in a society, such as that in ancient Israel, where a religion based upon written texts (sacred Scripture) was a central feature.

[70] Among the diverse pieces of evidence that would support the argument for a somewhat *higher* rate of literacy among the Jewish population of Israel before 70 C.E. are the following: (a) the relatively high number of synagogues which included distinct "houses" of reading and learning (e.g., 480 in Jerusalem alone) (Gamble 1995:7); (b) "[i]n theory, every Jewish male was expected to [read the Scriptures].... The Palestinian Talmud reports the rule of Simeon ben Shetach about 100 BC that

1.2 Overview

even most, illiterate persons would have had access to texts, not in the same manner as a modern reader, but through the surrogacy of a skilled reader-performer—the lector" (2011:16). Thus, Robbins terms this a "rhetorical culture," which "features comprehensive interaction between spoken and written statement…. In practice this means that writing in a rhetorical culture imitates both speech and writing, and speech in a rhetorical culture imitates both speech and writing" (2006:127).[71] By the first century CE, then, various strategies (termed "memory technologies") had been developed to help orators and rhetoricians recall for public delivery texts that had already been written down, no doubt in anticipation of eventual oral expression.[72] The

---

all children should go to school" (Millard 2000:7); (c) the Qumran scrolls reveal that "a sectarian Jewish community…invested heavily in the production and use of literature (Gamble 1995:20); (d) while Jesus often used words of listening with the general audience ["you have heard it was said"], he also assumed that the religious leaders were able to read the Scriptures ["have you never read?"] (Millard 2000:158). Carr documents the fact that "[t]he earliest synagogues were primarily teaching institutions, and the Bible was used first and foremost as a holy teaching tool for the education-enculturation of young Jews (mostly males). Within the early synagogues and nonsynagogal schools students learned to recite and understand biblical texts, learning Hebrew and memorizing the Torah, Psalms, and portions of the prophets" (Millard 2000:111).

[71] Some scholars posit for this ANE time period a dichotomy between oral and written (scribal) texts that is rather too rigid, for example: "Oral style is designed to be heard, remembered, and transmitted by memory. Written style is intended to be preserved in print for publication and distribution" (attributed to Marcel Jousse by Harvey 1998:135).

[72] "Some of these techniques facilitated the fabrication of *ex tempore* speeches, but others allowed for the more or less verbatim performance of previously composed speeches. They also made possible a third category of oral performance, the repeated performances of previously composed material, which, while not identical as verbatim repetitions, were more nearly the same than the performances of the epic singers" (Shiner 2006:151). Shiner goes on to present a plausible hypothesis based on architectural visualization and symmetrical structuring (e.g., triadic and chiastic arrangements) to suggest how the entire Gospel of Mark may have been composed to facilitate the text's memorization and subsequent performances (ibid., 156–162). Harvey agrees that "the aural audience was capable of recognizing such (iterative) echoes over a considerable expanse" (Harvey 1998:58). Lee and Scott, on the other hand, feel that "compositional practice in the ancient world did not place a high value on crafting large, architectonic schemes to organize compositions…. Rather, well-selected units of remembered material that could be held in memory and viewed in the confined space of a writing surface [i.e., of a scroll or codex] were crafted and blended together using various artistic devices" (2009:174). Another area of contention is the nature of memory: was it stimulated and preserved more by visual techniques or oral ones? Some scholars focus on the former (e.g.,

importance in an ANE setting of memory, memorization, recollection, and a concern for the accurate transmission of primary traditions and texts naturally has great implications for our contemporary assessment of the process of transmitting biblical compositions, whether in oral or written form:

> *To remember was to live, to forget was to die.* Memory became the essential link to the past. There emerged a never-ending struggle to protect it from distortion and to prevent the threat of distortion.... The rhetoricians made memory into a matter of honor and shame.... The rabbis moved memory into the religious domain by developing it into the basis of a learned didactic discourse linked to a specific concept of sacred tradition.... [T]hey focused on memory as the stable guarantee and medium of successful transmission in a chain of teachers and students.... The early followers of Jesus thus lived in a milieu where memory and tradition were closely bound to each other in various sacred contexts and forms of communication. The Christian authors of the first two centuries—from Paul to Irenaeus—encoded into their writings different signs of mnemonic negotiation between the sacred past and the present to such an extent that *written and oral tradition became words to live by and to die for.* (Byrskog 2009:2–3, italics added)

There are of course degrees of memory or memorization with regard to the quality of *precision*, that is, the exactness that it is carried out with respect to a given text, e.g., rote reproduction versus variation in accordance with a particular setting of performance. How stable or labile, generally speaking, was the process of Scripture text transmission? Scholars disagree on this crucial point, and therefore some of the key issues involved will be discussed more fully in chapter three. But the factor of memory is also of considerable contemporary significance. To what extent is the *"memorizability"*—and the associated performance facility—of the biblical text a matter of consideration in today's translation work? If this dimension of actual speech is not afforded due attention, then a dynamic aspect of the Bible's implied communication cycle has been short-circuited and is regrettably left unrepresented. The various text studies later on will illustrate this concern.

Thatcher 2011b), others on the latter (e.g., Harvey 1998). Obviously, it would seem that *both* primary channels of communication were involved, one medium complementing and reinforcing the other, both to engage and also to enhance the operation of audience memory.

1.2.9 Tradition

What happens to the notion of "authorship" in an oral-aural society and a setting of prevailing "primary orality"? An "audience" is obviously the essential element of any public communication event. Accordingly, the people present on the scene play a pivotal role in the expression of any given instance of verbal art, whether a folktale, dilemma puzzle, joke text, praise poem, or ballad, by interacting with the principal speaker both formally (e.g., by singing the chorus of a narrative-embedded folk song) as well as informally (e.g., through personal verbal and non-verbal responses, whether supportive or critical) (Wendland 1976:v). However, the originator of a certain well-known story, for example, is typically unknown, and normally the tale itself is simply attributed to the "ancestors," having been absorbed at some time in the past as a vital constituent in a vast cognitive sea of ongoing communal oral tradition. In place of an author, then, an oral performer recreates a known text from memory, to which the audience both responds and also contributes, as it is being uttered and augmented by paralinguistic devices (gestures, etc.) in their presence. As Maxey explains:

> Tradition is central to the social function of performance. Foley prefers to discuss oral traditions that immediately connect any verbal art to a culturally specific set of traditions. More is being said and done than simply the words of a performance. The performer works within a cultural context where one assumes many important cultural connections with one's audience. The audience actively participates in the performance and interprets the performance from a context of that specific cultural tradition....
>
> Foley understands that meaning is created between the performer and the audience by the use of cultural references in the performance. Given that the performer and audience share much of the cultural traditions, references to them do not need to be full-fledged, but can be coded "metonymically," with a part standing for the whole. In this way, a word, phrase, gesture, expression can metonymically communicate an entire narrative that is not fully expressed in the performance,

but nonetheless is fully accessible to both performer and audience.[73] (Maxey 2009:98)

These observations, though very applicable to situations of primary orality and oral performance, become problematic, or at least controversial, when simply transferred to the compositional setting of the biblical literature. Thus, there is a tendency in certain scholarly circles, perhaps under the influence of postmodern criticism, to dispense altogether with the concept of authorship and to more or less attribute all of the texts that have come down to us in the written canon of Scripture as deriving from a hypothetical fluctuating, ideology-driven oral or scribal tradition of one form or another.[74] With reference to the New Testament, for example, one scholar posits the following development:

> The early church was not simply founded on a collection of authoritative writings; rather, the collection was created in close association with the apostolic tradition, which was regarded as foundational.... The New Testament manuscripts from the early (first) centuries suggest...that the traditioning process was from the very beginning characterized by a variety of versions (and translations) of the New Testament writings and that these existed with equal validity alongside each other.... Even before the origin of the Gospels there was a sphere of tradition made up of words of Jesus, early Christian teaching authorized by the Lord, topoi from Jewish-Hellenistic ethics, and citations from scripture. Within this sphere, out of which Christianity created its own tradition and associated it historically with the phenomenon called "the teaching of the apostles" (Acts 2:42), the distinction

---

[73] Maxey refers here to Foley 1991:2, 7. The "metonymic" nature of the operation of resonant *intertextuality* in oral tradition is a prominent aspect of Lévi-Strauss's classic studies of mythology, e.g., "The Structural Study of Myth" (1974). It should also be noted that "traditions" are not only verbal; rather, they refer to "the recurrence of the same structures of conduct and patterns of belief over several generations" (Shils 1971:123. Furthermore, "in every society, whether ancient or modern...most of what passes as knowledge comes from tradition" (Sparks 2008:26).

[74] From my perspective, a "canon" is "much more than a list of books"; rather, "[t]he canon represents a body of texts that has influenced each other in the formation and development of the full body....[T]he canon is an entity that indicates... inner-textual interdependence and logic" (Köstenberger and Patterson 2011:153–154). See also Thiselton 2006.

between the "genuine" words of Jesus and other traditions played no part at all.⁷⁵ What was decisive, rather, was that early Christian teaching as a whole was regarded as resting on the authority of the Lord.... Early Christianity and the early church understood the Jesus tradition from the very beginning to be a free and living tradition.... We may conclude from this that there was no fundamental difference in the first centuries of Christianity between oral and written tradition. Instead, in both spheres we observe the analogous process of a free, living tradition that adapted its concrete form to the understanding of the content in each case. (Schröter 2006:106, 108, 110, 120–122)

However, a key question remains largely unanswered regarding this fluid/flexible text supposition: How did such a "free, living tradition" become relatively fixed quite quickly and firmly so soon after the events that they record have occurred? This is a rather weighty creative load to lay to the charge of some nebulous, communal oral tradition,⁷⁶ analogous to the Chewa oral narrative tradition, for example—if that is what is being referred to. Thus, one cannot attribute to an anonymous, communal "it" the credence and capacity to evaluate, select, and transmit specific texts (while excluding others), hence also preparing the ground for the acceptance of the chosen corpus of sacred writings, which later became canonized as "Scripture."⁷⁷ Without the notion of widely accepted authoritative authorship, plus a reliable method of textual transmission deriving from

---

⁷⁵ The NT writers, however, do seem to point out that studious discernment and discrimination was involved in the formulation of the NT writings, e.g., Luke 1:1–4; Acts 1:1–3; 2 Pet 3:15–16.

⁷⁶ So also Kirk 2009:170–171. In contrast, David Carr draws attention to the fact that "the Hebrew Bible—a complex collection of texts from widely differing periods—testifies to a form of cultural reproduction that is intensely textual" (2005:112). Carr goes on to cite many passages from the Hebrew Scriptures from diverse settings that support this claim concerning its essential *textuality* (ibid., 112–121) along with "widespread evidence for literate specialists and literate officials in early Israel," which must, however, "be interpreted with caution" (ibid., 119).

⁷⁷ Associated with this is the perspective that "wants us to think of 'the early Jesus tradition as an insistently pluriform phenomenon' involving performative or rhetorical oral textuality as well as multiple chirographic forms, and where there likely never existed an 'original' text of Jesus' words but 'a plurality of originals'" (Graham 2010:235, with reference to Kelber 2010). But of course it did not take long for such "pluriformity," if indeed it was as rampant as suggested, to be assessed, sifted, and reduced to four authoritative and reliable written "gospel" witnesses.

that (i.e., eyewitness testimony and memory based on extant texts), it is extremely doubtful that the documents of the "New Testament" as we know it (with the exception of several disputed epistles) could have developed as they did into a diverse, but recognized religious "tradition" having the singular mandate that it commanded from the very beginning.[78] In fact, why would the NT tradents, whether scribes or oral transmitters, diverge from the practice of their OT counterparts, where accuracy in the transmission of "long-duration," especially religious, literature was a prominent characteristic?[79]

Though not without its own difficulties, more credible to my mind is Birger Gerhardsson's hypothesis with respect to the indispensable "factor of memory in tradition in terms of [a] memorization of more or less fixed [Scripture] texts through repetition, with faithful repetition also being the mechanism of transmission" (Kirk 2009:156).[80] This approach derives by analogy from traditional rabbinic memory training techniques and ancient

---

[78] The same principle applies to the OT, both as a canonical whole and also with respect to its constituent books, although there is admittedly less certainty about authorship in many cases. Nevertheless, the concept of recognized authorship (whether actual or traditionally attributed) was critically important, and such a concern is undoubtedly reflected in strict, text-focused, oral-recitative Jewish scribal practice. This ancient profession was tasked with the responsibility of passing on the religious tradition as precisely as possible—since ultimately, all the words inscribed were viewed as originating with God (YHWH), whether recorded in the Law, the Prophets, or the Writings.

[79] As Carr observes, "the main point of the textual production and reception process in the [ancient Jewish] educational/enculturational context was not to incise and revise texts on parchment, papyrus, or tablet. Rather, the aim was to 'incise' such texts word for word on the minds of the next generation. A form of ancient literacy was learned, but the whole process was much more than mere learning of letters and words. It was the appropriation of an entire vocabulary of episodes, poetic lines, narrative themes, and implicit values. Written copies of texts served a subsidiary purpose in this system—as numinous symbols of the hallowed ancient tradition, as learning aids, and as reference points to insure accurate performance" (2010:18).

[80] See also Gerhardsson 1998; cf. Harvey 1998:13. "Thus, *the mind* stood at the center of the often discussed oral-written interface. The focus was on inscribing a culture's most precious traditions on the insides of people. Within this context, copies of texts served as solidified reference points for recitation and memorization of the tradition" (Carr 2005:6).

It might also be noted here that in the ancient Hebrew context, scribes not only *preserved* the textual tradition by copying it, but they also *protected* it by disposing of all old or defective copies, which is another reason (along with time, the climate, fragile writing materials, and warfare) why relatively few very ancient copies of the Hebrew Scriptures are extant (Wegner 1999:163; cf. Carr 2010:29).

1.2 Overview

pedagogical practice (Gerhardsson 1964:17–21)—a contextualized perspective that has been complemented and refined by theories regarding the importance of "eyewitness testimony" in the transmission of oral texts having great historical, sociocultural, or spiritual value.[81] In this understanding, the compositions of Scripture that began as an oral proclamation of some type are assumed to have been "recorded" in a more or less stable, authoritative form immediately or soon thereafter, either by ear (i.e., in memory) or by the eye (i.e., in an inscribed document).[82] As a result, oral as well as visual texts coexisted, but the written form, or tradition, was clearly primary as far as establishing a basis for sacred "Scripture." Written texts thus began to be used as more consistent points of reference for precisely memorizing and transmitting subsequent oral traditions derived from them—namely, all proclamations of those sacred texts that followed. In this connection, Byrskog notes that "[t]he tradition is a text…and it is important to realize that its [written] preservation was separated from its [oral-aural] use."[83] Oral tradition was still essential in the transmission of the texts that were eventually canonized to form the Old and New Testaments, but there was a priority established in terms of the prophetic and apostolic authority that was attached to specific oral traditions and written texts. This rabbinic-oral historical approach will be discussed further in the third chapter.

1.2.10 Multimodality

This final, multidisciplinary area of contemporary research is related to orality studies in general and deals with the potential influence of one semiotic mode of signification upon another during a given verbal communication event. "Words may interact with still and moving images, diagrams, music, typography, or page layout."[84] Such inter-semiotic interfacing is especially

---

[81] For example, see Byrskog 2002.

[82] In this connection, it is important to remember that Jesus was a recognized teacher (rabbi) with a relatively stable religious message about "the Kingdom of God/heaven," not to be compared with an itinerant storyteller, whose claim to fame would lie in the relative entertainment value of his repertory of variable fictitious tales (Gerhardsson 2005:7). Thus, the "evidence for orality in the NT points to a controlled *didactic* orality, not a communal orality ('by many for many')" (Barnett 2005:137).

[83] Byrskog 2009:13; added italics and material in brackets.

[84] This is a quotation from an announcement for a conference on the theme "Translating Multimodalities," held on November 6, 2010 at the University of

applicable to multimedia (e.g., audio-visual) translations,[85] but these issues are very relevant also for print versions, in the first place, with reference to assorted options that pertain to the display of the translated text on the published page. For example, in terms of the *typography* and *format* one would want to determine reader preferences and documented needs concerning variables like these:

- the use of one versus two columns of print;
- justified versus ragged-right margins;
- the most readable and yet also economical size and style of print;
- the incorporation of different font styles (italics, boldface, underline, caps, etc.) for the purposes of highlighting and emphasizing;
- the use of vertical space to indicate principal discourse breaks and horizontal space to reveal major text parallels or contrasts, chiastic structures, or other patterns of formal and/or topical arrangement;
- a break-up and display of the text in terms of ideal "utterance units" so that it is more legible and easier to read aloud.

Portsmouth, United Kingdom. Another excerpt: "Translation is usually about the printed word, but in today's multimodal environment translators must take account of other signifying elements too.... Multimodal meaning-making is deployed for promotional, political, expressive and informative purposes which must be understood and accounted for by technical translators, literary translators, copywriters, subtitlers, localisers and other language professionals" (ibid.).

An example of a new Bible translation that is purportedly "multimodal" in nature is the *BasisBibel* of the German Bible Society: "The *BasisBibel* is designed to be equally *suitable for reading as a book and on screen*, and its structure and language are *easy to understand* for people who are familiar with new media. 'The *BasisBibel* uses clear, concise sentences and *very rhythmical* language. Every line contains a single idea,' says Dr. Hannelore Jahr, head of the Bible Society's editorial department.... And links at the bottom of each page point to further *information available online*, including maps and photos" (2010; added italics).

[85] Multimodal or multimedia translation involves "the interlingual transfer of verbal language when it is transmitted and accessed both visually and acoustically, usually, but not necessarily, through some kind of electronic device" (Chiaro 2009:141). This multimodal focus is receiving increasing consideration in biblical studies nowadays, for example, by scholars engaged in the investigation of "ancient media culture," which concerns the dynamic interaction of communications technologies involving public oral as well as written means with respect to both composing and also transmitting/proclaiming religious messages (Le Donne and Thatcher 2011b:1).

1.2 Overview

Of course, some systematic target audience-oriented research plus trial and testing would be necessary in order to determine whether such graphic features actually help or hinder average readers. If helpful, then which ones are most important to try to implement, in keeping with a project's guiding *brief* and primary *Skopos*?

In this connection, it is important to recall how different media of transmission interacted during the original event of communicating the Scriptures. The norm probably approximated a combination that may be described along the following lines:

> The oral performative nature of ancient reading, therefore, shows that we are dealing with texts that are inherently multidimensional. As 1 John, for instance, was first read or recited aloud to its recipients, its text was experienced aurally and visually by means of the voice, body, and character of the lector, through the ears and eyes of the audience. In addition, the total atmosphere, including the make-up and emotional disposition(s) of the gathered audience as well as the setting's backdrop of sights, sounds, and smells, rendered the ancient reading experience a multi-media event. (Bickle 2011:18)

How very much different from the way in which many of us often interact with the Scriptures today—silently, visually, and individually. This is not to say that the latter is a less valid or productive manner of encountering the Word, but rather that we must realize how much this diverges from the custom in ancient times. We will be considering this textual and contextual setting in greater detail in the chapters that follow.

The multimodality factor also concerns the potential and actual semiotic interaction of the biblical text with various *paratextual tools* used to convey different types of background information to a reader, e.g., footnotes, sectional headings, glossary entries, cross references, illustrations, etc. There is a great need for such supplementary helps nowadays, as in a "study Bible," in order to enlighten readers (and combat "biblical illiteracy") with respect to crucial presupposed aspects of the original context that cannot easily be communicated in a translation, including a "meaning-based" version. Indeed, certain circumstantial facts about the Ancient Near Eastern environment may be necessary in order for readers to correctly interpret (and perhaps also apply) the translation in their language and sociocultural setting. This would include notes concerning important features of contemporary history, politics, economics, society, geography, religion, flora and fauna, world-view, value-system, customs and cultural practices. But how might such a "paratext" be provided for listeners of audio Scriptures? A range of possibilities come to mind as signaling devices, for example: a distinctive "narrator voice" (voices) to indicate diverse kinds of content, or the use of "sound effects" to mark an expository aside by means of a special sound (gong, cymbal, drum beat), or a repeated characteristic melody line.

In the case of audio-video productions of Scripture texts, this sort of elucidating, cognitively enriching information can be readily furnished through pictorial means, for that is one of the advantages of the visual medium. However, some ingenuity and creativity would still be necessary in order to find a way to distinguish the background from the biblical text, and also to prevent a distortion of the original message or over-contextualization in favor of the target cultural setting. The need for undertaking a prior wide-ranging program of focused testing is evident, for example, as project planners endeavor to determine what type of content is most essential for (or required by) the intended text "consumer" group and how best to convey it (by which medium and means). Research in this field would thus include the identification of all possible "mismatches," where the message from one medium distorts or detracts from that being conveyed in another medium, for example: a culturally incongruous or offensive illustration in a printed Bible document (e.g., a certain hand gesture displayed that is vulgar in the TL culture), music that does not harmonize emotively with the topic or text that it accompanies (e.g., a happy melody for a somber scene), or character "voices" with timbres that do not jibe perceptually with the biblical personages that they represent (especially in the case of Jesus and the great "heroes" of Scripture).

In the next chapter we will see how some of the ideas and issues that pertain to the ten general concepts considered above relate to a number of different methodologies that are especially helpful in the application of orality and performance studies to the analysis and interpretation of the Scriptures. As in the preceding discussion, I will focus in particular on those theoretical notions and practical approaches that encourage or refine an oral-aural perspective on the work of Bible translation and text transmission via various media.

2

Methodologies for Investigating the Oral-Aural Analysis, Translation, and Transmission of Biblical Texts

2.1 Overview

Why is research in *orality* (and associated fields) becoming such an increasingly influential issue in contemporary hermeneutics and the discourse analysis of biblical literature?[1] There are probably a number of reasons for this development, ranging from the elementary (as when print-oriented scholars simply failed to consider the spoken word) to the more theoretical (when past students of Scripture were too absorbed in documentary text-centered approaches, like source, redaction, and form criticism). In the latter part of the twentieth century, however, when scholarship began to pay more attention to the *reception* side of the

---

[1] At the 2011 SBL Annual Meeting in San Francisco, for example, at least a dozen proposed "program units" featured or involved different aspects of *orality studies* in relation to Scripture interpretation and presentation. Theories and models of biblical *discourse analysis* may be found, for example, in Porter and Reed 1999 and Wendland 2011:chs. 5–6.

communication cycle,[2] the *phonic factor* of discourse began to be investigated much more seriously. In conjunction with this development, researchers discovered that the dimension of orality also figured prominently in the initial *composition* of the biblical texts, which, as it turns out, were actually articulated aloud while they were being verbally created.[3]

However, these studies then gave rise to an important methodological problem: What can the exegete do about the critical *loss of sonic significance* in the original text, that is, the unrecorded (and un-recordable) pragmatic meaning that was transmitted via the *suprasegmental* prosodic features of sound, such as stress, volume, tempo, pause, intonation, and vocal quality? The classic case to illustrate the relevance of this point is Pontius Pilate, who in response to Christ's self-testimony enigmatically responds: "What is truth?" (John 18:37–38): Was this, in fact, a genuine question expressing the governor's desire for some needed information from Christ? Its intonation would have undoubtedly revealed whether or not it was. Furthermore, when recording this passage in script, the Evangelist would have had the apposite sounds in mind as he uttered and (he or a scribe) simultaneously penned the text. Or was this, as most scholars assume, a *rhetorical question* indicating Pilate's personal doubt that "truth" (whatever *that* was) could be determined at all? If so, this query would have additionally conveyed the speaker's associated emotions and attitude towards his addressee and the current crisis situation that brought them together (e.g., frustration, doubt, anger, hostility, harshness *versus* eagerness, longing, reflection, or regret).[4]

---

[2] For example, Fowler 1991. More recently, its has been asserted that "[t]he modern audience also bears the responsibility of hearing between the lines, of creating the story with the ancient author. In our particular context as the people of God reading the Scriptures, we are all the more likely to be persuaded by the argument we help complete, astonished by the pictures we help draw, and formed by the story we help create" (Maxwell 2010:xiii-xiv; cf. 178). However, I would argue that such a perspective gives far too much "responsibility" (or "liberty") to today's audiences (or readers). Our task is not to freely "create" meaning together with the biblical author, but first and foremost rather to strictly "interpret" the contextually intended sense and significance that was inscribed by the original author in the canonical text (reading even "between the lines" of text) that has come down to us through the ages.

[3] For a classic study of this subject, see Achtemeier 1990.

[4] Often such intonational features are necessary to *contrast* one part of a discourse with another, as for example, when Christ shifts from condemning "teachers of the law" for "devouring widows' houses" (Luke 20:46–47) to praising a poor widow for her total, self-consuming offering in the temple treasury (21:3–4).

2.1 Overview

Such vocal overtones thus constitute a crucial aspect of significance that we can only guess at today, using the information available from the immediate context and the author's characteristic discourse style.

This type of evaluation with respect to any potential implicit meaning has to be made when rendering the biblical text in translation.[5] At the most basic level, in Chewa for example, Pilate's query must be explicitly marked

---

Obviously, a chapter break (ch. 21) has been misplaced here, thus separating two interconnected passages.

[5] My position is that the "meaning" of any text is to be determined from the perspective of presumed *authorial intention*, including any subsequent "editorial intention," to the extent that such activity was involved in the case of those texts that came to be regarded by the community of faith, Jewish and early Christian, as being divinely "inspired" (cf. Wendland 2004b:52–53; Osborn 2006:495–499). I thus distinguish a text's so-called "sense," or inscribed content, including all of the explicatures, implicatures, and other inferable semantic and pragmatic intent (Huang 2007:188–197), from its "significance." The latter then refers to meaning as perceived, understood, and expounded by subsequent hearers, readers, interpreters, and transmitters. How do we determine authorial intention when dealing with the biblical literature (sacred tradition and sacred Scripture)? The SL text itself, its literary macro- and micro-structures, situated in its presumed compositional context provides many hermeneutical clues, and so does the long line of recorded scholarly and ecclesiastical interpretation over the years (i.e., a text's hermeneutical "tradition"). How have reliable exegetes and serious students of Scripture understood what the biblical author wrote, as recorded after any editorial and scribal modifications in the final canonical document? (cf. Frank 2009). Of course, in some cases a range of credible interpretations are available, but the possibilities are then limited by recognized text-critical, literary and discourse analysis procedures, hermeneutical methods, published exegetical studies, and for some, at least, the theological, superintending and unifying principal of divine verbal "inspiration" (see, for example, Osborne 2006; Vanhoozer 1998; Thiselton 1992).

In those cases where the author of the text is either unknown (e.g., Judges) or disputed (e.g., Hebrews), perhaps it would be advisable to refer to what literary critics term "the implied author." I define this notion as the hypothetical "person" ("God" for inspirationists) who is posited as being the single unifying mind (conception) and voice (producer) behind the compositional-editorial process (e.g., Psalms, Luke-Acts) which has resulted in the document that exists in the canonical collection of the OT/NT. From a secular perspective, "[t]he implied author is the image of the author projected by the text itself as the creator of its art and meaning and norms…; the implied author forms a construct embodying the overall structure and may vary even from one work to another by the same writer…. The author/narrator exists only as a construct, which the reader infers and fills out to make sense of the work as an ordered design of meaning and effect" (Sternberg 1987:74–75, with reference to Wayne Booth's *The Rhetoric of fiction*). The issue of authorial intention resulting in an authoritative "canon" of written texts (each arising from, or leading to a sacred oral tradition) is an important hermeneutical perspective and a principle that will resurface periodically in the various chapters of the present volume.

as being either real or rhetorical through the use of an introductory question particle and the proper word order. In addition, an attitudinal overlay can be conveyed by means of short intensifiers as well as exclamatory and emotive particles. But what is to guide translators in making these decisions? Commentaries and the appropriate Translator's Handbook can help to a certain extent, but perhaps the greatest assistance may be afforded by the translators themselves adopting a "performative approach" to the biblical documents, especially where dialogue or dialogic texts (like the psalms, prophets, and epistles) are concerned. This means that they try to "imagine" themselves as being in the current social and communicative context described in the Scripture passage at hand and then actually vocalize how the different speakers might orally express themselves in that particular interpersonal situation within the local culture. Such a sound- and setting-responsive translation strategy will be discussed in further detail with reference to the selected texts that are considered in sections II and III to follow.

2.2 Investigating orality

The intertwined dimensions of orality and scribality (writing) in relation to the contextualizing ANE milieu and the various compositions of Scripture have been increasingly investigated by scholars in recent years.[6] As noted above, some of the more helpful of these studies have adopted the discipline of "performance criticism," which "embraces many methods as means to reframe the biblical materials in the context of traditional oral cultures, construct scenarios of ancient performances, learn from contemporary performances of these materials, and reinterpret biblical writings accordingly."[7] Several recent publications that give prominence to the oral-aural factor have gone on to apply these findings to the practice of Bible translation.[8] In addition to the preceding works, there is a range of other communication-based methodologies that encourage a serious

---

[6] Along with those mentioned in ch. 1, we have, for the NT: Dewey 1994; Loubser 2007; Thatcher 2008; for the OT: Schniedewind 2004; Ben Zvi and Floyd 2000; Edelman and Ben Zvi 2009.

[7] David Rhoads, from the introduction to the "Biblical Performance Criticism" series (Hearon and Ruge-Jones 2009:i).

[8] Maxey 2009; Wendland 2011; Rhoads forthcoming.

consideration of the presence and influence of orality in the Scriptures. All these investigations can assist exegetes and translators alike to probe this vital acoustic facet of meaning as it is manifested in diverse biblical texts, prose as well as poetry. The major approaches are briefly summarized below along with several key references that expand upon and further develop each distinct field of study.[9]

2.2.1 Conversational analysis

Conversational analysis is a methodology that is derived from the broader discipline of sociolinguistics.[10] It investigates what people *do* when they converse with one another (pragmatics)—over and above what they *say* (semantics). The emphasis here is upon *implicatures in discourse, that is,* implicit information which is conveyed by the communicative context, or social setting of speech, in conjunction with the words that are actually uttered. An implicature results when one of the so-called "Gricean maxims" of conversation is deliberately deviated from or exploited during the text-transmission process (Grice 1975:45–47). Thus, the varied sociolinguistic, contextually determined "felicity conditions" (Grice's term) that are associated with this so-called "cooperative principle" involve the four basic "maxims" of *quality* (concerning truthfulness), *quantity* (amount of information), *relevance* (utility, appropriateness), and *manner* (clarity, brevity, and/or orderliness).[11]

Take Job 3:3, for example, where we hear the suffering Job say: "Let the day perish wherein I was born, and the night which said, 'A man-child is conceived'" (RSV). It would seem from this formally correspondent rendition

---

[9] See also Rhoads 2006a, b, *passim;* Maxey 2009:ch. 5.

[10] "**Sociolinguistics** is the descriptive study of the effect of any and all aspects of society, including cultural norms, expectations, and context, on the way language is used, and the effects of language use on society.... Sociolinguistics overlaps to a considerable degree with pragmatics.... It also studies how language varieties differ between groups separated by certain social variables, e.g., ethnicity, religion, status, gender, level of education, age, etc., and how creation and adherence to these rules is used to categorize individuals in social or socioeconomic classes. As the usage of a language varies from place to place, language usage also varies among social classes, and it is these *sociolects* that sociolinguistics studies" (from http://en.wikipedia.org/wiki/Sociolinguistics, accessed 10/14/2010; cf. for application in Bible translation, see Wendland 2004b:277–280, 299–300; 2008d:92–95).

[11] For an elaboration of these concepts, see Hatim and Mason 1990:62–63; Hatim and Munday 2004:176.

that Job has indeed violated all of Grice's felicity conditions mentioned above. How can a "day," let alone one's own birthday, be done away with—or one's conception follow the day of one's birth? Why would a person, no matter how much s/he is in anguish, want to pronounce such a "curse" (v. 1)? And why all the apparent repetition in this imprecatory utterance? The problem becomes even worse in other translations. A literal rendering of the old Chewa Bible, for example, reads nearly unintelligibly as follows: "May the day on which I was born be thrown away, and that night spoke, 'It has stood still [i.e., become pregnant] with him, a boy-child." When one has access to a printed text, it is possible to go back over the words in the effort to derive some sense from them. Simply hearing this passage (certainly the Chewa version) read aloud, however, leaves the audience mystified; it is no wonder to them that none of Job's three friends wanted to "say a word to him" (Job 2:13b)!

The extent to which such maxims is evidenced in non-Western language-cultures has been questioned, but this methodology can, after the necessary research in local modes and patterns of conversation, be locally adapted and usefully applied in oral-aural translation testing procedures. These methodologies would help to determine which particular factors cause observed failures and miscues during interpersonal communication in different settings. For example, does the TL version violate felicity conditions in terms of *quality* by conveying to listeners wrong implicatures in their sociocultural context; of *quantity* by not building enough redundancy into the text, hence making it too difficult to understand (thus crossing the threshold of frustration); or of *manner* by a literalistic rendering that sounds unnatural in relation to normal patterns of speech usage in the current situation being depicted in the biblical text?

2.2.2 Relevance theory

Relevance theory (RT) focuses on a single Gricean maxim (see above) and considers all inferential communication, oral or written, to be governed by the twofold "principle of relevance." Accordingly, a specific text is deemed "optimally relevant" (conceptually satisfying and sufficient to listeners) if it does two things. First, the speaker's words must provide "adequate contextual effects" for the audience with respect to their current "cognitive environment," that is, the set of pertinent assumptions which are activated by a given

2.2 Investigating orality

text in its cultural context. On the other hand, the utterance must accomplish this "without requiring unnecessary processing effort," that is, without being too hard to understand (Gutt 1992:24–25). Hatim and Mason use *effectiveness* and *efficiency* to describe this same mental process, which is also called the "minimax" principle ("maximum effect for minimal effort") (1990:91).[12]

The term "contextual effects" refers to information that serves to (a) provide important facts (generating implications) that the listening community needs to know (and use); (b) guide them in perceiving and interpreting speaker/author-intended implications; (c) eliminate extraneous or erroneous assumptions; and/or (d) reinforce correct and necessary assumptions.[13] However, in keeping with the cognitive principle of relevance noted above, an internal default regulatory, or balancing mechanism is always operative. Thus, any mental interpretive exercise must not result in too much conceptual processing effort, thus outweighing the potential gain in contextual effects. Relevance theory underscores the fact that a particular utterance (or discourse) always requires its hearers to *infer* considerably more information than is furnished by the linguistic forms of the text itself. They accomplish such understanding by selecting, more or less automatically, the most helpful (relevant) inputs available at the moment—textual, contextual, and memory-based (including one's basic beliefs, presuppositions, cultural values, personal recollections, and so forth) (Brown 2007:35).

Relevance is, therefore, an essential criterion not only during the interpretation of a text, but also when assessing the *acceptability* of a given translation (Wendland 2008d:226–228). This relates to a particular target group's expectations of what the TL version should *sound* (read) like in terms of style (linguistic form) and content, as well as their intentions with regard to how they propose to use or apply it (that is, what its primary intended function is). In public communication settings, especially where non-literates are concerned, the only way to determine whether a certain translated text manifests the desired contextual effects, coupled with a suitable level of communicative efficiency, is through a range of extensive and comprehensive oral-aural testing techniques (e.g., Wendland 2004b:319–366). With reference to Job 3:3 mentioned above, for example, one way to aid an audience, at least one listening in Chewa, to perceive the intended

---

[12] See also Hatim and Munday 2004:60.
[13] Information derived from H. Hill 2009; cf. H. Hill et al. 2011:25–28.

purpose and relevance of such a passage would be to audibly signal the nature of Job's words—that is, in a way that fits the situational context more appropriately, e.g., with an intonation that resounds with deep sorrow and mourning. Further clarity might be gained by subtly shifting the focus somewhat from the past to the *present*—changing "cursing" the day of his birth (which sounds either foolish or impossible) to "bewailing" the current circumstances that he was in (e.g., using an introductory speech margin such as, "He *lamented* saying...," to indicate the discourse genre).

2.2.3 Speech act theory

As its very designation implies, speech-act theory is of great significance when issues of orality are considered with respect to the Scriptures. It is often used in conjunction with conversation analysis (see above). The term "speech act" denotes the interactive purpose for which a segment of discourse is expressed, whether the text is complete or partial, oral or written.[14] Every speech-act is commonly described as consisting of three components: (a) the *locution*, which is the overt act of verbal representation (utterance/sentence, i.e., its form + content); (b) the *illocution*, which refers to the focal functional force or communicative aim of the speaker/writer's words (e.g., to promise, warn, console, instruct); and (c) the *perlocution*, which denotes the actual effect or perceived outcome of the utterance (e.g., persuasion, surprise, offense, confirmation). In short, the locution is *what is said*; the illocution is *what happens* pragmatically when the locution is uttered; the perlocution is the *response* of the hearer to what was said (Brown 2007:33).[15]

Speech acts (their illocutions in particular) may be described with varying degrees of specificity. Various classificatory inventories have been proposed. I, for example, have proposed describing speech acts with reference to the literature of Scripture as being: informative, directive, expressive, evaluative,

---

[14] Speech-act theory originated with Austin's *How to Do Things with Words* ([1962] 1975). When applied to written discourse, *communicative acts* would probably be a better term than *speech acts*. Thiselton calls attention to the theological significance of such communicative acts: "According to the central traditions of the Old and New Testaments, *communicative acts of declaration, proclamation, call, appointment, command, worship,* and most especially *promise* are constitutive of what it is for the word of God to become operative and effective" (Thiselton 1999:151; original italics).

[15] "[I]llocutionary acts are intended by the speaker, while perlocutionary effects are not always intended" (Huang 2007:103–104).

aesthetic, commissive, performative, and interactive in nature (2004b:215–217).[16] These disparate speech acts usually occur in combination, both sequentially and simultaneously, to form complex "speech events." Any sentence, whether written or spoken, may therefore be analyzed on several levels and to different degrees of detail. The theory of speech acts highlights the *interpersonal* character of verbal communication, stressing the initial *intention* of the speech source (speaker/writer) as a point of beginning any analysis. On the other hand, the methodology also gives considerable attention to the *responsive* activity of message consumers (hearers/readers) in the process.

The amount of *correspondence* between illocution and perlocution in the speech cycle is an area of interest when evaluating the relative quality of communication, and no less so when translated texts (written locutions) are involved. Obviously, it is important for translators to be aware of this often implicit, pragmatic feature of biblical discourse in their initial analysis of a text of Scripture. They must then endeavor to duplicate in their translation the main speech acts, or functional aims of the passage. This would include its intended communicative effects, such as rhetorical force, esthetic appeal, and oral-aural vibrancy, which would be especially important when transmitting the text via audio (-visual) media. As already noted, it is important to clearly signal the nature of the speech act found in Job 3:3 in order to avoid possible misunderstanding in the TL. In many languages this will be a "lament" or "[formal] complaint" (Chewa: *-dandaula*), for example, rather than a "curse" (*-temberera*), which carries a rather serious negative connotation in the sociocultural setting concerned (relating to traditional religious beliefs). In this case, the Chewa verb can also be used reflexively, not simply directively, thus giving poignant vocal expression to the great personal agony and grief that one is experiencing, whether or not anyone else happens to be listening.

2.2.4 Argument-structure analysis

Argument-structure analysis extends the notion of speech acts to encompass a broader, rhetorically based system of analysis that situates a certain text

---

[16] In his generic "typology of speech acts," Searle includes: representatives (assertives), directives, commissives, expressives, and declaratives (Huang 2007:106–108).

within a specific setting of communication.[17] The key structural and pragmatic elements either explicitly or implicitly involved in the formal presentation of an argument are displayed on the diagram below, as they are assumed to exist in dynamic interrelationship with each other.[18] The central constituent of the entire argument strategy is posited as being the principal "speech act" of making a *problem*-initiated, *goal*-oriented *appeal*, whether an exhortation to adopt a particular thought or action or a prohibition of the same:[19]

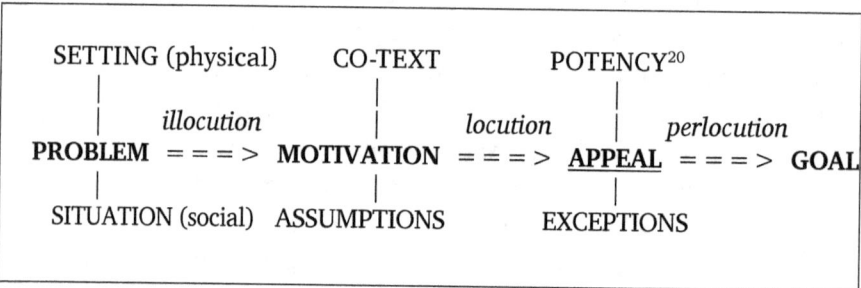

---

[17] This is not a simple task, and the manifold nature of communicating theological as well as literary, rhetorically-fashioned texts in complex, or "multiple social, cultural, and ideological contexts" (Robbins 2006:11) must be recognized and factored into the overall analysis process. The model presented here is an adaptation of S. Toulmin's proposed argument structure (*Uses of Argument*), where the "datum" (corresponding to "motivation" in the diagram) "is the evidence presented as the basis for the claim," (corresponding to the "goal"), which "is the conclusion the argument seeks to establish," and the "warrant" (corresponding to the "appeal") is the rational link between the two (Clark 1993:136). In addition, one may need to note a "qualifier" (corresponding to "potency") "to indicate the degree of strength conferred by" the datum on the claim, and one may also "want to spell out some of the reasons a conclusion might not follow"—the "rebuttal" ("exceptions") (ibid., 138).

[18] These components are presented in more detail and illustrated with reference to the epistle to Philemon in Wendland 2004b:219–24.

[19] This framework for text analysis must first be carefully "contextualized" with reference to the worldview and value system of the Ancient Near East, as is done in the approach known as "social-scientific criticism." This would include such basic sociocultural perspectives and distinctions as honor-shame, freedom-slavery, in group-out group, challenge-riposte, fictive kinship, imperial politics, polytheism, corporate personality, reciprocity, and patronage (see Pilch and Malina 1993, especially as such issues pertain to the practice of Bible translation (for some examples and case studies, see Neufeld 2008).

[20] The variable "potency," or verbal strength of an utterance (ranging from overt commands to implicit prescriptions/prohibitions), includes the relative authority of the speaker, that is, explicit or implicit references to his perceived ethos or ascribed status, prestige, and/or power to command the addressees.

2.2 Investigating orality

The *motivation* for the appeal consists of the different deductive and inductive types of reasoning that the author/speaker employs in support of his argument. This cause-effect sequence of [**problem** + **motivation** + **(verbal) appeal** → **goal**], along with its various textual extensions or transformations, constitutes the essential backbone of any Old Testament or New Testament hortatory (*paraenetic*) discourse, including segments of direct speech attributed to Christ (e.g., the "bread of life" teaching in John 6:25–59). The surrounding contextual factors give substance to the pivotal hortatory appeal (exhortation to or prohibition from) in terms of related presuppositions, assumptions, implications, implicatures, and other necessary background information.

Translators need to keep these distinct, but interrelated interactive variables in mind, especially when analyzing any argument-constituted text of Scripture, in order to transmit it both meaningfully and also with equivalent impact and appeal in their language. A good way of accomplishing this is by actually proclaiming the TL composition *aloud* in a public setting of performance, giving it the appropriate setting-sensitive intonation and paralinguistic modification, that is, in keeping with the overt content and implied sentiments being expressed. Much pertinent material concerning the original environment and circumstances may well have to be relegated to marginal notes or to the explanatory introduction of a given book, chapter, or section—with corresponding oral devices being utilized for an audio Scripture production (e.g., informative "asides" marked by a separate speaking voice, a drum/gong/bell/etc., or a readily recognized, repeated musical motif).

Job's plaintive lament of 3:3, for example, can be clearly identified by prosodic and paralinguistic means in most languages (e.g., Chewa) through the apt use of the correct oral intonation, pause, stress, tempo (slow), nasalization, and so forth. It is important in the case of such expressive speech that the correct personal emotions and/or attitudes get communicated along with the semantic content. In a printed text, on the other hand, such pragmatic implications would obviously need to be conveyed in writing, either within the text itself (e.g., by a verbal specifier such as "mourned" or "spoke sadly" in the speech margin of v. 2)[21] or indicated in the paratext (e.g., with an explanatory footnote).

---

[21] In a publication that features the creative use of format, certain prosodic features can be conveyed by changes in the font style, for example, boldface for loudness, italics for emphasis, small capitals for stress. Of course, such interpretive devices would need to be carefully explained in an introduction so that readers know in advance how to interpret them, ideally when actually reading the text aloud.

2.2.5 Functionalist strategy

A detailed functional approach to translation was being promoted and applied in the field for several years before the appearance of de Waard and NidA's popularization of this method for Bible translators (De Waard and Nida 1986). Thus, the notion of "function" was a prominent aspect of the *Skopostheorie* ('purpose-theory') school of translation pioneered by Reiss and Vermeer and further developed more recently in the scholarly research of Christiane Nord.[22] Functionalist writers stress the need for specifying, at the outset, the main communicative objective that a particular translation is designed to perform for its target ("client") audience within a specific sociocultural situation and organizational structure.

The importance of developing an explicit, generally approved operational framework for a translation project is also emphasized in functionalist studies. This is known as the translation *brief*, which explicitly sets forth a "job description" with reference to the total communication context. Such a description would include, for example, the major expectations of the TL addressee(s), the medium via which the message will be transmitted, organizational matters, available facilities and resources, the required qualifications of personnel, the proposed time frame, and, if necessary, also the motivation for the text's production and/or reception (Nord 1997:137). The chief component of a brief, then, makes explicit the precise purpose, or *Skopos*, for which the translation is being made, with due regard for its primary audience and context of use, and in keeping with the prevailing social and translational norms in the community. The whole preparatory stage of research and planning must therefore be fully interactive and freely "negotiated" between the proposed producer and consumer groups. A more complex brief and *Skopos* are normally called for when a sacred, manifold-use text, such as the "Holy Scriptures," is to be translated.

A specification of the communicative functions of the source language (SL) text according to its principal *genre* is the first part of the translator's task. This must be followed by a corresponding analysis of the target language (TL) in order to determine how to convey these inscribed intentions of the source document through suitable vernacular stylistic devices and rhetorical strategies in conjunction with the conventions that would

---

[22] Reiss and Vermeer 1984; Nord 1997; see also Wendland 2004b:50–53.

2.2 Investigating orality

apply to the designated text-type and setting. My own *"literary* functional equivalence" (*LiFE*) methodology, which is a development of de Waard and NidA's functional approach to translation (Wendland 2004b:ch. 11), is one particular application of an oral-aural focused *Skopos*.[23] The term "literary" (or "oratorical") conveys a twofold emphasis with reference to the *artistry* (forms) and the *rhetoric* (functions) of the biblical text as well as its translation (Wendland 2004b: ch. 8). Special attention is therefore accorded the TL and the search for oral and written (or mixed) genres that may serve as *functional equivalents* to those found in the Hebrew and Greek Scriptures.[24]

Different degrees of *LiFE* application are possible, depending on considerations of "relevance" (see above) in relation to a given project's "translation commission" (*brief*), including the major communicative goals (*Skopos*) of the envisaged version, the primary setting in which it will be used, the medium of

---

[23] *LiFE* is not really a new method of translation, let alone a new theory—but simply proposes a new application and option, an "extended range" model as it were, of the Nidan *functional equivalence* approach (e.g., de Waard and Nida 1986). Thus, a "literary" (or "oratorical") version is one that in some significant way capitalizes on available TL linguistic resources in order to duplicate or match general as well as particular artistic devices and rhetorical techniques that are found in a given biblical text, whether that be a selected pericope or a complete book. These features may range from the purely phonological (e.g., rhythmic, rhymed, euphonic style) to a complete genre-for-genre functional equivalence replacement. Such "special effects" may be applied to any type of translation, whether basically literal or idiomatic in nature—or somewhere in-between (depending on the project *Skopos*, primary audience, and principal setting of use). This is not a matter of "adding" a more dynamic dimension to one's translation; it is the effort to more adequately reproduce or recreate what is already there in the original text—that is, clearly manifested within the literature of Scripture.

Furthermore, as Carr rightly observes, the application of "literary studies" to the analysis of Scripture has "helped focus the attention of scholars on the present form of the text, including concentric and other patterns that may have played a prominent role in their memorization and performance.... Insofar as a literary approach aims to uncover literary dimensions that would have been recognizable to ancient writers, performers, or hearers, it must be attentive to the oral-written dimension of such texts and the aesthetics peculiar to such literature" (2005:292–293).

[24] Pym defines equivalence as "a relation of 'equal value' between a source-text segment and a target-text segment" (2010:7). Employed as a "paradigm" of translation, the notion of equivalence is foundational, but problematic in various respects, which Pym clearly documents (ibid., 20–21, 38–40). However, various paradigmatic alternatives are either integrally related to equivalence, for example, relevance theory and Skopos theory (ibid., 35–37, 44, 61), or they present even more problems in terms of practical application when translating (e.g., descriptions, uncertainty, localization).

text transmission, and the working competence of the translators. In the case of a longer passage like Job chapter 3, this may vary from a complete genre-for-genre transposition (e.g., from SL poetry to TL rhetorical prose), to a much more limited treatment, involving primarily the phonological structures (e.g., rhythmic lines) of a relatively literal, linguistically conservative "liturgical" version. A rather close oratorical equivalent of Job's lament in Chewa, for example, is found in the *ndakatulo* genre of expressive lyric poetry, which may be used on sad occasions as well as for joyful public celebration.[25]

2.2.6 Frames of reference

This approach offers a multifaceted, cognitive-based methodology for "contextualizing" a translation project,[26] not only the text per se, but also the entire supportive and enabling infrastructure, including the preceding methods of communication-centered analysis. In *Scripture Frames and Framing*, Wilt and Wendland (2008) posit a range of conceptual macro-constructs, moving from the most general, i.e., *cognitive* (world-view) frames, down through *sociocultural, organizational, conversational, intertextual,* and *textual* frames—to the most specific, i.e., *utterance* and *lexical* frames.[27]

---

[25] See examples of this poetic Chewa style in chapters 4 and 6.

[26] The concept of "frames of reference" originates in Gestalt psychological theory and is used to designate the coordinated systems that compute and specify the various possible spatial relationships from a certain *perspective* between an entity to be located (referent or *figure*) and an orienting landmark (or *ground*) (Huang 2007:149; Katan 2004:169). So also, by metaphoric extension, a complete text, or some element within it, may be cognitively "located" or specified in terms of a particular perspective with reference to one or more of the distinct dimensions of its wider contextual setting, including the prominent characteristics of its oral-aural environment.

[27] See also Wendland 2008d:passim. On the "macro-structure" of cognition, then, co-occurring *syntagmatic* (sociocultural, conversational, and textual) cognitive "frames" consist of *paradigmatic* "categories" of "collocates" which are "filled" by general/specific "instances," that is, with reference to some governing ("prototypical") frame in view and the prioritizing principle of "relevance" within a given setting of use and the current instance of verbal discourse. The frames of reference model is based on cognitive linguistic theory and essentially involves a "hyper-contextualized" approach to translation. In other words, it offers a heuristic method for investigating all of the diverse, but interrelated situational factors that inform and/or influence the interlingual interpretation and transmission of "meaning" during the multifarious process of communicating a source language text with a clearly defined audience group in a given consumer language and sociocultural setting.

2.2 Investigating orality

This simplified pedagogical, top-down perspective and strategy could, of course, be reversed. In any case, it is important to point out the hypothetical character of these posited categories and their assumed manifold interaction in the construction of meaning.

In past applications of basic frames theory and methodology to the practice of Bible translation, the approach tended to be presented in a manner that was rather static and rigid. In reality, however, hierarchically organized conceptual frames manifest fuzzy, flexible boundaries that typically relate to one another in many different ways (e.g., analogy/metaphor, association/metonymy) and are prioritized according to salience, relevance, appropriateness, etc. during perception and cognition, depending on the social setting and physical circumstances. They are dynamic, fluid mental constructs that are easily modified during any communication activity, especially live performance events, under the influence of a host of factors that vary according to who is speaking to whom and how, when, where, or why.[28] Such modification may occur more or less automatically by intuition or as part of an active communicative strategy of "negotiation" whereby one party seeks to persuasively present (or impose) his/her point of view to (upon) another in order to accomplish certain pragmatic objectives.

---

[28] The "why" question would subsume issues of *ideology*, that is, one's basic interpretation of reality, including one's fundamental beliefs, values, fears, goals, and philosophy of life—in short, one's "worldview." Thus, the activity of Bible translation is inevitably ideologically motivated, managed, and unfortunately at times manipulated by those in a position of social and/or religious "power" in relation to their collaborators, for example, with respect to the selection of translators (perhaps favoring a certain denomination or dialect), the specific type/style of translation being made (literal ⇔ idiomatic), the medium of transmission (favoring literacy over orality), the inclusion of supplementary helps (which ones, if any, and how many), etc. (cf. Maxey 2009:3).

Furthermore, Robert Bascom points out that "Once frames (or roles…) are seen as dynamic processes within the larger context of human interaction, all frame typologies and their interrelations (e.g., Wendland, *Contextual Frames*, 6) can be seen as the description of particular examples, or possible frozen moments in time. Which frame will encompass the other cannot be determined beforehand in more than a general or superficial way" (2010:51). However, as Mona Baker has observed in this connection: "The idea, then, is not to throw lists of apparently static components out altogether but to use them merely as starting points for analysis, to acknowledge that they are not all necessarily relevant in every context and, more importantly, that every element is open to negotiation in the course of a given interaction" (2006:328).

One might further refine the framing model so as to render it more discerning, in particular as a tool for analyzing oral-aural communication. To this end, one might posit ten, more precise cognitive concepts ("micro-" frames) that may be verbally evoked, in multiple interrelated sets, during the production and interpretation of any literary (also biblical) discourse.[29] These include mutually interactive relationships that may be temporal, spatial, substantive (involving entities), eventive, attributive (qualities, characteristics), social (interpersonal), logical (propositional), locutionary (dialogic speech-acts), textual (or intertextual), and literary/oratorical (genre based) in nature.[30] Such notions (among others possible) may be viewed as different aspects of the *textual* macro-frame, which functions as a constituent of the wider contextualizing sociocultural frames noted above. Together, in flowing, changeable, kaleidoscopic fashion and ordered according to one's current interest and concerns, they serve as the overall conceptual *framework* that may be associated with, or evoked by, a specific text when heard (or read) in a well-defined circumstantial setting.[31]

From an interpreter's perspective in relation to an explicit cotext and context, these distinct but overlapping and interactive frames, or "schemata,"[32] are evoked and construed semiotically on the basis of textual "signs" (phonological/graphological, lexical, syntactic) within the discourse at hand. They are then combined, prioritized, and "negotiated"

---

[29] As Robbins notes, "throughout the millennia humans have continually used forms, which cognitive scientists now call 'frames,' in one conceptual domain to understand and interpret forms in another domain" (2009:99). In a recent study V. Matthews employs "frame analysis" as a hermeneutical tool in analyzing the conversations of Hebrew discourse (2008:74–99).

[30] See Wendland, "Framing the Frames" (2010). Another proposed grid for classifying the various *metonymic* relationships between cognitive frames, or more specifically, the "conceptual relations that connect elements in mental spaces" is found in Gilles Fauconnier and Mark Turner: Change, Identity, Time, Space, Cause-effect, Part-whole, Representation, Role-value, Analogy, Disanalogy, Property, Similarity, Category, Intentionality, Uniqueness (2006:336–337).

[31] As noted in Wilt and Wendland 2008:ch. 1, cognitive frames not only influence perception and provide focus and perspective, but they are also conceptually *malleable* (they may be expanded or reshaped) and *interactive* with other frames in a given communication setting (e.g., through embedding, overlapping, and juxtaposing).

[32] The conceptual "activation" process for such interpretive frames undoubtedly involves the *situational context* of the extralinguistic communicative event as well as the verbal text. One's perception and comprehension is also guided by the cognitive inferential principle of *relevance*, as outlined above.

2.2 Investigating orality

in context according to the principle of salience (or "relevance") to form an interpretive mental framework—a "virtual text" (Katan 2004:169)—for deriving the overall "intended meaning" from the verbal passage being examined. Each mental frame, or perceptual "window" on the world of the text in its situational location, attaches various associated ideas, images, connotations, collocations, emotions, values, etc. to the frame. These "frame-fillers" are normally very culture- (> society- > area- > group-) and individual-specific. A progression is thus formed, moving from less to more particular, with the latter perspectives becoming increasingly difficult for others (who view life from outside a given sociocultural frame) to perceive, analyze, and evaluate precisely and/or correctly.

A flexible frames-of-reference approach, coupled with one or more of those already mentioned, e.g., specifying a descriptive, relevance, or functionalist perspective, can assist Bible translation planners and implementers in giving more nuanced attention to the issue of orality when carrying out the interconnected phases of their project. This would comprise practical measures such as selecting community-recognized vernacular text composers who are familiar with, or even experts in, the oral-aural and musical art forms of their language (e.g., the traditional musician-storyteller, *griot*, of W. Africa, or the *imbongi* praise poet of S. Africa). The selection process should include reviewers who are capable of evaluating draft translations for their phonological qualities (euphony, resonance, rhyme) and can propose improvements to render the text easier to articulate aloud and more "hearable" to a listening audience. Such qualities would be needed, for example, if the project brief stipulated a "lyric lament" as the genre to be adopted, or at least mimicked, when rendering Job's bitter elegy-like poem of chapter 3 into a cadenced TL oral, or even musical equivalent.[33]

2.2.7 Performance criticism

The crucial dimension of "performance" has already been touched on above, but in this section, I will briefly note several important applications

---

[33] As Dan Fitzgerald cautions, however, "musical genres, like discourse genres, cannot be 'adopted' or 'mimicked' as relevantly or easily as one might presume" (personal correspondence, 2012). Competent and experienced staff (in terms of training, research, etc.) must be available to guide and evaluate the choices made in terms of genre, musical style, appropriateness, and so forth.

of the discipline of "performance criticism" to Bible translation.[34] first of all, with regard to the "art" of translation and the consequent need to have verbal, especially oral, "artists" on a Bible translation team, the case could not be stated more clearly than in the following quote from David Rhoads:

> Translation is an *art*, because the act of rendering biblical works into contemporary languages is more than a purely technical process. It is an artistic achievement. Translation involves, first, understanding the profound content, the significant artistry, and the powerful impact of the original languages of the writings in the Bible in their context. Second, translation involves finding contemporary ways to express the meanings, the power, the vibrancy, the passion, and the potential impacts of the original compositions in modern tongues. (Rhoads forthcoming)

Since the diverse writings to be found in the Scriptures arguably *are* literature—*artfully* fashioned literature—a literary-rhetorical approach must be correspondingly applied to analyze and translate them, and this requires that adequate attention be given to the sound as well as the shape of the text.[35] Consequently, translation must be practiced with an artistic *eye*, as it

---

[34] "Performance criticism is a critical methodology used to analyze the way in which repeatable and socially recognizable events [featuring some public oral composition] use specific techniques to powerfully express social values and themes.... Performance criticism is concerned with identifying, describing and analyzing a performative event in which there is the presentation of character and event by actors using formal patterns that might include gesture, costume and speech in order to create a shared imaginative reality between actor and spectator" (Giles 2012:578, material in brackets added). Mathews provides a helpful "introduction to performance studies" in terms of a set of "performance themes" and a selection of "performance features" (2012:ch. 2).

[35] Although in the introductory chapter of his book on "the Bible's aesthetic secrets," Mazor argues that "the Bible is neither art nor literature, and following, there is no biblical literature" (2009:22), his subsequent detailed text analyses paradoxically demonstrate just the opposite. Even his closing chapter summaries express such a contradictory perspective, for example: "Thus, the biblical text creates an aesthetic intersection where two aesthetic devices (compositional and rhetorical) conjoin, not only for poetic purposes, but more importantly, as an enhancement of the ideological message that they corroborate and amplify" (ibid., 134). "In the biblical portion discussed [Hosea 5:1–3], the artistic virtue of the text is embodied in the dialectic interplay between structure and rhetoric.... Structure is not just an indifferent container into which one pours rhetorical thought; it is a framework that shapes rhetoric to achieve a particular effect. Therefore, one may

were, and an *ear* on the source language document as well as on the draft being rendered in the local vernacular. The paratext, descriptive footnotes for example, might include references to text-complementing gestures, facial expressions, body stances and movements, perhaps even appropriate indigenous musical accompaniments. Such creativity is especially relevant in the case of the poetic works of the Bible that give evidence of a mode of verbal communication in which the form, including the phonology, of the original message (the Hebrew/Greek text) is undeniably a part of the *meaning*. This functional import is not always specifically semantic in nature, but it is certainly *pragmatic* (having interpersonal implications) in terms of its aesthetic, affective, as well as imperative impact and appeal. Lyric texts, such as the Psalms, the Song of Songs, and many portions of Revelation, if not actually composed to be sung, were undoubtedly fashioned to have a melodic oral-aural effect that would be stimulated by a distinctive manner of public elocution, e.g., chanting, recitation, cantillation, or some type of creative musical expression.[36]

Of course, the oral-and-aural factor is not the only, or even the preeminent feature to keep in mind when translating the Bible, but it has so often and for so long been ignored or neglected, that it is important to underscore, perhaps even to over-emphasize its significance when selecting, training,

---

speak in the same breath of structural rhetoric (a rhetorical concept that lends itself to a particular framework) and rhetorical structure (a particular framework that lends itself to a rhetorical concept). There is nothing between them but the artist's genius" (ibid., 158). I seek to demonstrate the same intertwined artistically enacted structural principles and rhetorical purposes with respect to several smaller biblical books in *Prophetic Rhetoric* (2009).

[36] With regard to the additional communicative dimension of biblical songs, we note that "[t]hey make the unfamiliar familiar, aid in memory, help create feelings of belonging, preserve and pass traditions from one generation to the next, and communicate on multiple levels through rhythm, melody, and harmony, all in addition to the lyrics.... The songs are used to *reconstruct* the past in such a way as to assist in forming a *concrete social identity* among the reading and listening audience with the goal of creating a commitment or *obligation* to a specific ideal, value, or belief" (Giles and Doan, *Twice Used Songs* (2009), 2–3, 10; original italics). In the Scriptures then we have abundant evidence of this practical communicative principle in application: "Orality and writing technology are joint means for accomplishing a common goal: accurate recall of the treasured tradition" (Carr, *Writing* (2005), 7)—indeed, the very words of God and his spokesmen. The Apostle Paul refers to this vital trans-generational mnemonic function of the songs of the saints in Colossians 3:16, and adds the pastoral functions of "teaching and admonishing" (διδάσκοντες καὶ νουθετοῦντες).

guiding, and monitoring teams today. In fact, a "performance-oriented" approach can even be employed as a *hermeneutical* and also a *translational* technique in the extended compositional process. As one eminent scholar and practitioner suggests, from extensive personal experience:

> Translation is a demanding and exacting discipline, even while being significantly artful. I have found that the act of translating for performances I have done is one of the most significant means for understanding a biblical text. Translating for performance leads one to grasp in fresh ways the potential meanings of the composition, the oral arts evident in the text, the significance of sound as a medium for communicating the Bible, and the experience of the rhetorical impact on an audience. I believe that translating for orality can enhance the exegetical process such that exegetes become (oral) translators and that translators become (oral) exegetes—and that both try their hand at performing! (Rhoads forthcoming)

How should a performer of Job's lament (ch. 3), for example, orally articulate and visually display the translated text (assuming that an appropriate TL genre had already been selected and prepared for this public purpose)? Who would he envisage his *primary* audience to be—God, Job's three friends, the entire Joban community, himself (this is not specified by the text; any subsequent audience would be *secondary*). As already noted, in the case of any communal performance, it is not only a vocalization of this pericope that is involved (e.g., intonational shading and emphasis) but also overt modes of dramatic expression such as the orator's interpretive facial features, hand-arm gestures, as well as dynamic body movements and suggestive positioning (e.g., mournfully bowed low to the ground or facing up to God, as deemed appropriate in the culture concerned).

A performance-based methodology can also serve another vital function, namely, to get the translation's "host community" more actively involved in the project from the very beginning, while the first texts are being drafted, rather than at the very end, as happens all too often. Widespread public "acceptability" (transferred then to actual use) is the ultimate goal of any translation, and the sooner that the primary client audience can become meaningfully "engaged" in the process of evaluating and improving the team's drafts, the more effective the project will be in terms of accomplishing its communicative intentions (*Skopos*). This is because "[u]ltimately, the value of understanding Bible Translation as contextualization and performance must be measured by host communities who are the agents for translation and contextualization" (Maxey 2009:196). Thus, *from one language, culture, and community to another* the task goes on—the Word being contextualized and enriched by every human setting, sense, and sound in which it is verbally embodied and orally proclaimed.

2.3 Application of orality-oriented methodologies to Bible translation

To summarize this chapter, I might draw attention to three interrelated phases of the application of *orality research* to the practice of Bible translation, with special reference to the seven methodologies that were outlined above:

- **Analysis** of the **written** text: A full discourse analysis, comprising *form* (structure plus style), *content* (denotation, including implication, plus connotation), and *function* (major and minor pragmatic goals), is the foundation for any serious exegetical study. This necessarily incorporates an examination of the various *oral-aural* and/or *performative* dynamics that hypothetically underlie and are reflected in the biblical text (as recorded in the canon), whether expressed explicitly or implicitly. These facets of orality are especially evident—and important—in narrative dialogue portions and the proclamatory discourses of prophetic and epistolary literature (note, in particular, conversational, speech-act, and argument-structure analysis).

- **Translation** of the **analyzed** text: Corresponding oral-aural features must be carefully selected from the literary (oratorical) inventory of the target language so that the translation *matches* as closely as possible not only the semantic content (both expressed and implied), which is primary, but also the general *communicative functions*, the specific *speech acts*, as well as the principal artistic and rhetorical effects that were identified in the source text. In this effort, it is crucial for translators to capitalize on specific structural and stylistic devices that are not only *available* in the vernacular but also *natural* in relation to the primary medium of message transmission as well as the literary or oral genre being rendered (note the functionalist, frames of reference, and relevance approaches).

- **Articulation** of the ***translated*** text: The translation should be periodically tested and systematically evaluated with regard to the relative quality of its sound dimension. Such assessment is carried out both *orally* in terms of its relative ease of enunciation, and also *aurally*, that is, reviewing how the text "resounds" when it is publicly expressed aloud. Ideally, the text in question would be an "oratorical" version which is articulated by a practiced (experienced, recognized) performer who can dramatically proclaim, recite, chant, sing, or otherwise vocalize and display the target language version, including a judicious use of non-verbal performance features. This would be in keeping with its indigenous genre or sub-genre, the type of biblical content being expressed, and the preferred or designated audience-setting of communication (note the discipline and practice of performance criticism).

Each of the seven methodologies may be applied at *any* of the three phases of interlingual communication process, but they seem especially pertinent at the particular stages described above. It is clear then that considerations of orality and its influence on written compositions appreciably affect the foundational interpretation as well as the subsequent exposition and transmission of the assorted literary documents that comprise the Scriptures. Such attention would be most obvious in the production of audio (-visual) versions, but as has been suggested, this concern is relevant also in the case of published Bibles—perhaps more so, in view of the fact that the significance of the phonic dimension is not as apparent in a text that is normally read from the printed page, either in public or silently to oneself.[37] The translation program outlined above highlights the communicative capacity as well as the necessity of an oral-aural approach, the goal of which is to inject vibrant living sound, analogous to the original, back into the Scriptures as they are dynamically re-textualized in a contemporary vernacular version.

---

[37] It is arguable that a text that reads fluently and clearly aloud will be correspondingly more easily and understandably read silently to oneself.

In the next chapter, we will overview selected aspects of the current debate that has arisen with respect to various theories involving orality, scribality, and the transmission of the text of Scripture in ancient times—that is, in relation to both the Old and the New Testaments of the Christian Bible. These areas of controversy do raise a number of important hermeneutical questions that concern all biblical text analysts and interpreters, including those who are somehow involved in the interlingual, cross-cultural, oral-aural oriented communication of the Scriptures today. One's perspective on the quality, reliability, and indeed, the authority of the original text will inevitably affect how one handles it in translation.

3

Two Models of Oral-Based Scripture Text Transmission

3.1 Overview: A summary of the issue

In this chapter, I will survey a number of the major issues that are currently in debate with respect to how the media-related factors of orality and scribality interact in the original composition, transmission, and reception of the Scriptures.[1] This summary, which is carried out mainly through quotations from a selection of the pertinent scholarly sources,[2] will recall and further develop many of the core topics that have already been introduced in the first two chapters, especially those points that have generated a certain amount of controversy. The debate essentially concerns the degree of liberal scribal manipulation that was involved in transmitting the various recognized documents of "Scripture" versus the view that sees this textual

---

[1] For further discussion, see Wendland 2008b:4–48.

[2] The necessity of using a selection of citations brings with it the possibility (inevitability?) of personal bias. Therefore, I encourage interested (or unconvinced) readers to access the articles or books referred to in order to form an independent assessment of the various perspectives adopted and positions taken on these issues.

development rather as the product of a relatively constrained process of memorization.³ Accordingly, one may posit two hypothetical "models" based on the available evidence from ancient sources as well as subsequent scholarly studies, namely, a comparatively *flexible* as opposed to a more *restrained* recording of an "original" received written biblical text. These two contrasting perspectives have been chosen simply as a convenient means of organizing the discussion; there was undoubtedly a continuum of possibilities with regard to handling the received text in the actual practice of transmission, depending on the prevailing extratextual circumstances, the competence of the personnel involved, and the authoritative action of a succession of sometimes competing religious "gate-keepers," both Jewish and Christian.⁴

Perhaps the most significant area where a difference of opinion or scholarly uncertainty arises concerns the relative degree of variableness versus fixity with respect to the transmission of the verbal revelation of Scripture. How much malleability did the text of a given biblical author (whether known or unknown) manifest, first during its initial stages of oral existence and thereafter, when it was first written down by a scribe (or scribes) in the form of a communally accepted, authoritative (e.g., prophetic, apostolic) document? This debate comes to the fore with particular force when "the five books of Moses" or "the four Gospels" are considered. Is it feasible, defensible, or correct, for example, to posit a single "author" (or individual authors) and/or an "original text" in the case of these traditionally-recognized collections—or are such notions simply the unproven assumptions of scholars who are too thoroughly influenced by a typographical, print-based Bible text?

---

³ "Scripture" is in quotation marks in recognition of the fact that the process of canonizing the authoritative Hebrew Old Testament and Greek New Testament occurred over a number of years (c.a., 400 BCE–200 CE for the OT; 150–400 CE for the NT) and generally involved a gradual narrowing of the corpus of available textual candidates in circulation through scholarly debates, the writings of various church leaders, and the official decrees of a succession of rabbinic and ecclesial councils.

⁴ The process of developing a widely recognized (i.e., by the faithful adherents of a particular religious community), authoritative text of "Scripture" (the Word of God) is termed "canonization." It is important to note that "[t]he basis for the concept of canon containing authoritative information comes directly from the Scripture itself (Deut 4:2; 12:32; Jer 26:2; Prov 30:6; Eccl 3:14; 2 Pet 3:15–16; Rev 22:6–8, 18–19).... Several biblical texts indicate that even at a very early period some books of Scripture were treated with great reverence and were thought to be authoritative (Exod 17:14–16; 24:3–4, 7)" (Wegner 1999:100, 103; cf. also ibid., 99–116, 129–149). On the notion of "canon" and "canonicity," see Wilson (2008).

Along with a survey of some of the theoretical aspects of this dispute, which to a great extent also involve one's "theology of Scripture," I will focus upon several of the major positions regarding the compositional dimension of these two theories about the assumed nature of textual transmission:[5] How rigid or adaptable, persistent or variable, generally speaking, was the ancient process of oral and written sacred communication? In particular, how conservative or liberal were the textual "gatekeepers," the scribes, in carrying out their essential activities of transmitting the received tradition of Scripture? One's conclusion about such matters of message dissemination may have a number of important practical implications with respect to how strictly (literally, correspondently) or freely (idiomatically, periphrastically) one later decides to translate and convey via available media the received documents of Scripture (discussed further in III below). In other words, if the original scribes were free to modify, more or less, the *content* of the texts that they were transmitting in view of the current sociocultural and religious setting, what should prevent Bible translators today from freely contextualizing along the same lines in their language? In each section of the discussion, I will move generally from an OT to a NT perspective on the various theories and issues involved.

3.2 A More flexible model of text transmission

From the perspective of certain prominent orality studies in relation to the *Hebrew Bible*, the argument is that "scribes with more extensive grounding in literacy might act as full-fledged tradents, exercising in the chirographic transmission of their community's tradition a performative competence that significantly resembled that of the oral-traditional performer" (Kirk 2008:220). If the initial "performer" of the biblical text exercised such compositional freedom, so the argument goes, then why not also its later scribal "recorder" as well? Doan and Giles flesh out this premise in terms of the diverse "social power" relations that supposedly accompanied the transformative transition "from the prophetic performer to the scribal performer":

---

[5] I must acknowledge my own limited ecclesiastical "location" in this regard, i.e., conservative, evangelical Protestant; thus, I cannot offer a valid Catholic perspective, for example, on these issues.

> We posited the presence of a performative mode of thought still embedded in the prophetic literature.... We turn our attention to the role of the scribe responsible for the creation of the prophetic literature.... Conventional wisdom said that in the prophetic literature, the disciples sought to "re-present" their master in the centuries following his death. In terms of social power, the process was thought to be a relatively uneventful transformation of power from the charisma of the prophet to the pen of the scribe...."The view that the prophets had disciples who preserved and updated the sayings of their masters has never been supported by anthropological or literary evidence; it merely supplies a convenient mechanism whereby these edited compositions can be traced to an individual prophet."[6] (Doan and Giles 2005:19–20)

Similarly, according to Fishbane:

> When they copied their texts, the ancient Israelite scribes did not slavishly write the texts word by word, but preserved the texts' meaning for the ongoing life of their communities in much the same way that performers of oral epic re-present the stable, yet dynamic, tradition to their communities. In this sense, the ancient Israelite scribes were not mere copyists, but were also performers. (Fishbane 1985:85; cf. Persen 2010:47)

This pliable prophetic tradition thus appears to be the result of a transformation from the concrete revelation of messages from Yahweh to his Covenant people, originating in the works of individual prophetic messengers (the "authors"), into much more "human" religious texts that were essentially composed in free-flowing stages by a succession of scribal

---

[6] The final citation in this selection comes from Davies 1998:118. Seemingly clear contradictory evidence to this position from the Bible itself (e.g., Jeremiah 36) is dismissed as being merely an expedient ideological fiction, a literary device designed to establish or enhance the authority of the anonymous document at hand and apparently also the social status of the scribe, or scribal school, that was responsible for creating it. Thus, the text was supposedly attributed to a known prophet (e.g., "Jeremiah") in order to validate its message and to gain a wider hearing: "The prophet is a performer who exercises social power through the immediacy of [his/her?] performance [of a given prophetic discourse]" (Doan and Giles 2005:21). For an alternative summary of the compositional history of Jeremiah, for example, see Kitchen 2003:381–383.

3.2 A More flexible model of text transmission

self-assertive "performers." As suggested above, this incremental creative process is presumed to have involved an ideological struggle over power and prestige within the religious community of Israel. The compositional sequence might indeed derive to a certain extent from the inspired words of a recognized prophet, but the tradition would then purportedly continue to be developed, with one nameless scribe or school seemingly trying to "outperform" the other in order to gain a measure of personal/group status, security, and perhaps also some other socio-political advantage:

> The message has power because the prophet [*not Yahweh!?*] has power.... Permanence [for the message] can be achieved only by usurping the role of the prophet. And this is where tension results. Rather than a smooth transition from prophet to literature, it is much more likely that the evolution from prophetic performer to prophetic literature was characterized by a struggle for power. The prophetic scribe (or better, the prophetic playwright) is dependent upon the prophetic performer for his inspiration and derives his credibility from an attachment to the prophetic performer but, nonetheless, is bent on replacing the prophetic performer. Whether intentional or not, the effect of the literature is to script the prophetic performance and in so doing to control the prophetic performance.[7] (Doan and Giles 2005:21; material in brackets added)

---

[7] This hypothesis regarding rather loose or liberal scribal practice based on oral tradition would seem to be contradicted by Emanuel Tov's conclusion: "It stands to reason that literary texts were copied from written Vorlagen. There is no reason to assume that scribes who knew their biblical texts well wrote them from memory. Indeed, according to the prescriptions in rabbinic literature, scribes were forbidden to copy Scripture without a text in front of them, even if they knew the whole Bible by heart, in order to secure precision in copying (b. Meg. 18b and parallels)" (Tov 2008).
Undoubtedly, in the course of time and for various reasons, Hebrew scribes (soferim) did introduce certain changes (additions, deletions, corrections, etc.) into the manuscripts that they were copying. Tov classifies these as follows (1992:258): "(a) linguistic-stylistic changes, (b) synonymous readings, (c) harmonizations, (d) exegetical changes, (e) additions to the body of the text." In the last-mentioned category we find certain, not easily distinguished elements that "may have been added to the text upon its completion, in the margins, between the lines, or, in some scribal traditions, in the text itself, separated by a scribal sign"—including glosses, exegetical additions, interlinear and marginal corrections, remarks on the content, variant readings, scribal remarks and marks, and headings to sections in the text (Tov ibid., 275–276). This position regarding the relative stability of the ancient

Thus, as far as the corpus of prophetic literature is concerned, it is supposedly "a result of a social power struggle in which the prophetic performer lost control of the message, and prophecy came to an end" (Giles 2012:582).

Was there ever such a competition for power and control over a given text for personal ends, or could this be a different sectarian perspective seeking to hijack the primary interpretive tradition? If either option was in fact characteristic of the process of transmitting the prophetic record (messages from YHWH), then it is quite strange that there is no unambiguous intimation of this antagonistic or contrastive literary activity on record, either in the prophetic corpus itself,[8] or in the Hebrew historical

---

Hebrew text is supported by Wegner 2006:62–66; cf. Wegner 2012. The overall reliability of the Hebrew textual transmission is further generally supported by its earliest translation—the Septuagint (LXX), which at times arguably preserves an older, more "original" wording (Gentry 2012:164).

More recently, Gary Martin has drawn attention to the possibility of variant texts and translations in the Hebrew Bible that have arisen due to the "employment (or possible employment) of wordplay, so that, where applicable, variant readings are shown to reflect one of the intended or possible meanings. Translators of these texts into modern languages can then assess how they will incorporate word play and other literary devices into their versions" (2010:271; cf. *double entendre*, 95). "The scenario is this: at some definite point in time an author created a text that had never been recited, heard, seen, or read before. It was a real *Urtext, a single written original*. Within this text the author consciously created what we might call a *visual pun*, a consonantal string that could be vocalized in multiple ways, each of which had meaning within the immediate context.... [This was done] to demonstrate artistic, stylistic, or poetic finesse; to entertain; to embed political [or religious] satire; to encode a divine oracle; or for any number of other reasons" (ibid., 89; original italics; added words in brackets). Knut Heim (2010) has given evidence to suggest that such punning was a common literary device in Proverbs (and probably also other Hebrew wisdom literature). Heim concludes with reference to Prov 8:30: "the combination of polysemous and multi-lingual wordplay creates a kaleidoscope of meanings, all of which together enhance Wisdom's uniquely powerful role in, at, and beyond creation" (ibid., 16).

[8] The bitter verbal altercation that Amos reports as having taken place between himself and Amaziah (Amos 7:10–17), did not involve a power struggle between a prophet and his scribe, but rather, between a called prophet of the LORD (Amos) and a heretical priest of the shrine at Bethel. In the case of Elijah, it was two companies of pagan priests that God's true prophet had to deal with (1 Kgs 18:18–19). Similarly, Jeremiah's conflicts with King Jehoiakim and his officials over the prophetic record did not stem from the literary *manner* of writing (who controlled the way in which the text was transmitted), but rather from the theological *matter* (the content of what was actually written), which predicted disaster for the sinful nation of Judah (Jer 36:2–3). I do not deny the possibility that a certain amount of social

3.2 A More flexible model of text transmission

writings that report the momentous events of that religious era.[9] Does the significance of scribal inscription versus oral tradition not involve, primarily, issues of textual authority, stability, permanence, credibility, and ultimately divine truth, rather than intramural human struggles for social power? One wonders whether we are dealing here with history or indeed theology at all with regard to any of the named prophets or their prophetic books, if it is true that OT scribes normally took it upon themselves to "create prophetic *characters* out of the prophets themselves (prophetic *actors*),"[10] and if "[t]he difference between character and actor resides at the crux of the struggle for power and control between the prophet and the scribe" (Doan and Giles 2005:23–24; original emphasis).[11] Undocumented though it may be, so the argument goes, such was the authority of these scribes that they could actually engender some form of dynamic divine presence within the dramatic religious books that they artfully—some would argue even fictively—created:

---

and political control could have been exercised in ancient Israel by a predominant royal and religious "mode of textual education" in which "[s]cribal recollection of early traditions was ensured partly through teaching students to read and reproduce written copies of the key traditions" (Carr 2005:9). Such "power dynamics," however, concerned transmitting the corpus of completed inscribed texts, not the fundamental compositional process itself.

[9] This is not to deny the presence of different perspectives being reflected in Scripture with reference to the same biblical event or related series of events, either within the same document/scroll (e.g., Gen 1:1–2:3//Gen 2:4–25), or by different individuals (e.g., in the synoptic Gospels with regard to the life and mission of the Christ), or perhaps different religious groups and their scribal associates (e.g., concerning the monarchy in Israel/Judah as recorded in the book(s) of Kings versus Chronicles). However, I would not view these different accounts as being semantically contradictory or in ideological competition, but rather complementary to one another, with each record being internally coherent as well as consistent, the product of a relatively stable tradition of transmission—not the result of a long volatile period of considerable scribally generated accretion or modification.

[10] In other words, "the Hebrew prophets leave their role of actor to become characters, given life in the presentation of another actor: the scribe with pen in hand" (Giles 2012:582).

[11] The supposed struggle for control of the text between prophet and scribe is mirrored in the conflict that some secular theorists see involving an author and a translator (in another language): "[T]he mechanism of translation [is] an activity that provides a paradigmatic scenario for the underlying struggle for the control of meaning that constitutes both writing and interpretation as it involves the actual production of another text: the writing of the translator's reading of someone else's text in another language, time, and cultural environment" (Arrojo 2011:34).

> In the prophetic tradition, it was the prophet through whom God himself was present. In the scribal tradition, it was the scribe who, as actor, *created* the character of the prophet in order for God to be present. (Doan and Giles 2005:29)

According to this notion of malleable individual and communal text production with respect to the Hebrew prophetic Scriptures, we must necessarily distinguish two "performances" (or series of performances), only the second of which is literally reflected in the Bible, namely, the current, creative scribal "enactment of tradition" in a manner that was "responsive to the realities and crises of the tradent community" (Kirk 2008:222):

> Not only was there an original oral performance by the prophet, but there was a "re-performance" that must be considered as the scribe transformed the oral performance to written text.... The scribe of the prophetic performance enhanced the original performance by ordering, editing, and formalizing the prophetic utterance, thereby giving it "life in the present." (Doan and Giles 2005:30–32)[12]

In a similar, but more radical vein, van der Toorn conjectures that the prophets (actually the scribes) constituted a powerful subculture in early Israel—a school of religious intellectuals who more or less preached in writing only to themselves:

> Scribes wrote for scribes.... The text of the Hebrew Bible was not part of the popular culture. The Bible was born and studied in the scribal workshop of the Temple. In a fundamental sense, it was a book of the clergy.[13] (van der Toorn 2007:2)

---

[12] We thus have what amounts to a "neo-redaction-critical" approach to the transmission of the text of Scripture, a methodology that "analyzes the techniques by which a [scribe, scribes, or scribal school] assembled, shaped, and supplemented preexistent materials to form a new work, seeking insights into the literary dynamics of the product" (Biddle 2004:135, material in brackets added).

[13] In fact, according to van der Toorn, "Prophets, as a rule, do not write, nor do most of them have secretaries" (2007:112)—this affirmation despite "the biblical portrayal of Baruch as model secretary" (ibid., 111). Van der Toorn offers no credible evidence for this confident claim—a "pontification," which according to the late Anson F. Rainey, Emeritus Professor of Ancient Near Eastern Cultures and Semitic

3.2 A More flexible model of text transmission

Thus, the periodic biblical record of public, oral proclamations of the text of Scripture to a lay audience is apparently discounted (*contra*, for example, Deuteronomy and Nehemiah 8–9).[14] But more than that, without the efforts of these creative, proactive scribal scholars, so it is alleged, we would not possess any Hebrew Scriptures today:

> If the Bible became the Word of God, it was due to their presentation. Both the production and the promotion of the Hebrew Bible were the work of the scribes...[in fact] generations of scribes, each new one continuing the work of previous ones.[15] (van der Toorn 2007:2, 7)

In short, the whole notion of "divine revelation" becomes suspect, and we should rather look for the origins of Scripture in the realm of ancient "inspired" scribal practice relating to magic and divination, as was evident in "the world of the Babylonian and Egyptian scribes" (van der Toorn 2007:4). Thus, "[t]he mid- to late-twentieth-century consensus that formerly held about the history of the development of the Hebrew Bible—for example,... the assignment of the bulk of early prophetic writings to the prophets themselves (e.g., Amos, Hosea)...no longer holds" (Carr 2011:3). This means further that any quest for individual biblical authors is quite "pointless" because the making of the Hebrew Scriptures "is owed to the scribal class," who as a collective of textual artisans co-produced religious documents by committee, as it were, or "by means of a series of scribal redactions" (ibid., 5). In a sense then, our attempts to closely analyze the biblical books for

---

Linguistics of Tel Aviv University, "is total nonsense. It can hardly be reckoned as the product of serious scholarship" (2010:79).

[14] This opinion contrasts with a more responsible conclusion such as the following: "In the works of Ezra–Nehemiah...the law is viewed as authoritative, which means that it must have existed for some time in order to have attained that status. Likewise, the Chronicler treats Samuel–Kings as authoritative. The Prophets were also revered by this time. The implication is that 'by the time of Ezra-Nehemiah and the Chronicler the bulk of scripture must have already been in circulation. Thus it is logical to assume that since this could not have happened overnight, the origins of the majority of the biblical traditions—at least orally—must have lain in the pre-exilic period' (84)" (Hawkins 2012:6, citing Frendo 2011:84).

[15] Such a scribe-oriented, written perspective on the text transmission process also severely limits or downplays the ongoing oral performance tradition and any possible influence that this may have had either on preserving or modifying the biblical text, whether in greater or lesser degrees.

any sort of normative theology, too, become fruitless since these writings are mere convenient conglomerations and hence manifest no overarching plan or purpose. Van der Toorn's research leads him to a conclusion which challenges "the assumption that each book of the Bible should be considered a carefully crafted whole with a plan that is reflected in all its parts":

> The books of the Bible were not designed to be read as unities. They rather compare to archives. A biblical book is often like a box containing heterogeneous materials brought together on the assumption of common authorship, subject matter, or chronology. (van der Toorn 2007:16)

A rather different, yet similarly depreciatory perspective views the Hebrew text, its narrative portions at least, somewhat along the lines of "CliffsNotes," that is, as abridged written summaries or outlines that were meant to be fleshed out during performance in variable fashion according to the occasion and setting:

> [M]uch of the biblical narrative [should be viewed] as 'neither the record of the oral telling of a tale nor the skilled fashioning of a story as a work of literary art,' but as written outlines for oral elaboration (or omission in performance). Ancient editors were intelligent; they included several alternatives and options, perhaps to be chosen from by the bards.... The details of the story—descriptions of settings, for example—are provided by the storyteller in performance, based on the skeleton of the gobbets. The gobbets are the 'oral building blocks...varied at will according to the needs of the moment, and modified to suit new purposes and places.'..."[16]

Detailed stylistic and structural analyses, however, would not support the preceding negative, hypothetical assessments of the holistic nature and high literary quality of the various documents of Scripture, whether those written in Hebrew or Greek.[17] In any case, compositional artistry and

---

[16] Miller 2011:55–56, who cites Campell 1989:77, 80 and Westenholtz 2010:30.

[17] Wendland 2004b:passim; see also Wendland 2009 (studies of selected prophets); Wendland 2008b (studies of selected NT epistles). These works seek to demonstrate the principle that *good literature, as exemplified in Scripture, is not created*

3.2 A More flexible model of text transmission

architecture aside, as far as the origin of the text of the Hebrew Bible is concerned, for van der Toorn it is not a question of quality or authorship. His assumption is that the text is rather the outcome of *corporate* scribal enterprise. Accordingly, "the authorship that the tradition attributes to Moses and Jeremiah has to give way to the scribes as the actual producers of the biblical texts" (2007:141). Van der Toorn surveys "six ways in which [Levitical] scribes produced written texts," namely: transcription,[18] invention, compilation, expansion, adaptation, and integration (ibid., 110–141; cf. 90).[19] In this way, the "original text," if there ever was one, became subject to a series of scribal transformations until the time when the first steps towards the canonization of a select corpus of writings were taken, probably under the leadership and authority of Ezra the scribe around 450 B.C.E. (ibid., 248).

An analogous view of the pliable, rather uncertain compositional history of Scripture corresponding to that outlined above is applied by some scholars of orality also to the *New Testament* literature, the so-called "Gospel tradition"

---

by committee. An excellent example of a commentary that documents this principle with respect to one of the longest, most difficult books of Scripture is Norman Habel's masterful study of Job. Habel pays special attention to the "design" of the text, which "implies both the structured ordering of materials and an intention on the part of the author as a literary artist to create such an ordering," for example, "framing techniques, envelope constructions (*inclusio*), chiasm, adaptation of traditional forms or formulae, wordplay, double entendre, and irony.... Consideration is also given to the particular way in which the author has one speaker subtly appropriating or alluding to key ideas or terms used by a preceding speaker.... These allusions point to the author's technique of progressively integrating diverse themes and ideas as the plot and design of the book is unfolded. In this connection we explore those images and metaphors which convey major themes, and the traditional symbols employed by the author to add color and depth to the theological ideas held in tension throughout the book. All these literary features are viewed as part of a unifying scheme in which intricacies of poetic form, narrative plot, and theological motif are interwoven in a consummate artistic design of majestic proportions" (1985:24). Surely, reading Job from this unified literary perspective gives one not only a new understanding of the book, but arguably, also a deeper, more accurate understanding as well.

[18] For van der Toorn, even in the case of a transcription of an oral "prophetic" text, the real creator of the document is the scribe (or series/school of scribes): "Scribes, even in their most instrumental of roles, impose their style, language, and ideas on the text.... As prophecy turns into Scripture, when tale becomes text, the scribe transforms his data to suit the conventions of the written genre and his interpretation of the oral tradition" (2007:115).

[19] Again it is important to note the lack of reference here to any ensuing oral presentation (recitation, proclamation, performance) of the inscribed text.

in particular. As a result, considerable flexibility along with an extremely variable, unsettled process of text transmission is posited, apparently in accordance with Werner Kelber's "biosphere model" of ancient oral societies:

> [T]here can be no real "transmission of content" in an oral milieu, for every telling of a story is a discrete speech act operating within the dynamics of its own unique situation. An "oral tradition" should therefore be conceived as a loosely connected series of individual oral performances, not as a process by which fixed texts are handed down from one generation to the next, more or less intact.... The biosphere model also resists any notion of a "transmission," more or less accurate, of the content of a traditional saying or story.... It is therefore impossible to speak of "originals" and "variants" in an oral milieu.[20] (Thatcher 2008:10)

Such formal fluctuation and a disappearance of the notion of original sacred "content" is allegedly mirrored in the early written traditions of Scripture, where the practice of scribality is said to duplicate that of primary (as distinct from rhetorical, scribally-influenced) orality:

> Chirographic texts paralleled orality in at least four ways: a) variation in expression was the norm, not the exception; b) there were no single "originals" but rather a plurality of original and independent compositions; c) Jewish and Christian scribes attempted to keep texts relevant to the needs of their immediate audiences; in view of points a, b, and c, the early "manuscript tradition" should be understood as a series of active recompositions rather than as simple transmission and copying. This

---

[20] The "interactive speech environment" referred to by Kelber as a "biosphere" (perhaps more accurately labeled a "logosphere") is one "in which speaker and hearers live...an invisible nexus of references and identities from which people draw sustenance...and in which they make sense of their lives" (Thatcher 2008:4, with reference to Kelber 1994:159). More recently Kelber states that "we will henceforth have to proceed on the premise that the scribal tradition of Jesus sayings was characterized by an astounding fluidity.... Instead of fixation on the one original saying, this tradition was comfortable with multiple and variable versions, each of which claimed authority at one point. In analogy to oral performance, the scribal tradition moved with the flux of time by way of social adaptation, thus keeping itself alive by staying relevant" (Kelber 2008:254–255).

3.2 A More flexible model of text transmission

> conclusion calls for a complete rethinking of the status of the Masoretic Text (MT) and the Greek *textus receptus*. (Thatcher 2008:10)

A technical term has even been coined to refer to this postulated mutability, or "essential indeterminacy," of the manuscript/scribal tradition of the biblical text, namely, "*mouvance*," which, as in the case of the Hebrew tradition, spotlights the supposed central role of the scribes in the production of Scripture:

> In chirographic transmission, the person of the scribe was kinetically, cognitively, and existentially bound up in the re-creation of the text in such a way that is incomprehensible in our era of mechanically mass-produced documents. Transmission was a socially embodied *reading* that effaced any absolute distinction between reader and manuscript.[21] (Kirk 2008:225; original italics)

Such "textual mobility" is purportedly closely associated with "authorial anonymity":

> Anonymity suggested that a text was not regarded as the intellectual property of a single, individual author but was subject to recurring rewritings. By analogy, large parts of the ancient Near Eastern and Mediterranean textual tradition, including the early manuscript traditions of both the Hebrew Bible and the New Testament, may be understood as *mouvance*, that is, as a living tradition in a process of persistent regeneration. (Kelber 2010:118)

A more nuanced perspective on the process of orally transmitting the texts of the NT is proposed by James Dunn. This hypothesis puts forward a mixed model, one that incorporates lability as well as stability within the tradition:

---

[21] Thus, so it would seem, the text producer(s), the text itself, as well as its reader(s) would merge into some sort of a mystical social event (or experience) that was somehow meaningful in the moment of message transmission-communication.

Actually, the term "mouvance" has been adopted from medieval literary studies and applied now to the biblical literature, with essentially the same definition: "A concept formulated to describe *textual mobility* in medieval texts when the creation of a work is the *result of a communal process* rather than an individual act of literary production" (Doan and Giles 2005:171, italics added; cf. Kelber 2010:116–118).

> Oral transmission exhibits "an insistent conservative urge for preservation" of essential information, while it borders on carelessness in its predisposition to abandon features that are not met with social approval. Variability and stability, conservatism and creativity, evanescence and unpredictability all mark the pattern of oral transmission—the oral principle of variation within the same.[22] (Dunn 2003:200)

Another variant of the flexibility hypothesis draws attention more to the influence of the biblical text's variable performance tradition, especially during its earlier years of literary development. Only later then, in Second Temple times, and "[a]s the fixed, uniform text of Scripture became a cultural icon, scribes were increasingly reluctant to fold the results of the oral-performative interpretations of the text into its manuscript tradition" (Jafee 2001:19).[23]

In any case, the implication is sometimes given that if one does not subscribe, more or less, to this view of an unstable, manifestly changeable scribal tradition, one becomes guilty of a form of media blindness, an anachronistic outlook which simply does not recognize "the textual, typographic bias inherent in much of our historical and interpretive work" (Kelber 2008:237). This inherent instability of the biblical text in terms of its origin and transmission may, quite logically it would seem, be extended then to embrace any and all Scripture translations throughout the ages:

> Huge misunderstandings arise when people naively assume that their Bible is a faithful copy of the one and only original Bible, however that may be understood. If our Bible is not written in the languages used by the biblical authors, it is clear that we are not reading a faithful copy of the original.[24] (Fowler 2009:10)

---

[22] The quote comes from W. Kelber. For a detailed critique of Dunn's approach, see Witherington 2009a:ch. 10.

[23] It is interesting to note here that a "fixed, uniform text of Scripture" is referred to.

[24] It is rather disingenuous of the author to make this Islamic-sounding assertion about Bible translations, however, for he does not initially allow for the possibility of biblical "authorship" and an "original text," as traditionally understood: "In an oral/aural culture there is no such thing as an 'original' composition that is memorized and repeated verbatim. Rather, each performance of a story is itself a unique, new composition.... The scribes who wrote the manuscripts exercised tremendous freedom both in writing the original manuscript and in 'correcting' that

In sum, if translations of the Scriptures are unreliable, and if the original, supposedly God-given text itself is indeterminable, then, hermeneutically speaking, what are we left with? As one critic concludes with specific reference to the teachings of Jesus:

> More recent studies based on the culture of orality and communal storytelling have effectively closed off any pathway to the actual teaching of Jesus. Either way [i.e., following the form critics or certain orality specialists], the "real" Jesus and his teaching are seen as obscured by developments in the era after him. (Barnett 2005:136)

Now the preceding may well be an overstatement for impact, and one should not judge a particular methodology by the misuse by its practitioners, but it is true to say that many recent studies in the field of orality-oriented analysis often do cast substantial doubt on the authenticity and reliability of the Scriptures, chiefly for non-specialist readers who may not be able to distinguish the wheat from the chaff.

3.3 A more restrained model of text transmission

As indicated earlier, however, there is a significant alternative proposal to the preceding perspective, one that posits a much more fixed and stable Scripture text and manuscript tradition and does not "implicitly valorize oral over written communication" (Aune 2009:70).[25] This approach stems from the work of

---

same manuscript years later.... At the oral/aural stage, no two tellings of a biblical story would have been the same. Then, at the stage of manuscript communication, no two manuscript copies of a biblical book would have been identical" (Fowler 2009:7, 10, 16). But perhaps the critic is too anxious to demonstrate the topic of his article, namely, that "everything we know about the Bible is wrong," and thus also errs by making a universal negative claim concerning an unverifiable proposition (i.e., that no completely correspondent tellings/copies were ever produced at any time). On the importance of an *author*-oriented perspective in biblical hermeneutics, including any stylistic-rhetorical analysis, see Brown 2007:38–42, 47–50; Wendland 2004a:129–130, 242–243, 298.

[25] The following may be an example of such "valorization": "The manuscript was ancillary; it was the visual, material support—an external 'reference point' (Carr 2005:160; *ew: this is perhaps not a representative quote from Carr*)—for the primary existence and transmission of the text in the medium of memory. Likewise, it was not in minute textual dissection but in oral enactment out of memory that the text's meaning was actualized" (Kirk 2008:219). But in what

Birger Gerhardsson, whose Uppsala dissertation, *Memory and Manuscript*, was first published in 1961.[26] Mournet summarizes Gerhardsson's methodology, which favors a more constant as opposed to a flexible textual approach with regard to transmitting the Gospel tradition, as follows (2009:47–48):

> Among Gerhardsson's primary goals was to ask, "what was the technical procedure followed when the early Church *transmitted*, both gospel material and other material?" He expressed the view that Jerusalem was the center of early Christianity and that members of the Jerusalem church and other early churches formed a collegium which included leading men as the official possessors and transmitters of the teaching of Jesus himself. For Gerhardsson, the technical procedure was thoroughly indebted to the process of memorization, including the use of notebooks as an *aide-mémoir* for the disciples. Jesus was the authoritative teacher who intentionally engaged in a teacher-student relationship with his disciples.... Gerhardsson's work reawakened awareness of the Jesus tradition's thoroughgoing indebtedness to Judaism and Jewish pedagogical practices which were present within the Gospel texts all along.[27]

---

sense is a "reference point" to which all oral performances should be normatively evaluated simply "ancillary"?

Granted, we do not wish to return to the literary bias and patchwork text approach of the source and redaction critics. However, "[a]s Byrskog points out, the alleged polarity between orality and written texts, overplayed repeatedly by Kelber and his disciples, has skewed the discussion of the gospel traditions in various ways and even has led to a romanticizing of orality and oral performance over 'textual rigor mortis'" (Witherington 2009a:132—with reference to Byrskog 2002:33–40).

[26] Gerhardsson's approach has been refined and further developed by his student and successor at the University of Lund, Samuel Byrskog (2002), which has in turn been strongly supported by the massive recent study of Bauckham (2006). Bauckham's theory of an "eyewitnessed" historical tradition leading to the written Gospels has been recently affirmed also in Witherington 2009a:121–142.

With regard to the relative stability of the Gospel accounts of the Jesus tradition, Bauckham states: "The eyewitnesses who remembered the events of the history of Jesus were remembering inherently very memorable events, unusual events that would have impressed themselves on the memory, events of key significance for those who remembered them, landmark or life-changing events for them in many cases, and their memories would have been reinforced and stabilized by frequent rehearsal, beginning soon after the event" (2006:346).

[27] The initial enclosed citation is from Gerhardsson 1998:14–15, original italics. Mournet (ibid., 59) goes on to say, "While it is recognized that memorization should not be understood exclusively as an attempt to transmit tradition verbatim,

3.3 A more restrained model of text transmission

Gerhardsson's application of second-century rabbinic techniques of pedagogy and textual transmission to the Jesus tradition rendered his approach vulnerable to the charge of anachronism. However, "it would be fallacious to assume that these newly (i.e., post 70 C.E.) refined and/or adopted methods were created *ex nihilo* from within a cultural and historical vacuum" (Mournet 2009:48).[28] On the contrary, it is only logical to assume that:

> In order to be comprehensible and coherent, the didactic methods utilized by teachers during nascent rabbinic Judaism must have been, to some extent, continuous with those utilized by teachers and leaders during the time of Jesus himself. (Mournet 2009:48)

Jaffee documents the vital importance of memorization in the Hebrew religious tradition, where "the material form of the scroll encouraged readers to view it as a mnemonic safety device—a storage system for texts already held substantially in the memory"; thus a written "book" was correspondingly "a commodity that one heard through the medium

---

departure from verbatim transmission is explicable via an appeal to formalized, structured methods of transmission…[that is] through the model of rabbinic expansions and ongoing interpretations modeled on how the rabbis interacted with their own textual traditions."

Witherington adds (2009a:129, 131): "If one is going to deal with the orality of the early followers of Jesus, including the Gospel writers who wrote in Greek, Paul, and others, then one has to come to grips with the nature of a rhetoric-saturated culture and how oral traditions and sacred traditions function in a rhetorical culture. When you do assess the data in the light of rhetorical conventions and tendencies, rhetorically purposeful variation, rather than just flexible oral storytelling and traditioning, better explains most of the data…. What is in play here is not mere oral flexibility or variation on a theme but a purposeful editing or modifying of a tradition, whether oral or written, so that it adds to the persuasiveness of the material in Greek…. [R]hetoric is one of the keys to analyzing how the tradition was handled, shaped, and handed on, early and late."

[28] Carr views this tradition as stemming from and within the comprehensive educational-enculturating process of ancient Israel: "It is certainly possible that a scribe may have worked with a given manuscript on occasion. Nevertheless, well-educated scribes often could write out a verbatim, memorized form of an older, authoritative text…. Furthermore, having learned such precise, verbatim memorization in a text-supported oral educational system, Israelite authors were able… to echo their own writing. Their training in verbatim memorization in a text-supported environment gave them tools for exact or semiexact repetition that allowed them to produce works that features remarkably precise parallels" (2005:159–160). See also Safrai 2009.

of another human voice [and] 'reading' was the activity of declaiming a text before an audience in a social performance approaching the gravity of ceremonial ritual" (Jaffee 2001:17). Jaffee further describes the crucial relationship between written and oral texts:

> Literary culture was commonly delivered orally and received orally, the memory serving as the connector between mouth and ear. The intervention of the eye and hand was confined largely to creating the necessary material foundation for literary preservation. (Jaffee 2001:18)

In a recent essay which examines the "evidence for the interplay of memory recall and written technology in ancient Israel and surrounding cultures," Carr comes to the following noteworthy conclusion (Carr 2010:17, 32, emphasis added):

> One feature these three phenomena of *oral-written transmission* have in common is the overall focus of ancient tradents on preservation of written words from the past. Usually, this meant that they reproduced traditions with *virtually no change*. To be sure, as we have seen, such reproduction without change could include a variety of *memory variants*: changes of wording, order, or non-significant shifts in grammar or syntax. And graphically copied traditions could include various *copyists' errors*. Nevertheless, if we are to look empirically at the documented transmission of ancient texts, the first and most important thing to emphasize is the following: the vast majority of cases involve reproduction of earlier traditions with no shifts beyond the memory or graphic shifts surveyed so far. At the least, tradents aimed for preservation of the semantic content of traditions. Often, with time, traditions such as the later Mesopotamian and Jewish traditions developed various techniques for insuring more precise preservation of the tradition, often through processes of graphic copying and various techniques of proofing copies.[29]

---

[29] This was "an oral-written context where the masters of literary tradition used texts to memorize certain traditions seen as particularly ancient, holy, and divinely inspired.... This writing-supported process of memorization was how ancient cultures passed on to the next generation their most treasured written traditions, what might be termed 'long-duration' or 'literary' (in the broad sense of that term) texts" (Carr

3.3 A more restrained model of text transmission

According to this preservative memory model then (active during the ANE age of a "rhetorical culture"; Robbins 2006:127), there was substantial interaction between the oral and written media during Bible times, including the era when the Hebrew texts of Scripture were being composed, memorized, orally transmitted, recorded in writing—and during the entire process continually taught, both formally (in the Temple) and informally (at home) (Carr 2010:18). "Students in a culture such as Israel's learned the *written* tradition in an *oral-performative* and *communal* context" (Carr 2011:5, original italics). Thus, the principal, determinative record was always the *written* form of the text, also in the formative years of the Hebrew Bible. This inscribed text is attested, with emphasis, in both the OT and the NT traditions, internally (e.g., "write!"; "it is written"—Exod 17:14; Josh 8:31; Rev 1:11; Matt 4:6)[30] as well as externally, that is, in the comparatively large number of whole and partial ancient manuscripts available today.[31]

2011:4–5). Even "the archaic dialect/language and themes of such [ancient] texts marked them as special, worth the special effort to learn and preserve them" (ibid., 6).

[30] As Horsley observes, "The Gospel of Mark introduced 'quotes' and some of its other references with the formula '(as) it is written' (*gegraptai*; 1:2; 7:6; etc.). We can presumably conclude from this formula at least that the Gospel derives from a society in which the existence of authoritative written texts was widely known, even that their existence in writing gave them a special authority" (2010:98; cf. Graham 2010:238). With regard to the prophetic literature, Millard notes that "the written form carried authority in Mesopotamia and Egypt, and so, it may be deduced, it did in Israel and Judah. A prophet might revise and reorganize his oracles, but whether or not his disciples or later followers could alter them or bring them up to date, as often is alleged, remains hypothetical in the absence of early manuscripts" (2012:887–888) Furthermore, "the way scribes of cuneiform and Egyptian were trained to copy accurately—something essential for commercial, legal, and court matters—and to take letters from dictation might point in the other direction [i.e., from the popular scholarly supposition that they freely edited or altered prophetic texts], to ensuring that it was the words spoken that they recorded" (ibid., 886, material in brackets added from the context cited).

[31] For example, there are over 5400 complete and partial manuscripts of the New Testament, many of which date from within 200 years after they were written in the first century CE. By comparison, there are only 9–10 good manuscripts of Julius Caesar's *Gallic War*, composed in 58–50 BCE, but extant in manuscripts dating some 900 years later (Wegner 2006:40). This large number of NT Greek manuscripts is even more striking in view of the fact that many Christian scrolls and codices were certainly destroyed in the various persecutions that accompanied the growth of the early Church. The importance of the *written* text in the case of the Hebrew Scriptures is underscored by the careful practices that the earliest scribes adopted in order to stabilize and monitor the process of copying and transmitting the various received authoritative texts (ibid., 62–70).

Thus, criticizing scholars who would turn "Old Testament studies into a 'non-prophet-making' enterprise," Kitchen grants that "the first stage of almost every prophetic pronouncement was its oral declaration from the mouth of the prophet...," but argues that "just telling people by word of mouth was not deemed a sufficient means of record or diffusion" (Kitchen 2003:390, 392). Based on an extensive comparative investigation of the "history and functions of prophecy in the biblical world," Kitchen concludes:

> Throughout the centuries, across the biblical world, the firsthand external evidence shows clearly and conclusively that the record of prophecies among contemporaries and their transmission down through time was *not* left to the memories of bystanders or to the memory-conditioned oral transmission—and modification—by imaginary "disciples" of a prophet or their equally imaginary successors for centuries before somebody took the remnants at a late date to weave them into books out of whole new cloth, having little or nothing to do with a reputed prophet of dim antiquity whose very name and existence might thus be doubted.... Quite the contrary. When ancient prophets (from Mari onward) spoke out, witnesses could be summoned to attest the authenticity of the actual process of scribing the very words, the *ipsissima verba*, of the prophet, to ensure that the real thing was sent to the king, and to eliminate any querying of the wording and content of the message(s) concerned from the start. (Kitchen 2003:384, 392)

To this point, Millard adds:

> Writing was the principal means of ensuring that information of any sort was accurately preserved across generations, as the numerous legal deeds attest. In the same way, the written reports could continue to serve as witnesses to the prophets' declarations after they and their audiences were dead.... References to Hebrew prophets writing are few;[32]

---

[32] Although such references to writing are relatively rare, they cannot be discounted as possibly being the norm (e.g., Isa 8:1; 30:8; Jer 29; 30:2; 36; 51:60-64; Hab 2:2; cf. also significantly 2 Chr 9:29). If a certain prophet did use a scribe to record his words, like Jeremiah's Baruch, the latter may have been allowed to "put them into a recognized literary style," to make copies

3.3 A more restrained model of text transmission

however this should not be interpreted to mean that they did not normally write, but that the activity only deserved special notice when it had special significance. The possibility that their oracles were written down soon after they had uttered them deserves more attention than it has received in many commentaries. (Millard 2012a:886, 888)

The overall communication situation in the Greco-Roman age and time of Jesus is clearer of course, yet not entirely without controversy. The key notion here is the continued influence of the more conservative rabbinic mode of textual transmission, i.e., relatively strict memorization in conjunction with written documentation and oral performance, with reference to the various texts of the developing "New Testament":

> While orality closely interfaces with the written word, because the written word was intended for the ear, the culture in which Jesus lived was no preliterary society, [Gerhardsson] points out, and the Jesus tradition was never "pure" orality. The relationship between oral and written transmission was more complex than appears from comparisons with oral cultures. Scholars have to take into account how written texts, especially those from the Scriptures, constantly interacted with oral performance in the ancient Jewish milieu closest to early Christianity.... The words [of Jesus] were artistically formulated *meshalim* which were memorized, interpreted, and expounded in roughly the same way as Jewish *meshalim*. The mighty deeds of Jesus were mostly put into pointed narrative form after his departure. These narratives were memorized after the pattern of the sayings tradition.... [There was a] close interaction between the oral Jesus tradition and the scribal activities of the transmitters. Memory and memorization in early Christianity were...deliberate and sophisticated acts of preservation and cannot be equated with models of mnemonic performances of a more popular kind.[33] (Byrskog 2009:16–18)

---

and store them, as well as to proclaim the prophetic oracles to designated audiences—but all under the authority and supervision of the Lord's prophet (Millard 2012:886–887).

[33] "Gerhardsson, *Reliability* (2001:120), is not happy with the concept of 'performance.' While it may not be the ideal designation, it is by now thoroughly institutionalized in orality-scribality studies. It connotes the complex dynamics of oral

At this juncture, it may be helpful to consider Witherington's distinction between "oral history" and "oral tradition":

> Oral history is the testimony of eyewitnesses in the first place, and this is the bridge between past and present that is being actually mentioned in the NT itself, not an anonymous passing on of oral traditions in general between countless generations and voices.... Oral tradition may have passed from mouth to ear many times and is typically collective and anonymous; oral history is not.[34] (Witherington 2009a:134, 137)

In either case, the dimension of orality was a vital component of the process and practice of Scripture transmission, for the diverse religious writings of the Bible were undoubtedly all initially orally composed with a view towards their oral-aural proclamation to the author's intended audiences.

---

delivery in the ancient world, including the roles of the speaker and audience, social location, material context, emotive and kinetic dimensions, etc." (Kelber 2009:257).

I too am rather uncomfortable with the term "performance" when loosely used with reference to the textual transmission of the Scriptures, whether ancient or modern (Wendland 2008b:53–56), mainly because it seems to focus too much upon the audience-engaging role of the "performer" (tradent) rather than on the author-intended message of the original text. A similar concern arises when McLuhan's misleading overstatement "the medium is the message" is applied too freely in any Scripture "proclamation" event. The importance of authorial intention and a corresponding world-view during the communication process is illustrated by Paul's healing a crippled man at Lystra (Acts 14:8–20), a narrative that demonstrates the dramatic results of three very different religious perspectives on this "performance." I am happier with the use of "performance" when applied more strictly to the oral communication of an established, written tradition—i.e., the "performance of literature" (D. Rhoads, personal correspondence, July 27, 2010).

[34] In making this distinction, Witherington highlights the so-called "autopsy factor" (ibid., 133; "autopsy" from the Greek *autopsia*—'a seeing with one's own eyes') and builds upon the work of Byrskog (2002) and Bauckham (2006). Thus, according to Bauckham, "the period between the 'historical' Jesus and the Gospels was actually spanned, not by anonymous community transmission, but by the continuing presence and testimony of the eyewitnesses, who remained the authoritative sources of their traditions until their deaths" (2006:8).

Dan Fitzgerald observes in this connection: "The RC and Orthodox churches do not shrink from asserting that 'oral tradition' IS based on the testimony of eyewitnesses: they call that tradition 'apostolic'. They claim that this 'apostolic tradition' was not passed on anonymously, but through 'apostolic succession'—in two distinct though closely bound ways, that is, orally and in writing (i.e., oral and written 'modes')" (personal correspondence, January 23, 2012).

3.3 A more restrained model of text transmission

"Precisely because texts were composed under the assumption that they would be read in the setting of oral performance, their compositional styles drew deeply upon habits of speech and rhetorical traditions that had their living matrix in oral communication" (Jaffee 2001:18).[35] Furthermore, these texts were fashioned in an excellent oratorical style and in a powerful rhetorical manner so that they would be memorable and memorizable as well as having a captivating, persuasive effect on their hearers,[36] as befitting the supreme contents of their theological, ethical, and prophetic messages. It should be pointed out, however, that although the written compositions may have been "but surrogates for or transcripts of oral speech" (Witherington 2009a:133), they nevertheless retained their primacy in terms of referential authority and control with regard to stabilizing the textual tradition,[37] at

---

[35] However, as Jaffee also notes, "Even a text composed orally for the purpose of written preservation stands at an esthetic distance from the actual speech of oral communication, for literary diction in any form is not simply 'talking,' even though it might seek to place speeches in the mouths of literary characters" (2001:18).

[36] For example, "The majority of the authors of the New Testament, as we realize today, were highly literate, and not, it seems, all that reluctant to employ rather refined forms of the written medium as a means of communication" (Byrskog 2002:109). "The twenty-seven books of the NT reflect a remarkable level of literacy and rhetorical skill" (Witherington 2009a:8).

[37] "Only the Bible (the 'Written Law') was to be committed to writing; this served to fix and close the text" (Katz and Schwartz 1998:11). Furthermore, "These (usually) visually copied texts were a crucial reference point for further written and oral transmission" (Carr 2005:160; cf. Harvey 1998:50–51). "[I]t is through the written word that Christianity comes to define itself in the second and third centuries" (Haines-Eitzen 2000:124). In addition, it is important to recognize that "the [written] Jewish Scriptures was the 'Christian' Bible before the New Testament gradually came to formation" (ibid., 124).

This position is contrary to that adopted by Lee and Scott, at least with reference to Scripture: "Documents served as secondary references rather than sources of information storage…documents were not the repositories of authority…authors and not documents held authority" (2009:62–63). Hezser too seems to set up a false dichotomy between the written and the spoken word: With reference to John 7:15 ("How does this man know letters, having never learned?"), she comments: "John thereby stresses the higher, spiritual authority of Jesus' teaching (v. 16), which is not based on the written word of the Hebrew Bible. The assumption is that a Jewish scholar's learning would be based on the knowledge he gained from his reading of the scriptural text, whereas a Christian teacher's power goes back to the source of Scripture itself and is therefore independent of letters and writing" (2010:78). However, John 7:15 does not give evidence that Jesus was illiterate and/or did not refer to the written Scriptures to support his teachings (cf. Luke 4:16–21; 6:3; 10:26). Rather, the people's query here simply expresses the observation that he had not received the normal formal training under a recognized Jewish rabbi.

least within the particular tradent communities that took responsibility for preserving them.[38] "[A]t some point, the oral does not die, but its authority is subordinate to that of the written text" (van der Toorn 2007:218).

Furthermore, as the various text studies in Part II seek to demonstrate, the tightly woven, often multi-layered structural design of the biblical text (where confirmed) has two other significant implications concerning its transmission: (a) a perceptible,[39] memorable structural pattern would favor a more stable tradition, hence fewer major variations from the original literary arrangement; (b) such a rhetorically-motivated internal structure provides a helpful template today for the text's contemporary memorization and oral performance.

In summary,[40] a combined oral-history, scribal/rabbinic teaching model would seem to best explain the transmission process of most, if not all

---

[38] "Direct connections through letters would be established among community leaders on behalf of and as representatives of their local Christian co-religionists. These leaders, and especially Paul, would at least try to maintain control over lay Christians' beliefs and practices and divert attention from competitors ('false' apostles) who orally proclaimed alternative teachings. In this way, letters would still function as a means of executing authority and control..." (Hezser 2010:80).

[39] Such literary (oratorical) patterns must obviously be readily apparent in the text, aurally and/or visually, for them to serve their architectural, rhetorical, and mnemonic functions. With regard to the memory, for example, a typical structural pattern normally consists of from 5–9 constituent elements (Miller 1956), although some research would suggest that the lower number is more likely (Cowan 2001). On the other hand, by means of the cognitive process of "chunking," that is, grouping a set of related items together in the mind, a longer sequence of elements can be retained in the memory by breaking it up into smaller coherent units, especially threes (Simon 1983).

[40] See Wendland 2008b:ch. 1 for more details and additional documentation. Thus, my argument is that once an oral sacred text (there must be some distinction here—i.e., the "words of God") was recorded in writing, this inscribed version remained a relatively stable (yet not entirely iron-clad) reference point for the subsequent transmission of the tradition, whether widely regarded as "inspired Scripture" yet or not. The ongoing repeated public "performances" of that Hebrew/Greek text may have varied, but those variations, especially major ones, were not likely to alter the principal written versions in communal circulation. Nor would the scribes entrusted with making written copies of that text be very ready or prone to make significant alterations, other than various linguistic and perhaps also sociocultural updates.

I note Kelber's caveat that "one should not underestimate the degree to which prevalent needs and one's cultural horizon can exercise influence on nearly every aspect of historical inquiry, including the preference for one model over the other" (2009:184). Furthermore, to help avoid cultural and methodological bias, researcher-analysts would do well to become well-versed in all those disciplines that closely relate to their primary field of study.

3.3 A more restrained model of text transmission

Scripture documents, both in Hebrew and Greek, including narrative prose as well as the poetic and paraenetic genres. The different writings were viewed as being God-given, hence sacred and trustworthy in terms of governing the beliefs and morals of groups as well as individuals. These religious texts were either vocally generated in the first instance (e.g., most prophetic oracles) or deliberately composed (aloud!) in writing with oral elocution in mind (e.g., the apostolic epistles), generally by a single author-reporter (perhaps using an amanuensis) or a close disciple ("eye/ear witness"). Those texts thus recognized as being the trustworthy "Word of God" were therefore memorized to a greater or lesser degree and, if not already inscribed, were relatively quickly committed to some type of temporary or permanent written form (with or without subsequent scribal or editorial adjustments).[41] A stable written text was necessary for authoritative

---

I have attempted to sharpen my perception of orality studies in relation to the analysis of Scripture texts, among other ways, through a detailed investigation of traditional vernacular Chewa oral art forms (e.g., 1976), and on the other hand, through various insights gained from the context-centered *Jerusalem School of Synoptic Research*. This "school" posits the following three principles: "1. *Hebrew Language*: Hebrew was a living language in first-century [multilingual] Israel.... 2. *Jewish Culture*: The Synoptic Gospels must be interpreted within the context of first-century [rabbinic] Judaism; and they, in turn, contribute to our understanding of first-century Judaism.... 3. *Synoptic Gospels*: Tracing the linguistic and cultural data within the Synoptic Gospels leads to insights into their literary relationships" (http://www.js.org/Methodology/index.htm).

[41] Other scholars who support the hypothesis of a relatively early (and stable), written testimony of the early Christian message, the Gospels as well as the apostolic epistles are Gamble (1995) and Millard (2000). Richards comes to a similar conclusion regarding the Pauline epistles (2004:92–93).

"The place of the Torah and other sacred Scriptures set the book at the heart of Jewish society. No human ideas should be allowed to vie with God's Word or be mistaken for it. The written text stood as a control; it was read publicly in synagogue services and could be consulted whenever necessary; the fact that most scholars had committed it to memory did not reduce its final authority, for they had learned it from the written text, not from oral tradition, even if they sat in groups repeating what the teacher read. The presence of the text itself at the heart of Judaism and in its regular services should not be underestimated. It is a feature which weighs against characterizations of Herodian Palestine as an 'oral world'" (Millard 2000:204).

"That the earliest Christian writings are indebted to an already well-developed tradition of Christian exegesis shows that from the beginning Christianity was deeply engaged in the interpretation and appropriation of texts. That activity presupposed not only a mature literacy but also sophisticated scribal and exegetical skills. Arising within the matrix of a broadly literate Judaism, early Christianity was never without a literary dimension…" (Gamble 1995:29).

content preservation, to foster precise wider circulation, and to serve as a reliable memory aid, that is, "as *aides-mémoire* (in the sense of mnemonic devices that serve as aids to communal memory)"—and presumably individual memories as well (Aune 2009:79).[42] Documents with a more complex compositional history may well have been formed from the skillful redactional combination of a number of shorter, independent texts, either those originating from the same author on different occasions (e.g., the Isaiah scroll), or those knit together by a primary "compiler" from distinct oral and/or written sources (e.g., the Gospel of Luke).[43]

In short, it may be argued that the same reverential care that applied to the reading and preservation of the Hebrew Scriptures was either immediately or very soon applied to transmitting the documents that would eventually comprise the canonical NT. As the Apostle John stated this text-preserving principle:

> I warn everyone who hears the words of the prophecy of this book: If anyone adds anything to them, God will add to him the plagues described in this book. And if anyone takes words away from this book of prophecy, God will take away from him his share in the tree of life and in the holy city, which are described in this book. (Revelation 22:18–19, NIV)

It is my contention that this same stricture applied with equal force at a relatively early date in the history of the early Church also with respect to the process of *oral* text transmission and the public proclamation of the Gospels and Epistles.[44]

---

[42] Aune makes the twofold distinction between temporary *aides-mémoire* and more permanent *lieux de mémoire*, "sites of memory," "that is, texts that generated and transformed communal memory" (2009:79). My general view favoring, by and large, the *individual* authorship or compilation of biblical texts (i.e., not composition by a scribal or editorial committee) would make this distinction unnecessary.

[43] "The theory of oral history rather than somewhat flexible informally controlled oral transmission better explains what we find in the canonical Gospels. We have here in these Gospels 'Jesus remembered,' not just by anyone or everyman but by those who knew him best, those who were eyewitnesses and original heralds of the Word. The communities did not create these traditions—the eyewitnesses did. What the communities did do was to validate the tradition's veracity..." (Witherington 2009a:142).

[44] Many scholars would not agree with my linkage of canonicity and orthodoxy. For example: "The reasons for canon formation are usually seen in a defense against

3.4 Some unresolved issues

In a recent collection of articles that reflect upon Gerhardsson's seminal work and its significance (*Jesus in Memory*), Werner Kelber highlights in the form of questions a set of the unresolved issues that remain between the putative "orality" (or "performance-based") and "rabbinic" ("historical" or "didactic") models of biblical tradition/text transmission. With specific reference to the Synoptic Gospels, for example:[45]

- If it is granted that individuals played a role as carriers of the tradition, do the Gospel narratives attest to collected materials in terms, for example, of a Petrine tradition? *What implications, if any, would the latter development (the establishment of a "Petrine tradition") have with respect to the relative stability of the texts concerned in terms of both form and content?*

- Can one invoke "the evidence of reliable eyewitnesses" without consideration of the cognitive implications of memory? In other words, should we not think of eyewitness reports as ultimately the work of memorial processes? *And what about the possible influence on transmitting the biblical tradition(s) of ancient Jewish educational-enculturating practice, as proposed, for example, in Carr 2005:131–132?*

- How can we match the narrative causalities of the Gospels with the notion that these narratives are the result of and basically structured by apostolic preaching? In different words: can narrative critics and proponents of a strongly developed eyewitness theory ever find common ground? *What are the major issues that each side would have to concede or compromise on in order to find such "common ground" as a starting point for discussions?*

Marcionism, Gnosticism, and Montanism. One notes that the overall argument falls along the lines of orthodoxy versus heresiology, categories that are no longer quite fashionable in current historical scholarship" (Kelber 2010:124).

[45] Kelber (2009:184). I have added further interrogatory material (*in italics*) following each of the original questions proposed by Kelber (who is quoted verbatim).

- How can we sort out oral from scribal components inscribed in the Gospel narratives? For example, are the densely constructed miracle and pronouncement stories the result of oral, memorial economizing or of a literary tightening of a living oral tradition? *What would be the point and purpose of such a "sorting out"—what difference to our understanding of form and content might result? Would this differentiation in any way change our concept of a received canonical text that serves as the basis for any Bible translation?*

- Have the advocates of the orality model come to terms with performance as a key feature of tradition or are they still captive to the notion of transmission as a process of handing down and passing on words from person to person? *In addition, how does inscribing a given text at any stage affect the subsequent combined text transmission and performance (or proclamation) process?*

- Has the orality model taken seriously the inseparability of memory from tradition and has it integrated "the wide range of memorializing activities practiced within viable communities" into its mode of thinking? *Are there any significant differences between the Jewish Hebrew and the early Christian Greek traditions in this regard? Furthermore, how do such "memorializing activities" relate to inscribing a particular biblical text at any stage during its early process of transmission?*

These are certainly not all of the questions pertaining to such issues that could be raised;[46] another pertinent case concerns the apparent prioritizing by some researchers of oral over written communication in an ANE setting. For example: "[T]he few early Christian references to oral and/or written communication indicate that the communities of Christ and their nascent intellectual leadership did not just prefer orality, but were even reticent about or suspicious of writing" (Horsley 2010:101–102). This observation is supported by a quotation from Papias, an early 2nd-century theologian:

---

[46] For more queries relating to these diverse perspectives, see Wendland 2008b:32–48.

3.4 Some unresolved issues

> I inquired about *the words* of the ancients, what Andrew or Peter or Philip or Thomas or James or John or Matthew or any other of the Lord's disciples *said*, and what Ariston and the elder John, the Lord's disciples, were *saying*. For I did not suppose that things from books (*ek tôn bibliôn*) would benefit me so much as things *from a living and abiding voice* (*zôsês phônês kai menousês*). (Horsley 2010:102)

This leads to the conclusion that "Papias' statement indicates both the oral mode of communication and the high valuation placed on the direct oral continuity of communication from the Lord through the previous two generations of disciples" (ibid., 102). However, as Bauckham has pointed out, "[i]n order to understand Papias's preference for the 'living voice' over written sources, we must first recognize that it was an ancient topos or commonplace" (2006:21), and that "what is preferable to writing is not a lengthy chain of oral tradition, but direct personal experience of a teacher" (ibid., 22).[47] Furthermore, ancient synagogue practice, which arguably served as a model also for early Christians reveals the liturgical custom of first reading the Scriptures (the Law and the Prophets) and then commenting on what was written there (Acts 13:15). Questions and controversies such as those outlined above are sufficient to suggest that continued research in the combined communication field of ancient text composition, memory, chirography, and performance is still very much necessary.[48] Perhaps a

---

[47] "[I]n the case of Papias's use of the proverb, as Harry Gamble points out, 'it is not oral tradition as such that Papias esteemed, but first-hand information. To the extent that he was able to get information directly [i.e., from eyewitnesses], he did so and preferred to do so'" (Bauckham 2006:23; Gamble 1995:30–31; words in brackets added from the general context). The same basic criterion would lead me to revise the following conclusion: "[W]hat led to [Mark's] inclusion in the canon was [its] repeated oral performance as increasingly authoritative, scriptural texts in the second and third centuries before standardized written copies were widely available" (Horsley 2010:110). Rather, it would be the increasingly and more widely copied, authoritative eyewitness testimony of the Gospel as recorded in Mark that, by divine provision, led to its immediate recognition as "Scripture" and eventual canonization.

[48] The text-critical issues pertaining to the transmission of the text(s) of Scripture (see further below) have become more intense in recent years due to the discovery of the Dead Sea Scrolls, which include a number of manuscripts with texts that vary in different, usually minor, ways from the Masoretic tradition. Thus, some would conclude: "It has now become clear that the texts of the Hebrew Scriptures continued to be edited and changed until much later than what has traditionally been assumed. Moreover, the evidence seems to suggest

greater meeting of the minds can be achieved in future, or at least a fruitful exchange of differing viewpoints,[49] but one additional matter needs to be addressed more immediately given the special focus of the present study, namely, the relevance of the preceding divergent theories for the practice of *Bible translation*.

3.5 Text transmission in relation to Bible translation

One might initially suppose that adopting a rabbinical, reliable-text theory of Scripture transmission might entail favoring a more literal as opposed to an idiomatic rendition, and vice-versa for the orality approach. But this is not necessarily the case, for Bible translators must deal, whether more or less concordantly, with what is by and large an established, canonical corpus, for example (one of several possible combinations), the Hebrew Masoretic Text (*Biblia Hebraica Stuttgartensia*) and the UBS[4] Greek New Testament edition.

However, the rabbinic method would seemingly encourage a more conservative text-critical approach, with only the most strongly supported textual emendations being possibly considered, for example, normally only "A" and "B" type variants in the Greek New Testament.[50] This would ostensibly

that the editing processes were more radical than assumed" (Weissenberg et al. 2011:3).

The current buzzword in text-critical theory then is "multiple originals" (cf. Martin 2010)—a concept that would appear to be a deliberate paradox, but one which has important theological as well as hermeneutical implications (as in the case of the "multiverse theory" of existence and reality; cf. Folger 2008). In this book, however, I am arguing in favor of a single "original text" or textual tradition (consisting of a set of author/orator-generated texts) of Scripture that has been preserved in the main by its divine Inspirer from the time of initial composition, then through continued memorization and oral proclamation and/or by means of a contemporaneous or a subsequent process of scrupulous scribal transmission and ecclesiastical canonization. The ultimate result is the corpus of documents that has come down to us today as "the Word of God" (Luke 24:25–27; John 21:24; 2 Tim 3:14–17; 1 Pet 1:10–12; 2 Pet 1:20–21).

[49] As expressed, for example, in Kelber and Byrskog, *Jesus in Memory* (2009).

[50] For a summary discussion of such matters relating to "the practice of New Testament textual criticism," see Omanson 2006:11–36; for a fuller discussion, see Wegner 2006:207–254. Wallace concludes with regard to the NT text: "In sum, although scholars may not be certain of the New Testament wording in a number of verses ['less than one percent of all textual variants'], for the vast majority of words in the New Testament the modern English translations accurately represent

contrast with the more flexible critical practice that is informed by orality theory, for which, strictly speaking, there is no such thing as an "original text" of Scripture,[51] and "variability would have been seen as a positive value, a kind of authorizing afflatus in itself":[52]

> Others have raised more radical questions about whether the search for a more "original" form is in fact a misguided enterprise from the start, failing to take seriously the oral nature of the tradition. Thus the model of peeling away later additions may be more determined by the editing of written texts (removing, e.g., "scribal" additions). But for the oral tradition, any idea of an "original" form may be flawed. For it is of the nature of oral tradition not to be fixed (in the way that the act of writing fixed the tradition on a written page). Rather than there being a fixed "original" form of the tradition which is recoverable by modern investigators, there may have been variation from the very

---

what the original authors wrote, and therefore these translations can be trusted as reproducing the very words of God" (2012:117; cf. Wallace 2011).

[51] On the other hand, at least some proponents of an orality-oriented methodology do recognize the fact that this perspective can shed some light on the certain "problems" that many text-critics find in the biblical text: "The media transference of the performed act-scheme into literature may account for the problematic duplications, inconsistencies and awkward transitions that sometimes occur…" (Giles 2012:582). Many such difficulties may also be "logically" explained through the application of an oratorical approach that is based on the principles of how texts are composed and performed in a typical oral-aural setting (see the study of Isaiah 66 in ch. 4).

[52] Doane 1994:433, cited in Kirk 2008:226. Such "scribal pluriformity" is alleged by some orality enthusiasts to characterize both the Hebrew as well as the Greek Testaments: "As far as the Hebrew texts that eventually evolved to canonical status are concerned, their observed pluriformity at Qumran is such that the existence of the Masoretic Text, the normative text of the Hebrew Bible, cannot be assumed any time prior to 100 C.E. Both in the early Jesus tradition and in the textual tradition of what came to be the Hebrew Bible, scribal pluriformity was a phenomenon *sui generis*…. The sense of verbal permanence assumed by typography was not what characterized early scribality. As was the case in oral tradition, criteria for originality and authorship seemed far more relaxed. Orality's propensity, moreover, to conduct itself in plural and varying renditions had been sustained in textual tradition" (Kelber 2008:255; cf. 2010:119–121). According to Kirk, such "multiformity is the mark of the tradition's authority," apparently since it is a reflection of "the oral-traditional register, the body of tradition carried by a community 'intermnemonically' and that is constitutive of its cultural identity" (Kirk 2008:216, 215).

beginning and the variations are simply reflections of different (oral) "performances" of the tradition.⁵³ (Tuckett 2009:33–34)

According to this theory then, we must conclude that "[i]n the end, there is no 'Hebrew Bible'; there are no autographs, and we will eventually have to abandon the image of textual variants derived from some fixed, authorized text we can discover by sifting through the competing readings" (Miller 2011:57).

The implications of such a "radical" perspective on the text of Scripture and the associated practice of textual criticism⁵⁴ might then, in fact, if misunderstood, be mistakenly applied also to its translation.⁵⁵ For if all scribal

---

⁵³ See also Kelber 2009:183. In support of *"a single original text"* with regard to most books of the Hebrew Bible (a more difficult case to argue than that for the books of the Greek NT), Tov observes: "In terms of logic and plausibility, the simplest assumption is that the biblical books were composed at a certain time, or developed in a *linear* way over a period of time. At the end of this process, each of the biblical books was completed in the form of one textual unit (a single copy or tradition) even though, before this final stage, there already existed earlier editions of the books which would have been circulated. From this textual unit, a single copy or tradition, all other copies of the book were derived. Textual criticism aims at the composition which is reflected in the textual entity here defined as one 'copy' or 'tradition'" (1992:172). This view of a "virtual" original text, viewed now only indirectly and with a certain amount of controversy, is nevertheless a compositional-transmissional model that is truer both to the text-critical facts that we have available to us today and the testimony of the Scripture itself (John 20:30–31; 21:24–25).

⁵⁴ "Serious attention to orality also has the capacity to undermine one of the chief presuppositions of textual criticism: the quest to reconstruct 'the original manuscripts'. If a story has been given life within an oral culture, there simply is no original text to be reconstructed, but rather an ongoing, multi-generational interaction between tellers and audiences with scribes acting as tradents in the traditioning process" (Le Donne and Thatcher 2011b:3). So then, is the notion of (human) biblical "authors" just as "simply" to be abandoned? And what about Luke's claim to have composed "an orderly account" of the Jesus gospel for Theophilus so that he might "know the certainty of the things you have been taught" (Luke 1:3–4)? Indeed, there is some serious undermining that has occurred in such a "multiple originals" approach to the biblical text and its transmission (cf. Le Donne and Thatcher ibid., 5; Kelber 2010:121).

⁵⁵ There might also be certain negative implications in this approach for interpreting the text of Scripture as well, for if there is no such thing as an original text, how can there be an "original author"? This broaches the subject of *authorial communicative intention* in the hermeneutical process—whether or not it is a valid, viable notion and one that inevitably impinges also upon the practice of Bible translation—as already noted above. To be sure, this is "our interpretation of the author's intent(s)" (Maxey 2009:159), but at least it is a single, specific, contextualized

3.5 Text transmission in relation to Bible translation

variants (additions, deletions, modifications, etc.) are supposedly "equal" in value or authority in relation to a vague, ill-defined or indeterminable "base text" (whatever this might have been), what is to prevent translators from freely choosing those alternatives that merely appeal to them,[56] or even adding certain context-specific or culture-accommodating textual variations of their own? Indeed, they might thus feel empowered, in the liberating spirit of post-colonialism,[57] to generate their own locally domesticated, periphrastic "oral tradition" within the text of their vernacular translation! Therefore, although the actual determination of a single "original [divine] text" in the case of a given biblical book remains an unrealizable ideal, the evaluative principle that there was, in fact, such a normative composition deriving from one author/compiler, according to which comparative text assessment and interpretation may be oriented and conducted, is preferable, in my opinion, to granting every textual variant more or less equal status for serving as the basis of a modern Bible translation.

As we turn now from the preceding hypothetical, rather controversial translation scenario and the ongoing debate over Scripture origins and disputed textual transmission to some more concrete, practical examples, it would be important to remind ourselves of one of the fundamental principles that has been established through the various debates concerning biblical text composition and transmission. This has to do with the vital

---

hermeneutical point of reference. The importance of intentionality during communication has recently been reaffirmed from a cognitive linguistic perspective: "That as listeners or readers we are continually trying to determine an author's or speaker's intentions, particularly communicative intentions, supports the emphasis on recognition of communicators' intentions in a variety of fields dealing with communication" (Huttar 2006). Such a hermeneutical perspective of course flies in the face of the current in vogue model of *postmodernism*, which stresses "the subjective nature of all kinds of literary research...maintaining that there is no such thing as meaning in [a] text and even less an authorial meaning" (Van Wolde 2009:4). To be sure, it is possible to complicate the notion of authorial intention with subordinate concerns, for example: "authors [may] have unintended meanings" (Sparks 2008:44), but this hermeneutical principle not only makes sense, but is eminently defensible as well.

[56] Thus, according to Ulrich, "should not the object of the text criticism of the Hebrew Bible be, not the single (and textually arbitrary?) collection of Masoretic texts of the individual books, but the organic, developing, pluriform Hebrew text—different for each book—such as the evidence indicates?" (1999:15). But what sort of "evidence" would there be to evaluate in such a text-critical enterprise, and what would be the objective, non-arbitrary principles whereby it could be carried out?

[57] See "Postcolonial Biblical Interpretation," in Soulen and Soulen 2001:38–39.

interactive and complementary relationship between the oral and written word. The basic nature of this complex, dynamic, and fluid interface is well summarized with reference to the Gospels by Holly Hearon as follows:

> [W]e need to view these written texts as being closely intertwined with spoken word. They reflect, on the one hand, the engagement of the Hebrew Scriptures (written word) as words read aloud and remembered, and as spoken word that is taught, proclaimed, and debated. They also reflect spoken word (proclamation and teaching) that finds its basis in experience recounted as spoken word; that is, spoken word that is independent of written word. Nonetheless, it is possible that this spoken word engages themes or images recorded in written word (the Hebrew Scriptures) that are encountered and employed primarily, if not exclusively, as spoken word, depending on the social context. Second, they suggest that these written texts would have been perceived as in some way an extension of spoken word. (Hearon 2010:71)[58]

All contemporary Bible translators must recognize this crucial principle of Scripture communication that should be reflected accordingly in the vernacular versions that they happen to be rendering today: The written

---

[58] This article is well worth reading in its entirety, for it provides a wealth of data, primarily from the NT, which supports the author's thesis concerning the elaborate, meaningful "interplay between the written and spoken word in the Second Testament." My point is simply that this media "interplay" did (and does, during subsequent interpretation) have a *stable* point of reference, namely, the *written* text of Scripture and the divinely motivated *authorial intention* that underlies it. As argued in this chapter, then, I would disagree with conclusions such as the following which propose a very flexible, pluriform model of biblical text transmission: "[J]ust as many of us have come to question the notion of 'normative Judaism' prior to the Second Revolt, 132–135 CE, so will we now have to be skeptical about the concept of a single 'normative biblical text' in that period…. [S]cribes were not merely copyists loyal to the letter of the text, but creative traditionists as well. This is the point where the picture of scribes meticulously copying the Torah needs to be modified" (Kelber 2010:120). The notion of a "single normative text" does not necessarily entail the corollary that this was the most popular or widely used text at any given point in the history of its transmission. However, I would maintain that it is the text which did ultimate emerge as the Masoretic *textus receptus*, and that the scribes who transmitted this text were "meticulous copyists" (whether orally, visually, and/or memorially) and "loyal to the letter" of that particular textual tradition, which came to be increasingly recognized as the divinely inspired *Scriptures*.

3.5 Text transmission in relation to Bible translation

text needs to "give voice to" the spoken word, at least to the degree necessary so that any given passage is eminently "readable" (recitable, chantable, proclamable, preachable, etc.)—also hearable and memorizable as well.

In the following section (II) then, we will examine in greater analytical detail a set of dramatic, speech-based pericopes of Scripture—Isaiah 66 (4), John 17 (5), and Philippians (6)—in order to explore their essential basis in orality. The aim is to suggest how some of the insights of an oral-aural perspective and approach might be applied to the interpretation of these vibrant theological passages and, in particular, to their meaningful translation and varied media presentation. The intricate discourse design, admirable artistic construction, and dynamically conceived rhetorical argument of these diverse biblical texts would tend to support the hypothesis that they were not only composed by individual authors, but were also transmitted in a very conservative, text-preserving manner, that is, in terms of form as well as meaning. The challenge for translators then is to reproduce this same artful, powerful expression of theological and ethical content correspondingly also in their language.

II. DOCUMENTATION

Examining the Dimensions of Orality in Selected Texts of Scripture

4

"Hearing the Word of the LORD" (Isaiah 66:5): Amplifying the "Orality" of the Original Text in Translations of Scripture

4.1 Overview

Bible translation is a very text-focused activity that tends to be carried out in relatively complete silence. That may not matter very much when dealing with documents meant to be read quietly to oneself. But what about texts that are also, or even primarily, intended to be read aloud and publicly in a formal, especially a religious, setting? How does (or should) this crucial *oral-aural factor* affect the translation process? In this chapter I present a case study from the Hebrew Scriptures, which were by and large not only composed aloud with oral proclamation in mind, but are also accessed today most frequently via some oral and aural means. How can a communication-oriented sensitivity towards orality be stimulated or sharpened as the case may be?[1]

In the first place, the translator (or team) must as part of a thorough discourse analysis examine the received canonical document in the source language (SL), especially a poetic passage, in order to specifically identify overt and covert characteristics ("clues," markers) of orality. That is the initial step, and a study to illustrate this process follows with reference to Yahweh's challenging oracle to his people recorded in Isaiah 66:1–16, a text which emphasizes the necessity of not only *hearing* God's words, but also of correctly *responding* to them in daily life.[2]

Second, translators should be trained to find effective ways of "re-oralizing" the biblical text in the target language (TL) with respect to both *structure* (including genre) and *style* (including the sound of the text), no matter what kind of version is being prepared, ranging, for example, from more or less formal correspondence to varying degrees of functional equivalence. During this stage, the translation itself also needs to be consciously shaped to fit the manner (or medium) whereby it will ultimately be communicated—that is, with a specific target group, situational setting, and sociocultural context in mind (as determined beforehand by the project's job commission and goal). A practical methodology for preparing such an "oratorical" version will be outlined and exemplified, again using Isaiah 66 as a sample text.

Finally, the drafted translation should also be systematically tested in order to assess the degree to which the intended *audience* is correctly (that is, within a range of acceptable exegetical options) "hearing" as well as aesthetically appreciating their vernacular, "soundable" version. These auditors, too—the text consumer community—must then be given sufficient "voice" so that they might, through their critical comments, contribute to any necessary revision of the initial rendering. To conclude the sound-centered procedures proposed in this chapter, I will summarize the main interdisciplinary

---

[1] "To read prophecy…is to enter the world of the spoken word, a word that can be fully understood only be the exercise of the whole person. The reader must be attentive to the effect of the message not only on the mind and eye but also on the ear and heart" (Patterson 1993:298).

[2] For more background regarding the text-intensive, literary methodology applied here, see Wendland 2004b:ch. 7; for some additional studies in the Hebrew prophetic literature, especially the so-called "minor" prophets, from an oral-rhetorical perspective (and "audition"), see Wendland 2009.

implications that arise from my contextualized study. The special aim of this exercise is to preserve the vibrant orality of the biblical text, to the extent possible, in a modern translation that is meant to be heard as well as read.

My examination thus highlights an important portion of the Hebrew Scriptures, one that arises from and continues to support both a stable memorized tradition and also an ongoing process of oral transmission through public proclamation. This ancient tradition, whether realized in communal memory, in writing, in cantillation, or in dramatic performance, is established, enriched, and encouraged by means of an engaging *poetic* mode of creation. Surely, that is what made the Hebrew prophets such powerful preachers—accenting in the very ears of their audiences the awesome "word of Yahweh" which they had been commissioned to announce to their people, those who "trembled" at these divine messages (66:5), as well as those who refused to listen at all (66:4). In the four types of discourse analysis to be illustrated below, I will first of all seek to identify certain explicit devices along with some less evident ways in which the dimension of orality is manifested in this penultimate pericope of the Isaiah scroll.[3] My attention here will center upon the specific linguistic markers which would suggest that this section has been composed (and/or edited) with the oral-aural factor definitely in mind. How do such sonic insights complement other methods of textual investigation to enhance our overall understanding of the prophet's urgent message? This source-centered study forms the basis in turn for an effort to communicate the same passage via a vigorous vernacular translation in a correspondingly sound-sensitive, memorable manner.

4.2 Situating Isaiah 66:1–16 in its textual setting

Before taking a closer look at Isaiah 66:1–16 in order to investigate its oral potential and the implications of this for Bible translation, it may

---

[3] I have investigated and found wanting the elaborate theories of various scholars who would divide the book of Isaiah into several portions deriving from different prophetic sources (e.g., chs. 1–35, 36–39, 40–55, 56–66). Nothing other than a single scroll of "Isaiah" is extant, and "[t]here is no manuscript evidence other than for the literature as its stands.... The Hebrew Text (MT) of Isaiah has come to us in fine preservation without any real doubt what the text means or a serious necessity of emendation" (Motyer 1999:27, 34; cf. Pieper 1979:37–61; Webb 1996:30–39).

be helpful to begin by orienting ourselves with respect to the placement of this pericope within the book (scroll) of Isaiah as a whole. As already noted, Isaiah 66 occurs towards the very end of this rather long collection of diverse prophetic genres,[4] all of which were clearly intended to be orally proclaimed: divine oracles of judgment (e.g., 13:1–22) and salvation (11:10–16); prophetic predictions (52:13–53:12) and apocalyptic visions (65:17–25); parables (5:1–7) and prayers (37:14–20); hymns of praise (12:1–6) and thanksgiving (38:10–20); contrastive national taunts (14:3–23), woes (31:1–3), and laments (e.g., 15:5–9); and prose narrative episodes (39:1–8)—to name several of the most prominent literary types.

It has long been recognized that the present book of Isaiah is divided into two major groupings, chapters 1–35 and 40–66, by the historical interlude of 36–39, which serves to shift the focus of attention from Assyria to Babylon as Israel's main oppressor and an instrument of the Lord's punishment upon a rebellious and ungodly nation. Throughout the text, however, there is a periodic stream of oracles of encouragement that promise deliverance and a blessed future for all those who remain faithful to Yahweh and his covenant principles, despite the prevailing wickedness that surrounds them both at home and abroad (e.g., 1:21–28, 65:1–16). These optimistic predictions coupled with praise occur more frequently and in greater length in chs. 40–66, but a number of significant instances appear also in chs. 1–35 (e.g., 2:1–4, 4:2–6, 9:1–7, 27:1–13, 32:15–20, 33:20–24, 35:1–10). So, despite the many dire forecasts of judgment and destruction for the wicked, the overall theme and tone of Isaiah is quite positive, namely, for those who "humbly and penitently" (66:2) "listen to (= obey!) the word of the LORD [and] tremble at his word" (66:5). This is a message of comfort and reassurance that literally "cries out" to be publicly heard by God's people (contra 66:4b). Accordingly, it is expressed with, and intends to evoke within its audience, feelings of great joy and a sense of peace (66:10, 12–13, 14a; cf. 65:18–19, 25) in the context of a covenantal community which is distinguished by the personal "motherly" presence of Yahweh (66:7–13).

As for the immediate co-text of 66:1–16, I would make the case for a composite but coherent section of prophetic discourse that begins in 61:1–6, with an individual (1st person) song of commissioning and promise that

---

[4] There were no chapter and verse divisions, of course, in the earliest Hebrew manuscripts.

4.2 Situating Isaiah 66:1–16 in its textual setting

may arguably be attributed by implication to the Messiah-Servant chosen by Yahweh (as also in 42:1–9, 49:1–7, 50:4–11, and 52:13–53:12). This inaugural passage is followed by texts that successively convey the following communicative goals:

- reiterate the LORD's eager desire to covenant and fellowship with his righteous believers (61:7–11);
- predict a glorious future for these "holy" people (62:1–12);
- declare Yahweh's intention to punish his people's enemies (63:1–6);
- present Isaiah's extended, emotional prayer of intercession for the impenitent, who are urgently called upon to repent of their sins (63:7–64:12);
- give Yahweh's twofold response to the preceding prophetic appeals, i.e., an ominous warning for the wicked, coupled with a word of comfort for the contrite (65:1–16);
- reveal the book's climactic eschatological vision of "a new heavens and a new earth" (65:17–25);[5]
- and finally, express Isaiah's dual concluding message on behalf of the LORD—an encouragement to obey God's word (66:1–16) and a closing contrastive exhortation for evangelists to "proclaim God's glory to the nations" (66:19), but for all evildoers in the world to repent in view of the final judgment to come (66:17–24).[6]

---

[5] In terms of content and theological significance, this visionary pericope is obviously a high point in the book of Isaiah, especially occurring here as it does near the close of the entire composition. The text chosen for the present study (66:1–16) then offers Yahweh's own response, as it were, to the prior eschatological passage and outlines the distinctive implications for all those who hear the prophet's messages, not only the preceding joyous prediction (65:17–25), but also all those exhortations that have come before it in the book, the critical and condemning as well as the encouraging. The poetic section of 66:1–16 was selected for examination and illustration particularly since it includes a more diverse array of literary-oratorical devices that stimulate and enhance an oral-aural setting of message transmission.

[6] One might wonder about the concluding communicative effect of the awful negative imagery with which the oracles of Isaiah end (66:24). However, this must be viewed and evaluated according to Ancient Near Eastern poetic and rhetorical norms—that is, *structurally*: discerning the chiastic arrangement that underscores the concluding character of the passage as an integrated whole, i.e., **A** (connotatively negative: 17–18), **B** (positive: 19–21), **B'** (positive: 22–23), **A'** (negative: 24), and *stylistically*: recognizing the apocalyptic hyperbole that motivates the shocking scenario of v. 24.

We turn now to a more explicit and systematic investigation of Isaiah 66:1–16, with special reference to its orality and the auditory dimension of discourse. We will therefore search the source document for clues that not only suggest that the text was cued for oral articulation, but that it was also correspondingly shaped to be retained more easily and accurately in one's memory. This methodology features a manifold, multilayered approach that analyzes the Hebrew text in several stages and from diverse perspectives in terms of form, content, and function. The goal is to determine those key communicative elements pertaining to structure, style, and purpose that need to be afforded explicit attention also when translating this segment with equivalent impact and appeal into another language. This would be a version that seeks to duplicate the vital *oratorical dynamics* of the biblical message—to the extent possible, given the limitations of our imperfect understanding of the original text, coupled with the challenge of reproducing this in a different historical, linguistic, literary, religious, and sociocultural setting.

4.3 A linguistic, literary-rhetorical analysis of Isaiah 66:1–16

A linguistic, literary-rhetorical analysis is normally the principal type of detailed discourse examination that I carry out with respect to a specific pericope (Wendland 2004b:229–245). It involves a combined *linear* (sequential, syntagmatic) as well as a horizontal (vertical, paradigmatic) visual "spatialization" of the text. The particular aim is to discern any unusual word orders, parallel expressions, and prominent lexical or sound patterns based on some linguistic *correspondence*, whether exact (repetition), similar (synonymy), correlative (e.g., cause-effect), or contrastive (antithetical).[7]

Obviously, any sort of lexical or morphological reiteration will also have some manner of acoustic significance within the text, which must then be

---

[7] At a basic level, the principal clues to look for are these five: (a) syntactic constituents that are shifted out of the normal, default prose order (V–S–O, Hebrew being written from right to left); (b) full noun phrases in pre-verb position; (c) any expanded (e.g., by a construct phrase) syntactic "slot," whether Subject, Verb, Object, or Adjunct; (d) non-verbal predications; and (e) all explicit conjunctions or transitional expressions (or the absence of *waw*).

4.3 A linguistic, literary-rhetorical analysis of Isaiah 66:1–16

determined with regard to other, cotextually-related structural and stylistic qualities. The "linguistic" aspect of such study accordingly deals with all of the verbal forms of the composition under consideration. The "literary" aspect focuses on those features that are distinctive or "marked" in relation to their cotext, and the "rhetorical" aspect seeks to explain the communicative function of all marked constituents as part of the author's immediate or global strategy of audience persuasion and motivation. Religious rhetoric, which is abundantly exemplified in the Hebrew prophetic literature, thus aims to strongly encourage receptors either to change their current contrary thinking, attitudes, and behavior in the light of the principles and precepts of Yahweh as recorded in Scripture, or alternatively, to reinforce their current correct beliefs concerning these matters in the face of widespread pressures or temptations to abandon them—whether socio-political pressures from within, or paganistic practices from without.[8]

My composite linguistic discourse analysis technique thus differs somewhat from the "sound mapping" procedure that is endorsed by Lee and Scott:

> A sound map is a visual display that exhibits a literary composition's organization by highlighting its auditory features and in doing so depicts aspects of a composition's sounded character in preparation for analysis." (2009:168)

However, this approach appears to over-emphasize the organizational capacity of sound in discourse at the expense of its syntax and sense:

> *Sound itself* trains an audience's ear.... Because the New Testament compositions were spoken aloud and processed in real time through listening, sound necessarily served as their *primary organizing device*.... An audience cannot afford to rely primarily on semantic meaning to make sense of a written composition.... Because *sound* imposes structure on compositions at both the micro and macro levels, it organizes speech

---

[8] The messages of the prophets were not really about giving the people *new information* about Yahweh and his will for their lives; it was rather about calling them back to what they already knew (or should have known), based on past divine revelations and recorded texts (those regarded and revered as "Scripture").

into comprehensible units and is therefore the *most reliable guide* to compositional structure." (ibid., 40, 385, 135, 175; added italics)

To be sure, sound is a vital, in many cases the most perceptible indicator of structure and emphasis in an oral composition; however, it is certainly not the only factor that contributes to one's overall apprehension of a text's meaning. Syntactic organization and the developing sense of the larger discourse that is being progressively articulated are also involved and must be taken into joint consideration as the words are being conceptually processed and interpreted in time. The importance of syntactic selection and arrangement in the construction of meaning in texts (whether oral or written) is demonstrated also by Steven Runge in various studies of "information structure" in the NT Greek (2010:*passim*). Hence I prefer to carry out these analytical operations together, to the extent possible (as illustrated below), and to zero in then on particular features of literary-rhetorical interest later, once the formal and semantic contours of the whole have been determined.

The discourse segmentation display chart below (4.4) was prepared to document this exercise. The Hebrew text[9] was first segmented linguistically (sound, syntax, and sense) into putative poetic lines ("cola"; utterance units) and strophic (paragraph) divisions.[10] It was then analyzed with re-

---

[9] The Hebrew base used for this analysis is the Masoretic Text as reproduced in the *Paratext 7.1* program (© United Bible Societies, 2010); however, the font has been changed from *Ezra SIL* to *SBL Hebrew*. A relatively literal English translation, the *English Standard Version* (©), is provided in the footnotes.

[10] This segmentation process thus involves an appreciable amount of guesswork and hypothesis-making. How long was the "average" (natural) poetic line in Biblical Hebrew (BH)? Did this tend to be relatively long or short, and did the length vary according to genre, for example, in the lyric (e.g., Psalms) as distinct from the prophetic literature (Isaiah)? The ancient Hebrew scribal scholars, the Masoretes (ca. 5th–10th centuries CE) employed an elaborate system of vocalization, accents, and other diacritical markings (termed the Masorah) to assist lectors in reading the biblical text. But these conventions were introduced long after the Hebrew original consonantal text was established. Therefore, they too are open to debate with regard to both major and minor sentence divisions (e.g., *athnah*—the principal verse-internal divider and various disjunctive accents). In most cases, I have adopted the Masoretic proposal for segmentation, but in cases where they have allowed for poetic lines which I feel are too long, I have divided the segment into two (sometimes more) cola. Thus, I tend to interpret the phonic symmetry with a preference for shorter, rather than longer cola (utterance units), also on the basis of other prominent lexical and syntactic patterns within the text, which naturally may be questioned.

spect to the syntactic constituents that occur both before and after the *verb*, with the former generally being of more importance in terms of their diagnostic "signaling value." Selected items of interest are highlighted on the chart in grayscale and discussed in accompanying footnotes. With regard to word-order shifts in Hebrew (a VSO language), there are several important distinctions noted. A particular syntactic constituent, usually a subject, less often an object or adjunct, may be advanced either to the head (*pre-verb*) of its clausal unit or, less frequently, placed at the very end. Constituent advancement, or "front-shifting," has two principal discourse functions: topicalization and focalization:

- **Topicalization**: introduces (or reintroduces) a new major or minor "topic" into the discourse, usually as a full noun or noun phrase within the main clause of a sentence (e.g., 2c "and-unto=this-one"). The relative strength of a given topic is greater if it is an agent (vs. a patient), human (vs. inanimate), and/or definite (vs. nonspecific).

- **Focalization**: refers to the linguistic marking of certain information, other than the topic, as being pragmatically "in focus," that is, having a special salience or holding the greatest attention within a particular clause or sentence (e.g., 2a "and-DO[11]=all=these-things"). This process normally involves some sort of contrast, disjunction, restriction, expansion, replacement, specification, or shift of emphasis within the prevailing flow of information.

If both functions occur in the same poetic line, which is thereby especially marked, the first item is the new (or renewed) *topic* while the second is the constituent in *focus*. These functions need to be distinguished from

---

It may also be noted that the terminology that I am using favors the analysis of a written text. A more sound-based, orality-oriented set of terms has recently been proposed by John Hobbins (2005): "Translated into the terms of this hypothesis, a stress unit is equivalent to a 'prosodic word,' a verset to a 'phonological phrase,' a line to an 'intonational phrase,' and a strophe to an 'utterance.... A phonological phrase [i.e., colon] as understood in prosodic structure theory is marked off from its context by pitch accents, focus tones, phonological caesurae, and/or other closure phenomena. A phonological phrase is a prosodic, not a syntactic unit"—and the two do not always coincide.

[11] DO = direct object marker.

intensification, which refers to a very localized heightening of the qualitative nature of a specific concept or proposition within a clause ("Pay attention to this!"—e.g., the comparative series of NPs in v.3). Intensification may be produced by immediate exact repetition, use of a graphic or novel figure of speech, an exclamation, a deictic particle, or any close combination of such literary forms (cf. Wendland 2011:199–200).[12]

4.4 Discourse display chart of Isaiah 66:1–16[13]

Ref.	Post-Verb 2	Post-Verb 1	VERBAL	Pre-Verb 2	Pre-Verb 1 + Link
	Strophe 1				
1a[a]		יְהוָה	אָמַר		כֹּה
1b		כִּסְאִי	--------		הַשָּׁמַיִם
1c		הֲדֹם רַגְלָי	--------[b]		וְהָאָרֶץ
1d			תִּבְנוּ־לִי	אֲשֶׁר	אֵי־זֶה בַיִת
1e	מְנוּחָתִי	מָקוֹם			וְאֵי־זֶה
2a[c]			עָשָׂתָה	יָדִי	וְאֶת־כָּל־אֵלֶּה
2b	נְאֻם־יְהוָה	כָּל־אֵלֶּה[d]	וַיִּהְיוּ		
	Strophe 2				
2c			אַבִּיט		וְאֶל־זֶה
2d	וְחָרֵד עַל־דְּבָרִי	וּנְכֵה־רוּחַ	--------		אֶל־עָנִי[e]
3a[f]		מַכֵּה־אִישׁ	--------	הַשּׁוֹר	שׁוֹחֵט[g]
3b		עֹרֵף כֶּלֶב	--------	הַשֶּׂה	זוֹבֵחַ
3c		דַּם־חֲזִיר	--------	מִנְחָה	מַעֲלֵה
3d		מְבָרֵךְ אָוֶן	--------	הַשֶּׂה	מַזְכִּיר[h]

---

[12] In a comprehensive study of these syntactic-pragmatic phenomena in relation to NT discourse, Runge employs the terms "frame of reference" and "emphasis": Thus, in clause-initial (pre-verbal) position, a new topical *frame of reference* creates "an explicit mental grounding point for the clause that follows," whereas *emphasis* refers to "focal information (that which is already the most important in the clause) that is placed in a marked position or construction [that is, in the second syntactic slot/frame in the clause] in order to attract more prominence to it" (2010:190–191).

[13] My analysis is carried out with primary reference to the "verbal" (finite or non-finite) of a posited clausal utterance unit. The "link" is normally a conjunctive word of some type. I have allowed for two "pre-verb" positions (often elements of "topic" and/or "focus") and two "post-verb" positions.

4.4 Discourse display chart of Isaiah 66:1–16

Strophe 3

3e		בְּדַרְכֵיהֶ֣ם	בָּחֲר֔וּ		ⁱגַּם־הֵ֗מָּה
3f			חָפֵ֑צָה	נַפְשָׁ֖ם	וּבְשִׁקּוּצֵיהֶ֖ם
4aʲ		בְּתַעֲלֻלֵיהֶ֗ם	אֶבְחַ֣ר		ᵏגַּם־אֲנִ֞י
4b			אָבִ֣יא	לָהֶ֔ם	וּמְגוּרֹתָם֙
4c			קָרָ֙אתִי֙		יַ֤עַן
4d			עוֹנֶ֔ה		וְאֵ֣ין
4e			דִּבַּ֖רְתִּי		לֹ֥א
4f			שָׁמֵ֑עוּ		וְלֹ֣א
4g	בְּעֵינַי֙	הָרַ֣ע	וַיַּעֲשׂ֤וּ		
4h	ס		בָּחָֽרוּ׃	לֹא־חָפַ֖צְתִּי	וּבַאֲשֶׁ֥ר

Strophe 4

5aᵐ	הַחֲרֵדִ֖ים אֶל־דְּבָר֑וֹ	דְּבַר־יְהוָ֔ה	ᵐשִׁמְעוּ֙		
5b	שֹׂנְאֵיכֶ֜ם	אֲחֵיכֶ֨ם	ᵒאָמְרוּ֩		
5c	לְמַ֣עַן שְׁמִ֗י	מְנַדֵּיכֶ֜ם			
5d		יְהוָ֔ה	ᵖיִכְבַּ֣ד		
5e	בְשִׂמְחַתְכֶ֔ם		וְנִרְאֶ֣ה		
5f			יֵבֹֽשׁוּ׃		ᵠוְהֵ֖ם
6aʳ	קוֹל שָׁאוֹן ˢ מֵעִ֔יר		--------		
6b	ק֖וֹל מֵֽהֵיכָ֑ל		--------		
6c	ק֣וֹל יְהוָ֔ה מְשַׁלֵּ֥ם גְּמ֖וּל לְאֹיְבָֽיו		--------		

Strophe 5

7aᵗ			תָּחִ֖יל		ᵘבְּטֶ֥רֶם
7b			יָלָ֑דָה		
7c	לָ֖הּ	חֵ֥בֶל	יָב֥וֹא		בְּטֶ֨רֶם
7d		זָכָֽר׃	וְהִמְלִ֥יטָה		
8aᵛ		כָּזֹ֗את	שָׁמַ֣ע		ʷמִֽי־
8b		כָּאֵ֔לֶּה	רָאָ֣ה		מִ֚י
8c	בְּי֣וֹם אֶחָ֔ד	אֶ֙רֶץ֙	ה֤יּוּחַל		הֲ
8d	פַּ֣עַם אֶחָ֑ת	גּ֖וֹי	יִוָּ֥לֵֽד		ˣאִם־
8e			חָ֛לָה		כִּֽי־
8f	אֶת־בָּנֶֽיהָ׃	צִיּ֖וֹן	גַ֥ם־יָלְדָ֥ה		גַּם־
9aᶻ		אַשְׁבִּ֖יר			ᵃᵃהַאֲנִ֥י
9b	יֹאמַ֣ר יְהוָ֑ה		אוֹלִ֔יד		וְלֹ֣א
9c			הַמּוֹלִ֛יד		אִם־אֲנִ֧י
9d	ס ᵇᵇאָמַ֥ר אֱלֹהָֽיִךְ׃		וְעָצַ֖רְתִּי		

	Strophe 6			
10a[cc]		אֶת־יְרוּשָׁלִָם	שִׂמְחוּ[dd]	
10b	כָּל־אֹהֲבֶיהָ	בָהּ	וְגִילוּ	
10c	כָּל־הַמִּתְאַבְּלִים עָלֶיהָ	אִתָּהּ מָשׂוֹשׂ	שִׂישׂוּ	
11a[ee]			תִּינְקוּ	לְמַעַן[ff]
11b		מִשֹּׁד תַּנְחֻמֶיהָ	וּשְׂבַעְתֶּם	
11c			תָּמֹצּוּ	לְמַעַן
11d	ס	מִזִּיז כְּבוֹדָהּ	וְהִתְעַנַּגְתֶּם	
	Strophe 7			
12a[gg]		יְהוָה	אָמַר	כִּי־כֹה[hh]
12b	כְּנָהָר שָׁלוֹם	אֵלֶיהָ	נֹטֶה	הִנְנִי[ii]
12c	כְּבוֹד גּוֹיִם	וּכְנַחַל שׁוֹטֵף		
12d			וִינַקְתֶּם	
12e			תִּנָּשֵׂאוּ	עַל־צַד
12f			תְּשָׁעֳשָׁעוּ	וְעַל־בִּרְכַּיִם
13a[kk]			תְּנַחֲמֶנּוּ	כְּאִישׁ[ll] אֲשֶׁר אִמּוֹ
13b			אֲנַחֶמְכֶם	אָנֹכִי כֵּן
13c			תְּנֻחָמוּ[mm]	וּבִירוּשָׁלִַם
	Strophe 8			
14a[nn]			וּרְאִיתֶם[oo]	
14b		לִבְּכֶם	וְשָׂשׂ	
14c		תִפְרַחְנָה	כַּדֶּשֶׁא	וְעַצְמוֹתֵיכֶם[pp]
14d		וְנוֹדְעָה[qq]		
14e	אֶת־עֲבָדָיו	--------	יַד־יְהוָה	
14f	אֶת־אֹיְבָיו	--------	וְזָעַם	
15a[ss]		יָבוֹא	יְהוָה בָּאֵשׁ	כִּי־הִנֵּה[tt]
15b		מַרְכְּבֹתָיו	--------	וְכַסּוּפָה
15c	אַפּוֹ	בְּחֵמָה	לְהָשִׁיב	
15d	בְּלַהֲבֵי־אֵשׁ	וְגַעֲרָתוֹ	--------[uu]	
16a[vv]		נִשְׁפָּט	יְהוָה	כִּי בָאֵשׁ
16b		--------	אֶת־כָּל־בָּשָׂר	וּבְחַרְבּוֹ
16c	יְהוָה[ww]	חַלְלֵי	וְרַבּוּ[xx]	

[a]"Thus says the Lord: 'Heaven is my throne, and the earth is my footstool; what is the house that you would build for me, and what is the place of my rest?'"

[b]Two verbless, topic-oriented clauses (i.e., "heaven and earth"—a merismus) followed by a pair of rhetorical questions referring to each place in turn (i.e., heaven—house, earth—place-of-my-resting) help to distinguish the

opening of this major poetic unit (also Strophe 1), a divine oracle of direct discourse.

c"All these things my hand has made, and so all these things came to be, declares the Lord. But this is the one to whom I will look: he who is humble and contrite in spirit and trembles at my word."

dA front-shifted object ("all-these-things") in 2a, reiterated to form a chiastic syntactic construction (O–V=V'–O') in 2b, serves to foreground (constituent *focus*) the comprehensiveness of Yahweh's creation and hence also the extent of his royal domain. The rhythm created by the initial verbless clauses and the repetition in vv.1–2b serves to phonologically highlight this first short strophe as the aperture of the entire pericope (vv. 1–16). The formulaic נְאֻם־יְהוָה utterance closer appears also to mark the end of this opening strophe.

eThis phrase ("unto=the-humble-person") belongs syntactically in the predicate along with the two other items in the series, i.e., after the implicit verb "I-will-see (esteem)". It is placed here on the chart simply for the sake of space and also to visualize its being in structural parallel with the front-shifted constituent of the preceding line 2c, which announces a new *topic* ("and-unto-this-one") and hence initiates a new strophe. The most prominent descriptive in this sequence of three is the last item "and-the-one-trembling upon=my-word"—namely, the person who not only hears Yahweh's message, but also takes it to heart and life.

f"He who slaughters an ox is like one who kills a man; he who sacrifices a lamb, like one who breaks a dog's neck; he who presents a grain offering, like one who offers pig's blood; he who makes a memorial offering of frankincense, like one who blesses an idol. These have chosen their own ways, and their soul delights in their abominations;..."

gInitial asyndeton (absence of a conjunction) helps mark the onset of a rhythmic sequence of four verbless comparative clauses, each of which features a pair of lexical components on either side, as it were, of an implicit complement. This device effectively highlights the contrast between this negative series and the content of the preceding verse, as we move from Yahweh's description of the person that he honors/blesses ("looks-upon") in v. 2c–d to those whose actions (various ones listed) break covenantal fellowship in v. 3a–d.

hA notable overlapping wordplay—*dam-chaziyr* ("blood-of=a-pig") and *mazkiyr* ("a-person-offering")—in 3b and 3c coupled with alliteration in [m] help to vocally signal the close of the strophe covering verses 2c–3d.

ʲThe "focus particle" *gam* followed by a fronted subject constituent marks the onset of a new strophe, one that now highlights both the wickedness of all the covenant-breakers in the land and also the punitive response of Yahweh. In this case we see a correlated contrastive construction where גַּם־הֵ֫מָּה "whereas they" in 3e is paralleled in antithetical fashion by גַּם־אֲנִ֫י "accordingly I" in 4a. This contrast is reinforced by a repetition of the main verb in these two clauses: "they/I choose" בחר (cf. van der Merwe 2009).

ʲ"I also will choose harsh treatment for them and bring their fears upon them, because when I called, no one answered, when I spoke, they did not listen; but they did what was evil in my eyes and chose that in which I did not delight."

ᵏThe two *gam*-initial sentences establish a chiastic structure and a resultant mental template that organizes Strophe 3 as follows: A (3e–f) focus on the wicked ("they") – B (4a–b) focus on Yahweh ("I") = Bʹ (4c–f) Yahweh – Aʹ (4g–h) wicked. A minor break between the two halves of this arrangement is marked by the causal conjunction יַ֫עַן in 4c. Several chiastic sentence constructions are also found within this strophe, serving to highlight the contrast between the behavior of the wicked and God's consequent punishment, e.g., A and-they-did / B the-evil in-my-eyes // Bʹ and-in-what not=I-am-pleased / Aʹ they-chose.

ˡThe free "choice" (בָּחָ֫רוּ) of the ungodly in their evil actions is highlighted at the beginning and ending of Strophe 3 (3e/4h, *inclusio*). Therefore, they had nobody but themselves to blame for the punishment that Yahweh duly "chose" (4a) to inflict upon them. According to the Masoretic system of punctuation, This strophe ends in a "closed paragraph" as indicated by the symbol ס (*setumah*).

ᵐ"Hear the word of the Lord, you who tremble at his word: "Your brothers who hate you and cast you out for my name's sake have said, 'Let the Lord be glorified, that we may see your joy'; but it is they who shall be put to shame."

ⁿThis is a very clearly formally and semantically signaled discourse aperture, including asyndeton, an imperative, a prophetic proclamation formula similar to that of 1a (an instance of structural *anaphora*), a reference to "sound" that complements what was said in the preceding verse (i.e., "when I called, no one answered"—"hear the word of Yahweh!"), and a repetition of the word "word" (דְּבַר—with reference to יְהֹוָה).

ᵒThe emphasis on speech continues with an explicit mention of it (אָמְר֫וּ). However, there is an initially unmarked shift in reference of the 3rd pl. from God-fearers to haters of the godly. Thus, the dramatic contrast between the righteous and the wicked that was introduced in Strophe 2 now reappears, as suggested audibly also by a reiteration of the thematic expression "one/you who tremble at my/his word" (2d/5a, more strophe-initial *anaphora*). The topical spotlight is thrown on the wicked

4.4 Discourse display chart of Isaiah 66:1–16

by means of an unusually long descriptive appositional construction (5b–c) that leads off with the ironic paradoxical pair "your brothers—the ones who hate you!"

ᵖAn unmarked direct quote of the wicked here explicitly blasphemes Yahweh in ironic contrast with the mention of "his name" (שְׁמִי) in the preceding line (5c). A thematic contrast is thus forged also with 4c–d: there the Lord called but no one answered; here they answer with a sarcastic taunt directed at the God–fearers: "Let the *Lord* show his greatness and save you, so that we may see you rejoice" (GNT).

ᑫA contrastive focus construction highlights the thematic shift that occurs at this point: In the end, it will be the wicked, not the God-fearing who "will be shamed" (i.e., utterly defeated, demoralized, damned).

ʳ"The sound of an uproar from the city! A sound from the temple! The sound of the Lord, rendering recompense to his enemies!"

ˢ*Sound* (repeated terms, alliteration), *sense* (a dramatic reversal), and *syntax* (parallelism, strophe-final constituent lengthening) converge to mark this climactic segment (6a–c), which proclaims (in "sound" קוֹל) the Lord's ultimate judgment upon an ungodly nation (Israel). The drama of the battle scene being evoked in 6a–b is foregrounded through verbless predications that feature a shocking revelation at the end of the triad (6c): The awful "sound" emanating from a city (even the Temple!) being destroyed by invaders (prophetically, the Babylonians) has actually been orchestrated by Yahweh himself as he rightfully ("in recompense" גְּמוּל) punishes his people (now ironically referred to as "enemies") for repeated violations of his covenant with them.

ᵗ"Before she was in labor she gave birth; before her pain came upon her she delivered a son."

ᵘFrom verbless constructions, the text suddenly shifts to an alliterative (l/r), verb-packed segment at the onset of Strophe 5. The two temporal ("before") bicola also introduce in parallel (general—specific) fashion the graphic imagery of a paradoxical childbirth (delivery without pain!), which extends like a cohesive thread throughout the strophe (vv. 7–9). However, the sharp break in content at 7a–b (actually, the major division within the pericope of 66:1–16) seems to introduce an apparent *enigma*: How do these images apply to the current context, especially the immediately preceding judgment passage of Strophe 4?

ᵛ"Who has heard such a thing? Who has seen such things? Shall a land be born in one day? Shall a nation be brought forth in one moment? For as soon as Zion was in labor she brought forth her children."

ʷA pair of rhyming rhetorical questions (8a–b) highlight the incongruity of the preceding paradox and also form a transition to a corresponding figurative application—that of ᵡa "nation" (i.e., many people) being "born" in a day (8c–d), which is another parallel construction that begins with a rhetorical question and concludes with end rhyme. But again the mystery continues: to what or whom are these poetic images referring?

ˣAn emphatic pair of correlative particles (כִּי-–גַּם-) introduces the bicolon that finally provides the surprising answer to the topical riddle—namely, the subject of all the birthing activity, "Zion," which is strategically delayed until the end of the bicolon (8f), with this whole line being foregrounded by the focus particle גַּם. Why the surprise? Destruction of the city of Jerusalem (and its Temple) was graphically predicted in v. 6; now here in v. 7 a "new birth" is being prophesied. However, this "Zion" is not the same old ungodly Jerusalem; a *new* people of God, miraculously begotten by the LORD himself, are in view. This fact, the theological point of the whole passage, is underscored in the modified birth imagery of v. 9.

ʸSound similarity highlights the sequence of four verbs referring to "birth" that form the topical backbone of v. 8: *yûchal* (8c)—*yiwâlêd*—*châlâh*—*yoldâh*.

ᶻ"Shall I bring to the point of birth and not cause to bring forth?" says the Lord; "shall I, who cause to bring forth, shut the womb?" says your God.

ᵃᵃAnother parallel pair of rhetorical questions highlights the conclusion of Strophe 5. There is another surprise here too: Yahweh, the agent of the city/nation's destruction in v. 6, is now presented as the agent of her rebirth (the antithetical strophic conclusions are an instance of structural-thematic *epiphora*). Thus, Zion can give birth (v. 8) only because Yahweh enables it as the primary agent; this is formally and phonologically indicated by the string of *hiphil* causative verb forms in 9a–c, a series that is ended in contrastive fashion by the figurative verb וְעָצַרְתִּי "I shut up [the womb]/prevent birth" (9d), which is negativized by implication from the preceding rhetorical questions that demand the answer "of course not!" (a vivid reversal of אַשְׁבִּיר "I break open [the womb]/cause birth" in 9a).

ᵇᵇThe parallel utterance-final divine declaration formulas ("says the LORD"–9b, d) intensify the thematic point being made in a subtle reflection of the section's opening strophe: Yahweh the Creator of the material universe (2a–b) is responsible also for generating a (spiritually/morally) new nation (v. 9). A Masoretic paragraph end marker ס again confirms our decision to conclude another strophic unit at this point.

ᶜᶜ"Rejoice with Jerusalem, and be glad for her, all you who love her; rejoice with her in joy, all you who mourn over her;..."

ᵈᵈA trio of rhyming imperatives emotively announce the beginning of Strophe 6 in a brilliant paean of praise over the object of Yahweh's new creation—"Jerusalem." This aperture is formally underscored by initial sibilant alliteration (שׂ/שׂ) and

4.4 Discourse display chart of Isaiah 66:1–16

by the complete lack of any pre-verbal elements, in clear/audible contrast to the preceding strophe (5). Sound-sense repetition also distinguishes the end of this opening tricolon כָּל...עַל ("all...over [her]").

ee"...that you may nurse and be satisfied from her consoling breast; that you may drink deeply with delight from her glorious abundance."

ffTwo parallel declarations of reason (לְמַעַן) explain why the preceding call to rejoice was made in a figurative prediction of abundant blessings to come. The preceding imagery of birth and delivery is extended here into that depicting the satisfying nursing of a newborn babe. Word-final sound symmetry within each bicolon (11a–b and 11c–d) further emphasizes the notion of complete fullness that is being expressed by this verse as a whole, which is indicated by another concluding Masoretic marker ס.

ggFor thus says the Lord: "Behold, I will extend peace to her like a river, and the glory of the nations like an overflowing stream; and you shall nurse, you shall be carried upon her hip, and bounced upon her knees."

hhA prophetic proclamation formula echoing that found at the beginning of this pericope (1a, cf. also 5a) announces the onset of Strophe 7 (structural *anaphora*, i.e., parallel unit beginnings). The initial כִּי ("For/As a result...") in 12a serves to link Strophe 7 with Strophe 6 by giving an outcome that derives from what was said in the former unit, in this case, an intensified development of the imagery found there.

iiThe visualizing focus particle "Look, I am [about to do this...]!" (הִנְנִי) initiates the content of this strophe, which prophesies a future setting of "peace" or better, "prosperity and total well-being" (שָׁלוֹם—in clause-final focus position) for the believing community of Yahweh (lit. for "her," i.e. "Zion" 8f), which will include also Gentile (non-Jewish) "nations" (גּוֹיִם). The notion of superfluity of blessing is conveyed in the liquid imagery of flowing water—one of the crucial needs and a source of life in the Middle East even today.

jjThere is some uncertainty over how 12c should be translated. I have construed it as a verbless predication in parallel with the preceding colon: "like-a-river peace"—"like-a-stream overflowing wealth-of nations." The subsequent verb "and-you-will-nurse" (וִינַקְתֶּם), which the Masoretes interpreted as part of 12c, I have taken together with 12e–f to form a triad of parallel images relating to the tender care of a nursing infant: "at=[the]-side/hip you-will-be-carried; and-upon=[the]-knees you-will-be-fondled." The apparent problem of the lack of a connective *waw* at 12e may be viewed as a type of enjambment resulting in the fusion of lines 12d (consisting only of a verb, "and-you-will-suck") and 12e into one.

^{kk}"As one whom his mother comforts, so I will comfort you; you shall be comforted in Jerusalem."

^{ll}The imagery of loving motherly care (with the key verb נחם repeated) continues in a comparative construction involving the first two cola (13a–b): "Like/as...so [also]" (בְּ...כֵּן). The antecedent of the full (separable) pronoun "I" (אָנֹכִי) in the second line, namely Yahweh himself, is foregrounded (in focus).

^{mm}This emphatic strophe-concluding line (13c) features the third successive iteration of the figurative verb "comfort" (נחם) plus a reintroduction of the topic "Jerusalem" (יְרוּשָׁלָם) in fronted position (cf. 10a), thus forming a boundary-marking *inclusio* around the closely related strophes 6 and 7. This repetition has further hermeneutical significance in that it helps to clarify the antecedent for the 2nd pl. pronoun "you": those who once "mourned" over the destruction of Jerusalem (10a) will, as a result of Yahweh's rejuvenating action, be "comforted" (13b–c).

^{nn}"You shall see, and your heart shall rejoice; your bones shall flourish like the grass; and the hand of the Lord shall be known to his servants, and he shall show his indignation against his enemies."

^{oo}This is another case where the focus on verbal constituents does not result in a complete poetic line; thus the pair of initial *waws* is correlative ("when...then"), and 14a–b together form a single utterance unit. This transitional explicitness may also be a pragmatic marker that ironically recalls the reference to the wicked in 5e, who desired to "see" the "joy" of the oppressed people of God. Here in 14a (cf. 5f) the unexpected fulfillment of that sarcastic appeal is fulfilled, much to the predicted "shame" of their enemies.

^{pp}The vivid simile ("and-your-bones [= bodies] like-the-grass they-will-sprout [= flourish]") complements the preceding reference to "your heart" (14b); thus, one's whole being will rejoice on account of Yahweh's intervention and blessing. The long lexical items of 14c poetically complement the short ones of 14b.

^{qq}A rather unusual construction introduces the main thematic antithesis between what will happen to the righteous as opposed to the wicked: A passive verb "and-it-will-be-known-[that]" (14d) introduces a pair of verbless object clauses (14e–f): "the-hand-of=Yahweh [is] with=his servants; and-[his]-anger (repointing the MT) [is] with-his-enemies."

^{rr}The similarity in sound between the two line-final object constructions in 14e ("his-servants") and 14f ("his-enemies") masks their contrastive fates as determined by Yahweh, i.e., the "hand" of blessing versus the "anger" of his punishment.

ss"For behold, the Lord will come in fire, and his chariots like the whirlwind, to render his anger in fury, and his rebuke with flames of fire."

tt Immediately after predicting the LORD's coming to vindicate his saints and to castigate his enemies, the poet-prophet evokes by means of a typical introductory expression ("Indeed, just picture this!" כִּי־הִנֵּה) some powerful eschatological battle imagery in the remainder of this strophe to dramatize his message. This is highlighted by the focused constituent "with-fire" (בָּאֵשׁ), a highly symbolic, emotively-charged term that is echoed also at the close of the verse (15d) as well as at the onset of the next (16a). The juxtaposition with "Yahweh" (יְהוָה) in chiastic fashion in 15a and 16a reinforces the fact that the predicted divine discipline upon all the ungodly ("all flesh" 16b—כָּל־בָּשָׂר) will most surely take place.

uu Two verbless utterances (15b, d; cf. also 16b) and one based on an infinitive (15c) serve to heighten the fiery "judgment" (שׁפט 16a) scene that is being verbally depicted—that is, before the very eyes and ears of the listening audience.

vv "For by fire will the Lord enter into judgment, and by his sword, with all flesh; and those slain by the Lord shall be many."

ww After no mention at all in Strophes 6 and 7 (cf. 6c), the divine name (יְהוָה) reappears 4x in concentrated fashion here in Strophe 8, notably also in audibly prominent strophe-final position. This important literary-rhetorical feature no doubt signals the fact that we have reached the thematic peak of the entire pericope that covers 66:1–16.

xx There may be another wordplay involving the consonants רבו in the initial words of 16b and 16c that subtly link the notion of judgment ("sword") upon the "many" enemies of Yahweh. In any case, the content of this verse is a euphemistic version of the message that is expressed in horrific explicitness at the end of the book (v. 24; structural *epiphora*—similar unit endings).

4.5 Summary of the strophic structure of Isaiah 66:1–16

As the preceding discourse analysis would suggest, the collection of oracles in Isaiah 66:1–16 form a coherent and well-defined poetic unit within the book as a whole. Its opening in v. 1 is very clearly demarcated from the preceding verse, namely 55:25, which marks the close of the eschatological oracle set that began in 55:17. After an initial statement of Yahweh's right to judge all humanity, based on his manifestation of supreme power and authority at creation (strophe A, 66:1–2a; cf. Isa 40:12–41), the just judicial fates of the righteous and the wicked are contrasted in alternating fashion throughout the text (66:2b–16). The difference between these two groups is highlighted in particular on the boundary between Strophes 3 and 4, as their contrastive responses to "the word of the LORD" (דְּבַר־יְהוָה) are juxtaposed: the wicked do not listen at all (v. 4b), while the righteous "tremble" with reverence (חָרֵד) at these hortatory divine messages (v. 5a, cf. 2b). That would appear to be the twofold message of the prophet (or his editors), as it has reverberated throughout the book (scroll)—a message of warning and condemnation to all evildoers in the audience, in contrast to one of comfort and encouragement to those who remained faithful to the covenant principles of Yahweh.[14]

The next principal section, which is the book's closing pericope (66:17–24), shifts again to a more eschatological perspective (e.g., 66:18, 20, 22–24), along with a more expansive prosaic style of writing (e.g., less distinct parallelism, longer utterance units). However, a depiction of the contrasting fates of the wicked covenant-breakers and the faithful followers of Yahweh is again kept in thematic focus, with graphic references to the former establishing a structural boundary (*inclusio*, vv. 17, 24) around the latter: vv. 18–21, 22–23, the sub-sections being delineated by variants of the divine speech formula at the end of verses 17, 21, and 23. Appropriate to the climactic nature of these final prophetic words, the family of God is again viewed in Isaiah as including people of all nations in a glorious vision of "the new heavens and the new earth" (66:22; cf. 56:1–8).

The tightly organized poetic organization of 66:1–16 reflects the great competency and artistic skill of the author (editor) and further suggests that this text was prepared for oral-aural proclamation, being composed

---

[14] The general rhetorical strategy of the author then was to persuade his receptors towards repentance or fidelity, no matter what the circumstances happened to be in which they were currently living. Thus, although the precise historical and situational setting of the book of Isaiah is an issue of considerable debate (e.g., whether pre- or post-exilic and by how many years either way), this matter is of lesser relevance to my particular literary-oratorical analysis and application (for such contextual background information, see Motyer 1999:5–20; Webb 1996:19–25).

4.5 Summary of the strophic structure of Isaiah 66:1–16

in relatively short, well-balanced, rhythmic, visually graphic—and hence also memorable—segments.[15] The sevenfold formal and thematic structure of this prophetic passage (a complex divine "oracle") is summarized on the chart below (the closely related Strophes 6 and 7 have been combined into a single unit F). For each strophe (poetic paragraph), the primary structural markers that define the constituent are noted. It may also be observed that the strophes get progressively longer in length as the section moves to its dramatic, contrastive close in which the blessed destiny of the addressees, i.e., "his [Yahweh's] servants" (עֲבָדָיו, "you"—v. 14) is clearly distinguished from that of "his foes" (אֹיְבָיו), namely, all those who disrespect and disregard the word of the LORD (vv. 15–16; cf. v. 4).

The following structural-thematic summary of this poetic pericope (now employing simple two-part verse divisions, a/b) may serve then as the foundation for its subsequent translation into another language as well as its transmission via diverse media (e.g., with respect to potential break/pause points within the text):

Strophe	Literary-oratorical structural markers of thematic significance
A: 1–2a	*The strophe begins and ends with the authoritative divine utterance formulas ("Thus says YHWH…utterance of YHWH"; two internal rhetorical questions highlight the theme of Yahweh as Creator-God: He will also give birth to a new people/nation (cf. E-F).*
B: 2b–3a	*Topical front-shift marks a new strophic aperture: "And [DO] this one…"; internal cohesion is created by parallel constructions that feature descriptive participles, which further stress the contrast between covenant keepers (2b) and law-breakers (3a).*
C: 3b–4	*The strophe is introduced by a contrastive construction, employing the double correlative conjunction gam: "Just as…so also"; 4-term chiastic constructions appear throughout, except for the focal bicolon of 4b, describing the sins of the wicked and their just punishment from Yahweh.*

---

[15] The finely tuned literary structure of this pericope (and many others like it in the Hebrew Scriptures as well as the Greek NT) provides additional support for the argument that we are not dealing here with a text that has been gradually transformed over time by a succession of zealous scribes, where "additions to the manuscript text were incorporated through copying into the next version of the text in an incremental process of textual transformation" (Jaffee 2001:18). *Too many cooks spoil the broth!*

D: 5–6   This strophe is introduced by formulaic divine call to listen and an anaphoric (unit-initial) repetition of the expression those who "tremble at [Yahweh's] word"; it again foregrounds the contrasting attitudes of the obedient and disobedient; it concludes with some dramatic sound imagery (each colon of v. 6 beginning with "sound"—qôl) that evokes a scenario of the total devastation of Jerusalem (implied) on account of her many sins.

E: 7–9   Extraordinary mother and child imagery begins here and extends cohesively through strophes E and F; E is constituted by a tightly linked twofold structure: a proclamation of birth followed by two rhetorical questions; Yahweh thus brings forth a new people devoted to him; the unit concludes with the divine utterance formula.

F: 10–13   F opens with the surprising triple call to "rejoice!" over the new "Jerusalem", which begins and ends the strophe (inclusio); related images appear of mother nursing and abundantly providing for her young child (God's new people); as in strophe E, a bipartite structure is manifested, with part two beginning with another divine utterance formula in 12a (cf. 1a).

G: 14–16   G begins with anaphoric (strophe-initial) mention of "rejoicing" (cf. v. 10); cohesive reiteration of "Yahweh" throughout the strophe; imagery shifts from comforting mother-child references to awful scenes of warfare ("chariots") and judgment/punishment ("fire" repeated); a shocking strophe/section closure: "many slain [enemies] by Yahweh!" (an epiphoric echo of v.6), in sharp contrast to "you"—the happy covenant people of God!

4.6 The oral-aural basis and background of Isaiah 66:1–16

The following is an overview of some of the more common structural and stylistic characteristics of biblical oral-written discourses—that is, messages which were composed and transmitted orally but also written down for the sake of accurately preserving the sacred tradition. Prominent examples of each device or technique are cited from the preceding analysis of Isaiah 66:1–16 in order to indicate how this passage as a coordinated whole illustrates the *purposeful* (i.e., having thematic and/or rhetorical implications) amplification of orality, in the Hebrew Scriptures. These different features thus reflect and enhance the inherent orality of the text and thereby "program" it for public articulation:

4.6 The oral-aural basis and background of Isaiah 66:1–16

- Over and above the normal redundancy that one expects with poetic, oral-aural discourse, a significant recycling of major, culturally relevant themes, concepts, and images, producing what Bailey terms "a rhyme of ideas" (2011:34), e.g., rejoicing "heart," sprouting "grass," the protective "hand" in contrast to the burning "wrath" of Yahweh (14).

- Cohesive and strategic (boundary-marking) repetition, restatement, and paraphrase, e.g., the "sound" of Yahweh recompensing his "enemies" (6b) and executing "fiery" judgment upon "all people" (16b)—this structural *epiphora* suggesting that the objects of God's anger are the same, i.e., that "all people" is a hyperbolic reference to his "enemies."

- Use of standard opening and closing transitional formulas, e.g., "So speaks Yahweh" (1a/12a, *anaphoric* aperture); "utterance of Yahweh"/"says Yahweh…says your God" (2b/9a–b, *epiphoric* closure).

- Much parallelism and patterning in doublets/triads or terraced and chiastic arrangements, e.g., the series of verbless cola in v. 3, in which the topic refers to a type of improperly motivated ritual offering (one sacrificing a bull) linked and likened to a comment that lists a serious violation of the law (one killing a person, 3a).

- Preference for graphic, "memorable" imagery, figures of speech, sayings, epithets, catch-words, familiar symbols, acrostic-alphabetic arrangements, e.g., the evocation of battle sounds and imagery in v. 4—a "sound" with an ironic twist in that the "enemies" being destroyed are his chosen people Israel because of their persistent wickedness.

- Frequent dramatic, interactive discourse (interjections, imperatives, vocatives, rhetorical or real questions, etc.), e.g., the two sets of emotively toned (Yahweh is speaking!) rhetorical questions, all emphasizing a negative affirmation, that form the structural-thematic backbone of strophe E (vv. 8–9).

- Periodic poetic or rhythmic, euphonic, sound-sensitive sequences of utterances, e.g., the pounding punitive rhythm of a trio of cola each beginning with "sound" (*qôl*) in v. 6, the repetition thus reinforcing the fact of divine judgment being inflicted upon all the guilty.

- Inclusion of as much direct "character" speech as possible, e.g., the sarcastic, self-incriminating quote of the evil "brothers" in v. 3b, who verbally humiliate their righteous counterparts in the name of the LORD!

- Citations of, and allusions to religious information that is already assumed to be known, e.g., the reference to the universe that Yahweh both created and now also rules in strophe A, the verses of which recall texts from both inside and outside the Isaiah scroll, i.e., God enthroned in heaven—v. 1/37:16, 40:22 => Ps 2:4; God creating all things—v. 2/37:16, 40:26 => Ps 19:1, 124:8, 148:5.

This last-mentioned device, *inter*textuality, is worthy of further comment because it is such a prominent feature of all biblical discourse, in poetic texts as well as in the various genres of prose literature. Clear expressions as well as fainter echoes of important texts found in other books of the Hebrew Bible abound in Isaiah.[16] Examples from strophe A (1) have just been given; another case in this same poetic unit is a reference to the "building" of God's "house," which strongly alludes to King Solomon's prayer at the dedication of the first Temple in Jerusalem: How could the Creator of heaven and earth deign to dwell in a human "house," no matter how grand? (66:2 => 1 Kgs 8:27). The various prophetic formulas indicating divine discourse ("Thus says the Lord...," "Hear the word of the Lord," etc.) are another obvious example of this well-known literary-oratorical

---

[16] The issue of textual dating also arises here: Thus, citing instances of intertextuality operates under the assumption that the passages given as "pre-texts" come from books that were composed prior to the one under consideration. I regard Isaiah, the unified edited whole, to be a pre-exilic document that was composed in stages/sections over the period between 710 and 680 BCE. I thus concur with Webb's conclusion that "the account that the book of Isaiah itself gives of its own origins is far more plausible than any alternative that has so far been proposed" (1996:37). I, therefore, also subscribe to the hermeneutical position that allows for "predictive prophecy" within the canonically received text.

4.6 The oral-aural basis and background of Isaiah 66:1–16

attribute, one that authorizes, authenticates, and validates the message that follows, or less often precedes it. This function is evident also in the contrastive imagery that anthropomorphically depicts the varied emotions of Yahweh himself: first, as he tenderly comforts his faithful remnant, just like a loving mother (!) attends to her baby (66:13 => Num 11:12)—later, as he comes in fiery anger with his heavenly host to inflict massive punishment upon all his enemies (66:15–16 => Psalm 68:17–23).

But the recall of significant concepts, images, utterances, and even entire scenes within the fabric of prophetic discourse is stimulated also from within the writing itself—that is, from passages that have sequentially preceded a given verse, i.e., instances of *intra*textuality. These formal and semantic correspondences consist not only of verbal parallels and analogous visualizable imagery, but they also involve phonological associations, which further aid in the recollection of earlier texts in the scroll for the purposes of thematic reinforcement or elaboration in a new compositional setting. Just in the section at hand, we see that every verse in Isaiah 66:1–16 resonates with at least one earlier antecedent, as summarized in the following table:

Summary of intratextual "pre-texts" in Isaiah 66

66:verse	pre-text	66:verse	pre-text
1	40:22	9	37:3
2	40:26, 57:15	10	25:9, 52:9, 57:19, 65:18
3	1:11, 65:4, 44:19	11	60:16, 25:6, 49:23
4	10:12, 65:7, 41:28	12	9:6, 33:21, 52:10, 60:4–5
5	60:15, 44:9	13	49:13, 15, 40:1
6	59:18, 65:6–7	14	25:9, 60:5, 41:20, 54:17
7	54:1	15	1:31, 5:28, 34:2, 42:25
8	64:4, 49:19–21	16	1:20, 27:1, 30:30, 13:9

In this manner, earlier utterances of the text are recycled in either similar or novel contexts as the prophetic message is progressively augmented and developed to reach a thematic peak of intratextual convergence here at the very end of the scroll in chapter 66. The sound of the recurrent words and the mental pictures of the similar imagery reinforce each other as the content and intent of prior passages provide a background for what Yahweh has to say in concluding his message to Israel—to the righteous, who are thereby encouraged and rendered hope for the future, as well as to the wicked, who are vigorously warned of the certain fiery judgment to come if they refuse to repent. A good example of this effective preaching technique is found in the final verse of the section under consideration, verse 16 of Isaiah 66, as shown in English translation (NRSV) by a selection of pre-texts that intertextually inform and emphasize this closing pericope. Several descriptive-explanatory comments (*italicized*) are supplied along the right-hand column of the following chart:

Thematic significance of the intra-textual pre-texts in Isaiah 66:16

Pre-texts for Isaiah 66:16	Semantic-pragmatic significance
If you are willing and obedient, you shall eat the good of the land; but if you refuse and rebel,	*The ever-present "obedience option" lies alongside all the prophetic judgment texts; if fiery punishment befalls the wicked, it is their own choice.*
you shall be devoured by the sword; for the mouth of the LORD has spoken. (**1:19–20**)	*Like a pounding hammer, the prophetic message repeatedly underscores the divine Source, namely, "the mouth of Yahweh."*
On that day the LORD will punish with his cruel and great and strong sword	*The "day of the LORD" refers to a time when God will ultimately judge all humanity; this is the scenario evoked also in 66:16.*
Leviathan the fleeing serpent,… (**27:1**)	*Mythic imagery evoked in passages denouncing pagan nations comes by association to apply also to the ungodly among the people of Israel.*
And the LORD will cause his majestic voice to be heard and the descending blow of his arm to be seen,	*As throughout these divine oracles, the appeal to actual sound qualities complements the graphic visual imagery that both reinforces the message and also renders it more memorable.*

4.6 The oral-aural basis and background of Isaiah 66:1–16

in <u>furious anger</u> and a <u>flame of devouring fire</u>,... (30:30)	*By the time that 66:16 is reached in the scroll, the figurative linkage between destructive fire, furious anger, and divine punishment has been clearly established as a major theme of Isaiah's message.*
See, the <u>day of the LORD</u> comes, cruel, with <u>wrath</u> and fierce <u>anger</u>,	*This punitive scenario will reach its peak at the end of world-time, when the Lord's "day" suddenly arrives and all options for his enemies end.*
to make <u>the earth</u> a desolation, and to destroy its <u>sinners</u> from it. (13:9)	*All of human history will then terminate, and there will be a permanent separation between "sinners" (their fate) and the righteous people of God.*
For by fire will the <u>LORD</u> execute judgment, and by his sword, on all flesh; and those slain by the <u>LORD</u> shall be many. (66:16)	*Verse 16 focuses only on the wicked (cf. vv. 3–4, 5b–6, 14b–15). However, these dire passages of warning must always be viewed in the light of the gracious, heartwarming promises of abundant blessings for the faithful, who in humble contrition obey the word of the LORD (2b, 5a, 7–14a).*

The orality of the biblical literature, as explored from several perspectives in the preceding analysis, is shaped not only so as to stress and evoke memorable sounds, but through its diverse, vibrant imagery the prophetic preacher-poet also appeals to the inner sight of the audience. However, the aim of this manifold artistry is not primarily aesthetic; it is rather to emphasize the urgency and the importance of the divine message being communicated from the mouths and in the minds of successive proclaimers and audiences throughout the ages. The two dimensions, the *audio* and the *visual* complement each other in the transmission process, for what is orally articulated and aurally apprehended in language stimulates the entire sensorium, and this will naturally make a much greater impression than a document that is silently read to oneself.

To be sure, there is no way in which all of the dramatic impact and appeal of the biblical text can be duplicated precisely in another language and cultural setting. However, that does not give translators the right or the excuse simply to ignore this property of the Scriptures, for this sacred corpus manifestly incorporates a variety of religious compositions having the inherent literary beauty, oratorical power, and rhetorical objective operating in concert to highlight the specific "word of the LORD" being conveyed. It is to this second, contemporary half of the communication cycle that we will direct our attention in the remainder of the present study of Isaiah 66. That is to say, having analyzed the Hebrew text, the challenge now is to discover suitable ways of accurately re-presenting it in the most dynamic, functionally equivalent manner possible. Perfection is never achievable, of course, but varying degrees of approximation in terms of form, content, and purpose are feasible. It is to this lesser ideal and goal that we aspire—namely, where the circumstances, including many local contextual variables, do allow such a multifaceted oratorically-oriented enterprise to be undertaken.

4.7 Investigating the Orality of the Target Language

The first step in preparing a literary (artistic-rhetorical)—or, in view of the proposed oral medium of transmission, an "oratorical"—translation is to embark upon an investigation of the form-functional resources that are on hand in the target language. This is not a matter that can be left either to chance or to the pure intuition of the translator(s). Of course, they probably are all mother-tongue speakers, but this does not guarantee that they are competent linguists, let alone literary experts, with respect to this most familiar language. On the contrary, some sustained and focused research is necessary into the verbal art forms (oral and, if existing, also written genres) as well as the stylistics of the TL. This may be done either by a designated member of the translation team, who is assigned this special task, or, better, by the team as a whole. But how might such research be effectively carried out?

I need not repeat what I have written elsewhere on this subject,[17] but simply by way of summary, the following are several suggestions that may

---

[17] See, for example, Wendland 2004b:ch. 8; 2002b:237–51; 1993:chs. 3–4.

4.7 Investigating the Orality of the Target Language

be considered towards this end, that is, to develop an inventory of potential *form-functional equivalents*:

- In a few cases, quite a sizable *corpus* of published literature on the TL may be already available, including scholarly as well as popular studies of different genres and authors or oral composers. All materials of potential value should be gathered and critically appraised in the search for information that might be useful in the translation task, most notably, those works that investigate the artistic (poetic) and/or rhetorical dimensions of discourse.[18]

- In situations where such published *research* is either unavailable or insufficient, the translation team (or a designated member) will have to conduct its own systematic study with respect to oral as well as any existing written genres. Oral texts are often obtainable as broadcasts on the radio (nowadays especially FM), while written compositions will sometimes appear in the popular press before established publishing houses. *Radio* texts may turn out to be especially valuable in the search for translational equivalents, for example, written transcripts that are intended for public oral articulation, which obviously approximates the performance setting of many Scripture readings or adaptations.[19]

- Recorded oral texts, whether formal or informal in nature, need to be accurately *transcribed* so that they may be analyzed in terms of their stylistic and oratorical characteristics, which can then be *categorized* for reference in various ways according to the disparate devices that are manifested, e.g., on the macro- or micro-structure; phonological, syntactic, lexical, or discourse level; poetic or prosaic; etc. The same

---

[18] For a brief comparison between the "cognitive linguistic" and "corpus linguistic" approaches and their relevance for Bible translation, see Wendland 2003:225–228. For information on how to set up a corpus linguistic research project, see Luz et al. 2010.

[19] For example, Wendland 2004a; 2005. The dramatic works recorded, transcribed, and translated in the former book were scripted, those of the latter book were not (i.e., spontaneous vernacular studio performances broadcast on the radio).

procedure would apply also to literary features in the case of written/published creations.

- The categorization process should, ideally, seek to identify and classify the TL oratorical or literary devices in terms of both form and function. A *functional* perspective is essential since it may be the case that a particular TL form corresponds to that found in the biblical text, but it typically has a different communicative function and/or pragmatic implication, for example, rhetorical questions, irony, hyperbole, parallelism, the textual "overlap" (tail-head) construction. The aim is to discover as many all-around form-functional "matches" as possible, for these will be definitely useful in translation.

- Consideration must also be given to the comparative *distribution* of certain stylistic qualities within the text, the specific genres of discourse in which they normally occur, and/or the performance settings in which they are regularly used—in case there are any *restrictions* or limitations concerning a distinct TL form/function in relation to its SL formal correspondent. Furthermore, perhaps there are definite performance "additions" that are necessary before a local oral genre sounds "natural," e.g., an accompanying musical instrument or, indeed, an actual singing voice.

- A sufficient amount of *testing* will be required to determine the extent to which (or if at all) the diverse aspects of artistic oral discourse may be used naturally in written compositions, especially in the case of sacred Scripture, or to what degree they may be modified formally or functionally to suit a defined biblical text or genre category. Thus, a common idiomatic device that is effective when spoken aloud may turn out to be quite inappropriate for inclusion in a printed Bible translation not only with regard to usage, but also in terms of density, emotive connotation, or pragmatic impact, e.g., the ideophone in most African languages, which may be used for dramatic effect, but which often conveys unwanted humorous overtones.

The goal, in short, is a categorized inventory of potential form-functional features accessible to translators (at least within their mental repertory), which either closely correspond with or can be used to replace (i.e., compensate for) those which are identified as being crucial in the SL document. In the case of a literary or oratorical version, special interest will be centered on those artistic and rhetorical devices that can generate the necessary verbal beauty, forcefulness, and feelings to duplicate what has been demonstrated to be present in the original. In this regard, it is important to note that "functional equivalence" is needed also with respect to the biblical text's oral-aural dimension—so that the translation not only "sounds" natural but is also suitable for publicly articulating the text in question as the audible "Word of the Lord."

4.8 Re-oralizing the biblical text in translation

We might begin the discussion of re-oralizing the biblical text in translation by first illustrating the need for a more idiomatic, sound-discerning translation. This can be done by presenting a short sample of the long established ("KJV-type") version in the Chewa language. That version has been reproduced, exactly as formatted in publication, below—namely, Isaiah 66:1–3a (accompanied by a literal English back-translation to reveal something of the vernacular structure and style):[20]

---

[20] The (chi)Chewa language is a major language of east-central Africa spoken as a mother tongue and lingua franca by some 15 million people in Malawi, Zambia, Mozambique, and Zimbabwe. This translation, the *Buku Lopatulika* ("Sacred Book") was first published in 1922; the Bible Society of Malawi currently holds the copyright. In the Chewa text, hyphens indicate where line breaks akwardly occur in the published text.

Atero Yehova, Kumwamba ndi mpando wanga wacifumu, ndi dziko lapansi ndi coikapo mapazi anga; mudzandimangira Ine nyu-mba yotani? ndi malo ondiyenera ku-pumapo ali kuti? 2 Pakuti zonsezi mkono wanga wazilenga, momwe-mo zonsezi zinaoneka, ati Yehova; koma ndidzayang'anira munthu uyu amene ali waumphawi, ndi wa mzimu wosweka, nanthu-nthumira ndi mau anga. 3 Wakupha ng'ombe alingana ndi wakupha mu-nthu;...	So speaks *Jehovah*, In the heaven is my royal throne, and the earth is a place for placing my feet; you will build for Me a house of what kind? and a worthy place for me to rest is where? 2 For all these things my arm has created them, in this way all these things appeared, says *Jehova*; but I will look upon this person who is impoverished, and of (ancestral) spirit broken, and trembles with my words. 3 One who kills a cow resembles one who kills a person;...

It may come as no surprise that this literalistic, "missionary" translation is just as taxing to understand in Chewa as it apparently reads here in English.[21] Furthermore, the formatted text makes it rather difficult for readers, as well, due to the relatively small print and short, justified lines, which occasion many hyphenated words. The end of verse two is especially challenging to interpret because of its opaque reference to a poverty-stricken person (male or female), who is apparently afflicted with a "broken ancestral spirit." This unnatural expression might possibly be mistaken as referring to a guardian spirit that is depressed for some reason, perhaps, as seemingly explained in the following line, on account of "Jehovah's" frightful "words."

A new, "popular-language" translation of the Bible was finally (after nearly 30 years) published in 1998. Subsequent research has indicated that this modern, meaning-oriented version is much easier for most people to read and understand.[22] The published format also features greater legibility, but it is still more difficult than necessary on account of the justified two columns of rather small print. This version does facilitate an oral elocution and aural

---

[21] In addition to being a literal (formal correspondence) rendering, the *Buku Lopatulika* employs a number of archaic terms and being dominated by missionaries is not entirely natural in its sentence construction.

[22] This is the *Buku Loyera* ("Holy Book"; Blantyre: Bible Society of Malawi). For some information about the history, philosophy, and character of this version in comparison with the *Buku Lopatulika*, see Wendland 1998:chs. 4–5.

4.8 Re-oralizing the biblical text in translation

apprehension of the text, but more could actually be done towards this end. Such an "oralized" version is demonstrated in the following revised poetic rendition, which corresponds to the *Buku Lopatulika* selection given above:[23]

¹Chauta Mulungu akulengeza mau akuti,	*Chauta* God proclaims (these) words saying,
"Thambo lam'mwamba m'mpando wanga waufumu,	"The sky above is my royal throne,
dziko lapansi ndiye chopondapo mapazi anga.	the earth below is a place for setting my feet.
Kodi ndi nyumba yotani imene	Say, what kind of a house is there which
inu mungathe kundimangira?	you are able to build for me?
Alipo malo otani amene	What kind of place exists which
inu anthu mungandikonzere	you people can prepare for me
kuti Ineyo ndizipumuliramo?	so that I can rest myself for a while (in) there?
²Zinthu zonsezi ndidazilenga ndine,	All these things I've created (them) myself,
tsono zonsezi nzanga," akutero Chauta.	and so they all belong to me," so says *Chauta*.
"Anthu amene ndimakondwera nawo naŵa:	"The people whom I am pleased with are these:
odzichepetsa, olapa, ondiwopa, omvera mau.	humble, penitent, reverent, obedient.
³Koma pali ena anthu amene	But there are some people who
amangochita zoŵakomera okha.	simply do what pleases themselves alone.
Kwa iwo nchimodzimodzi	To them it's all the same thing
kupereka ng'ombe ngati nsembe,	(whether) to offer a cow as a sacrifice,

---

[23] The entire pericope studied in this essay (Isa 66:1–16) was translated afresh for this exercise and then field-tested (see below), but in the interest of space, only verses 1–3b are reproduced here.

| kapena kupha munthu mnzawo!... | or to murder a fellow human being!... |

This translation, which has been substantially adapted from the *Buku Loyera* version, reflects these meaning-enhancing and orality-oriented features:[24]

- Additional formal restructuring in general for better understanding and also to create greater aural impact and appeal (e.g., lines 1–2 of v. 3);

- Poetic lineation throughout the text to reflect the various lyric and acoustic characteristics that have been introduced into this rendering;

- Shorter lines (yet each still manifesting a complete syntactic construction) to generate a rhythmic pronunciation of the translation (e.g., the final three lines of v. 1);

- A break-up of the composition into strophic units (e.g., vv. 1–2a) in accordance with the preceding discourse analysis of the Hebrew source text;

- A deliberate effort, e.g., through word order variations and lexical redundancy, to introduce oral-aural-enhancing features into the Chewa text overall, e.g., alliteration, assonance, some rhyme, and euphony whenever possible (e.g., the final line of v. 2);

- More explicit boundary and transitional markers, such as the speech margins at the beginning and ending of the initial strophe (1a/2a);

---

[24] How to deal with the intra- and intertextual factor of the present pericope needs further thought and experimentation. The use of cross-references and footnotes are still the most effective way of resolving this issue in the case of a published text (in print) and a reading public, but what can be done in the case of an oral text? Experimentation and testing is needed not only with regard to supplying such contextualizing information, but also concerning how to "package" it, for example, to differentiate the actual biblical text in translation from any supplementary helps that are provided together with it.

4.8 Re-oralizing the biblical text in translation

- Introduction of parallelism in certain lines, whether adjacent or separated, to distinguish significant correspondences or contrasts in content (e.g., lines 4 and 6 of v. 1).

So, for whom is such a poetic, oratorical version intended? Of course, that is a question that would have to be asked and answered *before* the translation is undertaken on the basis of potential audience, constituency-based research. This exercise would undoubtedly need to incorporate an ample amount of pre-education concerning the nature of Bible translation and the various stylistic and publishing options that exist nowadays, depending on the circumstances, such as the history of translation in the area, already available versions in the TL and related languages, the participating churches involved, and the medium of text transmission to be used. The specific target audience and communicative purpose (*Skopos*) in mind would also have to be precisely defined with respect to a "job commission," including its guidelines and its terms of reference (*brief*), drawn up for the envisaged project.[25] In the case of the Chewa poetic version illustrated above, for example, these variables might be specified as follows: a fresh, lively translation intended to serve the younger generation (e.g., choir or drama groups) as a means of getting youth interested in Bible reading through a vernacular composition that is both appealing artistically and also easier to understand in terms of content. Perhaps this version could also provide the basis or stimulus for a musical arrangement that the young people could readily memorize for joint performance (singing) sessions as well as an evangelism tool to attract outsiders to join their group.

Turning to English, a language that most current readers will be more familiar with, we might investigate several of the issues raised above by means of a critical comparison of micro-structural translation techniques. The *New Living Translation* (Second edition, 2004), reproduced below in the left-hand column, is a popular version that seems to have made the greatest effort in "poeticizing" the biblical text (based on a comparative study). However, it too does not seem to have gone far enough, especially in the direction of "re-oralizing" the original message for a public proclamation. I have made an effort to do that in the modified rendition given in

---

[25] For details regarding these project-related organizational principles and procedures, see Wendland 2004b:50–53.

the right-hand column. This version also takes into consideration some of the principal results of the structural, stylistic, and rhetorical analyses that were carried out earlier on this pericope. The changes are indicated by the words in italics, and readers are invited to evaluate these adjustments and adaptations for accuracy as well as quality with respect to the primary goal of providing a liturgically acceptable (i.e., for use in public worship) "oratorical" translation of Isaiah 66:1–16. The designated "target audience" may be defined as follows: a relatively sophisticated, biblically literate church membership of mother-tongue English speakers.

New Living Translation (slightly reformatted)	**New Living Translation (modified for orality)**
¹This is what the LORD says: "Heaven is my throne, and the earth is my footstool. Could you build me a temple as good as that? Could you build me such a resting place? ²My hands have made both heaven and earth; they and everything in them are mine. I, the LORD, have spoken!	This is what the LORD *God* says: "Heaven is *indeed* my throne, and the earth is my footstool. *Can* you build me a temple as good as that? *Could* you *offer me* such a resting place? My hands have made both heaven and earth; they and everything in them are mine *alone*.ᵃ *This is what I, the LORD, have declared!*ᵇ

4.8 Re-oralizing the biblical text in translation

"I will bless those who have humble and contrite hearts, who tremble at my word.	"I will bless those *with humble contrite* hearts, all *those people* who tremble at my word.
³But those who choose their own ways—ᶜ delighting in their detestable sins— will not have their offerings accepted.	But *all* who *follow* their own *wicked* ways— *who take great delight* in their detestable sins— *they* will not have their offerings accepted.
When such people sacrifice a bull, it is no more acceptable than a human sacrifice.	When such people sacrifice a bull, it is no more acceptable than a *man*.
When they sacrifice a lamb, it's as though they had sacrificed a dog!	When they sacrifice a *choice* lamb, it's as though they had sacrificed a dog!
When they bring an offering of grain, they might as well offer the blood of a pig.	When they bring an offering of *ripe* grain, they might as well offer the blood of a pig!
When they burn frankincense, it's as if they had blessed an idol.	When they burn *fragrant* frankincense, it's as if they had blessed a *dumb* idol.
⁴I will send them great trouble— all the things they feared.	I *am about to give* them great trouble— *everything* they *ever* feared *in this world*.
For when I called, they did not answer. When I spoke, they did not listen. They deliberately sinned before my very eyes and chose to do what they know I despise."	For when I called, they did not answer. When I spoke, they did not listen *at all*. They deliberately sinned before my very eyes; *they* chose to do what they know I despise."

⁵Hear this message from the LORD, all you who tremble at his words: "Your own people hate you and throw you out for being loyal to my name. 'Let the LORD be honored!' they scoff. 'Be joyful in him!' But they will be put to shame. ⁶What is all the commotion in the city? What is that terrible noise from the Temple? It is the voice of the LORD taking vengeance against his enemies.	Now hear this message from the LORD, all you who *fear and obey* his words: "Your own people hate you *for this; they expel* you for being loyal to *me*. 'Let the LORD be honored!' they scoff. 'Be joyful in him *when you suffer so!*' But they will *surely* be put to shame. What is all the commotion in the city? What is that terrible noise from the Temple? It is the voice of the LORD *of heavens* taking vengeance against his enemies.
⁷"Before the birth pains even begin, Jerusalem gives birth to a son. ⁸Who has ever seen anything as strange as this? Who ever heard of such a thing?	"Before the birth pains even begin, Jerusalem gives birth to a son. Who has ever seen anything *like* this? Who*'s* ever heard of such a *strange* thing?
Has a nation ever been born in a single day? Has a country ever come forth in a mere moment? But by the time Jerusalem's birth pains begin, her children will be born. ⁹Would I ever bring this nation to the point of birth and then not deliver it?" asks the LORD. "No! I would never keep this nation from being born," says your God.	Has a nation ever been born in a single day? Has a country ever *emerged* in a mere moment? But by the time Jerusalem's birth pains begin, *all her children will* be born *fully grown!* Would I *bring* this nation to the point of birth, *then* not deliver it?" asks the LORD, *the Creator.* "No! I'd never keep *my people* from being born," *That is what the LORD* your God *declares.*

4.8 Re-oralizing the biblical text in translation

¹⁰"Rejoice with Jerusalem!
Be glad with her, all you who love her
and all you who mourn for her.

¹¹Drink deeply of her glory
even as an infant drinks at its mother's comforting breasts."
¹²This is what the LORD says:
"I will give Jerusalem a river of peace and prosperity.
The wealth of the nations will flow to her.
Her children will be nursed at her breasts,
carried in her arms, and held on her lap.
¹³I will comfort you there in Jerusalem
as a mother comforts her child."

¹⁴When you see these things, your heart will rejoice.
You will flourish like the grass!
Everyone will see the LORD's hand of blessing on his servants—
and his anger against his enemies.
¹⁵ See, the LORD is coming with fire,
and his swift chariots roar like a whirlwind.
He will bring punishment with the fury of his anger
and the flaming fire of his hot rebuke.
¹⁶The LORD will punish the world by fire
and by his sword.
He will judge the earth,
and many will be killed by him.

"Rejoice with Jerusalem, *all you who hear me!*
Be glad with her, you *people* who love her!
Be happy, all you who *now* mourn for her.

Drink deeply of her *blessings from God,*
as an infant *nurses from* its mother *in peace.*"
This is what the LORD says *to his people*:
"I will *grant* Jerusalem a river of peace*ful* prosperity.
The wealth of the nations will flow to her.
Her children will be nursed at her breasts,
carried in her arms, and held on her lap.
I will comfort you there in Jerusalem
just as a mother comforts her *own* child."

When you see these things *happen,*
all your hearts will *greatly* rejoice.
You will flourish like *growing* grass!
Everyone will see the LORD's hand—
a hand of blessing on his servants—
but one of anger against his enemies.
See, the LORD is coming with fire,
his swift chariots roar like a whirlwind.
He will bring *disaster on the wicked*
with the *punishing* fury of his anger
and the flaming fire of his hot rebuke.
The LORD will punish the *wicked* world
by *his fierce* fire and his *sharp* sword.
He will judge *all his enemies—yes,*
multitudes will be *executed* by him!

^aThe addition of "alone" highlights the chiastic construction of the divinely-focused Hebrew text.

b Many English versions (ESV, NRSV, NAB, NJB) do not recognize a strophic break here.

c The NLT has reordered v. 3 and therefore it is not possible to retain the two-strophe division of vv. 2b–4 as proposed in the earlier literary-structural analysis of the Hebrew text. This would be an example of a perceptual/conceptual clash between an analysis of the SL text and its reproduction in the TL.

The following is a listing of some of the literary devices specifically employed to promote poetics as well as orality in the modified version on the right (in certain cases these differ from the original Hebrew; all changes are subject to further revision, as is the English text itself):

- balanced lineation throughout, e.g., vv. 14–16;
- a strophic structure approximating that of the prior poetic analysis (as indicated by the internal line divisions), e.g., again, vv. 14–16;
- free, semi-rhythmic "meter," with occasional rhymes, e.g., 4e–f, 14b–c;
- use of synonyms and qualifiers to fill out lines (less exact repetition), e.g., v. 10;
- reduction in number of *ands*, insertion of several contrastive conjunctions, e.g., v. 14 (cf. the Hebrew text);
- inclusion of idiomatic lexical adjustments to create auditory appropriateness, e.g., 4a–b, 8;
- more explicit boundary formulas and demarcators (aperture, closure) within the text, e.g., vv. 9c–10a;
- general aim for euphony of expression (in English), e.g., v. 3.

Until one actually attempts in one's mother tongue to produce a new rendition (or revise an existing version) that is both poetic and aurally attractive, the issues involved in such endeavors will either remain rather opaque and perplexing, or they may not seem worth the time and effort. Having seriously embarked upon these innovative tasks, however, people soon discover their intellectual and aesthetic, as well as hermeneutical and religious value. Consequently, they find themselves frequently engaging in such compositional exercises in future, thus adding a new and fruitful dimension to their study and personal expression of Scripture. The following

4.8 Re-oralizing the biblical text in translation

recent rendition of Isaiah 66:1–2 is an example of such insightful creativity—in terms of textual format as well as verbal style:[26]

> **The Lord speaks**
> **this way**
> **the sky**
>
> and all ways behind it
> is a royal seat for me
> space
>
> is where I rest
> and the earth my footrest
> in time
>
> where could you build a house
> for me
> where a place
>
> especially for me to rest
> as if I would sleep or abide
> there or there
>
> when I made all this
> all of it comes from my hand
> all that is came into being
>
> **from me**
> **my Lord**
> **is speaking**

---

[26] Rosenberg 2009:267–268. The text is reproduced and punctuated as published. Obviously, to achieve its full effect the text must be orally articulated and correspondingly apprehended aloud. A valid critique of this new version is as follows: "If one is seeking a modern, trendy, and imaginative abridgement of selections of the Hebrew Bible that by and large have been rendered as poetry, then one will be quite satisfied. But those seeking a translation that reflects more of the actual language of the text rather than its perceived sentiments should look elsewhere" (Engle 2010).

> but I look at man especially
> for the man or woman oppressed
> poor and powerless
>
> when he knows he is
> brokenhearted and
> filled with humility
>
> his body trembling with care
> open to the others
> to my words.

4.9 Testing the translation in public performance

The production of a more aurally attuned "oratorical" translation is indeed a commendable accomplishment for any translation team, assuming that this goal fits the audience profile and communicative setting for which this version is intended. However, a draft translation, no matter how excellently conceived and constructed in the opinion of the translation team, is in fact simply a creative "hypothesis" until it has been "proven" through a sustained formal and informal process of evaluation.

This means that the rendering must prove to be "acceptable,"[27] as a minimum, in the general opinion of its principal target audience, whether the main medium of transmission is actually oral-aural or something else, e.g., print. Therefore, a particular translation (whether just a draft or a professionally published version) should satisfy two primary criteria—compositional quality (including accuracy) and economical viability. Of course, if the overall quality is poor or even mediocre, the salability (or marketability) will surely suffer. On the other hand, it does happen—perhaps all too often—that a well-crafted text does not

---

[27] But "acceptability" must, among other things, include the quality of "accuracy." Therefore, in my opinion it is not correct to claim that "any utterance of more than trivial length has no one translation; all utterances have innumerably many acceptable translations" (Bellos 2011:8). Thus, a particular rendering of a certain biblical passage may be acceptable in terms of grammar and lexical choice, but exegetically inaccurate and hence unacceptable as a translation option, for example, a version that simply omits, or even ameliorates, the final verse of Isaiah 66 (v. 24) due to its original graphically negative imagery.

4.9 Testing the translation in public performance

sell either. In such cases, the reasons for such poor sales must be thoroughly investigated so that the problems discovered may be avoided or corrected in a revised version. (Several probable negative factors are mentioned below.)

How is such translation testing, or "consumer" research to be carried out in an efficient and effective manner? Again, it is not possible here to go into detail,[28] but assessment procedures should involve both ends of the communication process, that is, in the case of an audio version, the translation's "performance" as well as its "reception." Thus, as regards its performance, since this translation is intended for oral elocution, it must first be evaluated with respect to how well average speakers and also trained lectors are actually able to articulate the text in public proclamation. Assuming that they have not memorized the words (memorization may well have been the case in the earliest stages of transmission), how easily and naturally do different readers verbalize the formatted text (see above) from a printed page? Places where they mispronounce the text, stumble, or hesitate in the process need to be investigated for potential problems of syntax, sense, and perhaps even the format itself (e.g., an awkward line break that disturbs normal patterns of intonation or pausing).

As regards audience testing for the evaluation of a translation's reception, there are a number of variables and assessment factors to keep in mind; the following is a summary of some of the more important of such considerations:

- The test, ideally varied according to the type of target group sampled (e.g., professional/pastoral or non-professional/lay), must have clear parameters, criteria, and questions.

- Those who present the text for evaluation by an audience must thoroughly practice it beforehand so that the evaluation process is not compromised by their poor elocution; in certain cases, experienced performers might be available for this purpose, artists who themselves may be able to offer suggestions for stylistic improvement.

---

[28] See Wendland 2008d:ch. 10; cf. also Wendland 2011:ch. 7.

- The persons carrying out the appraisal should have explicit instructions as to how to conduct the test, keeping the circumstances as similar as possible (including non-verbal performance attributes, such as gestures, facial expressions, vocal variables—stress points, volume control, intonation patterns, etc.) on each occasion in view of the primary listening group that the translation team envisioned when doing its work.

- Specific features of form (e.g., language/literary style), content (intelligibility), and connotation (e.g., emotive power and esthetic quality) should be selected for individual assessment during several readings of the same test sample (not everything all at once, unless simply a general reaction or opinion is required). Several options might be offered at a given juncture to better gauge audience preferences.

- The preceding requirement might necessitate also a careful pre-testing time of instruction for the audience (testees) so that they know what the test entails (e.g., that there are not "right" or "wrong" answers), how they will be tested, and why—what is the objective of the research (and the contribution that they can make to the translation under review). The use of such pre-test explanation may itself be evaluated since there is the possibility that such a procedure could skew the results.

- Although the focus in on the translation's orality, and in the case of Isaiah 66 its poetry as well, it would be advisable to include written reviews of the TL text, scholarly in particular but also non-scholarly, especially in the case of versions that will also be transmitted in published form.

- Comparative-choice tests, e.g., a sample of the Chewa *Buku Loyera* in comparison with the *Buku Lopatulika*, are usually easier to conduct with non-professional audiences since respondents can readily recognize differences and express personal preferences even if they are not able to articulate the nature of, or reason for them.

4.9 Testing the translation in public performance

- The more testers, audiences, settings (in keeping with the translation brief), types of assessment, and time allowed for the testing process, generally the more credible and useful the results—provided that these can all be objectively classified, evaluated, and then correctly applied in terms of revision and correction to the version at hand.

- In the case of an initial translation draft, it may be possible to produce a revised draft and then carry out the testing process again; in the case of a published version, this will probably not be feasible very soon, but the accumulated results of the testing process should be safely stored in electronic media for future use when an improved rendering is prepared. In any case, no text is completely "final" because no translation is ever perfect, but any given version always "leaks" in diverse ways that may be repaired and improved in a subsequent attempt that has carefully learned from past mistakes, shortcomings, and suggestions for improvement.

To be sure, many potential variables and associated options must be taken into consideration during any translation testing exercise. A significant amount of time and expense is also involved, and for this reason many translation programs simply omit it as an expendable luxury. However, as has been suggested above, this assessment process is essential not only for the translators themselves, assisting them to improve their ultimate product, but it also helps to popularize a new translation. It thereby encourages the target constituency to become personally engaged in the text's qualitative enrichment and expanded transmission, normally, as in the case of the testing itself, through oral-aural, word-of-mouth means.

Turning then to the two translations examined earlier, the modified Chewa and English (NLB) renderings of Isaiah 66:1–16, it may be reported that the testing process, so far relatively restricted in scope, is still in progress. Preliminary indications are that both versions generate substantial interest and attention when competently read aloud (though not as yet "performed" by a skilled professional mother-tongue speaker). The English version is more popular, perhaps because it was tested with audiences that are more literate and thus familiar with poetic texts that exhibit more unconventional usages and a style that diverges extensively from that of ordinary speech. The Chewa translation, on the other hand, was based on a particular oral-written genre of poetic discourse (*ndakatulo*) that is not as well-known to the masses. Therefore, it took a certain amount of time to explain to listeners not only the purpose of this new translation but also some of the features of its novel structure and style. It is anticipated that the Chewa version will become more acceptable once it has been adapted ("re-oralized") still further by an experienced composer to serve as the basis for a musical rendition that can be performed by local church choirs. The English version, however, will probably not reach even that level of limited distribution, but will rather remain as an illustrative text used mainly for instruction, namely, regarding the nature of Hebrew poetry and how the impact and appeal of the biblical text can—and must—be somehow duplicated in translation.

4.10 Conclusion: On the importance of orality for translation studies

My concluding remarks specifically concern literary compositions that are subsequently translated for written representation in another language. Thus oral to oral, or intersemiotic print to oral and/or video cross-media renditions are not directly discussed, although these comments may well apply also to such productions. Surprisingly, one does not read very much about the factor of orality in contemporary studies of secular translation theory and practice, except of course where issues of "interpreting" are being considered, that is, the simultaneous "oral translation of speech" (Munday 2009b:200).[29] However, my examination of Isaiah 66:1–16 based on the Hebrew source text clearly indicates that the vital oral-aural dynamic is a component of communication that is very important, not only in translations of Scripture, which are frequently transmitted aloud in some

---

[29] In this recent volume that overviews the contemporary translation scene, the key term "orality" (or something similar or related) is not found either in the listing of chapter "contents" or in the subject "index" at the back. The closest that one comes is in the article that deals with "issues in audiovisual translation" (Munday 2009a:141–165), but even here the principal emphasis is on the technical, technological side of the subject. The same absence may be observed in the *Routledge Encyclopedia of Translation Studies* (Baker and Saldanha 2008).

4.10 Conclusion: On the importance of orality for translation studies

public venue, but also for other kinds of non-religious, literary texts, for the following reasons:

- As was emphasized earlier, the study of orality begins with a thorough *exegesis*, or interpretation of the SL text, especially when any type of *poetic* piece is being analyzed. A significant part of the artistry of lyric composition obviously lies in the phonic dimension. Therefore, this must be an explicit aspect of a complete examination of the original document, for example, with regard to rhythm, rhyme, word plays, alliteration, assonance, and pure euphony or cacophony—a sequence of sounds perceived as being pleasing or jarring in the target language.

- A sound-responsive analysis of the source text is an essential part of a larger literary-structural type of study. It also has additional potential benefits with respect to other aspects of hermeneutical work, for example, textual criticism, especially in the case of *ancient* manuscripts, as well as subsequent sentence- and discourse-level exegesis.[30] Whether a secular or a religious literary composition is being translated, in particular a poetic, vocally-resonant one, a careful phonological examination of the source text usually pays great dividends in terms of the translator's better understanding of the total "meaning package" that s/he must re-express in the TL. *Where poetry is concerned, sound not only enhances, it also constitutes meaning!*

- Most literary translations are meant to be received *aloud* (often being popularized during public "readings"), as is surely the case for all Scripture versions. Therefore, the factor of orality must also shape their composition as well as their expression, or enunciation, since

---

[30] One example will suffice to illustrate several of these issues. In Isa 66:8b the expression הֲיוּחַל אֶרֶץ "Can the land be in labor..." occurs, but there is a problem in that the noun is feminine and the verb masculine. This apparent grammatical incongruity prompts proposals for emendation, for example, inserting a masculine noun: "people of the land" (עַם אֶרֶץ) to create agreement, as in the *BHS*. However, in poetry, such "disagreement is common in an impersonal passive construction" (Watts 1996:360). Furthermore, from a sonic impression, the addition of another word, even a monosyllable, disturbs the balanced accentual pattern of this verse, i.e., 3+3, 4+4, 2+2+2 (ibid., 358).

phonological form can contribute to a text's overall communicative significance (especially connotation, emotions, attitudes, values, etc.)—but only when it is actually heard.

- Thus, an important element in the testing of any type of religious translation is its public *delivery* and how a typical audience reacts pragmatically to a proficient oral expression of the text. This is especially true for a literary-poetic rendition, in particular, a dramatic presentation that includes non-verbal expressions and interpretations. In this case, the proof of the poetry is in the *sound* thereof—as determined by professional performance critics, on the one hand, and also ordinary average listeners.

- Systematic *research* into the orality of the target language, that is, a study of various oral genres, is frequently necessary before a literary translation project can be undertaken simply because little information on the subject is available to begin with. Such explorations will make the translator more effective then when preparing written versions, for example, when seeking to incorporate vital oral-aural clues regarding the text's structure (boundaries, peak/climax) and style (beauty or aesthetic appeal, and impact, its rhetorical power).

- Taking the preceding facets of orality into consideration during the translation process will render the consumer language text more *memorable* as well as *memorizable*. In other words, sound makes an immediately perceptible contribution towards distinguishing a translation formally with respect to its literary/oratorical properties in the vernacular. As a result it will be more likely that certain key passages (at least) will be remembered and perhaps even learned by heart or deemed important enough to be transmitted by additional media (e.g., in the form of a song). This captivating, inspiring sonic quality will contribute not only to a given version's popularity, but it may also affect its ultimate survivability as well.

- The KJV is a venerable example of the relevance of the oral-aural, elocutionary dimension in any translation that is intended, to an

4.10 Conclusion: On the importance of orality for translation studies

appreciable degree, for a public proclamation of the text. It is indeed a most worthy model to emulate.[31]

The prophet Isaiah exhorted his audiences to "hear," that is, pay close attention to, "the word of the LORD" and to "tremble"—to reverently obey what they were listening to (66:5). Surely there is more that contemporary translators can do as they carry out their work to help ensure that the actual audio rendering of their version, too, is worthy of the Word. By carefully attending to the oral-aural component of the sacred message along the way, they may be better able to accomplish this goal—*amplifying the orality of the original text* (as it has been received in canonical transmission)—thereby augmenting the rich phonic resonance of their translation in their own ears even as they seek to echo correspondingly compelling "sound effects" in the minds of those with whom they are communicating.

> *Before they call, I will surely answer them—*
> *While they are still speaking, I will listen! (Isaiah 65:24)*

---

[31] 2011 marked the 400th anniversary of the *King James Version* of the Bible, which was completed in 1611. This English translation has been termed "the book that changed the world"—at least a significant portion of the so-called "Western world" (King James Bible Trust). Could there ever be another "KJV"?! On the other hand, a recent study of the KJV suggests that the translators themselves were not really all that concerned about stylistic matters; rather, their emphasis was upon accuracy and faithfulness to the biblical text (Norton 2011:ch. 4).

5

Rhetorical Oral-Aural Dynamics of the Word: Revisiting John 17

5.1 Overview

A number of years ago, I found occasion to write several articles on the oral-aural qualities of John 17 and their implications for contemporary communication (Wendland 1992, 1994). Since orality is the subject of the present volume, I thought that it might be worthwhile to revise and update my earlier study. There are two reasons in particular for returning to the same subject: first, a *prayer*, such as we have recorded in John 17, is an obvious candidate for an investigation on the subject of orality and how it is manifested in the literature of Scripture. And second, this passage is not one that seems to have attracted overly much scholarly attention by way of a detailed analysis, perhaps because it occurs at the end of the so-called "upper room discourse" of John's Gospel (chs. 13–17). I will combine and develop aspects of my earlier studies in order to investigate the textual organization and interpretation of John 17 as a preliminary exercise to a more focused examination of its phonological constitution. This will provide the basis for an illustrative re-expression of the first portion of this "Lord's prayer" in the Tonga language of Zambia.

5.2 Understanding John 17 from a "speech-act" perspective

Prayer normally takes the form of some type of petition addressed to a deity, and it is therefore especially amenable to a speech-act analysis.[1] Speech-act theorists apply a functional approach to the analysis of literary (and other) discourse (oral and written), with an emphasis on what the text *does* in addition to what it *means*. They seek to examine texts as utterances "not only in terms of their surface grammatical properties but also in terms of the context in which they are made, the intentions, attitudes and expectation of the participants, the relationships between participants and the generally unspoken rules and conventions that are understood to be in play when an utterance is made and received" (Pratt 1977:86).[2] The pericope of John 17 presents a rather clearly defined "communicative event" in that it delineates a speaker (Jesus), an addressee (his heavenly Father), a group of witnesses on the scene who hear what is being said (and who are, arguably, secondary addressees, i.e., Christ's disciples), a specific setting (an evening meal, perhaps even the Passover dinner itself; 13:1–2), and a message—in this case, an explicitly demarcated prayer (cf. the corresponding inclusive marginal narrative comments in 17:1 and 18:1).

In order to describe the nature of this crucial Christological communication event more fully, it is helpful to consider it within the framework of "speech-act exegesis," which holds that "a biblical, that is religious, text

---

[1] Speech-act theory was summarized in ch. 2. From a social-science perspective, "Prayer is a socially meaningful symbolic act of communication directed to persons perceived as somehow supporting, maintaining and controlling the order of existence of the one praying. It is performed for the purpose of getting results from or within the interaction of communication" (Malina and Rohrbaugh 1998:246). "Like other types of language, prayer can be" instrumental, regulatory, interactional, self-focused, heuristic, imaginative, and/or informative (ibid., 246–247).

[2] Briggs adds: "Speech-act theory is concerned with the many and various things done with words.... Perhaps the most important point about speech-act theory for biblical interpretation [is] that it offers an integrative and balanced account of the many factors that go into a text's being encountered by a reader—or a hearer" (2008:75–76). See also Neufeld 1994:37–60.

5.2 Understanding John 17 from a "speech-act" perspective

should be viewed as a religious act" (Patte 1988:92). In other words, the discourse itself both constitutes and is constituted by a series of individual or composite speech acts, each manifesting, in addition to its denotative (semantic) content and connotative (emotive-attitudinal) implications, a distinct *locutionary* (linguistic) form, an *illocutionary* (functional) intent, and a *perlocutionary* (consequential) effect or response (cf. 2.2.3). Patte goes on to add the qualification that "religious discourses are peculiar speech-acts which cannot be assimilated to other kinds of speech-acts" (ibid., 100). However one decides to describe this special, or "peculiar," quality of biblical literature (qualified, for example, by the term "inspiration" and related notions), the adoption of such a hermeneutical perspective clearly affects one's interpretation of the content of these Scripture texts as well as their communicative function and ultimate outcome on people's thinking and behavior (including the assumed operation of the Holy Spirit).

There is another important issue that needs to be examined when considering the speech acts, or indeed, the more inclusive genre-related "text acts," of a book or pericope of Scripture, and this is the matter of *perspective*. In other words, from whose point of view should one discern and evaluate the functional aim of a given section, whether large or small—from that of the internal narrative participants, from that of the (implied) author and his (implied) readers/hearers, or from the viewpoint of receptors today? It is somewhat easier to adopt the internal perspective, for example, that of Jesus praying to his Father in the hearing, and thus also for the benefit of, his disciples in John 17. A certain amount of controversy arises, however, when one tries to establish the external perspective: Who is the real/implied author of the Gospel of "John"—if not John, the historical disciple of Christ, then who? If not the former, then it is likely that the rhetorical and theological purpose of individual portions along with the composition as a whole might well differ in significant respects. However, since I have not found convincing evidence to the contrary, I will assume the traditional understanding that the Apostle John is author of the Gospel that bears his name,[3] but the text of chapter 17 will be analyzed primarily in relation to the most overt, participant level of interpersonal interaction.

---

[3] For a full discussion of the issues, see Morris 1995:4–25: "It is a matter, then, of accepting that solution which best accounts for the facts and which has the fewest difficulties in its way. It is for this reason that I accept the view that John the Apostle was the author" (ibid., 24).

Accepting Johannine authorship makes it relatively straightforward then to postulate an overarching "macro-illocution" (communicative goal) for the Gospel as a whole. The rhetorical (and evangelistic) objective for this passage is clearly enunciated in 20:31—namely, to persuasively influence the implied, or intended, readers to "believe" all that has been written in this scroll about "Jesus the Christ" so that they might "have life." And since the divine authority of the Lord himself (e.g., John 11:25–26) stands behind this expressed intention on the part of the writer, as the attesting witness (21:24), its illocutionary force is augmented from that of being a strong assertion with the desire to persuade, to that of an even more forceful performative act having the capacity to fulfill Christ's "promise" of spiritual "life." The corresponding perlocutionary effect for those who believe is not merely one of "assurance" with respect to a certain fact, a point of information, but an immediate "appropriation" of that which has been promised, namely, eternal salvation.[4] These key theological truths are clearly reflected also in Christ's prayer recorded in the 17th chapter of the Gospel of John the Apostle.

I therefore undertake this analysis under the assumption that the text of John 17 is a substantially accurate record of the essence of Christ's closing prayer after the evening meal with his disciples (cf. 18:1).[5] The present Greek text may be a selective reworking or re-composition, perhaps, of an Aramaic original, but it is surely not some fictive creation by an unknown "implied author."[6] In any case, the harmonious and intricate welding together of form, content, and function within the specified textual context and the situational setting as described would seem to argue for viewing the discourse as being a historically reliable report and also a complete artistic, rhetorical, and theological whole. This chapter in fact occurs as the climax of Christ's pre-paschal ministry at a final fellowship meal with his closest disciples. It also constitutes an *intratextual* realization of the motivation attributed to Jesus at the very beginning of the section in 13:1–2.

---

[4] Those who do not believe do not receive the "life" that Christ here promises nor the associated blessings.

[5] Some commentators posit a different situational setting for John 17, for example, a text that developed much later in connection "with celebrations of the Lord's Supper in the early [Christian] churches" (Beasley-Murray 1987:294). Such views are common among redaction critics like Rudolf Bultmann (cf. Carter 2006:156–157).

[6] Contra, for example, Petersen 1984:45.

5.2 Understanding John 17 from a "speech-act" perspective

Thus, we see in this prayer a general development in parallel of the three main themes which are introduced in 13:31-35 at the onset of the farewell speech(es): *Glory* (13:31-32 > 17:1-5), *Departure* (13:33 > 17:6-19), and *Love* (13:34-35 > 17:20-26).[7] In view of his imminent departure through bitter suffering, death, and resurrection into heavenly glory, Christ's prayer is an intimate expression of the deep affection that he felt for all those who were "his own in the world" (17:9-10). In relation to the overall structure of John's Gospel, this passage is a critically-placed summary of the Lord's notion of "discipleship"—as exemplified ultimately and vicariously in his own sacrificial mission to save humanity, a "glorious" endeavor that he was just about to commence (18:1ff.).

There is also some strong *intertextual* resonance from the Old Testament and Jewish intertestamental literature which highlights this pericope's positioning in the Gospel at this juncture.[8] Such a concluding, culminating prayer is a familiar feature of the final "testamental" hortatory discourse uttered by a great leader to his followers just before his death, for example, Jacob (Gen 49), Moses (Deut 32-33), Joshua (Josh 23-24), Ezra (4 Ezra 8:19-36), Baruch (2 Bar 48),[9] and we might include also Paul at Miletus (Acts 20:17-38). This would be especially appropriate given the prominent paschal character of the extratextual environment of the text as recorded by John. The Passover celebration itself normally closed with doxological psalms (the *Hallel*) and liturgical hymns in praise of God's mighty acts of protection and deliverance on behalf of his people (Agourides 1968:144). These were typically retrospective and commemorative in nature. John 17,

---

[7] Also supporting the integrity and significance of this prayer are many other instances of noteworthy intratextual resonance, for example in the first portion of the prayer alone: "the time ['hour'] has come" (v. 1; cf. 2:4, 7:30, 8:20, 12:23, 13:1); "glorify your Son that your Son may glorify you" (v. 1; cf. 1:14, 7:39, 13:31-32); "you granted him authority" (v. 2; cf. 5:27); "this is eternal life" (v. 3; cf. 3:15-16, 5:24, 10:10); "by completing the work" (v. 4; cf. 3:17, 4:34, 5:36, 9:4, 10:37); "in your presence" (v. 5; cf. 1:1-2, 6:46, 8:16).

[8] For a study of the dynamic, almost personified use of Scripture in the discourses of John, see Labahn (2011)—that is, "how Scripture functions as a 'witness' to Jesus in the Fourth Gospel...[and] how these written Scriptures act as a character that speaks to audiences both within and beyond the narrative" (ibid., 135).

[9] However, as Brant observes: "John 17 has been compared to other biblical prayers that come at the end of farewell addresses (Gen 49, Deut 32-33...), but the sentence structure of none of these bears the same distinct antithetical pattern produced by repetition and clauses" (2004:121).

on the other hand, opens a new perspective by presenting a discourse that is decidedly anticipatory and predictive.

> The distinctiveness of the prayer of John 17, over against other related compositions, lies in the uniqueness of him who prays and the setting of his prayer: Jesus, the Son of God, is about to depart to his Father through a death and resurrection for the life of the world; in that circumstance that the purpose of God may be perfectly fulfilled through what he now does and through his followers. (Beasley-Murray 1987:293)

Turning then to a more focused speech-act analysis of John 17, we might begin by reconsidering the nature of this composition as a whole: Should the entire text be viewed as a "prayer," like the initial disjunctive quote margin would suggest, also by recording the gesture of Jesus "raising his eyes to heaven" (17:1; cf. 11:41; Mark 7:34; Luke 18:13)—or would some other illocutionary type be more suitable as a generic description? The roots of this seemingly insignificant issue actually reach back deeply into church history, for early theologians roundly debated the same point. Bishop Theodore of Mopsuestia, also known as Theodore the Interpreter (ca. 350–428 CE), for example, regarded John 17 as a "prophetic" passage, while John Chrysostom, the Archbishop of Constantinople (349–407 CE), saw it more as a hortatory monologue (Haenchen 1984:156). However, the formulaic introduction as well as the situational setting (17:1), and indeed the very style of the text, would strongly indicate that it is a prayer—nevertheless one that realizes a number of other important communicative functions that interact during the course of its utterance.

The presence on the scene of Jesus' disciples, that is, as "secondary" addressees, would certainly inject a prominent *didactic* element into the discourse, as in the case of the so-called "Lord's [better: disciples'] prayer" of Matt 6:9–13 (Luke 11:1–4). This interpretation is substantiated by prayers of a similar nature found in the Gospels, for example, John 12:27–28, Luke 10:21–22.[10] This viewpoint is further supported by the exegetical tradition of the early church (Agourides 1968:137). Thus, Christ reviews the

---

[10] It is evident that the practice of utilizing prayer as a medium of instruction was familiar in Bible times (cf. Morrison 1965:259–260).

5.2 Understanding John 17 from a "speech-act" perspective

principal themes of his gospel message for the benefit of his faithful few just before he was about to be violently taken from them in order to bring the Father's saving plan to completion on the cross.[11] But why cast such instruction in the form of a prayer then, and a poetic one at that (see analysis below)? More had to be involved than mere tradition (i.e., the farewell of a revered master) or customary ritual (i.e., praying at the close of the Pascal meal). Perhaps the teaching could be more dramatically and memorably impressed upon their minds through the use of this genre (Ukpong 1989:53). In any case, the climactic nature of this text—whether in relation to the Gospel narrative plot as a whole, or this discrete segment (chs. 13–17)—undoubtedly had substantial influence on its mode and manner of composition. Such concerns must therefore be taken into consideration also today as this prayer is transmitted in translation via diverse media.

Didactic discourse may be realized in very different literary forms, and therefore it is not surprising to find a variety of more specific illocutionary aims revealed as the prayer unfolds—communicative aims that also need to be reflected in any contemporary translation. First of all, accepting the hermeneutical stance that we are dealing here with an actual prayer of Jesus the Christ, one directly addressed to his Father in heaven (the primary receptor), we observe that he opens with a forceful laudatory appeal that God would be glorified (greatly honored, praised, worshiped, etc.) through the character and activities of his Son (vv. 1–5). This extended supplication is then followed by a complex bundle of occasionally overlapping intercessory illocutions which is carried through to the end of the passage. The individual components may be designated in various ways, depending on one's perspective (i.e., who is being addressed, whether directly or indirectly) and the degree of specificity desired, for example: invocation (1, 5, 11, 21, 24, 25), confession (3),[12] commendation (6–8), mediation (9), revelation

---

[11] "Much of the Gospel's theology climaxes in this concluding section of Jesus' final discourse in the Gospel" (Keener 2003:1050). D. A. Carson puts it this way: "In some respects the prayer is a summary of the entire Fourth Gospel to this point.... To cast this summary in the form of a prayer is not only to anticipate Jesus' being 'lifted up' on the cross, but to contribute to the climax of the movement that brings Christ back to God—one of the central themes of the farewell discourse" (1991:551).

[12] Neyrey points out that "[t]he first part of 17:3 resembles the confession known as the Shema, the premier prayer of the synagogue (see Mark 12:29, 32; Deut 6:4)" (2009:392).

[reiterated] (11), confirmation (11–12a), explanation (12b), encouragement (13), commission (18–19), promise (24, 26), dedication (19), and petition (1, 5, 9a, 11b, 15b, 17, 20, 21b, 23a, 24). These interactional motivations may well be intended to achieve or inspire a corresponding assortment of perlocutionary effects, for example: fidelity (13), assurance (15), commitment (17, 19), harmony and unity (22–23), perception (21, 23), knowledge (25), confidence (24), and ultimately, brotherly love (26).

As might be expected, most of these interrelated illocutions are connotatively positive in tone. But there are several distinctly negative notions that emerge; these are contrastive at least by implication and always used with reference to "the world" and its master, "the Evil One" (v. 15), for example: the need for separation (6a, 9), warning (11, 14), disappointment [over "the one doomed for destruction"] (12b), rebuke and reproof (25). Such sharply antithetical elements are typical of the Johannine corpus and serve, among other things, to highlight the desired—but difficult—model of discipleship (6b) and fellowship (11b) that Jesus is setting forth for those whom the Father had given him (24a).

> John uses this dualistic language to depict the distinctiveness and alternative identity of those who have entrusted themselves to follow Jesus. It does so in part by contrast, denoting in negative terms human existence that does not participate in God's life-giving purposes. Positively, John's dualistic language also describes God's salvation and the distinctive life it creates, lived in relation to God, manifested in Jesus, and yet to be completed.[13] (Carter 2006:104)

The underlying antithesis just noted has been accentuated by the influence of the heightened inter- and intra-textuality made possible through the shift in medium that occurred when the original transient oral-aural event

---

[13] Such dualistic language, here attributed to Jesus himself, performs a vital sociological, or we might say, "ecclesiastical," function: "It identifies consenting readers of the gospel as believers in Jesus and sharply distinguishes them from nonbelievers by depicting the latter in negative terms" (Carter 2006:104). This is not just a matter of religious name-calling by "believers as part of a counterculture or 'antisociety' alienated from, and alternative to, the rest of society"; rather, such in-group language is a mutually-supportive and unifying verbal reflection of their "privileged and distinct identity" (ibid., 104) as disciples of the Lord Jesus Christ and children of their heavenly Father.

was visually fixed—first partially by chirography in the "rhetorical culture" of the age, and then much later typographically in a more permanent manner.[14] Despite certain undesirable effects of such a "technologizing of the Word", as Ong (1982) calls it, this development in communication technology also has a number of beneficial consequences, including several of appreciable rhetorical and theological relevance. For one, the medium-induced process of objectification has permanently altered the scope of Christ's prayer in John 17. Its reference and application have thereby been extended from the "secondary" level of receivership, that is, the Eleven on the scene at the time, to a "tertiary" and potentially universal level, namely, all his future believing disciples (17:20). But the text's nature and purpose have also been significantly affected. In view of its contextualization within the wider Scriptures and due to increased historical and sociocultural "distance," its didactic element has tended to become more prominent, and its theological function, too, has been magnified as well as diversified—that is, to cater for its new multicultural, worldwide, and timeless receptor constituency.

For this reason then, the communicative intent of the John 17 discourse at any point cannot be described or evaluated solely in terms of the individual illocutionary components which are seen to converge there. Nor can an exposition of the reception process be reasonably confined and idealized to an initial, a strictly linear, and an unbroken process (Berg 1989:188–90). It is rather the composite whole, interpreted in the light of John's complete Gospel and in whatever way is normal and/or natural for a given receptor (reader, hearer) under the influence of the Spirit of God, which conveys the desired perlocutionary effect(s). This applies not only to the first hearers, but also to all those who now apprehend the source text's words through translation and message transmission (publication, broadcasting, performance, proclamation) via various media.

In the light of the preceding discussion, I would like to conclude this section by proposing a particular illocutionary force for the prayer that is rarely considered, namely, to effect physical, psychological, and spiritual *reinforcement* for its hearers. In his humanity, Jesus needed to strengthen himself, first of all, for the tremendous corporeal suffering and mental

---

[14] Ong 1982:132–133. Robbins defines a "rhetorical culture" as "a culture where oral speech and written texts continually interact with one another" (1996:59–60).

anguish that lay just ahead. He thus turned to his accustomed way to accomplish such personal fortification—through fervent prayer to his Father (cf. Christ's subsequent prayer in Gethsemane as recorded in the Synoptic Gospels: Matt 26:36–46, Mark 14:32–42, Luke 22:39–46). But Jesus was also praying aloud in his disciples' immediate hearing in order to strengthen them to face the trials that would soon come their way (11), to confirm them in his teaching for the ministry (8) that he was consecrating them to carry on in his name (17), to encourage them with regard to the ultimate success of their message (20), to reassure them of his continual protection (15), instruction (26), and loving presence (together with the Father, 22–23, 26), and in every event at all times to sustain them in their mission with the joyous hope of future glory (13, 24). The particular derived "significance"[15] of this prayer for disciples in their current setting of communication is that by faith they could also apply this same divine reinforcement, in its multiple facets, to themselves in their lives as believers in Christ (20), no matter how disparate their respective external circumstances in "the world."

In present-day sociological terms, we might sum up this notion of "reinforcement" as it relates to John's central themes with respect to *power* (authority) and *solidarity* (unity). Knowledge (i.e., biblical "wisdom," e.g., Prov 1:2–7) is power, and from a diagnostic perspective "to know" (γινώσκω, i.e., to understand, believe, establish a personal relationship with, and/or to commit oneself to) the true Source of "eternal life" puts all genuine disciples of "Christ, the Son of God" in an incomparably advantaged ("blessed") position vis à vis "the world" (17:2–3, 9, 16, 23, 25; cf. 20:29, 31).[16] On the other hand, this same knowledge acts as a powerful bonding force to unite all true believers, not only with one another, but also with their Savior-Lord, and indeed, with the heavenly Father himself (17:21).[17] Having such

---

[15] Hirsch correctly (in my opinion) but controversially (from the viewpoint of modern hermeneutics) distinguishes between the author-intended "sense" (or meaning) that is embedded within a verbal text and its "significance," that is, the meaning as variously perceived and applied by later interpreters (1976:3).

[16] The characteristics of the Johannine community (and all genuine disciples of Christ) in contrast to those of the people of "this world" may be described sociologically in terms of an "antisociety," e.g., precarious condition, selectivity, multigeneity, antistructure, other-centered, antisecular, revealed knowledge, etc. (Malina and Rohrbaugh 1998:61, 245).

[17] John 17 "is a prayer asking God to create a shared community of honor between himself, Jesus, and the disciples of all generations. In that sense it shares much with the entire Gospel of John" (Malina and Rohrbaugh 1998:247).

knowledge is also a vital prerequisite for communicating the Word of God meaningfully and appropriately in another language and cultural environment. In conclusion, a manifold speech-act methodology provides an essential discourse perspective on a particular biblical pericope that further encourages the analyst, whether an exegete or a translator, to view it more discerningly with reference also to its oral-aural potential during the process of text transmission.

5.3 Analysis: John 17 as a system of complementary textual structures

Any viable "system," whether animate or inanimate in nature, is composed of a strategic arrangement of interrelated elements, which interact according to a set of internally defined rules to form a unified whole. The overall constitution of every system then may be described in terms of a "structure" consisting of discrete *units* and connective *relationships* on one or more levels of organization. However, a system involves more than just form alone; it also manifests a clear-cut "function" (or group of functions) in a specific setting of operation, one that may change in accordance with the immediate context and the prevailing circumstances.

A verbal creation, for example, whether oral or written, is a complex multi-system of linguistic signs designed for human communication. It consists of at least four formal complementary and integrated co-systems: phonological, lexical, grammatical, and textual—supplemented in the case of an oral presentation by non-verbal semiotic systems such as the gestural and proxemic. In the case of every text, it is also necessary to identify its accompanying functional system, like the set of embedded speech acts as discussed in the preceding section. Such a performance perspective may be augmented, where literary (or oratorical) communication is concerned, by a "rhetorical" system. This encompasses all those features selected from the four formal structures which are organized in response to contextual constraints and pragmatic motivations so as to inject the qualities of impact and appeal into the discourse. The aim of *rhetoric* is to facilitate the main communicative objectives of the realized text in its intended situational context, that is, to "persuade" (in the broadest sense) an audience (or readership) of the validity, reliability, and credibility of what is being said—the "message." This message therefore conveys a "meaning" that is manifold, consisting of semantic "content," pragmatic "intent," and various associated (connotative) aspects, such as feeling, tone, mood, attitude, and evaluation. All of these dimensions must be taken into consideration then when communicating a text in translation. Which one(s) will be given prominence depends on the nature of the composition (e.g., in the case of Scripture, the semantic content is often, but not always primary),[18] the medium of transmission, the principal audience in view, the setting or occasion, and in certain cases also the specific purpose of the communication event (e.g., an evangelism crusade versus an educational conference for church leaders).

A multi-staged structural analysis of the text of John 17 was completed as part of the initial preparation for the present study,[19] which has as its special focus the oral-aural dynamics of this prayer with a view towards preparing a contemporary "oratorical" rendering of the passage in the Tonga language. Four distinct types of compositional investigation were applied (to be described and discussed below). The results of these individual studies provide a fuller conceptual frame of reference for understanding the biblical text in the first place and then also for identifying its chief structural, artistic, and rhetorical features so that these can be used as the basis for selecting literary functional equivalents in the target language, whether English or any other. A summary of the first three types of discourse analysis is given below; this set will act as the background for our present emphasis upon the text's phonological organization, as revealed by an *oral-elocutionary* analysis to be carried out in §5.6.

5.3.1 Paradigmatic-topical analysis

A paradigmatic-topical analysis of the textual organization and interpretation of John 17 deals essentially with its lexical and semantic organization. Fourteen key "topics" were identified by means of a simple charting process focusing on instances of verbal recursion (exact and synonymous) within

---

[18] In some biblical texts, or even entire books (e.g., the Song of Songs), the *pragmatic* function is primary.

[19] For the details, see Wendland 1992:71–88.

5.3 Analysis: John 17 as a system of complementary textual structures

the text. Some of these typical Johannine (Christological) motifs refer to simpler notions, like "life" or "word," while other designate more complex ideas, such as "faith/believe/know" or "unity/possession/oneness." The first topic, "speech/prayer margin," is rather different in that it incorporates all those expressions that introduce direct speech, e.g., vocatives, verbs of petition, and references to the beneficiaries of the prayer. The diverse topics were selected inductively, simply on the basis of their perceived prominence after many readings of this pericope as well as John's Gospel as a whole. Most topical units are relatively straightforward in their classification, but there are others that might be categorized differently. Furthermore, there are instances of mixing, overlapping, and a certain amount of ambiguity involved, for example, the notion of "separation" covers both a spatial (e.g., come/go away) and a spiritual sense (i.e., "sanctify").[20]

The results of this classificatory exercise give one a rough idea concerning both the density and also the distribution of the text's main topics. This, in turn, provides an indication of the primary themes of the prayer as it develops, based on the assumption that the most frequently occurring topics, whether interpreted in a literal sense or figuratively, have a definite bearing on the central message that the speaker/author wanted to get across to his hearers/readers. Thus, Christ begins with a strong emphasis on the concepts of "glory" and "giving" (vv. 1–5). The latter notion continues to be prominent in the second principal discourse section (6–9). The three topics of "unity," "preservation," and "separation" then intermingle (10–13) until the third comes to predominate (14–19) in conjunction with the antithetical concept of "world." The final portion of the prayer (20–26) is the most disparate topically, with "glory" being reintroduced along with an emphasis upon saving "knowledge" and solidifying "love," in contrast again with the world's inveterate "hatred." But the notion of relational "unity"—among fellow believers, between believers and Jesus, and between the Son and his heavenly Father—again prevails, as it does throughout the chapter.

---

[20] "Many of the terms are somewhat synonymous, with overlapping meanings denoting the experience and process of salvation (or its opposite)" (Carter 2006:104). Keener observes that "[t]he chapter also reflects standard Jewish motifs, such as the unity of God's people, their love for God, God's glory, obedience to God's message, the election and setting apart of God's people, and the importance of obeying God's agent (Moses in Jewish tradition).... In short, most of the motifs reflect common Judaism, yet reinterpreted in a christocentric manner and reapplied to the christologically defined community" (Keener 2003:1050–1051).

To summarize: Christ prays that the "fellowship" that exists between the heavenly Father and himself might be revealed among all those "believers" who have been "given" to him and whom he has, in turn, "commissioned" to carry on his ministry when he "departs." Such a demonstration of oneness is especially important, therefore, in view of his upcoming "separation" from them. This generally positive theme is highlighted by a secondary, but closely related, contrastive thought that features a fundamental paradox. This has to do with the need for Christ's disciples to be "preserved" and "set apart" morally and spiritually from the surrounding hostile environment in which they are, on the other hand, appointed to operate evangelically, thereby manifesting the "unity," "knowledge," and "love" characteristic of a common faith in the Lord while carrying out their mission to an unbelieving "world."

5.3.2 Syntagmatic-propositional analysis

A syntagmatic-propositional analysis of the textual organization and interpretation of John 17 deals with the text's syntactic and logical framework. It takes the form of a sequence of hierarchically arranged semantic relationships that link the various binary "propositional" segments (and their clusters) as they unfold in the pericope of John 17.[21] The development of the prayer's rhetorical "argument" (persuasion through personal petition) may be traced by noting in particular the relationships between the larger units (propositional clusters) of the discourse. Accordingly, the "grounds" (or basis) of the entire prayer is found in the initial proposition (v. 1a), namely, that "the hour had come" for Jesus to bring his saving mission to a climax in the crucifixion event (alluding back to many prior predictions, e.g., 12:23–24, 27; 13:1; 16:32). It was this ultimate fact that motivated the series of requests which he addressed to the Father on his own behalf and for the benefit of all his disciples, his immediate followers as well as all those who would one day come to believe their message (v. 20). The prayer consists of three principal discourse constituents, with an ever-expanding point of reference: 1–5 (Jesus, the pray-er), 6–19 (Christ's disciples), 20–26 (all believers in Christ).

---

[21] For a complete listing of these in John 17, see Wendland 1992:87–88. The methodology used for this type of propositional analysis is similar to that described in Sterner 1998:1–10.

5.3 Analysis: John 17 as a system of complementary textual structures

The first "petition" concerns Jesus himself as he requests that the Father would now "glorify [his] Son" (δόξασόν σου τὸν υἱόν) since he had completed the work which his Father gave him to do. This includes Jesus' past ministry of discipling and, by way of anticipation, also his impending passion. The motivation ("purpose") here is the Son's desire that his heavenly Father would also be glorified through these paradoxical events (i.e., an exultation to glory through the shame of the cross). The various theological ideas associated with this initial request,[22] which is reiterated for emphasis (*inclusio*) in v. 5 (δόξασόν με σύ, πάτερ) along with a reference to Christ's pre-creation glory (1:1–2; cf. 12:41), span the first major discourse segment, or propositional cluster (17:1b–5). Rhetorically as well as theologically, it is significant that Jesus begins with his most important petition, namely, the one that deals with his "glorious" divine relationship with his Father, which is integrally linked then with his mission to save mankind (v. 2) by making known to them "the only true God" and his "apostle" Jesus Christ (v. 3). This cluster of concepts and propositions constitutes the semantic "base" upon which subsequent requests in the prayer are established as successive stages of descriptive and petitionary "amplification."

Christ's second petition, an appeal on behalf of his own disciples for preservation from external evil through internal unity, is not explicitly expressed until midway within the second major section of the prayer (17:6–19). Thus, in v. 11b Jesus calls upon his "Holy Father" (Πάτερ ἅγιε) to "protect" (τήρησον) his followers "by the power of your name."[23] The preceding passage builds up to this peak by outlining the reasons for which the plea is made, namely, the disciples' knowledge, faith, and obedience (vv. 6–8), coupled with their beloved Master's imminent departure from them (9–11a). The essence of this request for "protection" (11b) is developed throughout this discourse unit (12–16) with increased emphasis. Jesus asks that the Father would "protect" (τηρήσῃς) his disciples from "the Evil One" (τοῦ πονηροῦ, 15), who exercises

---

[22] "In this passage as in others, a complex of associations clusters together, including Jesus' glory and love, God's name, and the revealing of God's word.... Thus Jesus' crucifixion and exaltation to the Father is the theophany that will reveal the divine name to the disciples" (Keener 2003:1052–1053).

[23] "Jesus revealed to the disciples God's 'name' (17:6), partly meaning his honor but very probably also implying his [holy/set-apart] character and identity (14:9, 17:26).... God expected his people [in turn] to sanctify his name (*kiddush haShem* was central to Jewish ethics), especially by righteous deeds" [v. 6b] (Keener 2003:1056, words in brackets added).

his rule in the wicked "world" that opposes ("hates") (14) and is completely alien to them (16). Indeed, one of their number is a negative case in point—"the one doomed for destruction" (12).[24]

A third petition leads off the short concluding unit (paragraph) (vv. 17–19) of the long middle portion of the prayer. Jesus now prays that the Father would "sanctify" (ἁγίασον) his disciples in/by the "truth" of his "word" (17) so that they are spiritually prepared to carry on with his ministry in the "world" at large (18). Thus, Christ's mediatory supplication was purposefully two-pronged: it had an immediate in-group, consolatory relevance, but it also presented a bold hortatory challenge for his followers to take the offensive with the true message of Scripture in a hostile earthly environment.

The third and final section of the prayer is also clearly divided by the vocative "Father" (Πάτερ, 24a; cf. 11b) into two segments (17:20–23, 24–26), each of which centers upon an additional petition. The first opens by expanding the scope of the entreaty to all believers (v. 20). It is another strong appeal for unity ("My prayer is...that they all might be one," 20–21a) based on the loving fellowship that binds the Father and the Son (21b–23). However, this is not a static, introverted notion, but rather one that forms the telic foundation also for the Church's evangelistic ministry into the "world" (21b and 23b, which parallel each other at the close of their respective paragraph sub-units). There is a definite overlap between the prayer's second and third sections as reference to Christ's current disciples ("not for them alone," 20a) extends to all future followers ("also for those who will believe," 20b). In this sense, then, the pronoun "them" (αὐτοὺς) in v. 23b may well be an instance of "semantic density" (Wendland 1990) by referring not only to the present "believers" but also to those out there in the "world" whom they will one day win for Christ.

The last paragraph (vv. 24–26) appropriately adds an eschatological dimension to the text in Christ's request that the elect might ultimately "see," and participate in, his "glory" (24b).[25] The Father would thus "glorify" believers, even as he is about to glorify his Son (cf. v. 1b). There is, however, also an immediate practical application of this future-oriented desire

---

[24] This graphic descriptive title as a substitute reference to Judas is an instance of (orally accommodating) rhetorical "antonomasia" (ibid., 1058).

[25] "The language is reminiscent of the Greek heroic tradition in which the witnesses to a death recognize its victim as a hero by praising his or her name and thereby share in the hero's glory" (Brant 2004:241).

5.3 Analysis: John 17 as a system of complementary textual structures   181

through an important extension of communicative roles. Just as Jesus made the heavenly Father "known" during his saving mission to bring "eternal life" to all people (cf. v. 3), so also Jesus would continue to do so through the message of his "sent" disciples (18, 25–26). There is in this connection also a subtle reversal that is articulated right at the end: The "glory" of Christ that believers will one day enjoy "with him" is to be experienced even now in the mutual "love" which should distinguish their temporal relationship with one another (26b; cf. 23b) while he is still with them (26a). Indeed, this is a divinely revealed "glory" that is as much worth working for as it is waiting for. Thus, the unified, loving relational character of the Father and the Son is to be complemented by their continuous salvation-motivated activity among believers, which these disciples are in turn to model in their daily lives. This "glorious" activity includes the verbal communication of the Lord's message—that of Christ himself and the Word of God in general—through the ministry of Bible translation, which is the special concern of the present study.

5.3.3 Poetic-architectonic analysis

The paradigmatic-topical structure considered earlier is viewed from a somewhat different perspective in this aspect of analysis, which investigates the text's larger patterns of thematic arrangement. The principal "topics" are now examined with respect to their "architectonic," or positional locations and relationships within the discourse as a whole. Repetitive, synonymous, and contrastive parallels in John 17 disclose more than a recursive style or even emphatic repetition; in addition, they manifest a prominent placement of topics within the composition, especially as boundary indicators for text elements (propositional clusters, "paragraphs") of all sizes. Hence, these correspondences are also of mnemonic significance, that is, in addition to reflecting a distinctly "poetic" prose style in general.[26]

---

[26] Recent studies that document the "poetics" of Johannine discourse in relation to the oral-aural character of the text and its context are Brickle 2011 and Thatcher 2011a. I do not mean to suggest here that the Apostle composed this passage by consciously following the poetic forms of Hellenistic literature. Rather, John selectively employed his own rhetorical devices and rhythmic patterns, I would argue, both to effectively express the subject at hand, perhaps as a liturgical restructuring of the original prayer, and also to render the text amenable to oral articulation as well as for memorization. It is interesting to note that current developments in

Notice, for example, the unfolding arrangement of parallels that creates a cohesive strand that unites the first constituent of section two in verses 6–8, that is: A–B–C=A'–B'–C' (where **A**: Father "gives" to Son; **B**: disciples "obey/accept" God's word[s]; **C**: "they know" whatever "comes from you"). There is a similar but larger, more general pattern that runs throughout the entire middle segment (vv. 6–19), that is, *background*: A (6–8) / A' (12–14); *reason*: B (9–11a) / B' (15–16); and *request*: C (11b) / C' (17–19). Other lexical-semantic similarities serve to reveal points of thematic emphasis and boundary markers, for example, *inclusio* (unit beginning and ending): the appeal to a revelation of "glory" (vv. 1, 24); *anaphora* (corresponding unit beginnings): explicit mention of Christ's "requesting" the Father (vv. 9, 15, 20); *epiphora* (corresponding unit endings): references to mutual "love" (vv. 23, 26); *anadiplosis* (unit overlap, or hinge, construction): references to "the world" (vv. 14b, 15a); *exclusio* (enclosing a well-defined unit): "I am coming to you" (vv. 11a, 13a, enclosing 11b–12).[27]

There are, in addition, several important "ring" (A–B–A') constructions that also function more specifically to define the boundaries of (sub)sections within Christ's prayer and to highlight different aspects of the major themes being conveyed as a part of his threefold "message" (i.e., to his heavenly Father, his disciples, and through this passage of Scripture, to all believers). We find various types of ring structure in the text's three chief divisions as follows (omitting verses 6–8 referred to above):

I. A (1–2):   Petition for "glory" and its goal, "life"
    B (3):   The goal is defined in terms of "knowledge"
    A' (4–5): The goal accomplished, the petition repeated

Hellenistic poetic technique, i.e., a certain measure of phonological simplification, appear to support the type of discourse analysis that I have carried out below: "From about the beginning of the Christian era, the distinction in colloquial Gr. speech between long and short vowel-quantities began to disappear, and the musical pitch-accent that had prevailed since archaic times began to be replaced by a tonic stress-accent similar to modern Gr. or Eng.... [B]y the beginning of the 6th c. A.D., the characteristic Byzantine versification was well established, its guiding principle no longer syllable quantity but recurrent stress accent" (Herington 1993:487).

[27] For further explanation of these structural devices, see Wendland 2004b:127, 421.

5.3 Analysis: John 17 as a system of complementary textual structures

II. A (9):   General reference to "prayer" on behalf of Jesus' disciples[28]

    B (10–11a):   Reason for prayer: Jesus "possesses" them and has revealed his "glory" through them in "the world", but he will soon be leaving "the world" to go to the Father

  A' (11b):   General petition for "protection"

    B' (12–14):   Reason for petition: Jesus who has been in "the world," "guarding" his disciples against the hatred of "the world" is now going to the Father

  A" (15–16):   Specific appeal for protection for the disciples against "the Evil One"

      C (17):   Christ's plea that his disciples would "be consecrated in truth" for their mission

        D (18):   Their mission is based on Christ's ministry "into the world"

      C' (19):   Christ "consecrates himself" so that his disciples might be "consecrated in truth" for their mission

III. A (20–21):   Petition for unity among believers so that "the world might believe" that God sent his Son[29]

    B (22a):   Motivation for unity: the "glory" that Jesus displayed to them

  A' (22b–23a): Petition for unity among believers so that "the world might know" that God sent his Son

      C (23b):   God's "love" for his Son and all believers

  A" (24a):   Indirect prayer that believers would be "with me"(Christ)

    B' (24b):   Motivation: that they might see "my glory"

      C' 24c):   God's "love" for his Son

        D' (25–26a): Emphasis on "knowing" and "making known"

      C" (26b):   God's "love" for his Son and all believers

---

[28] Here in section II we have an *extended* and *compound* ring construction (A–B–A'–B'–A" + C–D–C'), which was, as noted earlier, also preceded by a parallel panel arrangement (A–B–C=A'–B'–C') in vv. 6–8.

[29] This section III illustrates a *double*, interlocking ring structure (A–B–A'–C–A"–B'–C'–D–C").

We thus observe (and, if attentive, also hear!) an intricate interweaving of topics simultaneously being unfolded as the discourse progresses sequentially and also folded back into the prayer as the many reiterations and rewordings reflect upon one another in synchronic fashion. The different key concepts thereby gain in complexity and theological significance by virtue of the varied semantic contexts and mutually reinforcing structural positions in which they occur.

The central thematic term "glory/glorify," for example, is introduced as having a reciprocal implication already at the beginning of the prayer when Jesus prays that he would be "glorified" for the sake of the Father (v. 1). This notion is underscored and expanded at the close of the first main division as Jesus stresses the fact that such "glory" has been his unalienable attribute together with his Father from eternity (5). In between these occurrences, the abstract concept is made concrete by being integrally associated with the mission of revelation and salvation that Christ came into this world to perform (especially v. 4). The active and passive/stative aspects of this crucial topic—"glorify" and "glory"—are further extended to Jesus' (by implication also the Father's) relationship with his disciples in v. 10 and, in keeping with the ever widening scope of the prayer, to all believers in v. 22 and its parallel in v. 24. In the process of discourse development then, this foundational idea is related also to other key terms, such as "knowledge" (vv. 3, 23), "giving" (9–11), "separation" (11a), "preservation" (11b), "unity" (11, 22–24), "commission" (21), and "love" (24).

It is important to observe that "glory/glorify" as used in chapter 17 forms additional intratextual links with its other occurrences in the Gospel, notably, at the core of the Prologue, where all of the major themes are introduced (1:14), in the conclusion to the account of Christ's first "sign" (2:11), as opposition begins to build up against his person and ministry (7:18, 8:50), at the death of Lazarus (11:4, 40), in the final event of his public ministry as recorded by John, when Jesus predicted his death (12:23, 28), at the very introduction to the farewell discourse (13:31–32) as well as periodically within it (14:13, 15:8, 16:14). A final occurrence once more connects the active and relational force of "glory" with that of ministry as allusive reference is made to the manner in which Peter would eventually "glorify" his Lord in death (21:19)—ironically, as the tradition goes, also by means of a crucifixion!

5.4 Rhetoric: The persuasive logic of the logotactic word in John 17

The preceding analyses illustrate the extensive, exquisite verbal rhetoric of John's Gospel. The result of such a skilled manipulation and arrangement of Christological concepts is the formation of an elaborate semantic network, one that traverses the composition from beginning to end, diachronically as well as synchronically. A convergence of core topics, such as we have in the final three verses of Jesus' prayer, produces a rhetorical peak that emphasizes both its overall theme ("glory" from beginning to end) and functional intent (consolation, encouragement, motivation, etc.). In this manner, form is expertly wedded to meaning as rhythmic diction and a harmonious arrangement of utterances constitute a congruous linguistic framework that supports the speaker's content, attitude, and purpose (the dimension of sound will be examined more closely below). It is, in short, an appeal for concord in terms of both form and content, which underscores the author's pragmatic aim of unifying Christ's followers of all ages with one another and corporately with their "glorious" Lord.

The reason why John 17 was fashioned in poetic form, if not actually as a poem, is not hard to discern. Such formalization is yet another instance of a tendency towards multi-leveled communication, which is exemplified in the Scriptures from beginning to end. Biblical discourse of an especially crucial nature, whether uttered by God (Christ) or one of his chosen spokesmen, typically reflects an artful convergence of structure, content, function, and feeling. Thus, the text is generally marked in a distinctly "special" way, using a variable range of the poetic devices available in ancient Hebrew and Greek. Such formal embellishment is not gratuitous, but it is always motivated by a number of rhetorical aims, notably, the creation of emotive impact and esthetic appeal to complement the essential thematic highlighting. As was noted above, this is a prominent characteristic of Johannine composition too, many passages of which manifest most of the same literary features found illustrated in John 17, though not always in such heavy concentration.

There is, accordingly, a pronounced "logotactic" quality about John's writings, that is, a strategic verbal rhetoric with a pronounced focus upon the very one who was called "the Word" (ὁ λόγος—John 1:1). Every lexical item counts, often in more ways than one (i.e., "semantic density"), not only with respect to its individual selection, but also in terms of its placement within the text in conjunction with other words of similar semantic import. The potential significance of meaning then arises on several semantic and pragmatic planes, both syntagmatically by conjunction and paradigmatically by association, literally as well as figuratively. The farewell "prayer" of Jesus to his Father in the presence of his disciples (and ultimately, all believers) is a natural place for such heightened discourse to occur. There is no doubt that the text's style and structure contribute a great deal to the profound impression that these words create for listeners in particular, for it was certainly meant to be uttered aloud (see below).

It is somewhat paradoxical then to observe that the "heightening" to be found in this Johannine discourse is rather different from what one might expect, based on other rhetorically embellished NT passages, such as Matt 5–7, Luke 14–16, 1 Cor 9, Heb 9, or 2 Pet 2. Most poetry depends in large measure upon the principle termed "defamiliarization" (*ostraneniye* 'making strange') by the Russian Formalist literary critics. This refers to language which deliberately diverges in a recognizable way from what is normal or expected, thereby giving it a special forcefulness and/or beauty of expression:

> The technique of art is to make objects "unfamiliar," to make the forms difficult, to increase the difficulty and length of perception because the process of perception is an aesthetic end in itself and must be prolonged. (Shklovsky 1965:12)

This is just the opposite of what we see in John 17, however. The style differs, in fact, from some of Christ's other discourses recorded in John in terms of its transparency and directness, reflecting little of the ambiguity that occurs elsewhere "to focus attention and urge interpretive effort" (Kotze 1987:57). Accordingly, the grammar and vocabulary (and as we shall see, the phonology too) is unusually simple and straightforward. There is a virtual absence of novelty with regard to syntax and sense. The classical lexical figures of speech, including poetic images, are virtually non-existent. There are no rhetorical questions, exclamations, radical ellipses, hyperboles, ironic/sarcastic utterances, explicit quotations, or direct citations. The overall effect of this text in terms of clarity, impact, and appeal is almost entirely a product of the selection of a basic set of key topics and their deployment in a diversity of recursive and overlapping patterns. These not only facilitate the listener's apprehension of the sense of the whole, but they also enhance one's perception of its euphonious, rhythmic, and balanced properties of sound.

And yet, the style of John 17, however plain and unadorned in a literary sense, would appear to me eminently appropriate, not only for the genre of personal prayer, but also with respect to the function which it was designed to carry out and the essential message that it was—and is—intended to communicate. In his role as the original "Paraclete" (cf. John 14:16, 1 John 2:1), Jesus addresses an appropriate "paracletic" appeal to his Father on behalf of all his followers. After attending to his own personal needs (vv. 1–5), he devotes the rest of the prayer to supplication with reference to the immediate and long-term needs of his disciples, and indeed, all believers. He thus stands as their companion, teacher, mediator, and advocate before his heavenly Father and intercedes for them, even as he also commissions, counsels, and encourages them for their forthcoming ministry to/in the world by recalling some of the central aspects of his Gospel message. In the process, Jesus draws attention to the indissoluble bonds which link himself, the Father, and all believers in a triangle of loving fellowship (v. 26), a divinely established relationship that is foregrounded verbally throughout the discourse by the many interwoven parallel and chiastic constructions.

Instead of defamiliarization, then, the composition of this chapter might be more accurately characterized as manifesting the technique of "re-familiarization"—a manifold reiteration of sound, sense, and syntax the rhetorical purpose of which is to consolidate as well as to motivate his followers with what they already (*should*) know. There are no special dramatic peaks or troughs and nothing really new here as far as content is concerned—just a basic review of what Jesus had been telling his disciples during his entire ministry (from John's unique point of view). The key topics (life, glory, truth, faith, love, etc.) and the themes which they embody appear in many other pericopes of this Gospel. This "Lord's prayer" thus represents a fundamental summary of Christ's theology at an especially critical juncture in the carrying out of his Father's saving plan.

The remarkable fact, from a literary as well as a pastoral perspective, is that such repetition is so artfully and affectively articulated. The rhetorical consequence of the Word at work is cumulative. Listeners are immediately attracted by the simplicity of style, the familiarity of content, the rhythmic flow, and the depth of feeling conveyed (both explicitly and implicitly throughout). As they are carried along conceptually by its fluid forward progression, the audience is subtly but inevitably drawn into the internal narrative event of communication. As a result, by the time that the message is actually applied to them as contemporary "believers" (vv. 20ff.), they are already embracing the words and thoughts of this prayer as if they were original auditors on the scene—listening reverently and hopefully as disciples of their beloved Master, the ever-living Word. What a challenge there is, then, to see to it that the vital force and feeling of this prayer emerges along with its content also in translation!

5.5 Orality: Markers of a literary text's "rhythmic envelope"

The three types of discourse analysis carried out above (from a *paradigmatic-topical*, *syntagmatic-propositional*, and *poetic-architectonic* perspective) provide a supportive textual and hermeneutical foundation for the focal point of the present study, which is the resonant sound fabric of John 17. Phonological qualities thus complement the lexical, syntactic, and larger textual organization of a given passage both to express additional aspects of, and also to enhance the already established features of denotative as well as connotative "meaning."[30] Such features—the standard tools of "oral

---

[30] Scott and Dean delineate a "sound mapping" approach to the analysis of NT discourse: "Our analytical approach proposes to map in graphic form a composition's sounds and then to analyze those sound effects according to the listening conventions in place when the compositions were created" (2009:2). This a more detailed variant of the method that I proposed in 1994 ("Oral-Aural Dynamics of the Word"), which was also developed more fully by Thomas and Thomas (2006). In contrast to my studies, including the present analysis, and also that of Thomas and Thomas, Scott and Dean appear at times to overly privilege and depend upon the pure sound structure of discourse for making their analytical observations and conclusions with respect to selected NT texts. For example, they claim with respect to the Pauline corpus that "[t]he real letter is not the manuscript, but the letter's spoken sounds" (2009:37). Thus, it would follow that "*sound creates structure*, sound trains the ear, and sound balances the importance of signifier and

5.5 Orality: Markers of a literary text's "rhythmic envelope"

typesetting" (Parunak 1981)—thus provided essential markers of structure, progression, deviation, and prominence within an ancient text.[31] This was true for written creations as well as more natural oral-aural ones. These phonic techniques and devices constitute the text's "rhythmic envelope" of semiotic significance,[32] which must accordingly also be seriously evaluated during any holistic, comprehensive examination. By altering such characteristics as the volume, stress, tempo, pitch, pause length and spacing, vowel color, and other paralinguistic variables, one can appreciably alter or modify the functional import and pragmatic attitude of a certain utterance. Therefore, responsible exegetical decisions need to be made with respect to this particular dimension of the text as with any other.[33] For example, the statement "I am not praying for the world" (John 17:19), can be understood quite differently depending on the rhythm and intonation with which it is pronounced. Thus, the various distinguishing features of sound, considered together in concert, are an important constituent of the overall discourse structure, for they convey a specific auditory impression of the emotive tone and attitude of the composition as it was first conceived of by its author-orator.[34]

---

signified.... *Sound itself* trains an audience's ear.... Attention to a composition's ear training may be *the only* access an interpreter can gain to a composition's structural organization, a feature that is fundamental to its meaning.... [Sound mapping] *contends with* semantics, but also recognizes the independent contributions to meaning made by sound itself in cultures that relied on public performance for literary publication" (ibid., 80, 140, 389, 2–3; italics added). I would prefer, however, to apply a more balanced, integrated methodology, one that recognizes the complementary, mutually reinforcing contribution to a text's meaning, including its rhetorical and esthetic dimensions, that is made by sound, lexis (e.g., serial and disjunctive repetition), syntax (e.g., significant word order variations), and macro-structural organization (e.g., formulas, transitional expressions, boundary markers such as *inclusio*, etc.)—an approach that is well demonstrated by Thomas and Thomas (2006) with respect to 1 Peter.

[31] Köstenberger and Patterson summarize a number of the oral features that characterize Hebrews, often considered to be one of the most literary of the NT letters: reference to it being a "word of exhortation" (13:22; cf. Acts 13:15); repeated use of "speak" (5:11, 6:9, 8:1, 13:6); "a large speech" and "dull in the ears" (5:11); "a conversational tone in order to diminish the sense of geographical distance"; use of diatribe (e.g., 3:16–18), and periodic rhythmic segments (e.g., 1:1–4) (2011:477–479).

[32] This term is from Kelber 1987:117.

[33] For an elaboration of this point, see Thomas 1990.

[34] I support an author-text-oriented hermeneutical approach to the biblical text and would therefore agree with the implied negative response to L. Silberman's

But what substantial evidence may be adduced from an ancient written document with regard to its original or intended oral elocution? There are three main sources for the diagnostic markers that, when examined together, serve to suggest the most likely oral—and rhetorical—"reading" of a given Bible passage. The most perceptible of these indicators, when available, is found in the text's quote margins, e.g., "Jesus was troubled in spirit and testified..." (John 13:21). This criterion must be used of course in conjunction with the immediate cotext in which it occurs, e.g., "[Jesus' disciples] kept asking, 'What does he mean by "a little while"? We don't understand what he is saying'" (John 16:18).

A second complex indicator of the authorial/speaker attitude or emotion that may have influenced a particular segment of Scripture is one's interpretation of the text-critical quality of the composition itself, the discourse genre, and the motivation or function of the speech event (text act) as a whole. It makes a difference, for example, to one's "oral interpretation" of John 17 if Christ's words are understood as a later redactor's pious addition to the Johannine text to be used as part of a Eucharistic liturgy in contrast to how they ostensibly appear to be originally intended—namely, as an intimate prayer by the Son to his heavenly Father, an implicit hortatory speech to Jesus' closest disciples, or as a subtle blending of both. In any case, the discourse genre of John 17 would differ in certain respects from what would be expected in John 12:44–50, for example, the last sermon of Christ's public ministry, in which he "cried out" (ἔκραξεν) to a crowd of listeners around him. However, the rhetorical differences are not all that

---

rhetorical question: "What if the text is vocally constructed? *Can the author's voice be silenced?*" (1987:4, italics added; cf. Schneidau 1987:138). This interpretive stance would conflict, for example, with a contemporary "reader-response" approach, in which meaning in literature (including the Scriptures) is considered to have little if anything to do with the original author's intentions, but is rather viewed as "the product of the interaction between a literary 'text' and a reader" within his or her present sociocultural setting (Tate 1991:194). So also Scott and Dean assert that "[c]onsistent with the insights of modern reception theory, meaning arises in reception" (2009:386). But how did that meaning become encoded into a verbal text in the first place? Surely, it was conceived, formulated, and expressed, whether orally or in some form of writing, in accordance with the communicative design of the original creative "voice." As in the case of the Hebrew Bible with its long-established Masoretic tradition of vocalization and accentuation (the *Masorah*), so also there is strong evidence to support the conclusion that "elocutionary traditions" arose in certain areas alongside a written one to guide the interpretation of NT discourse by means of the human voice (cf. Bartholomew 1987:74–75).

5.5 Orality: Markers of a literary text's "rhythmic envelope"

great, for both texts constitute what may be termed a "climactic pronouncement," a literary form which in the Gospels is usually distinguished through some distinctive formal means—phonologically, lexically, and/or syntactically (e.g., John 11:25–26). Such potential connotative variation is greatest when Jesus' speech is contrasted with that of other speakers, especially the unbelieving masses or hostile Jewish religious leaders, who are often characterized by their ignorant assertions, misleading questions, false conclusions, misinterpretations, and unreasonable demands (e.g., John 11:37, 47–50, 56).

A third important textual guide to the rhetorical dynamics of spoken discourse may be found in its manifest "style," that is, in its selection and arrangement of words and combinations of words on all levels of structural organization. This includes a great diversity of literary and oratorical devices, notably those that involve a deviation from normal or expected ("prosaic") verbal patterns, for example, an unusual order of syntactic components in the clause, parallelism of lexis and/or grammar, rhythmic arrangement, alliteration and assonance, exact and synonymous repetition, contrast and antithesis, condensation and elaboration, figurative language and imagery, or a combination of the preceding elements.[35] Such notable features, which may vary in the frequency in which they are used from one language to another, effect rhetorical functions such as "wholeness, aesthetic appeal, impact, appropriateness, coherence, cohesion, focus, and emphasis" within the discourse (De Waard and Nida 1986:80). All these contribute, in turn, to the essential "rhythmic envelope" of a composition which renders it more memorable, enjoyable, inspirational, etc., and yet also more challenging to reproduce with equivalent beauty and effect in another language, especially when the text is uttered aloud in translation.[36]

---

[35] De Waard and Nida observe: "These rhetorical processes may involve any and all levels and types of discourse structures, but in actual practice they are far more frequent at the micro-level of discourse structure rather than at the macro-level of the larger units" (1986:86). On the other hand, it should be pointed out that at least some of these features may also perform important delimiting (boundary marking) and distinguishing (peak-marking) functions on the larger domain of discourse—the periodic repetition of key terms and expressions, for example.

[36] For studies of Johannine aural-aural compositional technique in relation to 1 John, see Dudrey 2003 and Wendland 2008b:147–205.

5.6 Display: The oral-elocutionary structure of John 17

The discourses of Christ are not only orally constituted, but many of them, in John's Gospel at least, exhibit a definite "poetic" quality. Whether one designates these passages as poetry or prose (or "poetic prose"), it is clear that they have been structured and stylistically embellished in an elaborate and artistic manner. They have undoubtedly been composed in order to be recited or even chanted aloud to an audience that has the oratorical competence in Greek to appreciate what they were listening to.[37] My hypothesis concerning the basic discourse framework of John 17 is based on what I view as being its "oral-elocutionary" structure (see below). This phonological organization is not an isolated aspect of the text, however, but should be perceived and interpreted as a creative element that harmoniously complements, even as it is carefully integrated within, the corresponding paradigmatic and syntagmatic components of formal textual organization, as discussed earlier.

The following poetically formatted Greek text of John 17 is distinguished by its putative sequence of short, rhythmic "utterance units." These appear to be delineated by prominent patterns of repetition, both chiastic and parallel, complete syntactic constructions (but not necessarily complete clauses), and instances of alliteration (in particular, but also vowel assonance).[38] Some of the main points and patterns of oral-aural significance within this "elocutionary structure" are highlighted by typographical means (gray background, underlining, boldface and italic type). A line space indicates a boundary between smaller strophic (poetic) units, while a single extended underline marks a discourse "paragraph" break and a double underline breaks the text up into its three principal thematic divisions.

---

[37] "In the prayer with which he ends his farewell speech, Jesus delivers a long series of carefully balanced lines that, from the beginning…(17:1), to the end…(17:25), match the themes of glory and unity with measured majestic delivery. These are lines to be recited rather than words on a page to be scrutinized" (Brant 2004:121).

[38] A transliteration of the Greek text, which is that of UBS_4 (as found in Paratext 7.1) is given in Wendland 1994:33–36; the present format (below) reflects a slightly revised analysis of the source-language discourse.

5.6 Display: The oral-elocutionary structure of John 17

Ταῦτα ἐλάλησεν Ἰησοῦς   1[39]
καὶ ἐπάρας τοὺς ὀφθαλμοὺς αὐτοῦ
εἰς τὸν οὐρανὸν εἶπεν,
==

Πάτερ, ἐλήλυθεν ἡ ὥρα·
δόξασόν σου τὸν υἱόν,
ἵνα ὁ υἱὸς δοξάσῃ σέ,
καθὼς ἔδωκας αὐτῷ   2[40]
ἐξουσίαν πάσης σαρκός,
ἵνα πᾶν ὃ δέδωκας αὐτῷ
δώσῃ αὐτοῖς ζωὴν αἰώνιον.

αὕτη δέ ἐστιν ἡ αἰώνιος ζωὴ   3[41]
ἵνα γινώσκωσιν σὲ
τὸν μόνον ἀληθινὸν θεὸν
καὶ ὃν ἀπέστειλας Ἰησοῦν Χριστόν.

ἐγώ σε ἐδόξασα ἐπὶ τῆς γῆς   4[42]
τὸ ἔργον τελειώσας
ὃ δέδωκάς μοι
ἵνα ποιήσω·
καὶ νῦν δόξασόν **με** σύ, **πάτερ**,   5[43]
παρὰ σεαυτῷ
τῇ δόξῃ ᾗ εἶχον
πρὸ τοῦ τὸν κόσμον εἶναι
παρὰ σοί.
==

Ἐφανέρωσά **σου** τὸ ὄνομα   6[44]
τοῖς ἀνθρώποις
οὓς ἔδωκάς μοι ἐκ τοῦ κόσμου.

---

[39] At the beginning of each verse, the *English Standard Version* will again be given for reference.

17.1: "When Jesus had spoken these words, he lifted up his eyes to heaven, and said, "Father, the hour has come; glorify your Son that the Son may glorify you,..."

[40] "...since you have given him authority over all flesh, to give eternal life to all whom you have given him."

[41] "And this is eternal life, that they know you the only true God, and Jesus Christ whom you have sent."

[42] "I glorified you on earth, having accomplished the work that you gave me to do."

[43] "And now, Father, glorify me in your own presence with the glory that I had with you before the world existed."

[44] "I have manifested your name to the people whom you gave me out of the world. Yours they were, and you gave them to me, and they have kept your word."

σοὶ ἦσαν κἀμοὶ αὐτοὺς ἔδωκας
καὶ τὸν λόγον **σου** τετήρηκαν.

νῦν ἔγνωκαν   7⁴⁵
ὅτι πάντα
ὅσα δέδωκάς μοι
παρὰ σοῦ εἰσιν·
ὅτι τὰ ῥήματα   8⁴⁶
ἃ ἔδωκάς μοι
δέδωκα αὐτοῖς,
καὶ αὐτοὶ **ἔλαβον**
καὶ ἔγνωσαν ἀληθῶς
ὅτι **παρὰ σοῦ** ἐξῆλθον,
καὶ ἐπίστευσαν
ὅτι **σύ με** ἀπέστειλας.

ἐγὼ περὶ αὐτῶν **ἐρωτῶ**,   9⁴⁷
οὐ περὶ τοῦ κόσμου **ἐρωτῶ**
ἀλλὰ περὶ ὧν δέδωκάς μοι,
ὅτι σοί εἰσιν,
καὶ **τὰ ἐμὰ** πάντα σά ἐστιν   10⁴⁸
καὶ τὰ σά **ἐμά**,
καὶ δεδόξασμαι ἐν αὐτοῖς.
καὶ οὐκέτι εἰμὶ **ἐν τῷ κόσμῳ**,   11⁴⁹
καὶ αὐτοὶ **ἐν τῷ κόσμῳ** εἰσίν,
κἀγὼ πρὸς σὲ ἔρχομαι.

Πάτερ ἅγιε,
τήρησον αὐτοὺς
ἐν τῷ ὀνόματί σου
ᾧ δέδωκάς μοι,
ἵνα ὦσιν ἓν
καθὼς ἡμεῖς.

---

[45] "Now they know that everything that you have given me is from you."

[46] "For I have given them the words that you gave me, and they have received them and have come to know in truth that I came from you; and they have believed that you sent me."

[47] "I am praying for them. I am not praying for the world but for those whom you have given me, for they are yours."

[48] "All mine are yours, and yours are mine, and I am glorified in them."

[49] "And I am no longer in the world, but they are in the world, and I am coming to you. Holy Father, keep them in your name, which you have given me, that they may be one, even as we are one."

5.6 Display: The oral-elocutionary structure of John 17

ὅτε ἤμην μετ' αὐτῶν   12[50]
ἐγὼ ἐτήρουν αὐτοὺς
ἐν τῷ ὀνόματί σου
ᾧ δέδωκάς μοι,
καὶ ἐφύλαξα,
καὶ οὐδεὶς ἐξ αὐτῶν ἀπώλετο
εἰ μὴ ὁ υἱὸς τῆς ἀπωλείας,
ἵνα ἡ γραφὴ πληρωθῇ.

νῦν δὲ πρὸς σὲ ἔρχομαι   [cf. 11a]   13[51]
καὶ ταῦτα λαλῶ **ἐν τῷ κόσμῳ**
ἵνα ἔχωσιν τὴν χαρὰν τὴν ἐμὴν
πεπληρωμένην ἐν ἑαυτοῖς.

ἐγὼ δέδωκα **αὐτοῖς** τὸν λόγον **σου**   14[52]
καὶ **ὁ κόσμος** ἐμίσησεν αὐτούς,
ὅτι οὐκ εἰσὶν **ἐκ τοῦ κόσμου**
καθὼς ἐγὼ οὐκ εἰμὶ **ἐκ τοῦ κόσμου.**
οὐκ ἐρωτῶ ἵνα ἄρῃς αὐτοὺς **ἐκ τοῦ κόσμου,**   15[53]
ἀλλ' ἵνα τηρήσῃς αὐτοὺς **ἐκ τοῦ πονηροῦ.**
ἐκ τοῦ κόσμου οὐκ εἰσὶν   16[54]
καθὼς ἐγὼ οὐκ εἰμὶ **ἐκ τοῦ κόσμου.**

ἁγίασον αὐτοὺς ἐν τῇ **ἀληθείᾳ**·   17[55]
ὁ λόγος ὁ σὸς **ἀλήθειά** ἐστιν.
καθὼς ἐμὲ **ἀπέστειλας** εἰς τὸν κόσμον,   18[56]
κἀγὼ **ἀπέστειλα αὐτοὺς** εἰς τὸν κόσμον·
καὶ ὑπὲρ αὐτῶν ἐγὼ **ἁγιάζω** ἐμαυτόν,   19[57]
ἵνα ὦσιν **καὶ αὐτοὶ ἡγιασμένοι ἐν ἀληθείᾳ.**   [cf. 12a]

===

[50] "While I was with them, I kept them in your name, which you have given me. I have guarded them, and not one of them has been lost except the son of destruction, that the Scripture might be fulfilled."

[51] "But now I am coming to you, and these things I speak in the world, that they may have my joy fulfilled in themselves."

[52] "I have given them your word, and the world has hated them because they are not of the world, just as I am not of the world."

[53] "I do not ask that you take them out of the world, but that you keep them from the evil one."

[54] "They are not of the world, just as I am not of the world."

[55] "Sanctify them in the truth; your word is truth."

[56] "As you sent me into the world, so I have sent them into the world."

[57] "And for their sake I consecrate myself, that they also may be sanctified in truth."

Οὐ περὶ τούτων δὲ **ἐρωτῶ** μόνον, 20[58]
ἀλλὰ καὶ περὶ τῶν πιστευόντων
διὰ τοῦ λόγου αὐτῶν **εἰς ἐμέ**,
ἵνα πάντες **ἓν ὦσιν**, 21[59]
καθὼς σύ, **πάτερ, ἐν ἐμοὶ**
κἀγὼ **ἐν σοί**,
ἵνα καὶ αὐτοὶ **ἐν ἡμῖν ὦσιν**,
ἵνα ὁ κόσμος πιστεύῃ
ὅτι σύ με ἀπέστειλας.

κἀγὼ τὴν δόξαν 22[60]
ἣν δέδωκάς μοι
δέδωκα αὐτοῖς,
ἵνα ὦσιν **ἓν**
καθὼς ἡμεῖς **ἕν**,
ἐγὼ **ἐν αὐτοῖς** 23[61]
καὶ **σὺ** ἐν ἐμοί,
ἵνα ὦσιν τετελειωμένοι εἰς **ἕν**,
ἵνα γινώσκῃ ὁ κόσμος
ὅτι σύ με ἀπέστειλας
καὶ **ἠγάπησας** αὐτοὺς [cf. 17a]
καθὼς ἐμὲ ἠγάπησας.

Πάτερ, ὃ δέδωκάς **μοι**, 24[62]
θέλω ἵνα ὅπου **εἰμὶ ἐγὼ**
κἀκεῖνοι ὦσιν μετ᾽ **ἐμοῦ**,
ἵνα θεωρῶσιν τὴν δόξαν τὴν **ἐμήν**,
ἣν δέδωκάς **μοι** [cf. 22a]
ὅτι ἠγάπησάς **με**
πρὸ καταβολῆς κόσ**μου**.

---

[58] "I do not ask for these only, but also for those who will believe in me through their word,..."

[59] "...that they may all be one, just as you, Father, are in me, and I in you, that they also may be in us, so that the world may believe that you have sent me."

[60] "The glory that you have given me I have given to them, that they may be one even as we are one,..."

[61] "...I in them and you in me, that they may become perfectly one, so that the world may know that you sent me and loved them even as you loved me."

[62] "Father, I desire that they also, whom you have given me, may be with me where I am, to see my glory that you have given me because you loved me before the foundation of the world."

5.6 Display: The oral-elocutionary structure of John 17

πάτερ δίκαιε,	25[63]
καὶ ὁ κόσμος σε οὐκ ἔγνω,	
ἐγὼ δέ σε ἔγνων,	
καὶ οὗτοι ἔγνωσαν	
ὅτι σύ με ἀπέστειλας·	[cf. 21b, 23b]
καὶ ἐγνώρισα αὐτοῖς τὸ ὄνομά σου	26[64]
καὶ γνωρίσω,	
ἵνα ἡ ἀγάπη	
ἣν ἠγάπησάς με	[cf. 24b]
ἐν αὐτοῖς ᾖ	
κἀγὼ ἐν αὐτοῖς.	

==

The most prominent characteristic of John 17, as visualized above and viewed as a poetic oral-aural discourse, is the abundance of relatively short utterance units, averaging roughly four words each. These lined segments (each one being presumably followed by a short or a longer pause, depending on the syntactic construction) form the basic framework according to which the prayer rhythmically unfolds as it is being uttered. The line breaks are not made arbitrarily, however, or simply following the progression of complete syntactic constituents. Rather, various literary-poetic devices, featuring different types of correspondence, contrast, variation, and parallelism, appear within the text to assist in the demarcation of lineal units. This is illustrated in the middle of the first strophe of v. 1, as reproduced below and accompanied by brief explanatory remarks:

...δόξασόν σου τὸν υἱόν,	A chiastic construction delineates the first two lines: δόξασόν σου + τὸν υἱόν
ἵνα ὁ υἱὸς δοξάσῃ σέ,	= ὁ υἱὸς + δοξάσῃ σέ.
καθὼς ἔδωκας αὐτῷ	Parallel endings serve to define lines 3 and 5 (see below).
ἐξουσίαν πάσης σαρκός,	Sibilant alliteration runs throughout line 4.
ἵνα πᾶν ὃ δέδωκας αὐτῷ...	ἔδωκας **αὐτῷ** + δέδωκας αὐτῷ.

---

[63] "O righteous Father, even though the world does not know you, I know you, and these know that you have sent me."

[64] "I made known to them your name, and I will continue to make it known, that the love with which you have loved me may be in them, and I in them."

Variations from established patterns constitute evidence for both boundaries (whether a new line, strophe, or larger unit) and also possible points of emphasis, as when lines are especially long. The latter are employed to highlight key concepts, e.g., "and the one whom you sent Jesus Christ" (καὶ ὃν ἀπέστειλας Ἰησοῦν Χριστόν) in v. 3b, and often for contrastive effect to accent some essential idea, often the concept of antithetical "world-system," e.g., "I do not ask that you remove them from the world (οὐκ ἐρωτῶ ἵνα ἄρῃς αὐτοὺς ἐκ τοῦ κόσμου) in v. 15a. The shorter segments, on the other hand, frequently form a series of familiar, reassuring theological concepts, e.g., v. 11b: Πάτερ ἅγιε, / τήρησον αὐτοὺς / ἐν τῷ ὀνόματί σου / ᾧ δέδωκάς μοι, / ἵνα ὦσιν ἓν /καθὼς ἡμεῖς.

The following is a selection of other important literary-rhetorical features of elocutionary significance in John 17 that illustrates the artistic diversity that this single passage exhibits. As displayed on the diagram above, these devices often operate in concordant concert to enhance the text's expression of content and emotion as well as to facilitate the pragmatic impact and appeal of its public oral articulation.

- *Vocatives* addressing the Father interrupt the rhythmic flow and usually mark the onset of a new strophe or major thought sequence, e.g., "Holy Father" (Πάτερ ἅγιε) in 11b (cf. also 1a, 24a, 25a). There are exceptions, apparently utilized to create a special rhetorical effect. For example, the line-final vocative heightens the entire utterance of 5a, for example, while the line-medial vocative in 21a underscores the unity of the Father and the Son: καθὼς σύ, **πάτερ,** ἐν ἐμοὶ.

- *Contrastive and complementary sound sequences* provide cohesion to certain lines and give the discourse as a whole a distinctive lyric progression. Such phonic techniques include the following (among others): patterns of contrastive vowel quality, e.g., the predominantly long vowels of 9a (ω, ου) with the shorter ones in 9b (ε, ι, ο, α) after ἀλλὰ; consonance, e.g., word-final ν in 3b; assonance, e.g., word-final η in 3a; phonological symmetry and word-play, e.g., the final utterance unit of v. 1: ἵνα ὁ υἱὸς δοξάσῃ σέ, where sibilant alliteration complements the final stress on "you" (Father)—or οὐδεὶς...ἀπώλετο / ὁ υἱὸς...ἀπωλείας in 12b; subtle rhyming sequences, e.g., the line-final

5.6 Display: The oral-elocutionary structure of John 17

words reiterating the 'μ' sound that focus on the first person (Christ) in v. 24—or the rhymed couplet ἣν (δόξαν) δέδωκάς **μοι** ὅτι **ἠγάπησάς με**, stressing the "glory" of God's "love" (also in v. 24).

- The *reiteration* of key words, phrases, and clauses can function to foreground the topics involved. This is evident in the following examples: "eternal life" in 2b–3a (chiastically arranged); "with you" in 5a–b; "give/gave to me/them" in 6–8; "keep them...your name...given to me" in 11b–12a; "out of/from the world/evil" in 14–16; "know" in 25–26; "that you have sent me" in 21b, 23b, and 25b; the "love" that bonds Jesus ("I/me") and all believers "in them" in 26b.

- *Parallel* and especially *chiastic patterns* of synonymous and/or contrastive elements in utterance-final position are sometimes used to demarcate lines. We see this, for example in: "glorify you/the son—the son/glorify you" (1b); "I-have-given/to-them—they/they-received" (8b); "not they-are of the world—I not I am of the world" (14b); "you, Father, /in me—and-I/in you" (21a). Alternatively, such patterns may indicate the *beginning* or *ending* of strophic units (poetic paragraphs). Examples are: "life eternal...eternal life" (2b–3a, *anadiplosis*); "I-manifested your the-name...the-word your I-have-kept" (6a–6b, *inclusio*); "concerning them I-ask—not concerning the world I-ask" (9a, *aperture*); "I-am/in the world—in the world/they-are" (11a, *closure*); "to you I am coming" (11a, 13a, *exclusio*); "sanctify them in the truth—that they too may be sanctified ones in truth" (17a/19b, *inclusio*); "and you-loved/them—as me/you-loved" (23b, *closure*; cf. 24b and 26b, *epiphora*).

- *Redundant* (independent) *pronominal forms* may be used for emphasis, contrast, and/or to "fill out" an utterance rhythmically or euphoniously, e.g., "glorify **me you** Father" (δόξασόν **με σύ**, πάτερ) in 5a; "and **they** received" (καὶ **αὐτοὶ** ἔλαβον) in 8a; "**as for me**, I have given them" (**ἐγὼ** δέδωκα αὐτοῖς) in 14a; "and **I too** I sent them... (**κἀγὼ** ἀπέστειλα αὐτοὺς) in 18b, which correlates with "**me** you sent" (**ἐμὲ** ἀπέστειλας) in 18a.

- *Word-order variations* too, that is, the front-shifting or back-shifting of an element out of its expected grammatical position in the clause, are employed for rhythmic purposes and especially to spotlight selected items of information. For example, we have "**your** son" (**σου** τὸν υἱόν) in 1b; "so that **everything that you have given to him**, he might give them..." (ἵνα **πᾶν ὃ δέδωκας αὐτῷ** δώσῃ αὐτοῖς) in 2b; "and **the one whom you sent**, Jesus Christ" (καὶ **ὃν ἀπέστειλας** Ἰησοῦν Χριστόν) in 3b; "the glory which I had...**with you** [back-shift]" (τῇ δόξῃ ᾗ εἶχον...**παρὰ σοί**) in 5b; "yours they were and <u>to me</u> them you gave" (**σοὶ** ἦσαν <u>κἀμοὶ</u> αὐτοὺς ἔδωκας) in 6b; "they know for sure that **from you** I came" (ἔγνωσαν ἀληθῶς ὅτι **παρὰ σοῦ** ἐξῆλθον) in 8b; "all **mine** <u>yours</u> is" (τὰ **ἐμὰ** πάντα <u>σά</u> ἐστιν) in 10a; "your word is **truth**" (ὁ λόγος ὁ σὸς **ἀλήθειά** ἐστιν) in 17a.[65]

- *Polysyndeton*, using a small set of reiterated conjunctions (especially *kai*, *hoti*, and *hina*), serves to establish line breaks and also to maintain the forward rhythmic progression. For example, each line in the sequence spanning the strophe of vv. 7–8 begins as follows: *nun* (now)...*hoti* (that)...*hosa* (as much as)...[from you]...*hoti*...*ha* (that which)...*kai* (and)...*kai*...*hoti*...*kai*...*hoti*.... Similarly, in the strophe covering vv. 9–10 we have: *egô* (I)...*ou* (not)...*alla* (but)...*hoti*...*kai*...*kai*...*kai*...*kai*...*kai*...*kagô* (and I). Therefore, asyndeton, the absence of any link word, is marked and often used to help signal the onset of a new strophe, e.g., in 1a–b, 4a, 6a, 9a, 11b, 14b, 17a, 20a, 24a, and 25a.

As has been mentioned, figurative language is notably absent in John 17 (see 16:25).[66] It almost sounds as if the discourse has been deliberately swept clean of all similes, metaphors, metonyms, synecdoches, personifications, and descriptive adjectives. The diction is profoundly iterative and relatively unadorned—arguably for both rhythmic and thematic purposes. The basic phonological patterns are uncomplicated and harmonic, sharply focused

---

[65] The English words in bold correspond to the Greek terms that are viewed as being highlighted through word order in the biblical text.

[66] I owe this observation to George Huttar—namely, the reference to Christ's significant assertion about no longer using "figures of speech" (παροιμίαις) when discoursing with his disciples (16:25).

5.6 Display: The oral-elocutionary structure of John 17

upon those recurrent lexical items of topical significance. Such patterning is, of course, most appropriate for a highly personal intercessory-consolatory prayer and serves as an excellent instance of what the Formalist linguist Roman Jakobson termed the "poetic function" of good literature:

> The poetic function projects the principle of equivalence from the axis of selection into the axis of combination. Equivalence is promoted to the constitutive device of the sequence.... The selection is produced on the basis of equivalences, similarity and dissimilarity, synonymity and antonymity, while the combination, the build up of the sequence, is based on contiguity. (Jakobson 1960:358)

In the case of a passage like John 17, varied formal instances and patterns of similarity with respect to sound, sense, and syntax re-appear as the text moves forward in time and presents the development of Christ's principal ideas and aims. These correspondences and contrasts continue to play off one another in each new context, thereby enriching the discourse semantically and empowering it pragmatically to reach an obvious peak of content and emotion at the final strophe, where a complex of themes converge: Father-Son-all believers, intimate fellowship, saving knowledge, confidence, love—and all these in contrast to what "the [unbelieving/hostile] world" has to offer.

The oral-elocutionary structure of John 17 as formatted above is a hypothetical proposal, of course, but it has been supported in its demarcation according to an assortment of recognized linguistic and literary criteria. The text manifests a number of variant readings, though none of these is in serious dispute.[67] Of greater concern is the fact that the ancient vocal tradition of the received New Testament text is not recoverable, and the actual pronunciation of Hellenistic (or *Koiné*) Greek is unknown.[68]

---

[67] R. Omanson lists seven noteworthy variants for the chapter, but the current UBS$_4$ Greek text reading is rated highly as "A" or "B" in each case (2006:206–7).

[68] In this connection, Scott and Dean observe: "We cannot know for certain how Hellenistic Greek was pronounced in any particular time or place in the Greco-Roman world, but we know that its spelling was phonetic and letters were pronounced consistently, whatever the pronunciation scheme" (2009:6). In addition, the formal analysis of the text of John 17, for example, is based on the essential principle of *repetition*, in which case the precise phonological quality of the text or its individual sounds is not a point of major concern.

Furthermore, there is little external evidence available, for instance, from ancient Christian commentaries, to confirm the proposed lyric style in this chapter. However, several detailed analyses of the biblical text, which were arrived at independently, generally support my results with respect to the individual lines and the main divisions in particular.[69] For example, Hansford's conclusion regarding 1 John, that "John intended it to be read aloud" and that "the author wrote much of [the work] in poetic parallelisms" is similar to my own about John 17 (Hansford 1992:129), except that we disagree somewhat in our criteria for establishing the onset of a new strophe.[70]

As a point of comparison, two major English translations (that I am currently aware of)—the *New Jerusalem Bible* and Eugene Peterson's *The Message*—also construe John 17 as a poetic composition and hence format the text as a poem. Many, probably most, of the proposed poetic lines in both of these versions are the same as those that I have indicated, though there are a number of differences too, notably in the case of potentially longer lines. In addition, these two versions do not segment the text into smaller strophic (paragraph) units. The NJB, for example, makes only a single break at v. 14, thereby eliminating even the obvious divisions of the discourse, that is, at v. 6 and v. 20.[71] Such a policy of formatting obscures the text's macro-structure as well as its micro-organization, the results of which could subsequently impact negatively on one's oral articulation of this pericope.

5.7 Implications: Seeking a rhetorical-poetic style for Bible translation

Rhetoric involves the functionally motivated use of linguistic form—actually a complex structure of diverse, but integrated, macro- and microforms—that serves to transmit an essential part of the original meaning (i.e., *form has meaning!*). Since these forms are language-specific, it might

---

[69] See, for example, Malatesta 1971; Hansford 1992. There are also some significant divergences in our proposals (e.g., Malatesta, ibid., 192).

[70] I would give more weight to a vocative phrase as a possible indicator of a poetic aperture, just as it would function also for prosaic paragraphs. In any case, Hansford's proposed poetic lineation of 1 John is very similar to mine for John 17.

[71] In *The Message*, discourse breaks occur before vv. 6, 13, 20, and 24.

seem at first that the translation of rhetoric from one language to another, especially in the case of poetry, is an utter impossibility. Indeed, many translators (teams) have come to this conclusion and simply ignore or overlook the rhetorical and poetic dimensions of communication during their work. Some translation teams may simply lack, for one reason or another, the competence or capacity to adequately deal with yet another new analytical task. They thus limit themselves to what they assume is an accurate rendering of the cognitive content of the biblical text, expressed in a more or less natural target language (TL) style.

The preceding text analyses have hopefully suggested how a significant portion of the inscribed "meaning" (connotative, emotive, esthetic, etc.) is lost when only the denotative aspect is dealt with. But more than that:

Denotative meaning can either be decisively clarified, obscured, and/or subverted by rhetorical and poetic formalizations. Thus, these forms, including those that involve the phonic fabric of the text, do not simply function connotatively, but practically speaking, function denotatively as well. This nexus of denotative and connotative meaning, I think, needs to be highlighted when we present our case to Bible translators.[72]

A helpful framework then for exploring the possibility of incorporating poetry (or "poetic" discourse) and rhetoric as part of the process of interlingual communication is provided by the "literary functional equivalence" (or *"LiFE"*) approach to Bible translation. The general framework within which such a method may be conceived in terms of its nature and purpose may be stated as follows:

> Translation is the conceptually mediated re-composition of one contextually framed text within a different cultural and sociolinguistic communication setting in the most accurate, relevant, and functionally equivalent manner feasible, that is, semantically correspondent and stylistically marked, more or less, in keeping with the designated job description agreed upon for the target language project concerned.[73]

---

[72] D. Fitzgerald, personal correspondence, 2012.

[73] This quote is adapted from the text found in Wendland 2011:68; for another description of "functional equivalence" translating, see de Waard and Nida 1986:36–37.

The communicative functions being referred to here include the text's incorporated sequences and combinations of "speech acts," which were discussed earlier, as well as its accompanying pragmatic features—that is, aspects of connotation, beauty, impact, and appeal. In a *"LiFE"* method of analysis and translation, then, special attention is given to the literary (or oratorical) dimension of discourse, in terms of the target as well as the source language.[74] In this case, "literary" refers in particular to both the artistic (form-oriented) and associated rhetorical (function-oriented) characteristics of a specific text.[75]

The manifold type of analysis applied to John 17 above was comprised of four discrete components: paradigmatic-topical, syntagmatic-propositional, poetic-architectonic, and oral-elocutionary. The results of these individual studies enable the analyst to develop a plausible "form-functional profile" of the source language (SL) document, which identifies those distinctive forms and combinations of form that carry out precise functions in the communication process. This enables a fuller interpretation of the original message to be made and lays the foundation for its rendering in another language. Accordingly, translators must seek to reproduce the most relevant and necessary facets of the overall meaning intended by the SL text, including its functional dynamics. They accomplish this by utilizing the appropriate formal resources available in the TL in accordance with the detailed "job commission" (*brief*) that has been agreed upon by project organizers.[76] An inverse type of compositional procedure must now be carried out as different structural and stylistic forms in the TL are selected in order to duplicate, to the extent possible, the assumed intended functions of the source text. The objective is to produce a translation that is not only accurate in terms of content, but is also formally appropriate for, acceptable, and even appealing, to the target community for whom it is being prepared.

I cannot elaborate upon the detailed principles and procedures of Bible translation here,[77] but will simply focus on the goal of preparing

---

[74] For some background regarding this methodology and its application to Bible translation, see Wendland 2011:chs. 1 and 3.

[75] I view "oratorical" as being the *oral-aural* equivalent of "literary" in terms of reference, simply to distinguish the two different modes of transmission—writing and speech.

[76] For details, see Wendland 2011:76–78.

[77] I elaborate my preferred approach in relation to a number of other methodologies in Wendland 2004b:ch. 2.

5.7 Implications: Seeking a rhetorical-poetic style for Bible translation

a *LiFE*-related "rhetorical oral-aural" rendering in a Bantu language. When embarking upon this study goal in the early 1990s (a personal investigation that has continued to the present day), I also wanted to discover the answer to this question: Is it necessary, desirable, or even feasible to replicate a "poetic" creation of Scripture by means of a corresponding rendition in a modern African language? As part of my research,[78] a set of additional questions had to be addressed; among them are the following:

- What are the precise socio-rhetorical functions of the diverse poetic sub-genres present in the TL tradition *vis-à-vis* those manifested in the SL text? Has sufficient research been done to enable one to answer this question, or is more, now focused investigation needed?

- Is there a certain lyric composition that is common in a given African sociocultural context, for example, one that is used for the purpose of expressing a prayer to the deity (or the ancestors), such as an appeal for rain in a time of drought, or healing in the event of an epidemic of some sort?

- How flexible are indigenous poetic genres and rhetorical devices with respect to form, content, function, and or setting—in other words, can such local forms be adapted for use in the Scriptures, in oral as well as written texts? What happens, for example, to a traditional oral-aural genre once its typical flexibility is firmly fixed by the written word?

- Can such a drastic shift in medium, i.e., from oral to written, be successfully accompanied by an analogous change in semantic content and communicative function to match that of the biblical document?

---

[78] See, for example, Wendland 1993; Zogbo and Wendland 2000; Wendland, 2013.

5.8 Translation: An experiment in intertextual generic re-presentation

In an attempt to answer questions such as those above (and others), an experiment was conducted at the seminary where I teach, involving a special workshop that compared Hebrew poetry with the Bantu poetic genres from six different language groups. Following a careful exegesis of a number of Psalm texts, the participants were invited to exercise their artistic talents when translating selected passages into their respective mother tongues, using an appropriate indigenous genre and seeking "literary (oratorical) functional equivalence" in the vernacular.[79] After ten weeks of practice, discussion, and revision, many successful versions resulted, including several that were performed in song. The participants were then assigned John 17:1–9 and the same procedure of trial and testing was followed. The most distinctive rendition that emerged from the group of about twenty performers was the expansive Tonga poetic text reproduced below, which is accompanied on the right by a relatively literal back-translation into English:[80]

1	Nteelela, Taataangu, ciya ciindi ncencico cino, Ta!	Pay attention to me, my Father, that very time—it's here, Dad!
2	Swiilila, Omuzyali, ndilemekezya ime ndemwanaako, Ta!	Listen, my Parent, honor me, I am your very child, Dad!

---

[79] In the case of a written/printed version "literary" criteria would be utilized as the basis for making a critical evaluation; in the case of an oral rendition, certain "oratorical" criteria would also come into play. Many of these diagnostic features would be the same, e.g., patterns of parallelism, but the oral version would be additionally judged according to its phonological qualities, e.g., rhythm, wordplay, euphony, etc.

[80] (Chi)Tonga is a southeastern Bantu language spoken as a mother-tongue by several million people living in southern Zambia and northern Zimbabwe. The following version was translated and performed by Salimo Hachibamba in 1992. The English back-translation was prepared by Hachibamba and Wendland; admittedly, it can provide only a poor image and rough impression of the original, which is a masterful adaptation of a traditional oral genre, ideally meant to be publicly performed. A corresponding translation in (chi)Chewa in a completely different vernacular poetic style (*ndakatulo*) was composed by the author working with several seminary students. It may be found in Wendland 1994:29–30.

5.8 Translation: An experiment in intertextual generic re-presentation

3	Komvwa, Omwaalu, ame lwangu mbubonya buyo ndakulemekezya!	Hear, my Elder, I for my part, in the very same way I have honored you!
4	(Wakacibona wakaambaati, "Lemeka kanike, akalo kakulemeke.")	(He who saw/witnessed it, he spoke thus, "Honor the little child, and it will also honor you.")
5	Langa mbookandisakizya, mbookandipa nguzu me, Ta.	Look how you got me ready, how you gave me power, Dad.
6	Omwaalu, nduwe ooti njendelezye mbwali muntu.	My Elder, you are the one who says that I should govern every person.
7	Oobo mbwepa buumi butamani kuli boonse, Taataangu.	That is how I give unending life to them all, O my Father.
8	(Bona, boonse mbookandipa, mbookapa mumaanza aangu, bubutambula buumi oobu.)	(See, all those you gave to me, those whom you placed into my hands, they receive this life.)
9	Taata, mboobu buumu butamani, nkuziba nduwe yebo.	My Father, here is life unending, it is to know you yourself.
10	Lwako olikke nduwe Leza, Leza mwinimwini ncobeni.	You alone, you are God—God genuine and true.
11	Nde Jesu okandituma, abandizibilizya ambebo, Omwaalu.	Me Jesus whom you sent, let them also know me, my Elder!
12	(Wakacibona wakaambati, "Maulu aamufu azibilwa kumwana.")	(He who saw it, he spoke thus, "The legs of the deceased are revealed in [his/her] child.")
13	Swiilila, Taataangu, nduwe ngwendemeka ansi aano.	Listen, my Father, you are the one I honor here on earth.
14	Nduonda mulimo ngookandituma—iiyi, ngooyu waba.	I've hammered out the work you sent me for—yes, here it is, all done!
15	Yebo, Omwaalu, ono ndelemekezye ndemwaaanaako, Ta!	You, my Elder, now you may honor me—me your own child, Dad!
16	(Ndacobonaace ciindi ncindakali aaTaaata, Mwalu wangu, mubulemu.)	(I have already seen it when I was with my Father, my Elder, in honor.)

17	Omwaalu, andibe abulemu kwako mbwindakajisi alili, Ta.	O Elder, may I receive honor at your place, that which I've always had, Dad.
18	Obuya mbwindakajisi nitwakali limwi ooko, Omwaalu wangu.	It is that [honor] which I possessed when we were together there, my Elder.
19	Ndakali bujisi alili, nyika eeyi kiitana akuba.	I possessed it always, even before this very land [earth] came into being.
20	Langa, babone mbondizandwide, balelwa, mbaaba mbobabede.	Look, see them, those you set apart for me, they've been well cared for—here they are, all of them!
21	Teelela mbubaambilwa, baiya aabo mbookampa kuti bakuzibe.	Listen to what they've been told, they have learned, the ones you gave me, to know you.
22	Tee, mbabakugaminide baya, mbabatakuumyi musako, Taataangu!	Isn't it true that they've been appointed for you—nobody would beat you with a rod on their account, O my Father!
23	Iiyi, okabapa kulindime, ncobaabamba majwi aako we.	Yes, you gave them to me, that's why they keep your words, right.
24	Langa, bazibe kuti zyoonse zyandime zizwa kooko.	Look, they know that everything of mine comes from there.
25	Majwi, mwaambo wako uulya ngookapa kuli ndime—	Words, that wise instruction of yours that you gave to me—
26	abalo ngonguwo lwawo wini ndubakatambula kuzwa kwangu.	as well as to them, that is really the very thing which they received from me.
27	Ani batazibili-nzi kuti ndakazwa kuli nduwe?	How could it be then that they would not know that I came from you?
28	Inga badonaika buti kuti wakandituma nduwe, Taata?	And how could they doubt that the one who sent me is you, O Father?
29	Nkoo iimbakombele me lwangu, mbe nebalombela kwako.	Say, just allow me to ask for them—me myself, let me make petition for them at your place.

5.8 Translation: An experiment in intertextual generic re-presentation

30	Mpailile buleya—nkumbilili buna bunji na? Kwalo pe!	Should I pray for others—should I plead for the public? Certainly not!
31	Nee, ndakombela baabo mbookandipa balikke pesi!	Noo, I will make petition only for those whom you gave me, that's all!

The preceding Tonga rendition of John 17:1–9[81] was composed according to the norms of the *ciyabilo* genre, a traditional popular, highly personalized, declamatory type of oral poetry. Typically, such poems are sung or rhythmically chanted in short stanzas of variable length, each unit being punctuated at the end by short musical bursts played on an ancient friction drum. The Tonga *ciyabilo* is a highly emotive, individualized lyric poem in which the singer normally expresses an often cryptic message to an audience of family, friends, and acquaintances.[82] It may deal with any of life's experiences, great and small, from the individual perspective of the poet-singer, but topics pertaining to love and death predominate. Each of the *lyric lines* corresponds to a single breath span, after which there is a short pause before the next line begins. Upon completing a strophe of several lines, the rhythm drum intervenes to provide artistic variety, dramatic relief, and an opportunity for the composer to mentally prepare the next verse. At times, in addition to the drumming interlude, a piece of traditional wisdom in prose will be inserted (indicated by the four lines in parentheses above), usually a proverb or an adaptation of one, which serves to support either what was just sung or a certain aspect of the content that will be expressed in the next strophe. In the preceding *ciyabilo* the nine strophes (demarcated by the alternating gray or white background for the verse numbers above) were kept uniform at three lines each; this structuring device would make it easier for another person to learn and perform the piece in public.

The *ciyabilo* based on John 17 features a number of the key stylistic devices that are normally associated with this traditional performing art

---

[81] Although it begins a new poetic segment, verse 9 was included in this reduced form of the discourse since it explicitly mentions "prayer" and was felt by the artist to be a good conclusion to his composition.

[82] It is getting increasingly difficult to find composers (and instrumentalists) of such ancient poems nowadays. The genre is not very fashionable among the younger generation, though a number of older performers are still popular on the radio and generate a strong nostalgia within older folk.

form. They are summarized below (the numbers in parentheses refer to specific lines in the preceding poem):

- There is an abundance of vocative phrases, which accent the highly emotive tone of the prayer (as in the traditional genre) and express the close interpersonal relationship of the poet and his divine addressee. The utterance-final *Ta* (1), for example, is an abbreviated, more familiar variant of *Taata* "my Father," which may be extended for rhythmic purposes to *Taataangu* "my Father mine." Another means of such extension plus emphasis is provided by a redundant vocative pronoun (as in the Greek), e.g., *yebo Omwaalu* "you, O Elder" (15).

- Poetic lines, especially strophe-initial ones, often lead off with a focus word of some sort to prepare the audience for what follows. In addition to a vocative (see [a] above), an imperative calling for perception may appear in this position, such as "pay attention / listen / hear!" (lines 1–3), or some type of intensifying particle, e.g., *Tee* "Isn't it true that...?" (22) and *Iiyi* "Yes!" (23).

- The alliterative rhyming concordial system of Bantu languages is capitalized on at times to focus upon the key concept of a particular phrase or clause, e.g., the /c/ of *ciindi* "time" in (1), or the /b/ of *boonse* "all [people]" and *buumi* "life" in (7–8). Alternatively, such phonic patterning simply adds to the euphony of the text and hence its aural appeal, e.g., *Langa, ba̱bone mḇondizandwide, ba̱lelwa, mḇaaba̱ mḇoba̱bede* (20), which initiates a new strophe as well as a major division in the prayer, as Jesus turns to his disciples.

- Appositional doublets are employed to underscore important topics in the discourse, e.g., "how you got me ready, how you gave me power" (5); "all those you gave to me, those you placed into my hands" (8). More extensive synonymous parallelism within a set of utterances, analogous to Hebrew poetry, also occurs, as in (2–3, 17–18, 29–31).

- Recursive interjective "comments" are an effective focusing device that immediately attracts attention on account of their incorporation of traditional proverbs and wisdom sayings. For example, "he who saw/witnessed it, he spoke thus" is a formulaic introduction to the proverb that follows, "Honor the child, and it will also honor you" (4). This gives an African flavor to Jesus' plaintive requests of (1–3) with regard to both conceptual perspective and situational style (assuming a non-liturgical, more informal public performance).

- Additional demonstrative, locative, and pronominal forms serve to spotlight certain notions of smaller semantic scope, e.g., "that very time—it's here!" (1); "you yourself" (9); "this very land/earth" (19); "that instruction of yours" (25).

- Redundant and implicit content, too, is employed either to fill out an individual poetic line, e.g., "Certainly not!" (the implied answer to the rhetorical question in 30), or even to add another line within a given strophe, e.g., "You alone, you are God—God genuine and true" (10).

- Carefully selected idiomatic expressions appear to foreground critical thematic concepts, e.g., "I've hammered out the work" (14); "here it is, all done!" (14); "here they are—all of them!" (20); "nobody would beat you with a rod on their account" [i.e., you have taken very good care of them] (22).

- Rhetorical questions are inserted for special emphasis, for generating audience engagement, and to add a perceptible emotive element to match what was felt to exist in the source text (e.g., 22, 27–28, 30).

- The use of unusual syntax offers a focused conceptual and affective perspective on selected items in the discourse. For example, an initially displaced relative construction highlights "those you set apart for me" in (20). Broken constructions also occur, such as the one that occurs across a strophic boundary in 25–26 to emphasize the Lord's "words—wise instruction" (another appositional doublet).

- For Tonga listeners, the incorporation of lexical items and syntactic constructions from related languages and dialects lends an authoritative tone to the prayer and also increases its audience appeal, e.g., *wakaambaati* (Ila language) and *kanike* (Lenje language) in (4); *Ndacobonaace* (Lundwe dialect) in (16).

These eleven characteristics, which offer only a partial illustrative listing, clearly (audibly!) mark the verbal style of the plaintive *ciyabilo* lyric, which was reckoned by mother tongue speakers to be the most appropriate and relevant genre to use for such a momentous and solemn occasion as Christ's farewell to his disciples. To some, this Tonga rendition, especially the English back-translation, might seem overly periphrastic and free, maybe even sounding too idiomatic for a prayer. But such an evaluation must be carried out in view of the text's designated target audience and medium as well as the proposed setting of use. Probably it would be judged too verbally vigorous to be presented as one of the liturgical readings in a public worship service. However, in a more informal religious situation, such as a parallel passage for the purpose of Bible study, this artistic translation might well add a helpful new perspective to the discussion. In any case, exegetes and translators alike must find some way to deal with the rhetorical poetics of the source text, the dynamics of biblical discourse, in a manner that is faithful to its intended function as well as its form. Christ's prayer is a section of Scripture that literally begs to be articulated aloud. A musical format might turn out to be even more effective, if a capable performer can be found and the genre demands it, that is, a sung version of the biblical text, perhaps also accompanied by a local instrumental arrangement.

5.9 Conclusion: Towards a more sight- and sound-sensitive translation

What can—or cannot—be done to modify established translation and publication procedures should, ideally, be guided not only by exegetical "control measures," but also by a consideration of what sounds natural and familiar to the text's envisioned users. What will enrich their understanding of, as well as appreciation for, the biblical message and also stimulate their engagement with its meaning and purpose in daily life?

5.9 Conclusion: Towards a more sight- and sound-sensitive translation

The latter objective includes the obvious but often neglected factor of the *published format* of a translation. Before one can publicly read any version (no matter what the language) clearly, correctly, and convincingly—aloud!—a printed text that is an adequate guide to enunciation and understanding must be provided. A reader who quickly recognizes and comprehends the crucial semantic and pragmatic aspects of a pericope of Scripture from a page of print will, all other things being equal, be better able to convey these features orally to a listening audience.

To this end, the importance of the typographical and spatial layout of published versions of the Bible cannot be overestimated. It is not only a matter of type font size and style, the amount and placement of strategic space on the page, the number of columns and whether they are justified or not. It is equally essential to arrange the printed text on the page so that it complements the discourse structure of the source text. In the case of John 17, for example, the lines of print should first of all match the sequence of utterance units and their grouping into strophic or paragraph segments. If possible and advisable in view of the intended readership, one could go even further and display the passage so that the layout represents a visual "isomorphic equivalent"[83] of the biblical message in terms of content organization (e.g., fronted focus), formal stylistic attributes (e.g., parallelism or chiasmus), and the function of specific rhetorical devices (e.g., to indicate special emotive emphasis or a thematic peak). This helps readers to visualize the discourse structure at a glance, thereby aiding both their comprehension and oral articulation of it.

The following are two examples that graphically illustrate what a difference the format and typography of a text can make as an integrated tool of message transmission, one that can either facilitate or detract from the quality of communication. The first selection is a close reproduction of John 17:1b–5 in a standard NIV publication (though only one of the two justified columns of print is shown, including disruptive hyphens). This is followed by a more dynamic, oral-elocutionary construction of the same passage (a slightly modified version of the NIV).

---

[83] This concept is discussed in De Waard and Nida 1986:118; for various examples, see Wendland and Louw 1993:*passim*.

"Father, the time has come. Glori-fy your Son, that your Son may glorify you. ²For you granted him authority over all people that he might give eternal life to all those you have giv-en him. ³Now this is eternal life: that they may know you, the only true God, and Jesus Christ, whom you have sent. ⁴I have brought you glory on earth by completing the work you gave me to do. ⁵And now, Father, glorify me in your presence with the glory I had with you before the world began.

Father, the time has come.   1b
Glorify your Son now,
That your Son may **glorify** you.
    For you granted him authority over all people   2
    that he might give eternal life
    to all those you have given him.
       Indeed, this is eternal life: 3
       that they all may know you, the only true God,
       and Jesus Christ whom you have sent.
    I have brought you **glory** here on the earth   4
    by completing the work you gave me to do.
Now Father, **glorify** me in your presence   5
with the **glory** that I had with you
before this world began.

Not everyone will agree with how the second text has been displayed. To be sure, the novel (but purposeful) arrangement needs to be tested with its intended audience to see what a difference, if any, it makes. The principal aim is to enable an experienced reader to move directly down the column of print and mentally process the discourse more quickly and accurately. This format should also greatly facilitate the performance of a lector and might also be used as the basis for a Bible class discussion regarding the function of structural form and rhetorical technique in the literature of Scripture.

5.9 Conclusion: Towards a more sight- and sound-sensitive translation

A comprehensive analysis of the biblical text, such as that conducted in the first part of this chapter, thus provides a foundation for any hermeneutical application, including a translation and subsequent transmission of the text. In the specific case of a *LiFE*-style version, the translation team might begin with an intensive group study of the composition as a whole from the point of view of its postulated initial linguistic and extralinguistic environment as compared with the communicative situation that is current within the current sociocultural context of the TL.[84] After such an intensive form-functional examination of a passage of Scripture, it would be left up to the "poet-rhetor" of the team, someone who is also trained in modern translation principles, to seek to reproduce the essential message of the original, including its recognized beauty, sonority (phonological resonance), impact, and appeal, in his or her mother tongue. This draft version would then be subject to extensive field testing, both text-based and exegetical (to ensure quality of content) as well as using oral-aural and practical techniques in order to assess the various responses of typical audience groups. This revision exercise would undoubtedly turn out to be an exercise in mutual compromise between the SL exegetes and TL communication experts, depending on how the translation is primarily to be used.

On the one hand, any qualitative appraisal of the draft version would have to take into serious consideration the possible loss, gain, or distortion of critical components of meaning in relation to the biblical text that may be occasioned by a dynamic equivalent translation. But this concern would need to be balanced by a corresponding evaluation of those aspects of authorial intention (built into the source document) which a more literary/oratorical restructuring is able to preserve.[85] The latter goal is particularly relevant with respect to the pragmatic (expressive, affective, imperative,

---

[84] The theory and practice of translation from an artistic and functional perspective was a characteristic feature of the mid 20th century "Prague School" of scholars—for example, Levý (2011): "Translation aesthetics" (ch. 3) and "On the poetics of translation" (ch. 4).

[85] Even from the point of view of secular translation theory "one needs to understand the underlying intention of a writer [in order] to translate effectively" (Katan 2004:172). In fact, this principle "has become a cornerstone of translation theory" (ibid., loc. cit.). "Every document has an author, and the resulting text is shaped by his or her intention. It is this authorial intention the interpreter [and translator] must aim to recover"—even in the case of writings whose original author may be unknown (Köstenberger and Patterson 2011:57–58; cf. Friedman 2002).

and artistic) dimension of communication, especially where a poetic and musical rendition is involved.[86] This is true even when the message transmission process is largely private and linear, as is the case with a written/published text. Furthermore, when the crucial element of the primary channel or medium of transmission is factored in, it is evident that a largely sound-oriented, lyric reproduction, such as the Tonga *ciyabilo* version, has much to commend it in comparison with a typical, relatively literal prosaic rendering, which is the usual alternative in the present setting of Christian communication in east-central Africa. The latter was surely not how the biblical text sounded in its initial environment.

Why, in fact, should the evocative power, the esthetic attraction, and the rhetorical dynamism of the Word of God be limited to those who happen to be familiar with Hebrew and Greek? In the final analysis, the commission of Bible translators today is quite straightforward: They have been given the task of conveying the Scriptures in every language-culture, meaningfully and in the manner in which the original creation was intended to be proclaimed (ideally orally). This challenging brief requires that sufficient attention and effort be devoted also to the poetic mode of expression in the Word as well as to an audio medium of message transmission. "Can the author's voice be silenced?" (Silbermann 1987:4). We would hope not—neither in terms of correctly *understanding* the intended sense and significance of the biblical text, nor more acutely and accurately *hearing* certain vibrant facets of that ancient voice also in a contemporary translation.

---

[86] On this issue, see Schrag 1992: For additional background regarding various translation testing and assessment principles and procedures, see Wendland 2011:ch. 7.

6

Modeling the Message: The Christological Core of Philippians (2:5–11) and Its Contemporary Communicative Implications

6.1 Overview

In this chapter,[1] I will examine the well-known Christological pericope of Philippians 2:5–11 from a combined structural and oral-rhetorical perspective in relation to its immediate cotext as well as the presumed situational setting of the epistle in its Ancient Near Eastern sociocultural environment. After a discussion of its manifest structural and poetic features, some of the manifold persuasive aspects of this impressive *encomium* are considered in terms of the proposed central theme, "modeling the message," now with more specific reference to a possible rhetorical occasion for the Philippian epistle from Paul's hypothetical perspective. The foundational and motivational thematic notion of "modeling" is then itself modeled in

---

[1] This is a thoroughly revised and expanded version of Wendland 2008c.

the form of an "oratorical" translation that seeks to duplicate the lyric, oral-aural dynamics of this critical passage in Chewa, a Bantu language of south-eastern Africa. These are some of the essential steps needed for accomplishing the goal of effectively communicating the text's continued theological, ethical, and ecclesiastical relevance to vernacular communities in diverse contemporary contexts where orality continues to be the much preferred mode of Scripture transmission.

6.2 Defining the epistolary epicenter of Philippians

In its non-geological, extended sense, an "epicenter" may be defined as the focal or crucial point of some material or verbal construction. I wish to apply this notion to Philippians 2:5–11 along with the insights derived from a discourse analysis of the letter to support my hypothesis that this "poetically organized discourse"[2] functions as the thematic nucleus of the entire epistle.[3] It does so by expressing several key notions that reverberate in their theological and ethical implications, both within the text's immediate cotext as well as throughout the composition as a whole. In magnificent lyric prose,[4] the Apostle Paul sums up how Jesus Christ not only models in himself the divine means of salvation, but also exemplifies the implications

---

[2] This term, originally from Banti and Giannattasio (2004:293–95), was suggested to me by D. Fitzgerald (personal correspondence, 2012; cf. Fitzgerald 2011).

[3] Fee describes this as "at once one of the most exalted, most beloved, and most discussed and debated passages in the Pauline corpus" (Fee 1995:192). The detailed examination of one section of a larger literary composition must be based on a corresponding study of the complete text. My method of "literary-rhetorical" discourse analysis, briefly applied to Philippians as a whole, is described in Translating the Literature of Scripture (2004b):ch. 7. For more comprehensive text-linguistic approaches, see: Banker 1997; Guthrie 1995; Reed 1997:ch. 2; and Heil 2010. It is interesting that the last mentioned and most recent study also espouses a "literary-rhetorical, audience-oriented method," one that gives special attention to putative "chiastic structures" in the epistle (Heil, ibid., 6–9, 10–31; cf. Wendland 2004b:31–35, 149, 198, 229–246, 335–336).

[4] Reed notes at least one scholar's opinion that in general Philippians, like most biblical letters, is stylistically "artless" (1997:150). My research leads me to the opposite conclusion, not only with respect to Philippians (e.g., Wendland 2004b:208–214), but also other NT epistles as well (cf. Wendland 2008b; see also Thomas and Thomas 2006).

of this universal message for all of his followers who seriously "think" (φρονέω) like he does.

This study illustrates how a close literary-rhetorical investigation of the source composition can reveal some vital text-critical as well as hermeneutical insights that influence how we understand and communicate this apostolic letter, especially, as in the initial event, via a *public oral proclamation* of the biblical text. The theme "modeling the message" is thus taken in a twofold sense: It pertains first of all to the form and function of the forceful exhortation that Paul was conveying to the Christians at Philippi. Second, the concept of "modeling" applies also to the manner in which this passage is expressed in a functionally-equivalent Bible translation via various media of transmission today.

6.3 Displaying the distinctive audio-visual structure of Philippians 2:5–11

Philippians 2:5–11 is obviously not ordinary epistolary prose; nearly all commentators and versions recognize that—the latter normally by means of a special print format. This section of the letter is clearly distinctive due to the significance of its Christological-theological content (which also distinguishes this text from its surrounding co-text), but the actual linguistic form of the discourse in the original Greek is also salient. The lyric character of this panegyric portion (i.e., poetic prose) seems to act as a hermeneutical cue to highlight its functional importance within the entire epistle. From a communicative perspective, this is also a very memorable pericope because, over and above its prominent subject matter, its reversed parallel organization of topics would render the passage easier to memorize and hence also to publicly proclaim, perhaps even as a corporate creedal testimony.

Commentators have posited a host of different antecedents, analyses, and potential structural arrangements for these verses.[5] I will not discuss any

---

[5] As Silva observes, "Unfortunately, a baffling diversity of opinion exists regarding the proper way of arranging these lines; indeed, at least a half a dozen arrangements can easily be defended" (Silva 2005:93). Silva goes on to quote Morna Hooker's tongue-in-cheek confession: "I myself have produced six or seven different analyses—and found each of them convincing at the time" (ibid., 93). This diversity of opinion gives further indirect support to the

of the proposed textual precursors of this section,[6] or whether it originates with Paul himself. In this study I am interested only in the final form of the text and its primary communicative purpose(s) within the Philippian epistle as it has ultimately come down to us.[7] I will consider just two of the possible arrangements of this passage, those that I regard as being the most plausible from a structure-functional perspective.

The first proposal views this passage as being constituted by a sequence of six short, three-line strophes (poetic paragraphs),[8] an arrangement that appears to climax in the middle with an extra-long alliterative and rhythmic (hence formally "marked") poetic utterance. The accompanying English rendition is a relatively literal back-translation of the Greek text:

[6]ὃς ἐν μορφῇ θεοῦ ὑπάρχων	Who being in the form of God,
οὐχ ἁρπαγμὸν ἡγήσατο	did not regard (as) an advantage,
τὸ εἶναι ἴσα θεῷ,	(his) being equal with God,
[7]ἀλλὰ ἑαυτὸν ἐκένωσεν	but he emptied himself,
μορφὴν δούλου λαβών,	taking on the form of a servant,
ἐν ὁμοιώματι ἀνθρώπων γενόμενος·	being in the likeness of humanity;

conclusion that this passage is indeed poetic in nature and crafted in this manner so as to attract attention to its content and function as well as to ensure its memorability.

[6] For an overview of a selection of scholarly options and opinions in this regard, see Basevi and Chapa 1993:338–344; Fowl 2005:108–113; and Hooker 2000:501–506.

[7] I consider the Apostle Paul to be the author of Philippians, one of the so-called "prison epistles" sent from Rome. For important background issues that pertain to the biblical source text, central themes, theology, authorship, intended readership, cultural setting, and other contextual issues pertaining to Philippians, I can simply recommend the comprehensive discussions in exegetical commentaries such as Fee 1995:1–53; Silva 2005:1–34; and O'Brien 1991:1–38. For some text-critical notes on 2:5–11, see O'Brien, ibid., 203.

[8] This proposal is adapted from the analysis of Lohmeyer (1928:5–6), which is supported by Silva (2005:93) and Köstenberger and Patterson (2011:473–474). Such a structure would not appear to be regular enough metrically to qualify as a "hymn or psalm derived from a worship setting" (Malina and Pilch 2006:305), unless it happened to be a translation or adaptation from an Aramaic original, and there is no solid evidence for this (cf. Hooker 2000:501; Silva 2005:99; Fee 1995:192–194; Fowl 2005:108–113; Breck 1994:256–257; Ryken 1992:456–457). Several other poetic structures, essentially variations of the following, are summarized in Harvey (1998:248–251). I have underlined the syntactically crucial conjunctions in the Greek text.

καὶ σχήματι εὑρεθεὶς ὡς ἄνθρωπος	and in appearance being found as a man,
⁸ἐταπείνωσεν ἑαυτὸν	he humbled himself,
γενόμενος ὑπήκοος μέχρι θανάτου	being obedient to death
—θανάτου δὲ σταυροῦ!	—even death of (on) a cross!
⁹διὸ καὶ ὁ θεὸς αὐτὸν ὑπερύψωσεν	Therefore also God exalted him
καὶ ἐχαρίσατο αὐτῷ τὸ ὄνομα	and granted him the name
τὸ ὑπὲρ πᾶν ὄνομα,	(that is) above every name,
¹⁰ἵνα ἐν τῷ ὀνόματι Ἰησοῦ	so that at the name of Jesus,
πᾶν γόνυ κάμψῃ ἐπουρανίων	every knee must bow of those in heaven
καὶ ἐπιγείων καὶ καταχθονίων	and those on earth and those under the earth,
¹¹καὶ πᾶσα γλῶσσα ἐξομολογήσηται	and every tongue should confess
ὅτι κύριος Ἰησοῦς Χριστὸς	that Jesus Christ (is) Lord
εἰς δόξαν θεοῦ πατρός	to (the) glory of God the Father!

Another, somewhat different yet also complementary perspective on this portion of the discourse views it as manifesting a compositional "inverted structure," that is, a reversed parallel or extended chiasmus.[9] In this case, the parallel segments (A–A', B–B', etc.) serve to underscore, through formal (lexical) *correspondence* as well as conceptual *contrast*, the central ideas of the section as a whole. This is shown in the reformatted and font-marked visual version below.[10] It reveals that as the various truths of this text are being unfolded in a linear, sequential fashion, at the same time these notions reflect back on what was already asserted to reinforce similar concepts as well as to forge new, especially contrastive ones that proclaim in

---

[9] See Breck (1994:264) for a rather different concentric arrangement, and Heil for a basic A–B–A' structure (2010:31). For a discussion of various criteria regarding the form and function of "chiasmus in the Pauline letters," see Thompson (1995:213–232) and Heil (2010:10). In contrast to viewing this unit as being hymnic or poetic in any form, Fee considers the "exalted and rhythmic" lines of 2:6–11 to "follow one another in perfectly orderly prose" (1995:42).

[10] I have used several different typographical styles (underlining, italics) simply to highlight the corresponding lexical items in each pair of parallel panels, A–A', B–B', etc.; the boldfaced words represent the sequence of significant syntactic utterance connectives, leading off from τοῦτο.

concise lyric summary the praiseworthy character and accomplishments of Jesus the divine Christ:

⁵ **τοῦτο** φρονεῖτε ἐν ὑμῖν	Introduction[11]
ὃ καὶ ἐν <u>Χριστῷ Ἰησοῦ</u>,	
⁶ **ὃς** ἐν μορφῇ θεοῦ ὑπάρχων	A
οὐχ ἁρπαγμὸν ἡγήσατο τὸ εἶναι ἴσα θεῷ,	
| ⁷ **ἀλλὰ** ἑαυτὸν ἐκένωσεν μορφὴν δούλου λαβών,	B
| ἐν ὁμοιώματι ἀνθρώπων γενόμενος·	
| | **καὶ** σχήματι εὑρεθεὶς ὡς ἄνθρωπος	C
| | | ⁸ <u>ἐταπείνωσεν ἑαυτὸν</u>	D
| | | | γενόμενος ὑπήκοος μέχρι θανάτου,	E
| | | | θανάτου δὲ σταυροῦ.	E'
| | | 9 **διὸ** καὶ ὁ θεὸς αὐτὸν ὑπερύψωσεν	D'
| | **καὶ** ἐχαρίσατο αὐτῷ τὸ ὄνομα τὸ ὑπὲρ πᾶν ὄνομα,	C'
| ¹⁰ **ἵνα** ἐν τῷ ὀνόματι Ἰησοῦ πᾶν γόνυ κάμψῃ	B'
| ἐπουρανίων καὶ ἐπιγείων καὶ καταχθονίων	
¹¹ **καὶ** πᾶσα γλῶσσα ἐξομολογήσηται	A'
ὅτι <u>κύριος Ἰησοῦς Χριστὸς</u> εἰς δόξαν θεοῦ πατρός.	

The basic outline of this dual concentric structure, including an "introduction" in v. 5 that links it to the preceding pericope (2:1–4), is formally displayed by lexical chiasms at its external borders as well as its core, viz. "Christ Jesus" (Χριστῷ Ἰησοῦ) and "Jesus Christ" (Ἰησοῦς Χριστὸς) in vv. 5 and 11. This focus on the divine "name" (10a) is supported by the great contrastive "transformation" in vv. 8a and 9a: "he lowered himself" (ἐταπείνωσεν ἑαυτὸν) and "him he (God) hyper-elevated" (αὐτὸν ὑπερύψωσεν).

The rest of the proposed composition is not as clearly defined, although commentators have long observed that the quasi-narrative, bifid arrangement obviously turns sharply after the emphatic repetition of "death" (θανάτου) in the middle at the end of v. 8. The *humiliation* of Christ is thus the subject of the first panel (vv. 6–8), while his post-passion *exaltation* comes to the fore

---

[11] This "Introduction" establishes the cognitive frame of reference for the following pericope and indeed the letter as a whole. Thus, the verb φρονεῖτε conveys the idea, not simply of "attitude" (NIV), but of "mindset," "mental map," even "world view" (cf. Rom 8:5–6; Col 3:2). This mode of thinking must affect how believers view one another (2:2) in contrast to the way of thinking of the ungodly (3:15, 19).

in the second panel (vv. 9–11). This latter half begins with the consequential conjunction "wherefore" (διό) and explicit mention of the divine agent, "God" (ὁ θεὸς), who is the subject of all subsequent events. Two major logical relationships balance each other in the inner portion of each portion of the composition, namely, *contrast* (ἀλλὰ) in v. 8 (i.e., B—what Christ lowered himself to) and *purpose* (ἵνα) in v. 10 (i.e., B'—what Christ was elevated to). If the principal *negative* thematic and emotive focal point occurs in the center of the poetic structure (E–E'), its positive counterpart appears at the end in the rhythmic "Christo-doxology" of the very last line (excluding the initial ὅτι): κύριος Ἰησοῦς Χριστὸς // εἰς δόξαν θεοῦ πατρός! (7 syllables in each hemistich).

Generally speaking, the putative lined "utterance units" are somewhat longer in terms of syllables in this proposal (as opposed to the first strophic segmentation), but they do become audibly shorter in the middle of the structure (vv. 8–9a), with the shortest one occurring right at the central turning point in v. 8c: "even death of a cross" (θανάτου δὲ σταυροῦ). In any case, the respective progressions of the two panels are clearly *antithetical* in nature, as Christ "empties himself" (ἑαυτὸν ἐκένωσεν) in the first (B), but is patently elevated in the second (B')—that is, above any living being "in heaven and on earth even under the earth" (ἐπουρανίων καὶ ἐπιγείων καὶ καταχθονίων). Finally, it is interesting to note that the two basic sections of this text are roughly equal with regard to their constituent lexical inventory: Introduction to E = 42 words; E' to A' = 43 words.

It is evident from the poetically composed character of this passage that the interlocking subject of Christ's humiliation and exaltation was not only of doctrinal importance to the Apostle Paul as he dictated this epistle to the congregation at Philippi; it also had a vital role to play in the particular pastoral exhortation and encouragement that he wished to convey to the Christians there. Jesus Christ was not only the Messiah sent from God to redeem mankind, he was to be for them something more—namely, a Model for their everyday attitudes and actions, both within (1:27) and without (1:28–29) the communion of "saints" (1:1b), especially those believers who like the Apostle himself happened to be experiencing trying times and difficult circumstances (1:30). It is clear that the artful manner in which this passage has been shaped would have contributed a great deal also to the impact and appeal that it would have had before a listening congregation of believers.

6.4 How does Philippians 2:5–11 relate to its cotext?

As the preceding analysis suggests, there is no doubt that 2:5–11 is a specially marked constituent within the text of Philippians. However, the next, perhaps more critical issue to consider is this: What is the significance of this distinctive formal structuring in terms of Paul's overall theme and argument strategy? Again, it is necessary to be brief at this point:[12] The initial present imperative phrase in v. 5, "Adopt this attitude…" (τοῦτο φρονεῖτε),[13] follows from two others that have preceded it as Paul develops the principal hortatory portion of this epistle. The letter's primary admonition "Only [= the important thing is to] conduct yourselves [lit. 'behave as a good citizen', i.e., morally; cf. Acts 23:1] in a manner worthy of the gospel of Christ" (Μόνον ἀξίως τοῦ εὐαγγελίου τοῦ Χριστοῦ πολιτεύεσθε…) in 1:27–28 sets the general evangelical tone for all to follow.[14] Second, Paul appeals to his own standing with the Philippian congregation as he asks them to "make my joy complete" (πληρώσατέ μου τὴν χαράν—2:2) by living in a manner that befits the gospel, despite the threats and troubles that they happen to be experiencing both within and without. With this in mind, then, the

---

[12] For much more detail regarding these issues, see for example: Fee 1995:196–199, 226–229; Fowl 2005:89–91; O'Brien 1991:203–205, 253–268.

[13] Some less prominent manuscripts include the postpositive conjunction γάρ at the beginning of v. 5, perhaps for stylistic reasons, that is, to more smoothly link Paul's exhortations to Christians in vv. 1–4 and the subsequent, motivating example of Christ in vv. 6–11. But as Omanson concludes in support of its exclusion, "If the conjunction γάρ were original, it is hard to understand why it would have been omitted" (Omanson 2006:403; cf. Fee 1995:197 and Hawthorne 1983:76). O'Brien, on the other hand, argues for inclusion (1991:203). The deictic nature of τοῦτο is roundly debated by scholars: Is this demonstrative *anaphoric* in its syntactic function (i.e., pointing back; e.g., Fee 1995:199 and Hawthorne, 1983:80) or *cataphoric* (i.e., pointing ahead; e.g., Banker 1997:85, and Loh and Nida, *A Translator's Handbook*—Paratext 7.1 (1977))? I would argue that this is an instance of "semantic density" in which *both* interpretations are possible and probably intended (cf. Wendland 1990).

[14] In Greco-Roman rhetorical terms, 1:27–30 constitutes the *propositio*, or main thesis statement of the letter. Thus, the general appeal τοῦ εὐαγγελίου τοῦ Χριστοῦ πολιτεύεσθε in v. 27a is restated and reinforced by στήκετε ἐν ἑνὶ πνεύματι, μιᾷ ψυχῇ συναθλοῦντες τῇ πίστει τοῦ εὐαγγελίου in 27b. And the ultimate motivation for such a contra-cultural life-style is "salvation" (σωτηρίας, v. 28b).

6.4 How does Philippians 2:5–11 relate to its cotext?

Apostle turns to a consideration of the perfect example to emulate in this life-and-death struggle for ecclesiastical survival, namely, "Christ Jesus," whose model mindset and character is poetically narrated in the dependent section that follows (vv. 6–11, introduced by a relative clause—ὅς...).

As in most of his epistles (e.g., 1 Corinthians, Ephesians), the Apostle is very concerned about the presence or absence of *Gospel-based unity* within the fellowship of believers—that is, how to promote the former and guard against the latter. Such corporate oneness must be built upon the solid faith-foundation established by the good-news message about Jesus Christ (cf. 1:12, 18), which has been proclaimed by Paul as well as by the Philippians themselves (1:5, 7). Furthermore, it must be manifested in the sanctified community through mutual good works that bring glory to God (1:6, 11; 2:1–4) and by actively contending for this Gospel, despite constant persecution (1:14, 20, 27–30).

As usual in biblical discourse (or any literary text for that matter), the author had a variety of linguistic-literary resources at his disposal for indicating points, areas, and degrees of topical emphasis and connectivity within the creation at hand. In the case of our focal passage, a lexical *repetition* of the verb "think" (φρονέω) in the verses leading up to 2:5–11 seems to be especially prominent in this regard. This verb first occurs in the letter as part of Paul's "thanksgiving" to God on behalf of the Philippian believers (1:3a). As the Apostle expresses his deep affection for them and their "partnership in the Gospel" (1:5), he underscores his emotive endorsement with the somewhat elliptical statement, "[So I thank God,] just as it is right for me to think this [way] about all of you... (καθώς ἐστιν δίκαιον ἐμοὶ τοῦτο φρονεῖν ὑπὲρ πάντων ὑμῶν...) (1:7a).

In addition to the oppression from outsiders that Paul as well as the Philippians were experiencing (1:30), the congregation appears to have been facing a persistent problem that virtually all Christian groups experience (no less so nowadays!), which was various sorts of dissension within the ranks, whether pertaining to leadership ambitions (1:17) or to squabbles between ordinary members (4:2). It is in this socio-ecclesiastical context then that the need for proper "thinking" which would correspondingly lead to righteous behavior came to the fore. Paul emphasizes this notion in connection with his imperative of 2:2: "Make me truly happy...!" (*New Living Translation*). In what way? By "thinking the same thing" (reiterated synonymously: τὸ αὐτὸ φρονῆτε...τὸ ἓν φρονοῦντες), which involves not so much a cognitive, intellectual activity as an emotive, dispositional one, i.e., "being united in your convictions" (*Jerusalem Bible*) or "having the same sentiments." How could this be done? Paul offers several concrete suggestions in contrastive fashion in v. 3: "Do nothing out of selfish ambition or vain conceit, but in *humility* consider others better than yourselves" (NIV), where in this cotext, the verb "consider" (ἡγέομαι) is a close synonym to φρονέω. "Humility" (ταπεινοφροσύνη), then, is the key; there seems to be a subtle pun here, for this is "a compound word from 'lowly' and 'mind' (from the verb in φρονεῖν v. 2), hence the KJV 'lowliness of mind'" (Fee 1995:187). Paul then makes his primary exhortation even more specific (and hard to ignore) in the admonition of v. 4: "Each of you should look not only to your own interests, but also to the interests of others" (NIV).

The first four verses of Philippians 2 have prominently set the stage for v. 5: "You should have the same attitude..." (τοῦτο φρονεῖτε ἐν ὑμῖν...). And where does Paul find the real-life model to exemplify his message (which is always a more effective teaching device)? Nowhere else but in the person of "Christ Jesus" (...ὃ καὶ ἐν Χριστῷ Ἰησοῦ!). We note here in passing the poetic balance and sound symmetry in the two halves of this verse (5a–b), which introduces the main creedal confession that follows. The crucial aspect of "humility" in Christ's attitude and behavior is reinforced by the verb that occurs in v. 8a: "he humbled himself" (ἐταπείνωσεν ἑαυτὸν), which is seconded then by the parallel contrastive action of God in v. 9a "he exalted him" (αὐτὸν ὑπερύψωσεν).

The importance of having this clear/correct sort of "thinking" (φρονέω) is reiterated by the Apostle periodically throughout the rest of his letter to the Philippians (the verb occurs 12 times in total). In 3:15–16, for example, Paul associates this mental state (3x) with Christian "maturity" (τέλειος) and then in v. 17 exhorts his readers to be "imitators" (συμμιμηταί) of him as a derived and hence secondary "model" (τύπος) to follow in Christian living. All this is in graphic contrast to those perverted and polluted people, who are "enemies of the cross" (3:18b), who are on the path to eternal "destruction" (3:19a), whose "god is their stomach" (3:19b), and who only "think about earthly matters" (οἱ τὰ ἐπίγεια φρονοῦντες—3:19c). Furthermore, in contrast to two individuals within the fellowship, who were apparently not able to get along or "agree with each other" (4:2; lit. 'to think the

6.4 How does Philippians 2:5–11 relate to its cotext?

same thing'—τὸ αὐτὸ φρονεῖν), Paul urges the Philippians to be actively concerned for those fellow-believers in need, as they had already demonstrated towards him (lit. 'to think on my behalf'—τὸ ὑπὲρ ἐμοῦ φρονεῖν) (4:10; cf. 4:14–18). Accordingly, the Apostle Paul, who imitated and aspired after the Model of Christ (e.g., 2:17–18; 3:7–11), was himself a model for the Philippian congregation, namely, with regard to his attitude (which they were to 'deeply consider'—λογίζομαι; 4:8), his teachings (4:9), as well as his Christ-oriented response to all sorts of trying circumstances in life (4:11–13).

The centrality of this theme of *joyfully* modeling the Christ-focused message in Philippians[15] also helps to explain a rather large section of the epistle that does not seem to fit in where it is found, a segment of text that appears on first reading or hearing to be some sort of an aside or topically of "little significance."[16] Thus, after exhorting his readers to continued obedience (2:12–14) as "the children of God" (2:15), both to serve Christ and to give Paul a reason for rejoicing" (2:16–18), he proceeds to announce the travel plans of Timothy (2:19–24) and Epaphroditus (2:25–30).[17] However, in the light of 2:5–11, it would seem that this latter por-

---

[15] Some analysts argue that "there is no one theme in the letter" to the Philippians (Reed 1995:101). In contrast, Heil considers the "main theme" to be "Let us rejoice in being conformed to Christ" (2010:1). Heil underscores the importance of the emotive mindset of "joy/rejoice" (χαρά/χαίρω) in this epistle—a leitmotif that colors all the Apostle's instructions and exhortations: "The various forms of the verb 'rejoice' and its cognates in the letter..., taken together, express Paul's exhortation for his audience to rejoice with him.... [This] is included in the closely related concept of 'grace' with its connotation of joy in both the noun form χάρις and the verb form χαρίζομαι.... A note of joy can also be readily detected in the various exuberant doxologies and expressions of praise to God throughout the letter..." (2010:1–2).

[16] Such a conclusion is criticized by O'Brien 1991:313. This seeming digression—or apparent conclusion—is also part of the reason for some commentators positing two (or three) letters to the Philippian congregation, involving roughly chs. 1–2 and 3–4. As Reed concludes: "The interpretive watershed of the debate over literary integrity has been and continues to be the beginning of Philippians 3" and the "noticeable shift in tone and mood" that occurs there (1997:131). However, Reed goes on to cite an impressive list of "[l]exical and thematic parallels found throughout the letter [that] point to its unity" (ibid., 140–142; cf. 412–418). That is the conclusion supported by my own literary-structural analysis of this letter (cf. O'Brien 1991:314, 10–18).

[17] The passages 2:17–18 and 3:1 link up closely in terms of content and function, e.g., in the command to "rejoice," and thus form a structural bracket (or *inclusio*)

tion of chapter 2 (vv. 19–30) also performs a greater thematic function. In this view, the two apostolic emissaries are, like Paul himself (2:17–18), concrete examples of believers who are "conducting themselves in a manner worthy of the gospel of Christ" (1:27) by being "concerned about the interests of others" (2:4). In imitation of their Lord they are thus, like their mentor Paul, human models of selfless service (vv. 22, 30), laboring on behalf of the entire community of Christ (vv. 20, 25), and hence worthy of sincere honor and emulation (v. 29).

6.5 The epistolary-rhetorical organization of Philippians

A preliminary discourse analysis (*not included for lack of space*) suggests the following as a basic *epistolary outline* for Philippians, that is, in relation to its periodic doxologies and the motivational theme of "Paul as Model":[18]

	Doxologies*	Paul as Model
A. Letter Opening (1:1–2)		
B. Thanksgiving-Prayer (1:3–11)	1:10b–11	1:3–8
C. Body (1:12–4:20)		1:12
1. Beginning (1:12–2:11)	2:9–11	1:25, 30
2. Middle (2:12–3:21)	3:20b–21	2:17–18; 3:12–17
3. Conclusion (4:1–20)	4:19b 4:20	4:8–14

---

* around 2:19–30.

[18] Harvey divides the "Body" portion into the following sub-sections: Letter-body A (1:12–2:18), Apostolic *parousia* (2:19–30), Letter-body B and *paraenesis*/summary advice (3:1–4:9), and Note of thanks (4:10–20) (1998:233). Witherington offers a partially corresponding outline of Philippians according to the technical principles of Greco-Roman rhetorical analysis: Epistolary Prescript (1:1–2), Epistolary Thanksgiving/*Exordium* (1:3–11), *Propositio* (1:27–30), *Probatio* (2:1–4:3), *Peroratio* (4:4–20), Epistolary Greetings and Closing (4:21–23) (2009b:127 [seemingly omitted is 1:12–26]). Compare the more detailed structure in Watson 1997:399–400. Watson too proposes a Greco-Roman "rhetorical outline" of Philippians (ibid., 404, 426), the 1988 version of which is criticized by Reed as being an over-reading of the text (Reed 1993:314–322; cf. Watson 1997:57–88). Fee suggests that the letter's organization simply "follows a basically chronological scheme" (1995:38).

6.5 The epistolary-rhetorical organization of Philippians

D. Letter Closing (4:21–23)

*<u>Christological</u>/<u>christocentric</u> passages:** 1:2, 6, 11, 18, 21, 27; 2:1, 5, 11, 16, 21, 30; 3:3, 8, 14, 20; 4:1, 7, 13, 19, 21, 23.

Some of the principal literary-structural and rhetorical markers that support the text segmentation proposed above include the following characteristics:[19]

- A "doxology" (or reference to the "glory" of God) concludes each major internal portion of the composition (i.e., literary *epiphora*). This structural-thematic feature serves to demarcate the epistle into its chief divisions. An extended *doxa* passage concludes the Body of the entire letter (4:20).

- The Body "middle" and "closing" sections each begin with Ὥστε "So then" to present a related, but refocused aspect of Paul's argument (i.e., literary *anaphora*; 2:12, 4:1; cf. 1:13; note: if Ὥστε is anaphoric in 2:12, then it is most likely the same in 4:1).

- The letter's generic, foundational exhortation "stand firmly in the Lord" occurs in a semi-independent summary verse at the onset of the Body closing (4:1). It appears in fuller form in 1:27b as part of the letter's main paraenetic thesis, or *propositio*: "…that you stand firmly *in one spirit, striving together with one soul* for the faith of the gospel." This then is what it means to "conduct yourselves worthy of the gospel" (1:27a). This in turn specifies Paul's prayerful summary of the Philippians' contribution through their "*defense* and *confirmation* (establishment) of the gospel" (1:7). These two vital Christian activities are foregrounded in each of the thematic "core texts."

---

[19] A "literary-structural" perspective focuses on the *form* of the biblical text, while a "rhetorical" perspective focuses on its communicative *function*. Often, however, it is difficult to separate these two types of analysis, and therefore I have not attempted to do so in the following discussion. For an explanation of the "literary-rhetorical" methodology that concluded with these results, see Wendland 2004b:ch. 7; 2011:ch. 3.

- Every major *hortatory* pericope in the letter includes a Christ-centered passage as a *motivating* factor to encourage Christ-like living and thinking.

- The epistle's most important christological statement, 2:5–11, is manifested as such by the elaborate structural patterning and poetic styling that it displays as well as by its crucial theological content and primary motivational purpose. This passage occurs in climactic location at the end of the epistle's Body opening.

- Christ is indeed the supreme Model for our faith-life, but his apostolic emissary, Paul, is also a credible, persuasive "model" (or "mentor") for such behavior and attitudes. This fact is pointed out repeatedly in the sequence of "Paul-as-exemplar" texts (see the listing above). Every sector of the letter (usually in a highlighted beginning or closing position) includes a reference to the blessed spiritual result of following the Christ-like model, namely, "joy/rejoicing."

- The general reference to genuine Christian *attitudes* and *behavior* in the summary section of 4:8–9 reverses the order of treatment of this pair of appeals in the back-to-back segments of 1:27–30 (behavior) + 2:1–4 (attitude).

- As suggested earlier, the verb φρονέω (and related terms) manifests itself as a key word in this epistle, appearing not only at the onset of the focal portion (2:5), but also in other important passages that have reference to the central theme of "modeling" (+ = positive, – = negative reference): 1:7 (+); 2:2 (+), 5 (+); 3:15 (+), 16 (+), 19 (–); 4:2 (+), 10 (+); cf. Rom 8:5 (–); 12:3 (–), 16 (+/–); 15:5 (+); 1 Cor 4:6 (+); 2 Cor 13:11 (+); Gal 5:10 (–); Col 3:2 (+).

The significance of the final point mentioned above is increased as one observes a number of hypothetical "parallel pericopes" in Philippians, namely, those which appear to emphasize Christ-like "models" and believers, in turn, modeling the Christ-like life:

6.5 The epistolary-rhetorical organization of Philippians

a epistolary opening (1:1–2)

  b focus on the Philippians, their partnership in the gospel (1:3–11)

    c focus on Paul, his devotion to the gospel (1:12–26)

      d appeal to "stand fast" in the faith of the gospel against all opponents (1:27–30)

        e emphasis on "like-mindedness" in humility (2:1–4)

          f the supreme Model of Christ's humiliation and exaltation (2:5–11)

            g hold on to the word of life in a wicked world (2:12–18)

              h the example of Timothy (2:19–24)

              h' the example of Epaphroditus (2:25–30)

            g' beware of false teachers who boast in their flesh (3:1–4a)

          f' Paul's example of self-emptying for the sake of Christ (3:4b–10)
          and ultimate exaltation at the resurrection (3:11)

        e' emphasis on "like-mindedness" in perseverance (3:12–16)

      d' appeal to "walk" according to Paul's "pattern," not that of the "enemies of the cross of Christ," and to "stand fast" in it (3:17–4:1) exhortation: Let peace reign in the Christian community through the power of Christ and according to the teaching and practice of the Apostle Paul (4:2–9)

c' focus on Paul and his devotion to the gospel (4:10–14)

b' focus in the Philippians and their partnership in the gospel (4:15–20)

a' epistolary closing (4:21–23)

The preceding outline is not intended to imply that this epistle was originally composed according to a chiastic arrangement.[20] However, it is interesting to observe the various topical parallels and the manner in which Paul recycles the main elements of his pastoral exhortation to the Philippian congregation. If it can be credibly established that other chiastic structures do appear in the discourse within larger or smaller stretches of text, then the implications for its oral presentation and aural reception would be as follows:[21]

---

[20] For a similar outline, see Luter and Lee 1995:92. Recently Heil has proposed a "macrochiastic structure" for the whole of Philippians consisting of ten individual chiastically arranged sub-units "with five pairs of parallel units and with the pivot of the entire macrochiastic structure occurring in the progression from the E unit in 2:1–16 to the E' unit in 2:17–30" (2010:31). While interesting and insightful at times, especially in the discussion of the organization of individual constituent sections, this proposal is on the whole not very convincing. There are two major problems in my view: (a) the alleged parallel panels, whether on the macro- or micro-structure (e.g., E and E'), are linked primarily by individual key words that do not often capture the principal content of the unit posited; and (b) most of the corresponding panels encompass content that is too extensive and diverse to be perceived as being related—that is, heard and interpreted as being similar by a listening audience. For example, macrochiastic section 5 covering 2:1–16 is viewed as manifesting the following inverted arrangement: A (1–5), B (6–7), C (8a)—C' (8b), B' (9–11), A' (12–16) (ibid., 17–18), and panels A and A', other than having several key words in common, are only related in the broad sense of presenting various paraenetic instructions.

[21] I have not examined this epistle closely with a view towards identifying such chiastic arrangements, but Heil refers to a number of studies that do this with respect to Philippians as well as other Pauline letters (Heil 2010:10–13). Bailey attributes such structures to Paul's "Hebrew literary heritage" (2011:53) and lists a number of reasons why these non-linear patterns are hermeneutically significant (ibid., 50–52).

> Chiastic patterns serve to organize the content to be heard and not only aid the memory of the one delivering or performing a document, but also make it easier for the implied audience to follow and remember the content. A chiasm works by leading its audience through introductory elements to a central, pivotal point or points, and then reaching its conclusion by recalling and developing, via the chiastic parallels, aspects of the initial elements that led to the central, pivotal point or points. (Heil 2010:12)

6.6 The thematic composition of Philippians

Of course, a well-organized *linear* outline, including one or more peaks of thematic significance, might accomplish the same mnemonic objective, possibly in conjunction with a corresponding concentric pattern of some kind. In any case, perhaps a more viable proposal for establishing a set of memory "hooks," or vocal prompts, for a composition like Philippians is to look for certain topical correspondences that appear individually and in clusters throughout the pericope. For example, an examination of the thematic constitution of this letter in greater detail reveals that that there are seven principal *motivational topics* that may be derived or abstracted sequentially from the nuclear "Christ-as-Model" text (2:5–11). They are shown below with reference to the concentric discourse arrangement for this passage (as earlier proposed):

Have this mind among yourselves, which is yours in

A: Christ Jesus, who, though he was in, the form of God did not count equality with God a thing to be grasped, ➔ **SELF-EVALUATION**

   B: but emptied himself, taking the form of a servant, ➔ **SERVICE**

      C: being born in the likeness of men. ➔ **FELLOWSHIP**

    D: And being found in human form

        E: he humbled himself   → **HUMILITY**
           and became obedient   → **OBEDIENCE**
           F: unto death,   → **PATIENCE**
           F': even death on a cross.   → **in SUFFERING**

        E': Thus God has highly   → **EXALTATION!**
           exalted him

    D': and bestowed on him the name which is above every name,

   C': that at the name of Jesus every knee should bow,
      (those) in heaven and on earth and under the earth,

  B': and every tongue confess that **Lord**

A': **is Jesus Christ**, to the glory of God the Father.

One or more of these "core values/activities" would appear to be highlighted in virtually every paragraph-sized unit of this letter, thereby demonstrating the thematically "nuclear" character of 2:5–11. Such a cluster of related thematic topics would also enhance the potential for memorizing certain prominent portions of this epistle, if not the whole text. The ultimate purpose of these attitudes and behaviors is to bring "glory" to God (Christ), i.e., an "exaltation" (motivation #7 in the sequence) of worship and praise, which is foregrounded in the second half of the inverted topical panel.[22] Thus, the first six values

---

[22] I might suggest that whereas the center of the chiastic structure, F/F' (v. 8), serves as the *thematic* "peak" of this pericope, its *emotive* "climax" comes as the end (v. 11), in the expression "the Lord [is] Jesus Christ" (κύριος Ἰησοῦς Χριστὸς). Furthermore, the fronted (focused) term "Lord" is arguably a theologically "dense" concept, pointing on the one hand to the fact that Jesus Christ is true "God" (κύριος being the term regularly used with reference to YHWH in the LXX), but on the other hand implicitly also our "Savior" according to prominent OT prophecies (e.g., Isa 45:15, 17, 21b–22; cf. 23b and Phil 2:10) as well as NT predictions (e.g., Rev 5:6, 9, 12). It would indeed be difficult to convey these nuances in translation without an expository note.

6.6 The thematic composition of Philippians

as exhibited by Christ are "active" in nature and should be modeled in turn by Christians. The last one is "passive" in that *exaltation* is received by "Jesus" (Savior; cf. 3:20) from the Father; on the other hand, he is also to be lauded as "Lord" by his people (in contrast to the self-deified Roman emperor). Furthermore, the first six involve some preeminent ways in which all believers are to unite in order to remain "standing firmly" in their faith (4:1), while the last refers to the "glory" that will be theirs when they stand together before Christ on the Last Day (3:21). It is this amazing divine plan of salvation that gives Paul and his fellow "gospel partners" (1:5) such a great cause for "rejoicing" despite the difficult circumstances in which they may be in life (another key theme in Philippians, i.e., χαρά—1:4, 25; 2:2, 29; 4:1; χαίρω—1:18; 2:17–18, 28; 3:1; 4:4, 10).

In support of the preceding selection of the focal concepts that pertain to "modeling" in Philippians 2:5–11 is a *paradigmatic* display of these same motivational topics as they are manifested in the major pericopes that comprise this epistle as a whole. Of course, both the choice as well as the attribution of apparent prominence of these seven themes in relation to the individual text units could be deemed arbitrary and hence debated. However, the point here is simply to illustrate the relative pervasiveness of these seven themes within the Philippian epistle as a whole. This recycled thematic cluster would also suggest that they served also as a conceptual *memory aid* to assist in the repeated oral proclamation of this letter to audiences throughout the Roman world and beyond, that is, wherever the Greek language was readily understood.

SELF-EVALUATION	SERVICE	FELLOWSHIP	HUMILITY	OBEDIENCE	PATIENCE	EXALTATION
		1:1–2				
		1:3–8				
	1:9–11					1:9–11
	1:12–18 (proclamation)					
1:19–26		1:19–26				1:19–26
		1:27–30		1:27–30	1:27–30	
2:1–4		2:1–4	2:1–4			

SELF-EVALUATION	SERVICE	FELLOWSHIP	HUMILITY	OBEDIENCE	PATIENCE	EXALTATION
2:5–11	2:5–11	2:5–11	2:5–11	2:5–11	2:5–11	2:5–11
	2:12–18			2:12–18		
	2:19–24 (Timothy)					
	2:25–30 (Epaphroditus)				2:25–30	
			3:1–4a			
3:4b–11					3:4b–11	
3:12–16			3:12–16			
3:17–21			3:17–21			3:17–21
		4:1		4:1		
	4:2–4a	4:2–4a		4:2–4a		
		4:4b–7				
4:8–9				4:8–9		
4:10–13	4:10–13					
	4:14–20	4:14–20				4:14–20
	4:21–23					

The listing below further indicates selected (not necessarily all) passages in Philippians that are related to one or more of its key thematic and hortatory concepts:[23] *Christ is the Christian's model* (the verses in **bold** are especially diagnostic):[24]

---

[23] In this connection, an interesting exegetical aside concerns the problematic interpretation of the semantically dense term τὸ ἐπιεικὲς in 4:5 (Greenlee lists 12 different translation glosses in 1992:242; cf. the *UBS Translator's Handbook*: "It denotes one's willingness to give and take instead of always standing rigidly on one's rights"). Could its range of reference perhaps include the complex bundle of six active attributes displayed by Christ in the thematic core text of 2:5–11, as shown above: SELF-AWARENESS + SERVICE + FELLOWSHIP + HUMILITY + OBEDIENCE + PATIENCE? Believers who demonstrate these qualities will receive their "reward" when the Lord returns in glory to glorify his saints (3:21; 4:19; i.e., structural *epiphora*). This then is the life-"model" that Christians are to display (since) their Lord, the Model, "is near," either temporally (to return) or spatially (in personal presence). This behavioral model is founded upon such complementary attitudes as those listed in 4:8, with the ultimate result being "peace," both within the unified fellowship and with their God (v. 10).

[24] Other "Christ/Paul as model" texts in the NT include the following: 1 Cor 4:16, 11:1; 1 Thess 1:6–7, 2:14; 2 Thess 3:7, 9; cf. Eph 5:1; 1 Tim 4:12; Titus 2:7; Heb 6:12, 13:7; 1 Pet 2:21, 5:3; in 1 Thess 1:7 we have the example of a Christian congregation serving as a model for others to "imitate." A number of commentators have

6.6 The thematic composition of Philippians

- **in suffering**   1:13, 1:17, 2:27, 1:29–30, **3:10**
- **in service**   **2:17**, 2:20–22, 2:30, 3:12–13, 3:17, 4:14–19
- in holiness/righteousness 1:10–11, 1:27, 2:12–15, 3:9, 3:12
- **in attitude**   1:20–23, **2:1–4**, 2:21, 3:7–8, 4:4–9
- **in steadfastness**   1:27, 3:13–14, **4:1**, 4:3, 4:11–13
- in love   1:7–8, 2:1–2, 4:1
- **in glory**   1:23, 3:3, 3:11, 3:14, 3:20, **3:21**

Finally, it is important from a rhetorical perspective to take note of a number of *negative* counter-examples that are positioned periodically throughout the epistle, serving as varied foils to the recommended models by contrasting good instances of belief and behavior with some notable bad cases. The latter group, not to be emulated in any way, would include Paul's rival preachers in Rome (1:15, 17), opponents of the congregation at Philippi (1:28a), representatives of the prevailing crooked and depraved generation (2:15), members of the Judaizing clique (3:2), antinomian libertines (3:18–19), a pair of contentious Philippian women, Euodia and Syntyche (4:2), and even some tight-fisted surrounding Christian congregations (4:15b). The model of Christ—and those believers who patterned their lives after their Lord (e.g., Paul, Timothy, Epaphroditus, Clement, and others)—are thereby further highlighted in particular by concrete cases of individuals and groups that "opposed" (τῶν ἀντικειμένων) the Gospel and who would one day face punitive "destruction" (ἀπωλείας) (1:28).

---

pointed out the strong intertextual relationship between Phil 2:5–11 and Isa 52:13–53:12. Breck, who also points out the concentric construction of the OT precursor (1994:262), observes: "This expression of Jesus' 'kenotic' obedience could hardly fail to evoke in the minds of Paul's readers the image of the Suffering Servant, who gave up his life voluntarily to atone for the sins of the people. Accordingly, the Christ-hymn of Phil 2 unfolds in such a way as to center upon the proclamation of v. 8, 'He humbled himself *unto death, even death on a cross*'" (ibid., 263). On the other hand, alleged contrastive allusions to Adam (e.g., Hooker 2000:504–506; Keesmaat 2006:194–197) are, to my mind, unconvincing. Furthermore, I would argue on the basis of 3:21 and other texts that the segment concerning Christ's "exaltation" (2:9–11) is not "extraneous to its present context" (Wendland 2004b:98, 110).

6.7 A model of discourse: A literary-structural overview of Philippians

The following outline of Philippians traces out the letter's epistolary structure to suggest how Paul arranged his composition sequentially as he develops his principal ideas, especially the key hortatory and Christological topics listed above, as they together serve to develop his overarching theme of modeling the Gospel message in one's everyday circumstances. This outline is further supported by an assortment of literary-structural markers, which are summarized afterwards. The important thing to note here is that these are not primarily literary devices, prepared for the visual reader, but rather *oral-aural* signals and signposts,[25] intended first of all to guide a lector when publically proclaiming the text (perhaps even to memorize critical portions of it) and then also to assist an audience to more readily perceive and understand the message that they were concurrently hearing.[26]

---

[25] From an ancient Greco-Roman literary perspective, a letter "ought to be written in the same manner as a dialogue…as one of the two sides of a dialogue…. intended to be expressions of friendship or of one's friendly feelings (*philophronesis*)" (Köstenberger and Patterson 2011:459), thus evoking the (re)establishment of *parousia*, or personal presence, despite the actual physical (and temporal) distance between the writer and his readers (or more precisely, hearers, that is, via a reader-proclaimer of the letter).

[26] In a sound-centered study of the epistle of James, David Rhoads (2009) focuses "on the way in which a composition such as James reflects memory arts that assisted the performer in remembering the composition being performed…. These memory arts were built into the composition from the start as means for the composer to recall later, for other performers to recall, and for audiences to recall" (cf. Wendland 2008b:ch. 2). In addition to the genre and structure of the text as a whole, Rhoads (2009) notes the various stylistic and rhetorical forms, including phonological features (e.g., word chains, synonyms, correlatives, contrasts, alliteration/assonance, and "rhythmic beats in certain lines") as well as emotive devices ("striking images; strong language; stark threats or promises; proverbs") within the discourse that made it memorable in terms of both performance and communicative effectiveness. Rhoads also points out the important of a text's syntax in this regard, its various conjunctions, for example, which "move the speech forward in connected ways, help memory flow to know what is next [and] how each line relates to what went before and what follows."

6.7 A model of discourse: A literary-structural overview of Philippians

1:1 Greetings from Paul/Timothy "to the saints"
1:2 "Grace to you"
    1:3–8   Thanksgiving for the Philippians' "partnership in the gospel"
    1:9–11   Prayer that the Philippians might manifest "the fruits of righteousness"
    1:12–2:11 Letter *Body Opening*: "humility" in action
        1:12–18   Paul's focus is on "preaching Christ," even in prison
        1:19–26   Paul's desire is to "magnify Christ," whether in life or death
        1:27–31   Appeal for hearers to exhibit conduct "worthy of the gospel of Christ"
        2:1–4   Appeal to "be like-minded" through "encouragement (from) Christ"
        2:5–8   Christ's model of humiliation
        2:9–11   Christ has therefore been exalted as "Lord"

2:12–3:21 *Body Middle*: Follow good examples when pursuing the heavenly "prize"
    2:12–18   Appeal to "hold fast to the word of life" unto salvation in Christ
    2:19–24   Appeal to "seek the things of Christ," like Timothy
    2:25–30   Emulate the example of Epaphroditus in "the work of Christ"
    3:1–4a   Appeal to "boast [take confidence] in Christ," not in oneself
    3:4b–11   Appeal to "consider" [acknowledge] Christ as Lord above all else
    3:12–14   Paul's model of striving to gain "the goal of God's call" in Christ
    3:15–21   Appeal to follow Paul's pattern of "walking" and "waiting" for Christ

4:1–4:20	*Body Closing*: Prepare for the Lord's coming by being united in His "peace"
4:1	Appeal to "stand fast in the Lord"
4:2–3	Appeal to work together in unity
4:4–7	Appeal to "rejoice" and "pray," guarded by "the peace of God"
4:8–9	Appeal to put Paul's example into practice
4:10–14	Paul is strengthened in every situation in life by Christ
4:15–19	Wish for God's blessings upon the Philippians for their generosity
4:20	"Glory" be to God!
4:21–22	"Greetings" from "the saints" to every "saint"
4:23	"Grace" be to you all!

The table below gives a summary of the main discourse markers of *discontinuity*, *continuity*, and *prominence* within the sequence of compositional (paragraph, sometimes larger) constituents in Philippians. For example, in the second unit (1:3–8), Paul opens with the distinctive "thanksgiving" portion of his epistles (the formulaic Εὐχαριστῶ τῷ θεῷ μου), a single sentence that features "you" (Philippians) and "all" at the beginning (πάσῃ...ὑμῶν) and ending (πάντας ὑμᾶς).[27] This is followed by a climactic emotive concluding utterance that leads off with a focal oath (μάρτυς γάρ μου ὁ θεὸς) and closes with "Christ Jesus," in reversed order from its occurrence at the end of the preceding constituent in v. 2 ("Jesus Christ"). There is also the mention of "God" in both of these unit-ending lines, an instance of structural *epiphora*.[28] This perspective on the text further illustrates how Paul

---

[27] Mitternacht surveys the various types of "epistolary formulas" that occur in a Hellenistic letter (2007:66–73). These serve as structural discourse markers, usually paragraph "openers," and thus also facilitate the text's oral proclamation and mnemonic potential. Mitternacht mentions other Pauline epistolary features that would promote "the oral performance of the letter in a group context" (ibid., 58)— for example, "basic indicators of situational interaction," such as devices for attracting attention (vocatives and other features of direct address, like 2nd person plural verbs/pronouns) and for engaging the audience, such as highly emotive-affective (confrontational, agonistic, empathetic, participatory, etc.) language (ibid., 59–60).

[28] The literary-structural devices of *anaphora* (unit-initial parallels), *epiphora* (unit-final parallels), *anadiplosis* (tail-head unit parallels), and *inclusio* (unit-initial and final parallels) are further explained and exemplified in Wendland 2004b:126–134; 2001:207–209; cf. §5.3.3 above.

6.7 A model of discourse: A literary-structural overview of Philippians

develops his central theme of *modeling the Christ-like message* from one paragraph to the next, from the opening salutation to his final greetings. The important point to note from an *oral-aural* communication perspective is how these different structural markers further serve as phonologically prominent signals to effectively "format" the text with memory hooks for all future preachers and also audibly for their audiences as this letter was/is being proclaimed aloud:[29]

Text Unit	Topic for Mutual Modeling	Structural Markers of Demarcation and Cohesion (**B** = beginning, **M** = middle, **E** = ending of the text unit)
1:1–2	Paul greets the Philippians with a fervent Christological wish.	Apostolic epistolary formula: Writer => Addressees + "Grace to you..."; repeated reference to "Jesus Christ"
1:3–8	Paul thanks and praises God for the Philippians ("fellowship").	**B**: formula = "I thank my God for..." **M**: a long periodic sentence in Greek, beginning and ending with "all [of] you" (3–7), followed by [+] a climactic closing utterance (an oath, "God is my witness," 8) **E**: the pericope concludes with an emotive figure: "bowels of Christ Jesus" (reversed from v. 2, structural *epiphora*)

---

[29] Additional details that reflect the orality of this epistle, e.g., instances of alliteration, assonance, rhyming, punning, lexical repetition, synonymy, epistolary formulas, antithesis, climax, vocatives, direct address, transitional expressions, graphic figurative language, personal examples, etc., may be noted in Heil's commentary (2010:*passim*), though our proposed structural boundaries do not always match. In this connection, see also Harvey 1998:233–245 and Davis 1999:chs. 3–4. Note that "the attention of the listening audience is triggered every time a new section begins" (Mitternacht 2007:75).

1:9–11	Paul prays for the Philippians (a continuation of the example of Christians thanking God and praying for one another on a regular basis).	**B**: illocutionary shift to "prayer"; front-shift [FS] "this" τοῦτο (cataphoric reference forward to what follows) **M**: prayer mode continues throughout the paragraph **E**: concludes with a doxology (11), with reference again to "Jesus Christ" and "God" (cf. vv. 2, 8; = *epiphora* again)
1:12–18	Fearlessly preaching the gospel to win souls for Christ in spite of opposition is Paul's supreme desire and goal (as it should be for all Christians).	**B**: apostolic disclosure formula: "I want you to know" + vocative ("brothers") **M**: cohesive expressions = "preach Christ" + "my bonds" **E**: ends with an emphatic rhetorical phrase τί γάρ + the repeated thematic "rejoice" motif
1:19–26	Paul lives for Christ and to serve the Philippians in a mutual joyful fellowship.	**B**: "For I know that" (cf. v. 12, *anaphora*) + shift in topic **M**: internal debate about alternatives: "dying" or "living" **E**: *inclusio* = "deliverance through your prayer" (19a) and "my coming again to you" (26b); in "Christ Jesus" cf. v. 11 (*epiphora*)
1:27–30	Paul encourages the Philippians to stand firm with him in unity and in remaining faithful to the gospel of Christ.	**B**: FS "Only worthily of the gospel of Christ" + letter's first imperative "conduct yourselves"; shift to 2pl. exhortation **M**: key word cohesion: "gospel—Christ—faith/believe" (2x each) **E**: P. closes by emphasizing his role as mentor (ἐν ἐμοί, 2x); *inclusio*: "see/hear" (vv. 27/30)

6.7 A model of discourse: A literary-structural overview of Philippians

2:1–4	Paul poetically appeals for total unity in selfless humility.[a]	**B**: elaborate iterative conditional series introduces Paul's second command regarding *inner* attitudes (cf. preceding pericope on *external* behavior) **M**: cohesive emphasis on unity and mutual concern **E**: back-shift [BS] focus on "each one" being involved in this unity, juxtaposed to "others" (τὰ ἑτέρων ἕκαστοι)
2:5–11	Christ is the divine Model of perfect humility and future glory that all Christians are to emulate.	**B**: FS "This" (τοῦτο)—cataphoric, pointing ahead to what follows in the text **M**: an extended *chiasmus* lends coherence to the entire unit **E**: this final segment of the Body Opening complements its beginning as the "content" of Paul's activity of preaching Christ (1:12–18); it concludes with a doxology (v. 11, cf. 1:11, structural corresponding end-unit *epiphora*)
2:12–18	Believers need to work hard to remain firm in the faith.	**B**: Paul begins to elaborate upon the points made in the Body Opening—Ὥστε + vocative ("my beloved ones"); 2pl. paraenesis continues (cf. 1:27) **M**: cohesion in words from semantic field of "work" (exerting effort in the Christian life) **E**: ends with emphatic double statement of the "rejoice" motif (vv. 17b–18; cf. 1:18, = *epiphora*); reference also to "faith" and mutual "sacrifice/suffering" "with" Paul (cf. 1:29b–30, = *epiphora*)

2:19–24	Paul commends the Christ-centered, devoted service of Timothy.	**B:** sudden shift in topic—Timothy as another "mentor" in the Christian faith-life **M:** cohesion through P's praise of and plan for Timothy—a model of "service" (cf. 2:17) "in the Lord Jesus" **E:** surprising shift to P's plan to "come" to Philippi (apostolic parousia); *inclusio* = "in the Lord" (ἐν κυρίῳ); another *inclusio*: ἐλπίζω/πέμψαι/ταχέως (19/23–24)
2:25–30	Paul praises Epaphroditus for his willingness to risk his life for him and requests a warm welcome for him at Philippi.	**B:** shift in topic and tone (*pathos*) to the distressing affairs of Epaphroditus **M:** the focus is on Epaphroditus throughout—a model of suffering on behalf of Christ and fellow-Christians **E:** marked syntactic arrangement of final clause, FS "because of the work of Christ"; BS "service"; *inclusio* 25/30: ἔργον and λειτουργία (cf. 2:17—*epiphora*)
3:1–4a	Paul warns against following the teachings and example of false Judaistic teachers.	**B:** transitional phrase Τὸ λοιπόν + vocative ("my brothers") + "rejoice" motif + return to 2pl. exhortation **M:** inner emphasis on "watch out!" (βλέπετε, 3x) **E:** chiastic close: A/A' "in flesh"—B/B' "confidence"

6.7 A model of discourse: A literary-structural overview of Philippians

3:4b–11	Paul contrasts the "rubbish" of personal "law righteousness" with righteousness by "faith in Christ."	**B**: hypothetical example (εἴ τις, cf. 2:1, structural *anaphora*) + overlap construction (*anadiplosis*) "confidence—in flesh" **M**: cohesive (pro)nominal references to "Christ" + "righteousness" + "consider" (ἡγέομαι) **E**: repeated reference to "resurrection" and "dead/death" (2x each); closes on a climactic note with another conditional (εἴ) construction (*inclusio* with v. 4b)
3:12–14	Paul determinedly pursues the theological goal of God's heavenward "call" in Christ.	**B**: begins with emphatic (FS) negative contrastive expression (Οὐχ ὅτι ἤδη ἔλαβον ἢ ἤδη τετελείωμαι); reiterated key term "laid hold of" (καταλαμβάνω, 4x); contrast also in v. 13, emphasized by vocative "brothers" **M**: repeated reference to personal (1st sg.) cognitive evaluation in relation to the goal of salvation **E**: Climactic close in "the upward call of God in Christ Jesus" (v. 12, *inclusio*), which is the "goal" that P. implies in v. 12, thus also setting up the following exhortation

3:15–21	Paul appeals to fellow believers to follow his example of desiring a glorious citizenship in heaven.	**B:** FS "Whoever therefore [are] mature" + repeated key verb "regard" (φρονέω, cf. 2:5) + return to 2nd pl. exhortation **M:** internal alternating contrast between earthly and heavenly matters and between some who may "think differently," who "live as enemies of the cross of Christ" and "those who live according to the pattern that we gave you," whose "citizenship is in heaven **E:** *epiphoric* reference to the "glory" (δόξα) of Christ and his Omnipotence (cf. 2:11); also a climactic reference to the believer's resurrection (cf. 3:11, more *epiphora*)
4:1ᵇ	Paul repeats his general appeal to "stand firmly (together!) in the Lord."	**B:** transition to letter's Body Closing: Ὥστε + ἀγαπητοί (cf. 2:11, *anaphora*) + vocative ("my brothers") + crucial imperative "stand fast!" (στήκετε ἐν κυρίῳ) (cf. 1:27) —how? through "the Lord's" enabling power (cf. 3:20–21) **M:** vocative reference extended in figurative terms **E:** vocative (ἀγαπητοί) reiterated at the very close; 4:1 acts as a "hinge verse" that links in both directions, back to 3:21 and forward to 4:2
4:2–3	Paul urges a renewal of unity and harmony in joint gospel ministry.	**B:** double "I appeal" (παρακαλῶ), preceded by foregrounded personal names "Euodia" and "Syntyche"; topical shift from group perspective to individuals within the group **M:** extended appeal to unity **E:** ends with major eschatological phrase, "the book of life"

6.7 A model of discourse: A literary-structural overview of Philippians

4:4–7	Paul encourages prayer in place of perplexity to attain the peace of God.	**B**: a double call to "rejoice!" (Χαίρετε) begins the unit + "in the Lord" (cf. 3:1, strong structural *anaphora*) **M**: a series of commands leads to their result—"peace of God" **E**: *inclusio*: "in the Lord" (4) / "Christ Jesus" (7; also *epiphora*: 3:14, 1:26)
4:8–9	Paul again calls for Christlike attitudes and appropriate behavior, according to his example.	**B**: the transitional phrase Τὸ λοιπόν + vocative ("brothers"; cf. 3:1, 4:1 = *anaphora*) **M**: repeated reference to abstract "things"; a poetic, rhythmic, alliterative style occurs throughout the unit[c] **E**: final focus on modeling Paul (cf. 1:30, *epiphora*); inverted key phrase "God of peace": ὁ θεὸς τῆς εἰρήνης (cf. ἡ εἰρήνη τοῦ θεοῦ in 4:7 = *epiphora*)
4:10–14	Paul rejoices in the Lord and is therefore content in every situation, whatever the circumstances.	**B**: new topic + δὲ + "rejoice in the Lord" motif (cf. 4:4, 1:18b = *anaphora*); double ref. to keyword "think, be concerned about" (φρονεῖν) **M**: P. refers to his continual contentment and mentions the Philippian gift at the beginning and ending of this unit, but speaks about his own attitude in the middle **E**: the A-B-A' topical arrangement of this pericope concludes with the thematic notion of "fellowship" (συγκοινωνέω); concessive πλὴν (cf. 3:16, = *epiphora*; also 1:18, 3:4a)

4:15–20 Paul thanks the Philippians for their gift of fellowship and blesses them for it.	B: P. addresses the "Philippians" directly (vocative); I "know," cf. 1:12, 19 (*anaphora*), overlapping reference to "fellowship"(κοινωνέω—v. 14, *anadiplosis*) M: P. refers to the generous gift of the Philippians throughout E: a closing wish for the Philippians' well-being "in Christ Jesus" (v. 19, cf. 4:1, 7; 3:14) leads to a paragraph-ending doxology and an affirmative "amen" (ἀμήν—v. 20)
4:21–23 Paul sends final greetings and concludes with a "grace" wish for the Philippian congregation.	The letter ends with a typical section of Pauline "greetings" with repeated reference (ἀσπάζομαι), corresponding to the opening salutation (1:1), plus the apostolic "grace" in farewell (χάρις v. 23, cf. 1:2, = macro-*inclusio*); also a chiastic *inclusio* for this closing paragraph: Χριστῷ Ἰησοῦ...Ἰησοῦ Χριστοῦ (21/23)

[a]The following poetic, threefold strophic arrangement of vv. 1–4, obviously conducive for memorizing and an oral elocution of the text, has been suggested by Black (1985:302):

A Εἴ τις οὖν παράκλησις ἐν Χριστῷ,
  B εἴ τι παραμύθιον ἀγάπης,
    C εἴ τις κοινωνία πνεύματος,
      D εἴ τις σπλάγχνα καὶ οἰκτιρμοί,
A πληρώσατέ μου τὴν χαρὰν ἵνα τὸ αὐτὸ φρονῆτε,
  B τὴν αὐτὴν ἀγάπην ἔχοντες,
  B σύμψυχοι,
A τὸ ἓν φρονοῦντες,
A μηδὲν κατ' ἐριθείαν μηδὲ κατὰ κενοδοξίαν
  B ἀλλὰ τῇ ταπεινοφροσύνῃ ἀλλήλους ἡγούμενοι ὑπερέχοντας ἑαυτῶν,
A μὴ τὰ ἑαυτῶν ἕκαστος σκοποῦντες
  B ἀλλὰ [καὶ] τὰ ἑτέρων ἕκαστοι.

[b]The beginning of ch. 4 offers a good example of the different discourse structures as proposed by myself here in comparison with Heil and Davis.

6.7 A model of discourse: A literary-structural overview of Philippians

I suggest three opening units: 4:1 (a transitional verse), 2-3, and 4-7, as summarized above. Heil proposes a rather unlikely chiastic arrangement covering 4:1-5, i.e., A (1-2), B (3a), C (3b)-C' (3c), B' (3d), A' (4-5) (2010:142; the division of v. 3 into four chiastic units is especially problematic). Davis, on the other hand, has two units, 4:1-3 and 4-7 (1999:140). However, he links 4:1-3 with a series of three segments beginning in ch. 3 (3:2-16, 3:17-21, 4:1-3). This simply illustrates part of the difficulties connected with these structural outlines. They may conflict with each other and hence confuse rather then enlighten readers. Thus, all such proposals, including my own, must be critically evaluated with regard to perspicuity, credibility, validity, comprehensiveness, etc. on the basis of explicitly stated criteria in relation to the purpose of the analysis itself. It should also be noted that such structural descriptions may differ with respect to the level of discourse being considered, that is, with a more or less inclusive perspective. In the reversed formulations of Heil, for example, 3:1-21 is regarded as a single macro-unit consisting of nine chiastically arranged micro-units (ibid., 114-115). Davis proposes three units, 3:1 as a transition, then 2-16 and 17-21 (ibid., 140). I differentiate four units: 3:1-4a, 4b-11, 12-14, and 15-21. Much of the same linguistic evidence is being considered, but it has been diversely interpreted. These structural differences will naturally have consequences as far as understanding the text as well as its actual oral articulation is concerned (e.g., pause and stress points, intonation patterns).

ʿThe poetic parallelism, with its corresponding appeal to orality, appears below:
ὅσα ἐστὶν ἀληθῆ,
ὅσα σεμνά,
ὅσα δίκαια,
ὅσα ἁγνά,
ὅσα προσφιλῆ,
ὅσα εὔφημα,
εἴ τις ἀρετὴ
καὶ εἴ τις ἔπαινος, ταῦτα λογίζεσθε·
ἃ καὶ ἐμάθετε
καὶ παρελάβετε
καὶ ἠκούσατε
καὶ εἴδετε ἐν ἐμοί, ταῦτα πράσσετε·

6.8 Modeling the message—another rhetorical perspective

The preceding *literary* examination of Philippians involved a systematic analysis of the matter and manner of writing, that is, the text's *structure* (the larger compositional units and their arrangement) and *style* (distinctive linguistic features on the micro-level of discourse organization).[30] This forms the basis for a subsequent *rhetorical* study, which deals more with the *functional* significance of literary form, that is, how an oral text (or one written for public performance) has been structurally and stylistically shaped in order to enhance its specific communicative purposes and overall pragmatic effects—its capacity to *convince*, to *persuade*, and to *motivate* the intended receptors.[31] In other words, one examines the way in which the art of composition is utilized in the service of promoting the author's message by exhorting and motivating his target *audience* (normally a group of listeners is in view) so as to reinforce, modify, or completely change their current beliefs and/or behavior. An "oral-rhetorical approach" (Wendland 2008b:viii–ix) offers an explanation, for

---

[30] In terms of its epistolary genre, Fee proposes that Philippians is a "hortatory letter of friendship" (1995:12; for the reasoning, see ibid., 2–14). For a listing of ancient "letter types," see Mitternacht 2007:65. Garland disagrees and prefers simply "a hortatory letter that is reinforced with appeals to examples" (2006:184). With regard to 2:6–11, Basevi and Chapa call this passage "not only an *exemplum*, but a praise, an *encomium*, of the real cause of Christian unity. Christ is praised because of his nature and because of what he did. If Christ had not been God and had not died, Paul's argument could not be maintained" (1993:349).

[31] My translation-oriented "literary-rhetorical" methodology (Wendland 2004b: 80–95) does not delineate all of the detailed aspects of a traditional classical rhetorical approach since these are often rather debatable and hence differ from one analyst to the next (Porter 1993:100–122; Köstenberger and Patterson 2011:467–468). In general, the three main "canons," or aspects, of Greco-Roman rhetoric normally investigated with respect to NT literature concern the argument(s) chosen in relation to text content (*inventio*), the structure or arrangement of the discourse in terms of the whole and its parts (*dispositio*), and style, or the choice of particular linguistic constructions and literary features (*elocutio*) (cf. Kennedy 1984:13; Murphy 1994:63–66; Wendland 2002:169–195). Two additional canons, namely, memory, the preparation for delivery (*memoria*), and pronunciation, including the use of non-verbal gestures (*pronunciatio*) (Kennedy ibid., 13–14), are generally not considered (e.g., Murphy ibid., 63), though the latter, in particular, is highly relevant to Bible translations, especially those that are meant to be read or recited aloud (as most are; see below).

6.8 Modeling the message—another rhetorical perspective

example, for why Paul withholds his pointed expression of thanks for the Philippians' concrete gestures of support until the very end of his epistle to them (4:14–20) so that "these are intentionally the last words left ringing in their ears as the letter concludes, words of gratitude, theology, and doxology that simply soar" (Fee 1995:17).

According to Aristotle (Murphy 1994:58), "rhetoric" may be defined as the formal practice of verbal persuasion through a personal appeal to *logos* (reason/logic), *pathos* (passion/emotion), and/or *ethos* (credibility/integrity).[32] The particular mode or manner of argumentation in a defined discourse, such as a NT epistle, may be further illustrated by means of the rhetorical "triangle," as shown below:

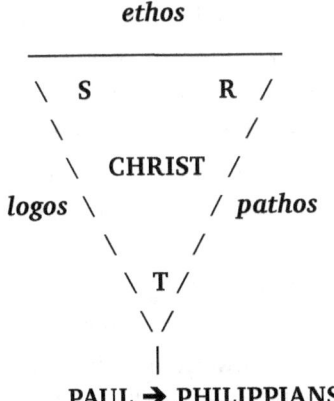

ethos = argument supporting the authority
(S ⇔ R) and reliability of the **S**ource

pathos = argument aimed at affecting the
(R ⇔ T) emotions/attitudes of **R**eceptor(s)

logos = argument based on the style and
(S ⇔ T) logical arrangement of the **T**ext

It is important to note the overall prominence of *ethos* as part of Paul's "argument" in Philippians. This aspect of *ethos* centers in his affectionate partnership with the Philippian congregation (e.g., 1:5, 7–8, 25–26), including his suffering (1:12–14; 2:17) and that of his colleagues (2:19–30) for the sake of the gospel (*logos*), which served as examples of their complete commitment to the cause of Christ.[33] Such devotion to duty serves as a

---

[32] Thuren suggests a differentiation here: "*Argumentation* aims at changing or modifying the audience's thoughts, while the goal of *persuasion* is action" (1993:468; italics added).

[33] "Within Philippians, Paul makes extensive and diverse use of identifications with the audience and with God/Christ to build the trustworthiness and authority dimensions of his ethos, respectively" (Marshall 1993:370). However, it is important to point out that in this epistle Paul clearly subordinates his "authority roles" (ibid., 370) to express the spirit of partnership (1:5; 2:17–18) as well as to model

Christ-like "model" (2:5–11) for his readers to follow in their lives of Christian service and in "standing fast" against all threats to their faith-life in Him. This particular interpersonal emphasis, involving also an appeal to their emotions (*pathos*), may have been necessary due to Paul's lack of detailed knowledge concerning what was going on in the Philippian congregation (hence his great desire to know more, cf. 1:27, 2:19). Based in their past expression of assistance and fellowship, Paul wished to encourage his listeners to remain faithful to and supportive of the saving message that he and others had "preached" to them, despite their current trials, deprivation, and attacks from diverse opponents (e.g., 1:7, 11, 14, 18, 27–30).[34]

It appears that Paul also employed the three standard "species," or types, of rhetorical argument in his letter to the Philippians, namely, *judicial*, which concerns the forensic determination of truth and justice or right and wrong with regard to certain controversial (debatable) words or actions; *deliberative*, which concerns the evaluation and encouragement (or dissuasion) of what is beneficial and expedient (or the opposite) with respect to some proposed action or decision; and *epideictic*, which concerns the celebration or condemnation (praise/blame) of a person's past or present behavior and character (Wendland 2002a:173–174).[35] Of course, these three considerations often overlap in their apparent manifestation within a given discourse, and as a result it is not always easy to distinguish among them. Furthermore, they may be realized within the framework of a single span of text, for example, in the first chapter of Philippians: judicial (1:28b), deliberative (1:3–6), epideictic (1:15–16). In any case, the crucial epideictic passage in this letter is 2:6–11, which lauds Christ as the ultimate (divine) example of humility and model of suffering for the sake of others. This should in turn motivate the various deliberative exhortations that surround the humility of his Lord (2:6–9), which is the "example" (τύπος) that he wishes his readers to follow (3:17; cf. 4:10–19).

[34] Paul makes various references (some rather pejorative) to those who oppose him and the Gospel about Christ: hypocritical preachers (1:15–16), adversaries/enemies (1:28), a perverted generation (2:15), self-seekers (2:21), dogs/evil workers/mutilators (3:2), the "perfect ones" (? 3:15), enemies of the cross of Christ (3:18), earthly-minded ones (3:19), stingy churches (4:15).

[35] Rhetoricians debate these categories with respect to a given text: For some, Philippians is an *epideictic* discourse (e.g., Basevi and Chapa 1993:349; Kennedy 1984:77); others claim, just as strongly, that it is *deliberative* in character (e.g., Marshall 1993:363; Watson 1988:59). On the other hand, I feel that most epistles (and prophetic books) manifest aspects or sections of all three rhetorical species.

6.8 Modeling the message—another rhetorical perspective

this pericope (i.e., 2:1–4, 12–18; 3:1–4, 3:15–4:1, 4:1–9) and ultimately, the primary communicative purpose of the epistle as a whole, namely, to substitute for his personal, pastoral presence (1:24–26; 2:24).

In view of the likelihood of ambiguity in following the ancient rhetorical manner of classifying and analyzing texts, it may be advantageous to examine an author's strategy of persuasion in a literary creation by using a more specific, pragmatic *speech-act* approach, already summarized in §2.2.3.[36] In brief, a "speech act" is comprised of three communicative aspects, namely, the formal verbal utterance, whether spoken or written, called the "locution"; the basic communicative goal or intention of that utterance (the "illocution"); and the actual cognitive or perceived behavioral effect on the hearer/reader of that utterance (the "perlocution"). Space does not permit me to carry out a precise speech-act analysis of Philippians, but I might venture a general overview of Paul's multifaceted purpose in writing this epistle. This takes the form of a synchronic synthesis of some of the letter's primary *illocutionary objectives*—that is, aims considered in relation to the text's overarching hortatory theme: how to "persuade" (in the widest sense) believers to persistently and consistently "model the message" of their communal faith in Christ. These mutually-supporting communicative functions are summarized below:[37]

- **Encouragement** to remain steadfast ("stand fast"—4:1) in loving fellowship, unity, good works, prayer, and faithfulness to the truths of the gospel—with joyful hope, despite their facing varied temptations and forms of persecution (e.g., 1:1, 3–11, 25–26, 27–30; 2:1–4, 12–18; 3:7–11, 12–14, 20–21; 4:1, 3, 4–6, 8–9, 21–22).

---

[36] See also Wendland 2004b:214–18.

[37] This is simply a sample listing (with illustrative passages) to use as a point of reference for others to critique and develop more fully if so desired (cf. Thuren 1993:469–470). Most of these communicative functions are anticipated, as is normal, in Paul's opening section of thanksgiving and prayer (1:3–11). For Fee, the *theology* of Paul "is confessional (cf. 1:18–24; 3:3–14) and doxological (4:19–20)" (1995:47), highlighting these key theological motifs (ibid., 46–53): *Gospel*-oriented (e.g., 1:5, 7, 12, 16, 25, 27; 4:15), *Trinitarian*—Father (e.g., 1:3,11, 28; 2:15), Son ("in Christ"—21x), Spirit (1:19; 2:1; 3:3). This provides an *eschatological* foundation for faith (e.g., 1:6, 10; 2:16; 3:14, 19–21; 4:5) and promotes a *steadfast, sacrificial Christian life in community* (e.g., 1:9, 27, 29–30; 2:2–4; 3:17, 20; 4:1–3, 8–9).

- **Admonition** (negative appeal) to avoid un-Christ-like behavior, especially that which causes dissension within the Body (e.g., 1:27; 2:3a, 14–15; 3:1, 15–16, 17; 4:2).
- **Provide information** about Paul's personal circumstances in prison (e.g., 1:12–26; 4:10–19).
- **Commission** of Timothy, a trusted co-worker, on a fact-finding assignment to the Philippian congregation (e.g., 2:19–24).
- **Commendation** of Epaphroditus, an exemplary Philippian believer, whom Paul was sending back due to ill health (2:25–30).
- **Warning** against false teachers, legalists as well as libertines (3:2–6, 18–19), indirectly also against religious opportunists (1:15–17), who disrupt or even destroy corporate unity.
- **Thanksgiving** for this congregation's supportive and generous gifts (e.g., 1:5; 4:10–18).
- **Reminder** of certain basic gospel teachings (e.g., 2:5–11; 3:9; 4:20–21).
- **Prayer** for God's blessings to rest upon them (e.g., 1:2, 10; 4:7, 19, 23).
- **Praise** to the glory of God and the Lord Jesus Christ (e.g., 1:11; 2:11; 4:20).

Considering this bundle of illocutionary aims with respect to the letter as a whole, we observe how they are for the most part positive and constructive in nature, thus reflecting the "love"-based "joy" that Paul felt when dealing with the Philippian congregation (e.g., 1:4, 7, 18; 2:2, 17–18; 3:1; 4:1, 10). It was this complex, all-embracing spiritual emotion that he as their pastor also wanted them to experience in their interpersonal relationships (e.g., 4:2–4) so that inner as well as outer "peace" would prevail (4:7, 9).

At some point during the pragmatic analysis of any biblical writing, it is important also to take into account also the so-called "rhetorical exigence,"[38] that is, the specific sociocultural context and religious environment in which it was originally communicated (as nearly as this can be determined on the basis of reliable evidence). The occasion or circumstances of composition and reception will obviously influence the author's method and means of argumentation and ethical appeal. One way to form a hypothesis concerning the setting and hence also the motivation for an

---

[38] For some details on this contextual feature, see Kennedy 1984:35; Wendland 2002a:173, 184.

6.8 Modeling the message—another rhetorical perspective

epistle, is to identify its main exhortations, that is, whether to continue in or desist from a particular manner of thinking or living. In the case of Philippians, several prominent references to instances of harmful speech and behavior seem to motivate Paul's varied encouragements to follow better, Christ-like "models," namely: [a] self-serving rival preachers (1:15–18); [b] external, non-Christian enemies (1:27–30); [c] Judaizing preachers and teachers (3:2–4); [d] members who demonstrate earthly, immoral life-styles (3:18–19; this category may refer back also to [a] or [c]); and [e] co-workers involved in petty, but disruptive disputes (4:2–3).[39]

The rhetorical exigence of a Pauline epistle would include, in addition to pertinent historical information, the prevailing Ancient Near Eastern cultural norms, values, attitudes, beliefs, and so forth. Accordingly, the situationally influenced "rhetoric" in Philippians needs to be further investigated in the light of a traditional Mediterranean worldview and way of life. The key thematic concept of "modeling," for example, is probably related to or based upon the "honor-shame" polarity—or "patron-client" relations. However, according to Pilch and Malina it is above all a feature of the core value of "group orientation," which "shows up in the constant injunction that disciples imitate their masters" (Pilch and Malina 1993:89). The following is a survey of just a few of the critical insights that a "social-scientific" perspective can provide for analysts of NT epistolary literature, with special reference to Paul's letter to the Philippians and the crucial motives of self-evaluation, service, fellowship, humility, obedience, patience, and exaltation (honor).

Christ, for example, the focal personage of this epistle, is a perfect model of "the obedient son" (Phil 2:6; Heb 3:2, 6), for he "valued obedience to his Father's will enough to die for it" (Pilch and Malina 1993:125). He was also a person of "patience" and "humility," that is, showing oneself as "powerless to defend one's status" (cf. Phil 2:8) (ibid., 132, 107). However, depending on the situation, "humility [may also be] a means value, that is, a course of action or behavior which facilitates the realization of *honor*, the core value of Mediterranean culture" (ibid., 108)—that is, by acting selflessly on behalf of the group (Phil 2:5–8), and subsequently being acclaimed by the group (2:9–11). On the other hand, Christ is the *anti-model* of someone who

---

[39] Cf. Banker 1997:14; Snyman 1993:327; contra Marshall, who "question[s] whether Paul knew exactly what he was writing against" (1993:361).

acts conventionally in accordance with the principles of "limited good" and "domination orientation" (ibid., 46), that is, in the concerted effort to preserve one's inherited status or to exercise "lordship" over others (Phil 2:6–7; cf. 2 Cor 8:9) (Malina 1981:90, 93). Therefore, "Jesus Christ" will receive in addition to his innate glory as the Son of God (2:6, 9) the "ascribed honor" (the highest "name") of all creation (2:9–11) (Pilch and Malina 1993:103).

For their part, Christ's followers (or "imitators) are to be "pure," that is, blameless (2:15) and innocent (3:6) (Malina 1981:53; Malina and Neyrey 1991a). This relates to the notion of the "dyadic personality" (Neyrey 1991b), e.g., Paul who, like his Lord, gave up his "ascribed honor" (3:4–6) for the sake of Christ (3:7–8). So also the fellowship or family of the Church, in Christ, should make a living testimony within secular society (4:8–9, 21–22) in accordance with the "holiness code"—especially "kinship" and "saints" (Malina 1981:29, 99, 115, 152). Similarly, obedient and loving "self-sacrifice," for example (see 2:1–4; 3:16), "is a [multifaceted] value that serves as a means of preserving honor which is rooted in the group and shared in by individual members of the group," i.e., within an "honor-shame society" (Pilch and Malina 1993:157–158). This involved "service" to one another, a contra-cultural activity that was divergent from prevailing social ideals in relation to one's fellow man but essential in the religious realm with respect to God. Hence, "the slave service…owed God in Temple worship is now to be displayed in the Christian's service to neighbor, which is service to Christ" (e.g., 2:22, 30) (ibid., 160), in keeping with the divine Servant's own ideal example (2:5–8).

So it was that "in Paul's view, those 'in Christ' need to reassess what they once considered honorable in favor of a new set of standards" (cf. 3:4–8) (ibid., 99–100). "Status" in the eyes of Christ is what counts, both now and at the last day (1:27; 2:16), not one's social standing in the community at large, or even within the fellowship of believers. Accordingly, the primary curse of sin, which initially stems from loveless, individual and/or social pride (1:15–17; 2:3–4), is to stand judicially "shamed" before God, rather than to be liable to specific punishments (3:8–9) (ibid., 95–104). Christ's followers thus acknowledge and live according to a new "dyadic identity" (ibid., 51), namely, as brothers and sisters in the family of God (4:1–3) and as citizens in his Kingdom (3:20). The Philippians' "sharing" of their meager resources with the imprisoned Apostle (4:15) was a commendable

6.8 Modeling the message—another rhetorical perspective

manifestation of the core social value of "hospitality" in relation to fellow members of the community of Christ (ibid., 104).

As far as he personally was concerned, Paul's public witness, expressed in his letter to the Philippians, demonstrated "assertiveness" (1:20) as befitting an "honor-able" citizen of the Empire (Pilch and Malina 1993:10), who defended the goals and principles of the Christian society. This "boldness" was based on his complete confidence in Christ and his total allegiance to his Lord (ibid., 180). Nevertheless, Paul also exhibited a deliberate "equivocation" with respect to his "rights" vis-à-vis others, that is, though he could lay claim to a certain status with its associated privileges, he did not exercise these rights, giving them up for the good of the Christian community and as a follower of the example of Christ (cf. 3:4–7) (ibid., 59–61). In short, Paul modeled himself on the supreme Model of Christ: "like Jesus…[Paul] forgoes the former value found in the Law and seeks only to be conformed to the dying and risen Jesus" (ibid., 89) (cf. 2:16–17; 3:7–10, 17).

We thus see that the "persuasive" component of rhetorical argumentation in the case of any socioculturally-oriented literary "text" is *behavioral* (not only verbal) in nature. It involves the explicit or implicit hortatory appeal to maintain one's actions in accordance with prevailing social standards and the popular (or the author's!) perception of what is fitting and proper, good, praiseworthy, etc.—as well as the norms of the religious, ethical and theological framework that controls one's thinking and behavior. This "Christian," forward-looking frame of reference, or world-view, is frequently made explicit at crucial junctures in any NT epistle, in Philippians, for example, not only in 2:6–11, but also in 1:6, 10; 3:10–11, 20–21; 4:3c, 7, 19. This includes, as indicated earlier, a largely implicit and allusive, but nonetheless significant *intertextual* framework of reference that stems from the Hebrew Scriptures (or, more likely, the Septuagint translation) which the Apostle assumes his hearers are quite familiar with. One of the clearest examples of this occurs, appropriately, at the close of the Christological hymn of praise:[40]

---

[40] Other such instances of intertextuality include 3:9 (cf. Hab 2:4b); 3:19 (Ps 73:4–6, 19); 4:4 (Ps 97:12, Hab 3:18); 4:5–6 (Ps 145:18); 4:7 (Ps 26:3–4); 4:19 (Ps 23:1).

> ...that at the name of Jesus every knee should bow
>> in heaven and on earth and under the earth,
> and every tongue confess that Jesus Christ is Lord,
>> to the glory of God the Father. (Phil 2:10–11, NIV)

> Before me every knee will bow;
>> By me every tongue will swear.
> They will say of me,
>> "In the LORD alone are righteousness and strength.
>> All who have raged against him
>>> will come to him and be put to shame." (Isa 23b–24; cf. Ps 95:6)

The text and cotext of the Isaiah segment add three significant elements to the public (note the *direct quote*) Christological confession of Philippians: (a) the explicit identification of Yahweh ("me") with "Jesus Christ" ("Lord"); (b) an expression of the Christ's soteriological role: "Turn to me and be saved, all you ends of the earth!" (Isa 45:22a); and (c) the supreme certainty of this belief, which is underscored by a personal oath by Yahweh himself (Isa 45:23a; cf. Phil 2:9).

6.9 Modeling the message in translation—An "oratorical" version of Philippians 2:5–11

It is one thing to competently *analyze* a literary document in the source language; it is quite another matter to *communicate* that same text effectively in another language and cultural context. This is not the place to discuss present (or past) translation theory and practice (Wendland 2004b:ch. 2), so at this stage I will simply recommend and apply one particular approach that seems most appropriate for the passage at hand, Phil 2:5–11. I term this a literary functional-equivalence (*LiFE*), oratorical method. Accordingly, the goal is to render in the "target language" (TL)[41]

---

[41] As already noted earlier, the term "target language" is not really the best since it implies a passive audience, which is certainly not the case in the making of meaning. The terms "guest" and "host language" have been suggested as alternatives, but such qualifiers do not work so well with "text" or "message," especially where the Scriptures are concerned. Language of course is a central aspect of the more inclusive domain of culture, including a people's worldview, value system, and way of life.

6.9 Modeling the message in translation

a vernacular version that accurately matches[42] the "source language" (SL) message with respect to its salient communicative functions (imperative, expressive, informative, esthetic, etc.) and also in a manner which manifests a similar degree of oral-aural dynamism that reflects the source-language composition.[43] This type of translation seems especially appropriate for conveying a pericope which is prominent, not only with regard to its literary-rhetorical qualities (as shown in the preceding sections), but one that is also of central thematic significance in the document at hand, Paul's epistle to the Philippians. It is in this extended sense then that such a more energetic and idiomatic rendition may be said to "model the message" that it transmits.

The importance of the *phonic* dimension in the analysis of biblical texts has already been pointed out above. In order to take this aspect of the SL discourse into consideration, one must devise a specific methodology to appropriately deal with it. Normally, this involves a careful examination of the Greek (or Hebrew) text in an effort to discern the various conjunctive and disjunctive markers of its "oral-aural envelope," for example: vocatives and exclamations; rhyme and rhythmic utterances; contrastive and complementary sound sequences; punning; any sort of reiteration of verbal form such as lexical chains or hook words; parallel, alternating, and chiastic arrangements; redundant personal pronouns; word order shifts from the norm; and polysyndeton or asyndeton.[44] This type of analysis was already carried out with respect to Phil 2:5–11 above (§6.3). A number of other significant instances of

---

[42] On the notion of "matching" in translation, Bellos poetically observes: "Translators are matchmakers of a particular kind. It's not as simple as the marriage of content and form. Just as when we match faces and portraits, we rely on multiple dimensions and qualities to judge when a translation has occurred.... Not all of them are great at their job, and not many have the time and leisure to wait for the best match to come. But when we say that a translation is an acceptable one, what we name is an overall relationship between source and target that is neither identity, nor equivalence, nor analogy—just that complex thing called a good match" (Bellos 2011:322; cf. Zogbo and Wendland 2000:ch. 4).

[43] On the importance of orality in the ANE with particular reference to NT times and its manifestation in the Philippians, see Davis 1999:ch. 1; cf. also Wendland 2008b:chs. 1 and 5.

[44] Cf. Wendland 1994:20–24, with the example of John 17 (ibid., 33–36; cf. the preceding sections of this chapter); see also Harvey 1998:231–58. A similar sound-based approach to biblical text analysis is extensively supported and exemplified (however, with no reference to Philippians) in Lee and Scott 2009.

sound structuring in the epistle were recorded in the subsequent literary-structural overview of Philippians, thus suggesting the importance of this oft-neglected procedure in biblical study.

In order to briefly illustrate this principle of communication and method of translation, I have chosen a semi-poetic (*ndakatulo*) style of oral or written communication in Chewa.[45] This version, which features rhythmically balanced lineation, poetic diction, idiomatic demonstrative shading, contrast, and euphony, is reproduced below, together with a relatively literal English back-translation:

Chewa poetic version—Phil 2:5–11	English back-translation
5. Motero mtima womwewo nanunso m'fanizire,	Therefore, the very same heart you too must imitate,
mtima umene adali nawo Khristu Yesu, indee.	a heart which Christ Jesus had, yes indeed.
N'chifukwa chake tikuyamikani, inu Ambuye!	For this reason we praise you, O Lord!
6. Zoona, inu munali ndi umulungu chikhalire,	Truly, you have always possessed deity,
komabe kulingana m'Mulungu simunayese	however, to be equal with God you did not consider
chinthu choti n'kuchidalira nthawi iliyonse.	something that [you] had to depend on at all times.
7. Mudadzitsitsa kotheratu, Yesu, munatero,	You lowered yourself completely, Jesus, you did
pakudzitengeratu umphawi wa ukapolo,	by taking to yourself the poverty of servanthood,
ndi kukhala munthu wonga onse anthu.	and becoming a human being just like all people.
8. Pokhaladi munthu, inu mudadzichepetsa;	By becoming truly human, you humbled yourself;

---

[45] I have considerably adapted this version from the modern "popular language" Chewa version known as the *Buku Loyera* ("Holy Book," 1997, *Bible Society of Malawi*; cf. Wendland 1998). My adaptation was critically reviewed by one of my current seminary students, who is also an experienced translator of Christian literature into Chewa, his mother tongue.

6.9 Modeling the message in translation

mtima womvera mudali nawo mpaka imfa,	an obedient heart you maintained up to death,
indedi, imfa yanu yopachikidwa pamtanda.	yes, your death was by being hung up on a tree.
9. N'chifukwa chake Atate adakukwezani zedi,	For this reason the Father elevated you greatly
nakupatsani dzina lopambana lina lili lonse.	and gave you a name above every other name.
10. Adachita izi kuti dzina la Yesu pakulimva,	He did this so that upon hearing the name of Jesus,
zolengedwa zonse kumwamba, pansipano,	all created things in heaven, here on earth,
m'paliponse, zikugwadireni mopembedza.	and everywhere must do you obeisance in worship.
11. Zonsezi zidzakuvomerezeni momvekatu	All these [creatures] should confess you publicly
ponenA'ti, "Yesu Khristu ndiye Ambuye!"	by saying, "Jesus Christ he is the Lord!"
Pakutero nawonso alemekezekedi Ataate!	In this way he too must be praised, your Father!

The poetic Chewa version recorded above appears to closely duplicate both the form and the function of the original praise poem, or *encomium*.[46] Notice, however, that a major shift in participant reference had to be made, i.e., from the initial 3rd to the present 2nd person pronouns (along with an appropriate introduction, v. 5c), in order to maintain a natural style for this genre in the TL. Such a lyric form would be especially suitable for use in a text that is intended for public oral articulation, whether liturgical or informal (e.g., a youth Bible study), as well as in a non-print media production, for example, as adapted in a musical (song) format. It is recognized that different types, or styles, of translation are needed in order to cater for

---

[46] Among the distinctive features of the encomium, Ryken lists the following: "a catalogue or description of the praiseworthy acts and qualities of the subject"—"[t]he indispensable or superior nature of the subject"—and "[a] conclusion urging the reader to emulate the subject" (1992:293; cf. with reference to Phil 2:5–11, ibid., 456–457; Malina and Pilch 2006:306). In the Philippians example, the command to emulate initiates, rather than concludes the piece.

the increasingly diverse range of settings in which the Scriptures are being used in the 21st century, ranging from local traditional dramatic performances to global electronic internet transmissions.[47]

As already noted, the closely related set of topics in a revolving sequence no doubt promoted the *memorizability* of Paul's epistle to the Philippians, or at least facilitated its public reading from a manuscript that was probably rather difficult in terms of its legibility, as was typical for virtually all handwritten texts in that age (cf. (§1.1). In addition to its structured arrangement of content then, this letter also manifests a great variety of literary and rhetorical features that aided and enhanced the oral and aural presentation of the text in a communal worship setting. It therefore behooves all contemporary communicators to make at least some effort to duplicate what they can of the powerful impact and appeal of Paul's exhortations and supporting examples in a translation that sounds, like the biblical message itself, as suitable to and for its intended audience as "a fragrant offering, an acceptable sacrifice, pleasing to God" (4:18). In this effort, it is helpful to keep the following advice in mind:

> Oral features are integral to a text. Therefore, attention to the oral characteristics of a written text is always part of a translator's task.... The universal features of orality are communicable in other languages. Certain oral features may be reproduced fairly directly. Other elements of a text are amenable to the use of functional equivalents, that is, to literary devices that make an impact similar to the original although they are not identical to the components found in the original. (Thomas and Thomas 2006:3)

---

[47] Additional translation-related considerations would include text formatting issues (e.g., setting off Phil 2:6–11 in a lined poetic layout) as well as the need to produce various setting-sensitive study helps that provide a "contextual frame of reference" for the Scriptures, for example, explanatory notes that elucidate some of the crucial ANE historical, religious, and sociocultural factors that pertain to this Christological passage (some of which were mentioned above).

6.10 Conclusion: Modeling the message in performance

Gordon Fee makes several insightful observations concerning the canonical and ongoing relevance of the christological confession of Philippians 2:6–11 (1995:226):

> In the light of the grandeur of this passage...one can easily forget why it is here. Paul's reasons are twofold: first, as throughout the letter, to focus on Christ himself, and thus, second, in this instance to point to him as the ultimate model of the self-sacrificing love to which he is calling the Philippians. That Paul himself has not forgotten where he is going becomes evident in the application that immediately follows, where the Philippians are called upon to "obey," just as the self-abasing One "obeyed" the will of his Father. But we should note further that both of Paul's concerns transfer fully into the ongoing life of the church and the believer.

We are masterfully presented in this epistle with an incorporative "chain" of modeling behavior, one that promotes a particular ethical ideal, namely, genuine humility and sacrificial love demonstrated for the sake of the worldwide Christian fellowship. The sequence moves, with increasing specificity, along these lines:

Christ →
   Paul and associates →
      the entire Philippian congregation →
         individual members of this fellowship (e.g., Euodia, Syntyche, and Syzygus?–4:3) →
            every contemporary hearer or reader within her/his local religious community.

Such an imperative, motivational example involves much more than a hermeneutical decision in terms of this pastoral letter, or an ecclesiastical ideal and a communicative choice with regard to its contemporary significance. When it comes right down to it, to the very end of the line, the implicational chain inevitably links up with each and every hearer or reader—in short, with "*me*." This includes the spiritual belief system, set of values, and way of life that I display on a daily basis, as I continue to "work out [my] salvation with fear and trembling" (Phil 2:12). Thus, "performance" not only includes the words uttered during the sacred text's proclamation, but it also embraces a crucial behavioral dimension that is reflected in one's overall life-style as well. If (or when) the strain of trying to follow Paul's example (3:17—let alone that of Christ!) becomes too great, then I must remember once more "to take hold of that for which Christ Jesus took hold of me" (3:12), and that "it is God who works in [me] to will and to act according to his good purposes" (2:13). With this assurance of ongoing strength and support from the divine Model himself (4:13), every believer and each believing community cannot fail to faithfully model his message until he returns (1:10–11, 3:20–21), that is, by continuing to "stand firm in the Lord" (1:27, 4:1)—no matter what the opposition (1:29–30, 3:18).

In the next section (III), we will begin a set of three chapters that aim to encourage readers to practice their own aural acuity more fully by engaging the biblical text directly and with specific reference also to the language in which they may be translating. First, the graphic prophetic and visionary chapters of Song of Songs 8 and Revelation 5 will be considered with special reference to their manifest phonic and performance potential both in the original and also a modern vernacular rendition.

III. APPLICATION

Discovering the Dimensions of Orality in Scripture Texts

7

Identifying and Displaying the Oral-Aural Dimension of Two Dramatic Biblical Texts

7.1 Introduction

In this chapter we will make a preliminary examination of a pair of pericopes, one Old Testament (Song of Songs 8) and one New Testament (Revelation 5) passage, with special reference to their respective oral-aural dynamics. Both of these passages have a great deal of performance potential in the sense that they contain much built-in dialogue and character differentiation. This vital interpersonal dimension of the biblical text must also be conveyed somehow in translation as well as in oral performance.

We will consider each of these two pericopes from three distinct but interrelated perspectives:

- **Formatting** the text—*visualizing* its structure and performance features;

- **Interpreting** the text—*justifying* the format in terms of structure and style;
- **Performing** the text—*re-oralizing* the Scriptures for a contemporary audience.[1]

It is not possible here to investigate these two texts in exegetical detail or with specific reference to the many, diverse recurring (alliterative, assonant, paronomastic, etc.) and euphonious phonological qualities of each passage in the original language.[2] The purpose is simply to examine certain general aspects of the *oral-aural dynamics* that have been built into (and arguably implied by) each pericope in order to explore how it might be communicated more appropriately today in a corresponding "sound-responsive" manner.

7.2 Song of Songs 8

I submit the following representation of Song 8 as one way of formatting and demarcating the text of Song 8 so as to visually demonstrate on the page of print the various shifts of speakers and scenes. Such a formatted passage would also be of assistance in guiding those who are presenting the passage orally in public. This display (including the indents and section headings or titles)[3] has been substantially modified from the *New English Translation* (NET), which goes into the most detail with regard to the speaker exchanges that are implicit in this chapter. The English rendering is my own adaptation, comprised of a combined selection of verses based on the *Good News Translation* (GNT)

---

[1] The earliest use of term "re-oralizing" that I have thus far discovered comes from a large modern English literary study in relation to "ethnopoetics"—e.g., the "reoralizing tendency of modern poetry" (Rothenberg and Rothenberg 1983:464). My use of this term focuses on the translation process whereby a literary (poetic) text is composed or rendered in the target language so that it is clearly manifested and ideally expressed in sound.

[2] I discuss SoS 8 in the context of the book as a whole in "Love Lyrics: On the Form and Meaning of the Song of Songs," in *Lovely, Lively Lyrics* (2013:ch. 6); an overview of Rev 5 may be found in Wendland 2008d:ch. 11.

[3] The *New English Translation*'s multitude of helpful text-based and explanatory footnotes has also been excised for the sake of this example. Verse numbers, too, have been removed (except for the major headings) so as not to disturb the smooth flow of the text as it is being read and heard.

and the *New Living Translation* (NLT). Thus, I have often adjusted these versions, at times quite significantly, so as to express what I felt was the sense and import of the original Hebrew in a more idiomatic way, as befitting the poetic style (e.g., parallelism), the dramatic scenario being depicted, and a vocal elocution of the text. Readers (oral!) are invited to critically interact with my rendition and format and to write in lyric modifications as desired:

The Beloved Expresses Her Heart's Desires (8:1–4)

The Beloved to Her Lover
Oh, how I wish you were my brother,
that mother had nursed you at her breast!
Then, if I met you passing in the street,
I could kiss you and no one would mind.
I would take you to my mother's home,
where you could teach me about love.
There I would give you spiced wine,
my sweet pomegranate wine to drink.

> *The Beloved about Her Lover*
> How I wish that his left hand would caress my head,
> and that his right hand would freely stimulate me!

>> *The Beloved to the Maidens*
>> O promise me, you women of Jerusalem,
>> not to waken my love until the right time!

The Awakening of Love (8:5a)

> *The Maidens about the Beloved*
> **Who is this sweeping in from the desert—**
> **that one who is leaning upon her lover?**

The Nature of True Love (8:5b–7)

The Beloved to Her Lover
I aroused you under the apple tree,
where your mother gave you birth,
where in great pain she delivered you.
Seal your heart to every love but mine;
hold no one else in your arms but me!
Surely love grips as strongly as death—
passion so powerfully as the very grave.
Our love flashes fiercely in flames;
such ardor blazes brightly like fire.
Water cannot extinguish it at all;
even a flood could never drown it.
If anyone tried to buy love with wealth,
surely utter contempt is all he would get!

Brothers' Concern for their Sister (8:8–10)

Brothers about the Beloved
Yes indeed, we have a little sister,
but she's too young to have breasts.
So what will we do about our sister
if someone comes asking to marry her?
If she is a virgin, closed tightly like a wall,
we'll protect her so precious with a fortress.
But if she's too loose, like a revolving door,
we will block her exit as with a cedar bar!

The Beloved to Herself
I am indeed a virgin, like a wall;
now my breasts are tall towers.
So when my lover looks at me,
he's delighted with what he sees.

Solomon's Vineyard like that of the Beloved's (8:11–12)

The Beloved to Her Lover
Solomon has a vineyard at Baal-hamon,
which he leases out to tenant farmers.
Each of them pays a thousand shekels,
silver of course, for harvesting its fruit.
But this vineyard is my very own to let out.
No "Solomon" can buy me for a treasure;
I will pay two hundred shekels to anyone,
who cares well for the fruit of my vineyard!

The Lover's Final Request and His Beloved's Response (8:13–14)

The Lover to His Beloved
Oh, my darling, lingering there in the garden,
friends delight to hear the sound of your voice.
So please let me, your lover, now hear it too!

The Beloved to Her Lover
Just come to me quickly, my lover, swift as a gazelle,
like a strong stag from hills scented with sweet spices!

As anyone who has studied this passage already knows, it is not very easy to determine how the condensed, sometimes cryptic text of this lovely "song" should be structured and understood, let alone translated. At times, one must remain content with a studied, contextualized guess (e.g., with respect to vv. 11–12). A comparison of the preceding modified rendition with the standard versions and commentaries reveals many differences in terms of both content and form. But most of the speaker-initiated breaks noted above are, in fact, supported by two or more scholarly sources, in particular, the basic organization of this chapter, which most agree is divided into four major segments (poetic "stanzas")—namely, 8:1–4, 5–7, 8–10, and 11–14.[4] To help make this

---

[4] These "stanzas" may, in turn, be sub-divided into smaller "strophes," e.g., [5 + 6–7], [8–9 + 10], [11–12 + 13 + 14].

decision, the analyst must depend on various typical signals or markers of *aperture* and *closure* within the discourse. Examples of these would include vocative forms and shifts in pronominal, topical, temporal, and spatial reference, as well as cohesion spans created by lexical reiteration along with terms that belong to the same general semantic domain and/or sociocultural scenario.

There is widespread agreement that the thematic core of this pericope (and perhaps the Song as a whole) occurs in the medial section covering verses 6–7, preceded by a short transition, v. 5a/b. Here one can almost feel the fervent heat of the text in the brilliant description of "love" as expressed by the Song's main personage and speaker, the female "Beloved." This central element seems to be encompassed by verses that allusively hark back to the two Lovers' childhood days, i.e., *he*—v. 5b and *she*—vv. 8–9, and possibly vv. 10–11 as well (cf. also the beginning of the Song, 1:5–8). This set of medial passages is, in turn, preceded and followed respectively by apparent introductory and concluding poetic segments, i.e., 8:1–4 and 13–14, which reiterate images and motifs that have recurred throughout the composition.

In *Lovely, Lively Lyrics* (Wendland 2013:ch. 6), I propose that reiterated "refrains" serve to mark the concluding boundaries of major "song" divisions within the Song, as shown on the chart below:

Song	Verses	Refrain markers	Summary of the set of seven refrains marking "closure"
1.	1:2–2:7	A, B, C, E, G	A = left/right arm embrace
2.	2:8–2:17	B, D, E	B = gazelle/doe/stag imagery
3.	3:1–3:5	B, C, F, G	C = do [not] arouse/waken love
4.	3:6–5:1	C, [D], E, F	D = I am my lover's/my lover is mine
5.	5:2–6:3	D, E, F	E = garden and related (fruit) motifs
6.	6:4–7:10	D, E, F	F = movement imagery (coming/going)
7.	7:11–8:4	A, C, [E], G	G = daughters of Jerusalem
8.	8:5–8:14	B, E, F[a]	

[a]According to my analysis, the *thematic* peak of the Song occurs in 8:5b–8, preceded by a short interlude (5a), and followed by a rather long epilogue (8:9–14). This is to be distinguished from the *pragmatic* (emotive) peak that is found at the close of "song" 4, i.e., at 4:16c–5:1.

A thorough discourse analysis and interpretation of the Song reveals that *not* to give any structural guidance at all, for example, by way of speaker headings and sub-paragraphing, results in a *mis*-translation. A completely unformatted, unmediated version, such as the KJV or the RSV, further complicated by a literalistic rendering of the source-language text, is virtually unintelligible, even to educated mother-tongue speakers of English. Thus, any type of multifunctional format, even one that is somewhat controversial (non-standard) or perhaps misleading in certain minor respects, is better than nothing. This is because it functions to alert the reader to the fact that completely different speakers alternate when uttering selected portions of the Song. This reality should ultimately alter one's understanding of the text—and its oral expression as well.[5]

Obviously, chapter 8, like the Song of Songs as a whole, is an instance of emotively intense, dramatic lyric poetry—a text that is intended to be vigorously articulated aloud, not quietly read to oneself.[6] Even a specially formatted, idiomatically styled translation like the one illustrated above is not adequate either to reproduce or to evoke the beautiful poetic wording of the original message, or to replicate its rhetorically heightened mode of passionate verbal expression. Certainly, one would need to be much more creative and dynamic if one wished to capture more of the intense feelings and illocutionary force being expressed by the lovers.[7] However, in order to accomplish such objectives poetically, one would undoubtedly need to move more in the direction of paraphrase and transculturation

---

[5] This passage could of course be presented dramatically by a single performer, but that person would face a considerable challenge when attempting to articulate the differences among the various character voices and moods. The various sectional headings too would require distinctive voicing or backgrounding, e.g., music or a special type of sound shading.

[6] The Song would be an excellent example of what House terms "closet drama," that is, literature which is "composed in dramatic style, but is written without the play [necessarily] ever meant to be staged...[with] dramatic characteristics, plot, character, dialogue, etc." (1989:50, words in brackets added).

[7] This would present an even greater challenge in the case of an audio rendition of this passage. Thus, "In the case of a recorded oral composition, should a translator supply the absent indicators of meaning? How should a translator convey the meaning of the text if varying interpretations of the illocutionary force are possible?" (Loubser 2004:296–314). An example of this would be the possible use of sarcasm (or "fraternalism") in the brothers' speech of 8:8–10: if present, how much of the text does it encompass, and how should this attitude be expressed?

(e.g., with respect to physical scenic features like sweet pomegranate wine, the desert, a fortress, cedar bar, tall towers, Baal-hamon, shekels, and sweet spices).

Instances of obvious oratorical composition like this (which in fact characterize many portions of biblical discourse)[8] offer clear evidence of the principle that in the case of excellent literature, whatever the language or genre, the *form* as well as the *function* (including the emotive value) of the text are both vital aspects of its intended meaning. Hence, to ignore or neglect to deal with these pragmatic dimensions in the interest of pure "content alone" is to diminish the resultant translation and ultimately to fail to fully convey the author's desired communicative intention. Since I have dealt with this subject sufficiently elsewhere,[9] I will move straight to the special focus of the present study, namely, how to express the *essential orality* of the biblical text in an indigenous translation, which would, of necessity, have to be an oral-aural rendition of some kind.

In this challenging endeavor as it concerns the preceding passage (SoS 8), a variety of detailed practical questions and issues would need to be dealt with during any pre-project planning consultation. I have simply listed for consideration a number of these below as potential reflection and discussion points, in no particular order of priority:

- In an audio text, the acoustic quality (timbre) of the different characters' "voices" is an important factor (e.g., with respect to pitch, resonance, tempo, intonation, etc. of speech); such properties are normally culture-specific and therefore need to be carefully researched in advance. For instance, what would be an appropriate voice for each of the two central speakers, the female "Beloved" and her male "Lover"?

---

[8] It is difficult to quantify this assertion. My various studies in OT and NT literature, at least, would suggest that artistically composed, rhetorically motivated discourse is the norm, especially in passages of direct speech, which would include most of the poetic books of the OT as well as the gospels and epistles.

[9] See, for example Wendland 2004b:79–97; 2009:190–204. My views on authorial intention would thus differ considerably from proposals such as this: "In the context of performance criticism, the idea of an author's 'intentions' has no meaning; what is important instead is what the performance of a text communicates to its audience" (Holland 2007:337).

7.2 Song of Songs 8

- How should the principal breaks in the discourse be indicated orally/aurally, for example, as the Song moves from one major division ("song") to another, and how long of a pause or transitional signal should there be between successive speakers?

- How can the poetic features of the SL text be duplicated by corresponding, functionally equivalent lyric devices in the TL, in particular, those that are phonologically prominent in the vernacular according to the genre selected to represent the Song? For example, in Chewa this might be done through parallel phrasing, alliteration and assonance, rhythm and euphony, word plays, descriptive ideophones (e.g., in vv. 6–7), exclamations representing distinct emotions (e.g., vv. 1, 4, 5b, 7b, 13–14), local imagery and figures of speech (e.g., vv. 2b, 5b, 6a, 8–9), added transitional expressions to mark new speakers and shifts in content.

- Do the different speakers or groups need to utter their "parts" more slowly (and loudly!) than normal in order to facilitate audience "tracking" of the poetic composition—or can a certain amount of poetic "redundancy" (e.g., paraphrase) be used to accomplish the same objective for a public performance?

- Would special, audibly marked (e.g., by a bell, gong, chime) "asides" be advisable in order to periodically present any necessary descriptive setting-related or explanatory information to the target audience? Some languages (like Chewa) may have a way of marking such "oral footnotes" within the main text itself, e.g., opening/closing transitional devices, distinctive backgrounding intonation, pre-/post-parenthesis pauses, singing them, etc.

- How might the prominence of the central portion of the text be underscored vocally—simply by extra volume, through an introductory aside, by means of a musical backdrop, drumming, or in another, more indigenous, locally-familiar manner?

- How can the persons speaking the parts best be coached so that they might correctly and effectively portray and vocalize their assigned characters, especially with regard to the appropriate oral expression of critical attitudes (e.g., doubt, frustration) and emotions (e.g., anger, affection)? This would include advice concerning the non-verbal aspects of performance—body movements, hand gestures, facial features, etc.

- Is a supplementary written "performance script," based on a careful exegetical and contextual study, needed to assist those impersonating the Song's characters? This would help them to prepare for and then "play their roles" with vibrant feeling as well as some measure of textual fidelity—that is, without overdoing it, or distorting the phonic "portrait" that is evoked for a given personage (e.g., the Lover).

- Ordinary text/print-oriented translation teams will probably not be properly equipped or prepared to make an acceptable audio version of their TL text, so how can they be trained to do this—or is a separate, professional drama team needed for this purpose?

Naturally, these performance-related issues are greatly multiplied when a *visual* as well as an audio presentation is being planned, for example, in a TV or video production, or a group dramatic skit on an open stage. In such cases, over and above the distinct vocal factors just discussed, additional properties would need to be built into an inclusive performance script. Such additions might include specific character gestures, facial expressions, body stances, symbolic movements, as well as other aspects of interpersonal interaction (e.g., relative proximity, direct/indirect facial contact, etc.). The inclusion of such properties would render the performance more natural in terms of the local sociocultural setting, especially in reference to the particular "scene" of the Song being verbally depicted.

7.3 Revelation 5

Many of the preceding considerations come to the fore again as our next sample text is examined, namely, the second half of the impressive heavenly "throne room" scenario described in Revelation 5. In order to highlight its performative attributes, this passage has again been specially formatted below. Three levels of indentation are used in order to reflect the broad organizational features of this chapter's discourse structure: most left column = the *narrative* progression, middle left = *descriptive* material, least left = *direct speech*. The aim then is to spotlight the content and intent of the quoted speeches, which move from the seer's inquisitive query (v. 2) to a revealing response (v. 5), and from there to successive, ever widening paeans of praise extolling the person, the work, and the honor that is due the sacrificial, but sovereign Lamb of God (vv. 9–10, 12, 13).[10] I have also tried to reflect the poetic prose and syntactic focusing of the original Greek, along with some of the flavor of the rhythmic progression of paratactic καὶ clauses. The following text is a modified English rendering that again draws mainly from the *Good News Translation* and the *New Living Translation*:

Who is worthy to open the scroll? (5:1–5)

Then I saw in the right hand of the one who was sitting on the throne a scroll.
    There was writing on the inside and the outside of this scroll,
    and it was sealed with seven seals.
And I also saw a strong angel, who shouted with a loud voice:
    "*Who is **worthy** to break the seals on the scroll and open it?*"
    But no one in heaven or on earth or under the earth—
    no one at all was able to open the scroll and read it.

---

[10] For an insightful, rhetorically-oriented overview of the throne room vision of Rev 4–5, see DeSilva 2009:97–102, 196–198, 258–263. "The worship scenes of Revelation 4 and 5 articulate a model of a well-ordered cosmos in which all created beings in every region of the map turn toward this one center—the throne of God and of the Lamb—to offer their grateful adoration" (ibid., 98). The challenge confronting all Bible translators is to duplicate something of the oral dignity and majesty of this discourse in their language, the periodic paeans of praise in particular.

Then I began to weep bitterly because no one was found
worthy enough to open the scroll and to read it.
But one of the twenty-four elders said to me,
> "Stop weeping!
> *Look, the Lion of the tribe of Judah, heir to David's throne,*
> *it is he who has won the ultimate victory—*
> *surely he is **worthy** to open the scroll by breaking its seven seals!"*

The LAMB is worthy to open the scroll! (5:6–14)

Then I saw standing between the throne and the four living beings and
among the twenty-four elders
> a Lamb that looked as if it had been sacrificed.
> He had seven horns and seven eyes,
> which represent the sevenfold Spirit of God
> that is sent out into every part of the earth.

He stepped forward and took the scroll
from the right hand of the One sitting on the throne.
And when the Lamb took that scroll,
the four living beings and the twenty-four elders fell down before him.
> Each one had a harp, and they held gold bowls filled with incense,
> which represent all the prayers of God's people.

And they sang a new song with these words:
> "You alone are **worthy** to take the scroll
> and to break its seven seals and read it.
> For you were sacrificed and have ransomed by your blood
> people for God from every tribe and language and people
>   and nation.
> And you have made it possible for them to become
> a Kingdom of priests for our God.
> And they will reign on the earth."

Then I looked again, and I heard the voices of angels,
> a thousand thousands, even millions and millions of them,
> encircling the throne and the living beings and the elders.

And they sang in a mighty chorus:

7.3 Revelation 5

> ***"Worthy** is the Lamb who was sacrificed—*
> *to receive power*
> *and riches*
> *and wisdom*
> *and strength*
> *and honor*
> *and glory*
> *and blessing!"*

And every creature in heaven and on earth and under the earth and in the sea, I heard them all as they sang this song:
> *"Blessing and honor and glory and power*
> *belong to the one sitting on the throne*
> *and to the Lamb forever and ever!"*

And the four living beings proclaimed,
> "Amen!"

And the twenty-four elders fell down and worshiped the Lamb.

The structure and style of this striking descriptive selection from the Apocalypse is quite different from the lyrics of the Song, and yet from a performative perspective, it is equally interesting and challenging in many respects. The climactic "crowded stage" and poetic choruses of the scene that John depicts would suggest that it is an early thematic peak point in the book of Revelation as a whole and one that sets the tone for graphic apocalyptic visions that follow (i.e., despite the horrors being depicted, the Lord is in supreme control). Therefore, this is a text that translators would do well to pay due attention to in their work. How then can they duplicate some of the grandeur of this heavenly setting along with the rhetorical power of the varied words that give praise to the central figure—the paradoxical living Lamb who had been slain?[11]

---

[11] The following is the attempt of the new German *BasisBibel* to produce a modern translation that is accurate in terms of content and also sensitive to the oral-aural dynamics of spoken discourse; the text is Revelation 5:11–13:

[11] Dann sah ich viele Engel
und hörte ihre Stimmen.
Sie standen rings um den Thron,

The problems—or complications—confronting those who would prepare a sound-and-structure sensitive print version, an audio recording, or an audio-visual production of this passage are similar to the ones listed earlier with reference to SoS 8, for example:

- Does the novel format of print actually help readers to articulate the text interpretively in public (e.g., modulating their voice to distinguish among its narrative, descriptive, and dialogue segments)—and does it assist the audience, in turn, to better understand this pericope as it is being interpretively read? What further modifications might be made in terms of the structure (e.g., possibly remove the section headings), the typography (e.g., use different font styles to indicate repetition or emphasis), or the translation (i.e., change to a more literal or a more idiomatic version—one that most listeners deem more "sound-worthy")? What are the reasons for any proposed modifications?

- What about written versus oral diction: are certain terms and expressions more appropriate for print, but not so appealing in an oral rendition, e.g., the "sacrificed" (instead of "slaughtered/killed/slain"

---

die Wesen und die Ältesten.
Es waren zehntausend mal zehntausend
und tausend mal tausend.
[12] Sie riefen mit lauter Stimme:
"Dem Lamm, das geschlachtet wurde,
steht es zu,
die Macht zu bekommen.
Dazu auch Reichtum und Weisheit,
Kraft und Ehre,
Herrlichkeit und Lob."
[13] Und alle Geschöpfe im Himmel,
auf der Erde und unter der Erde
sowie auf dem Meer –
alles, was in der Welt lebt,
hörte ich rufen:
"Gott, der auf dem Thron sitzt,
und dem Lamm sollen Lob und Ehre zuteilwerden.
Sie regieren in Herrlichkeit und Macht
für immer und ewig."

—ἐσφαγμένον) Lamb in v. 6? On the other hand, a number of adjustments in the interests of orality have already been made, e.g., v. 5 "...open the scroll by breaking its seven seals"—since the breaking presumably occurred first; v. 8 "And when the Lamb took..."—to clarify the antecedent "he."

- In the case of an audio version then, what is the best way to "slow down" (or prolong) the narrative account in a natural manner in order to allow the content of what is being described, and uttered in praise, to make the desired aural and evocative impression upon an alert listening audience?

- It is necessary to interpret and then correctly represent, also in emotive overtones, those speech acts that allow for several interpretive alternatives, for example, the narrator's initial question (real or rhetorical?), "Who is **worthy**...?" (v. 2: *is this an assertion of conviction or doubt—is any anger or frustration involved?*); the response of the elder, "Do not weep...!" (v. 5: *is it a gentle or impatient imperative?*); and surely the final "Amen!" (v. 14: *is it subdued and reverential, i.e., "said," or a resounding acclamation, i.e., "proclaimed"?*).

- How does one develop a procedure for identifying commanding, culturally appropriate "voices" to give utterance to unfamiliar, celestial creatures, such as the "mighty angel" (v. 2), "one of the elders" (v. 5), "the four living creatures and the twenty-four elders" (vv. 9–10), the "myriads and myriads of angels" (v. 12), and ultimately, "every creature" anywhere and everywhere (v. 13)?

- Not only must the preceding series of distinct vocal groups be properly "voice-typed," but the sequence as a whole should also sound as if it is gradually moving to a climax and crescendo, which is finally reached in the all-embracing superlatives of v. 13. Perhaps, over and above the voices themselves a certain type of accompanying, accentuating background may be needed; for example, along with a simple increase in volume, one might add some impressive music, selected instrumentation (e.g., drums, gongs, shakers, cymbals, etc.), or special sound effects (e.g., thunder, rushing wind, raging water—whatever would be most suitable in the local cultural setting).

- The primary panegyric quotations of vv. 9–10, 12, and 13 are reported as having been "sung," so this may present an added obstacle for the translators, who may not be especially gifted in the field of poetry and music. In this case, expert local composers and songwriters will have to be sought out who can not only create the desired powerful lyrics but can also render these in a vernacular song genre that fits this precise context of Scripture as well as the principal audience environment in which this version will be used.[12]

- A visual (video) portrayal of this passage brings with it even more difficult challenges, and a considerable degree of focused, medium-specific research will undoubtedly be necessary to give direction for resolving these issues, for example, how to portray the *dissimilar creatures* referred to in this text—in particular, the scene-central "Lamb, looking as if it had been slain…with seven horns and seven eyes" (v. 6, NIV). Perhaps, instead of a "realistic" figure, some sort of a graphic symbolic (impressionistic?) representation will be needed, but then the question is: How will the intended audience interpret this novel depiction? Again, the use of extratextual "asides," clearly distinguished from the main story line, might be experimented with to accomplish this explanatory objective.

- A portrayal of the disparate, otherworldly personages incorporated in this heavenly vision presents a special challenge in any video production. Several of the "props" and actions reported also present various difficulties due to the text's lack of explicit descriptive detail—for example: how to represent the "scroll with writing on both sides and sealed with seven seals" (v. 1); how to position the Lamb "standing in the center of the throne" (v. 6) upon which "him who sat on the throne" (v. 1) is also present; how to stage the "four living creatures and the twenty-four elders falling down before the Lamb" (v. 8).

---

[12] Some suggestions for holding a Psalms ("songs") workshop for Bible translators may be found in Wendland 2002b:238–251.

7.3 Revelation 5

- How well (clearly, beautifully, accurately, etc.) does the Word sound in *The Voice*? The following is a sample of this new translation that seeks to produce "an amplification of the voice of God so it is more clearly heard by today's readers."[13] Evaluate this rendition of Rev 5:1–10 with special reference to the text's accuracy, artistry, and orality.[14]

[5:1] And then I saw a scroll in the right hand of the One seated upon the throne, a scroll written both on the inside and on the outside. It had been sealed with seven seals. ²Then a mighty heavenly messenger proclaimed with a loud voice,

Mighty Messenger: Who is worthy to break the seals and open the scroll? ³No creature *of creation* in all heaven, on all the earth, or even under the earth could open the scroll or look into its *mysteries*. ⁴Then I began to mourn *and* weep bitterly because no creature *of creation* was found who was worthy to open the scroll or to look into its *mysteries*. ⁵Then one of the elders consoled me.

One of the 24 Elders: Stop weeping. Look there—the Lion of the tribe of Judah, the Root of David. He has conquered and is able to break its seven seals and open the scroll.
⁶I looked, and between the throne and the four living creatures and the *twenty-four* elders stood a Lamb who appeared to have been slaughtered.

---

[13] This and the following quotation are from *The Voice* website, the page entitled "About the Translation" (http://hearthevoice.com/about-the-translation, [accessed on 12/07/2012]). This version aims at "artfully presenting truth": "Today's translations often present the Bible as a reference book filled with facts. *The Voice* expresses Scripture as a narrative with engaging conversations, passionate poetry, and beautiful literature. *The Voice* brings literary art to the Bible. This Bible lends itself to dramatic readings; first, because of the beauty of the language, and second, because of the unique acting-script format. It is the Good Book that reads like a good book." How credible are these claims based on your examination of the portion reproduced here? There is one immediate correction to the preceding quote to begin with: *The Voice,* indeed no translation in any language, "brings literary art to the Bible." In fact, literary art is already embodied in the original text; it is up to a translation faithfully to reflect it, to the extent possible.

[14] This selection is reproduced as formatted on the website: http://www.hearthevoice.com/compare-translations (accessed on 12/07/2012).

The Lamb had seven horns and seven eyes (the eyes are the seven Spirits of God sent out over all the earth).

John hears that the Lion of the tribe of Judah, the Root of David, has arrived and will open the seals to reveal the scroll's mysteries. But when he turns to see the Lion, he sees a Lamb instead. Not everything is as it appears. The Lamb stands, even though He has been slaughtered as a sacrifice, because He has been resurrected from the dead. And now in his vision, John sees things as they truly are: the Lamb-King has seven horns and seven eyes, signifying the perfect power and perfect sight He possesses to rule the world.

⁷The Lamb came and took the scroll from the right hand of the One seated upon the throne. ⁸And when He took it, the four living creatures and twenty-four elders fell prostrate before the Lamb. *They worshiped Him, and each one held a harp and golden bowls filled with incense (the prayers of God's holy people).* ⁹Then they sang a new song.

Four Living Creatures and 24 Elders:
>You are worthy to receive the scroll,
>to break its seals,
>Because You were slain. With Your blood,
>You redeemed for God
>people from every tribe and language,
>people from every race and nation.
>¹⁰You have made them a kingdom; You have
>appointed them priests to serve our God,
>and they* will rule upon the earth.

7.4 Conclusion: Putting theory into practice

Ultimately, all of the scholarly theories discussed in Section I of this book—concerning orality and performance as they relate to the ancient composition and transmission of the biblical text as well as its current interpretation—must be transformed into proficient practice when it comes to actually rendering ("re-oralizing") the Scriptures in a new language and

7.4 Conclusion: Putting theory into practice

cultural setting. At this point then, it is up to a competent, resourceful, and sufficiently educated local translation committee (perhaps assisted by invited specialist-consultants) to agree upon a comprehensive functional job description (brief) including the specification of one (or more) principal communicative goal(s) (*Skopos*). What kind of audio (+/- visual) rendition are they capable of producing in view of the human and material resources available, the proposed client audience, and the primary setting of use? Even in the most limiting of circumstances (e.g., a more formally correspondent type of translation), there is always something vocally creative that can be done to allow a measure of the dynamic phonic dimension of the biblical text to be heard by attentive listeners today. This would be true whether the aurally attuned version is intended for informal individual use, e.g., to introduce a Bible class or Sunday school to the artistry of Scripture, or in a formal liturgical venue, as a joint proclamation by the entire congregation present, or to serve as the vocal basis for a musical rendition of the passage.

Some of the major practical issues that arise from the preceding discussion will be further developed for critical reaction and application in the next two chapters. Here we will examine two complete passages, namely, Philemon (ch. 8) and 1 Corinthians 13 (ch. 9). Special attention will be given to their oral potential with respect to both exegesis, understanding and interpreting a passage of Scripture in the original, and also transmission—communicating the biblical text today via a corresponding functionally equivalent "oratorical" translation.

8

Notes on the "Sonic Structure" of Paul's Epistle to Philemon

8.1 Overview

This chapter presents a selective sonic commentary on the putative "sound structure" of a short Pauline epistle. The purpose is to further highlight the importance of the oral-aural dimension in the composition and transmission of the Scriptures. Readers are encouraged to *first* engage the Greek text on its own terms and in *audio* form before critically consulting the accompanying descriptive, explanatory, and comparative footnotes. One might note in particular which aspects of often implicit *semantic* and *pragmatic* significance may be discovered when a closer examination (or "audition") of the acoustic formation of a biblical document is undertaken on an individual verse by verse basis. This initial "hearing" of the text may then be complemented by further analytical reflection with reference to its detailed linguistic and literary structure.

My analysis will be selectively compared with the results of a study of "persuasion and conversion—Paul's letter to Philemon" by Lee and Scott, which I consulted after completing my own work on this epistle's phonological organization (Lee and Scott (hereafter, L&S) 2009:225).[1] The authors assert that their methodology "illustrates the *independent* contribution of sound to meaning apart from semantics" (ibid., 225; added italics).[2] However, I prefer to view all linguistic facets of the text—*sound, sense, and syntax*—operating as a meaningful nexus to convey the author's intended communicative goals, ideally, expressed orally and apprehended aurally in community. Readers are invited to come to their own conclusion on this matter as they "speak-listen through" Philemon on their own. The Greek text used is UBS$_4$, with reference being made also to the new SBL/Logos Greek NT; the English translation on the right is that of the relatively literal RSV. This is a practical exercise intended to encourage a careful *hearing* of the Word in terms of its *hermeneutical* import with regard to the author's intended message as it was actually articulated aloud.

8.2 Sonic structure display and commentary

Παῦλος δέσμιος Χριστοῦ Ἰησοῦ	[1] Paul, a prisoner for Christ Jesus,
καὶ Τιμόθεος ὁ ἀδελφὸς[a]	and Timothy our brother,
Φιλήμονι τῷ ἀγαπητῷ **καὶ** συνεργῷ ἡμῶν	to Philemon our beloved fellow worker
καὶ Ἀπφίᾳ τῇ ἀδελφῇ	[2] and to Apphia our sister
καὶ Ἀρχίππῳ τῷ συστρατιώτῃ ἡμῶν[b]	and to Archippus our fellow soldier,
καὶ[c] τῇ κατ' οἶκόν σου[d] ἐκκλησίᾳ:	and to the church in your house:
χάρις ὑμῖν καὶ εἰρήνη	[3] Grace to you and peace
ἀπὸ θεοῦ πατρὸς ἡμῶν	from God our Father
καὶ κυρίου Ἰησοῦ Χριστοῦ.[e]	and the Lord Jesus Christ.
Εὐχαριστῶ τῷ θεῷ **μου** πάντοτε[f]	[4] I thank my God always

---

[1] For my earlier analysis of the literary-rhetorical structure of Philemon, see Wendland 2008b:207–282. Corresponding features in the Greek text are highlighted through the use of similar font styles (boldface, italics, underlining) and gray shading.

[2] I also disagree with several aspects of the authors' interpretation of this letter, but will not discuss these differences here; for example: "Nowhere does the letter explicitly state or even imply that Onesimus has run away, nor are any of the technical terms for this situation invoked" (Lee and Scott 2009:225; cf. Wendland, ibid.).

8.2 Sonic structure display and commentary

μνείαν **σου** ποιούμενος ἐπὶ τῶν προσευχῶν **μου**,	when I remember you in my prayers,
ἀκούων **σου**[g] τὴν ἀγάπην καὶ τὴν **πίστιν**,	[5] because I hear of your love and of the faith
ἣν ἔχεις **πρὸς** τὸν **κύριον Ἰησοῦν**	which you have toward the Lord Jesus
καὶ εἰς πάντας τοὺς ἁγίους,[h]	and for all the saints,
ὅπως ἡ κοινωνία τῆς **πίστεώς** σου	[6] and I pray that the sharing of your faith
ἐνεργὴς γένηται ἐν ἐπιγνώσει παντὸς ἀγαθοῦ τοῦ ἐν ἡμῖν εἰς Χριστόν.[i]	may promote the knowledge of all the good that is ours in Christ.
χαρὰν γὰρ πολλὴν ἔσχον καὶ **παράκλησιν**[j]	[7] For I have derived much joy and comfort too
ἐπὶ τῇ ἀγάπῃ σου,	from your love,
ὅτι τὰ **σπλάγχνα** τῶν ἁγίων[k]	because the hearts of the saints
ἀναπέπαυται διὰ σοῦ,[l]	have been refreshed through you
ἀδελφέ.[m]	my brother.
Διό, **πολλὴν ἐν** Χριστῷ **παρρησίαν**[n] ἔχων	[8] Accordingly, though I am bold enough in Christ
ἐπιτάσσειν σοι τὸ ἀνῆκον,	to command you to do what is required,
διὰ τὴν ἀγάπην μᾶλλον **παρακαλῶ**,[o]	[9] yet for love's sake I prefer to appeal to you,
τοιοῦτος ὢν ὡς Παῦλος **πρεσβύτης**	I, Paul, an ambassador
νυνὶ δὲ καὶ **δέσμιος** Χριστοῦ Ἰησοῦ[p]	and now a prisoner also for Christ Jesus --
παρακαλῶ σε περὶ τοῦ ἐμοῦ τέκνου,[q]	[10] I appeal to you for my child,
ὃν ἐγέννησα ἐν τοῖς δεσμοῖς,	whose father I have become in my imprisonment,
Ὀνήσιμον,[r]	Onesimus.
τόν ποτέ σοι **ἄχρηστον**	[11] (formerly he was useless to you,
νυνὶ δὲ [καὶ] σοὶ καὶ ἐμοὶ[s] **εὔχρηστον**,[t]	but now he is indeed useful to you and to me).
ὃν ἀνέπεμψά σοι, αὐτόν,[u]	[12] I am sending him back to you,

τοῦτ' ἔστιν **τὰ ἐμὰ σπλάγχνα**ᵛ	sending my very heart.
ὃν ἐγὼ ἐβουλόμην πρὸς **ἐμαυτὸν** κατέχειν,ʷ	¹³ I would have been glad to keep him with me,
ἵνα ὑπὲρ **σοῦ μοι**ˣ διακονῇ	in order that he might serve me on your behalf
ἐν τοῖς δεσμοῖς τοῦ εὐαγγελίου,ʸ	during my imprisonment for the gospel;
χωρὶς δὲ τῆς σῆς γνώμης	¹⁴ but without your consent
οὐδέν^z ἠθέλησα ποιῆσαι,	I preferred to do nothing
ἵνα μὴ ὡς κατὰ ἀνάγκην τὸ ἀγαθόν σου ᾖ	in order that your goodness might not be [done] by compulsion
ἀλλὰ κατὰ ἑκούσιον.ᵃᵃ	but of your own free will.
τάχαᵇᵇ γὰρ διὰ τοῦτο ἐχωρίσθη πρὸς ὥραν,	¹⁵ Perhaps this is why he was parted from you for a while,
ἵνα αἰώνιον αὐτὸν ἀπέχῃς,	that you might have him back for ever,
οὐκέτι ὡς **δοῦλον**	¹⁶ no longer as a slave
ἀλλὰ ὑπὲρ **δοῦλον**,	but more than a slave,
ἀδελφὸν ἀγαπητόν,ᶜᶜ	as a beloved brother,
μάλιστα **ἐμοί**,	especially to me
πόσῳ δὲ μᾶλλον **σοὶ**ᵈᵈ	but how much more to you,
καὶ ἐν σαρκὶ καὶ ἐν κυρίῳ.ᵉᵉ	both in the flesh and in the Lord.
Εἰ οὖν **με** ἔχεις κοινωνόν,	¹⁷ So if you consider me your partner,
προσλαβοῦ αὐτὸν ὡς **ἐμέ**.ᶠᶠ	receive him as you would receive me.
εἰ δέ τι ἠδίκησέν **σε** ἢ ὀφείλει, A	¹⁸ If he has wronged you at all, or owes you anything,
τοῦτο **ἐμοὶ** ἐλλόγα.ᵍᵍ B	charge that to my account.
ἐγὼ Παῦλος ἔγραψα τῇ* ἐμῇ χειρί,* C	¹⁹ I, Paul, write this with my own hand,
ἐγὼ ἀποτίσω*.ʰʰ C'	I will repay it—
*ἵνα μὴ λέγω **σοι**ⁱⁱ B'	to say nothing of your
ὅτι καὶ **σεαυτόν** μοι προσοφείλεις.ʲʲ A'	owing me even your own self.

8.2 Sonic structure display and commentary

ναί, ἀδελφέ,	²⁰ Yes, brother,
ἐγώ <u>σου</u>ᵏᵏ ὀναίμην <u>ἐν κυρίῳ</u>·	I want some benefit from you in the Lord.
ἀνάπαυσόν μου τὰ σπλάγχνα <u>ἐν Χριστῷ</u>.ˡˡ	Refresh my heart in Christ.
Πε**ποιθὼς** τῇ ὑπακοῇ <u>σου</u> ἔγραψά **σοι**,	²¹ Confident of your obedience, I write to you,
εἰδὼς ὅτι καὶ ὑπὲρ ἃ λέγω ποιή**σεις**.ᵐᵐ	knowing that you will do even more than I say.
ἅμα δὲ καὶⁿⁿ ἑ**τοίμαζέ μοι** ξενίαν·	²² At the same time, prepare a guest room for me,
ἐλπίζω γὰρ ὅτι διὰ τῶν προ<u>σ</u>ευχῶν **ὑμῶν**	for I am hoping that through your prayers
χαρισθήσομαι **ὑμῖν**.ᵒᵒ	I may be granted to you.
Ἀ<u>σ</u>πάζεταί σε Ἐπαφρᾶς	²³ Epaphras sends greetings to you,
<u>ὁ</u> <u>σ</u>υναιχμάλωτός <u>μου</u> ἐν Χρι<u>σ</u>τῷ Ἰη<u>σ</u>οῦ,	my fellow prisoner in Christ Jesus,
Μᾶρκος, Ἀρί<u>σ</u>ταρχος, Δημᾶς, Λουκᾶς,	²⁴ so do Mark, Aristarchus, Demas, and Luke,
<u>οἱ</u> <u>σ</u>υνεργοί <u>μου</u>.ᵖᵖ	my fellow workers.
Ἡ χάρις τ**οῦ** κυρί**ου** Ἰη<u>σ</u>**οῦ** Χρι<u>σ</u>τ**οῦ**ᵠᵠ	²⁵ The grace of our Lord Jesus Christ
μετὰ τοῦ πνεύματος ὑμῶν.	be with the spirit of you all!

ᵃThe reiterated -ος endings draw aural attention to the close cooperation between Paul and Timothy.

ᵇThe second half of this line (v. 2b) rhymes with the corresponding portion two lines above (1c), with an emphasis on Christian fellowship, i.e., συν- + ἡμῶν.

ᶜThe reiterated *kais* highlight the assumed unity of the group mentioned in the letter's greeting (1–2).

ᵈThe syntactic "envelope construction" in v. 2c highlights the information in the middle, i.e., "[that meets] in your house," thus again calling attention to the significant ecclesiastical role of Philemon.

ᵉThis chiastically worded paired phrase "Christ Jesus…Jesus Christ" (1a/3c) forms an *inclusio* that demarcates the letter's "opening" in a manner that "brings attention to Jesus' defining identity for the ἐκκλησία" (L&S, 227). L&S analyze the text in terms of Greco-Roman "commata" (roughly, syntactic phrase units), "cola" (roughly, syntactic clauses), and "periods," which are initially defined rather ambiguously as consisting of "cola that can be spoken in a single breath and easily comprehended by hearing" (109). A more detailed, hence helpful definition is this: "Well-formed periods are typically characterized by *rounding* (the repetition at the period's end of sounds heard at the beginning, *balance* (parallel or antithetical cola) and *elongation* (long final colon and/or multiple long vowel sounds" (ibid., 171; added italics).

There appear to be as many arbitrary decisions according to this "classical" system as in my more intuitive linguistic method, which breaks the text into smaller "utterance/breath units," based on lexical parallelism and significant instances of phonological or syntactic symmetry. Readers must judge our respective proposals for themselves based on the textual evidence. For example, L&S consider "period 1" of Philemon to encompass the first three verses. But how that chunk of text could be uttered easily in "a single breath" is not clear, especially when a logical and physical break would be most probable at the end of v. 2 after the greeting. Thus, this first period crosses a semicolon in the Greek text (at the close of v. 2), whereas the posited period 2 ends at a semicolon at the end of v. 6 (ibid., 227–228). The boundaries of colon 1 in this case would seem to be determined by the verbal characteristics listed above, rather than the physical breath-span (note the contradiction in primary criteria; ibid., 109–10). However, L&S do recognize that "different sound maps might display colometric divisions of the same passage differently, depending on the particular sound features to be exhibited" (ibid., 170).

[f]This word "always" could modify either the preceding line, the following one, or both.

[g]An alternating series of genitive pronominal forms emphasizes the close connection between "me" (Paul) and "you" sg. (Philemon).

[h]A chiastic construction links the activities of "love" => "saints" and "faith" => "Lord Jesus"; "faith" and "love" are mentioned again in chiastic order later in this same paragraph (vv. 6a, 7b) to underscore their spiritual and ethical interconnection.

[i]L&S point to the sound similarity between Εὐχαριστῶ (4a) and Χριστόν (6c) as marking the external boundaries of "Period 2" in Philemon (ibid., 171), and also Paul's "thanksgiving" (ibid., 228). However, the conjunctive connective γάρ in 7a coupled with the disjunctive conjunction Διό in 8a would suggest that the Apostle's word of thanksgiving must be extended to include v. 7, and that the "body" of the letter actually begins in v. 8 (contra L&S, 228–229). The content of v. 7, e.g., the

repetition of "love" and "saints" from v. 5, would also indicate a closer connection with the preceding rather than the following material.

ʲThis is the third in a series of three lines that manifest a discernable internal rhyme scheme, thus creating phonological cohesion within the paragraph. Such rhyming is especially evident in the first of the three lines (6b), which foregrounds the "energetic knowledge" of what is ours in Christ (6c).

ᵏAssonance in "a" links the thematically key terms "joy," "comfort," "love," and "bowels" in v. 7.

ˡThe last two clauses in the paragraph, except for the final vocative, end with an emphasis on "you" (σου) – Philemon—the "brother," who is about to be requested to provide additional brotherly "refreshment," this time directed towards a very unexpected, indeed a new "brother" in Christ!

ᵐAn instance of syntactic back-shift focuses the spotlight on "brother" and thus concludes the paragraph unit. That would be a genuine instance of a dramatic rhetorical "comma" (L&S, 111).

ⁿA front–shifted syntactic construction (as also at the beginning of v. 9), here with an enclosed ἐν phrase, highlights the fact of Paul's apostolic authority—which he is about to forgo "for love's sake." Note also the parallelism in the overlapping between these two paragraphs—one ending in v. 7: πολλὴν ἔσχον...**παράκλησιν**, the other beginning in v. 8: πολλὴν...**παρρησίαν** ἔχων.

ᵒAssonance in "n," along with the initial Διό, helps to aurally announce the onset of this new paragraph.

ᵖAlliteration in "p" (note also 10a) overlaps with the preceding "n" sequence, then also with "s" to throw the phonological spotlight on Paul, the "elder"—but now also a "prisoner of Jesus Christ" (cf. 1a). The word πρεσβύτης is possibly intended also to reflect the more authoritative term πρεσβεύτης "ambassador" (cf. Eph 6:20; Metzger 1994:588). L&S arbitrarily conclude their "Period 4" here in v. 9c—based on the artificial "rounding" forged by a lexical link with "Christ" (9c/8a; ibid., 230)—despite the more prominent syntactic-semantic evidence that the utterance (and thought sequence) begun in v. 8 continues on into v. 10, as suggested by the reiterated verb παρακαλῶ (cf. v. 9a; the SBL Greek text indicates a continuative pause between vv. 9 and 10). This verb picks up on Paul's argument and his "appeal"—that is, after the brief personal digression in which he refers to his own situation (9b–c).

ᑫLine-ending assonance in –ου (10a) echoes that of the preceding line (9c), thus forging a cohesive phonological linkage that continues Paul's line of reasoning and foregrounds the mystery concerning Paul's "son": Just who could that be? And what might be the apparent connection with "Christ Jesus"? The answer to this personally pressing (note the emphatic ἐμοῦ) enigma is about to be revealed.

ʳAnother prominent verbal back-shift, coupled with clause-initial and –final sound similarity, foregrounds Ὀνήσιμον –in an ironically similar way to Paul's "brother" (Philemon) at the close of the preceding paragraph (7e). The two antagonists of this personal epistle are thereby syntactically linked!

ˢL&S claim that "hiatus emphasizes ἐμοί" (ibid., 232; *hiatus* is created by two words, the first that ends in a vowel and the second that begins with one; it allegedly "interrupts the flow of sound," but that claim is both difficult to perceive aurally and hence also to prove; ibid., 192). In contrast, it would seem that *both* σοί as well as ἐμοί are syntactically foregrounded in 11b and hence emphasized. It is true that the fuller form ἐμοί might be somewhat more "sound stressed" than its shorter correspondent μοι (cf. 13b), but it could also be argued that ἐμοί was chosen to pattern phonically with σοι to anticipate the sound of the following key term εὔχρηστον.

ᵗThe wordplay here, "useless"—"useful," is almost too obvious, but it makes Paul's point: a drastic transformation has taken place in the person being referred to—left unmentioned, but unambiguous in the context, Onesimus!

ᵘAlthough Onesimus is not mentioned by name again, the reiterated object pronominal references (in -όν) emphasize that Paul is definitely referring to "him," with the protagonists in the discussion—Paul (ἀνέπεμψά) and Philemon (σοι)—in juxtaposition between the two references to Onesimus.

ᵛRepeated mention of the highly emotive expression "bowels" implicitly connects Onesimus with Paul on the one hand (12b) and with Philemon on the other (7c), who was known for manifesting such "loving concern" for fellow believers in Christ ("the saints"), whose group Onesimus had now joined! The affective, emphatic (word order plus assonance in "a") phrase τὰ **ἐμὰ** σπλάγχνα here corresponds to and identifies with τοῦ **ἐμοῦ** τέκνου in v. 10a, further underscoring the close relationship between the Apostle and his beloved "bowels." L&S perceptively comment that "[i]n this context, τὰ σπλάγχνα metaphorically depicts Onesimus as part of Paul's body" (ibid., 232), quite the opposite from how slaves were normally perceived (and treated) in that day and age. However, one cannot go so far as to claim that "Onesimus' own name, beginning and ending with -ον, becomes a sound signature for this transformation" (ibid., 232–33), since that would be true only when he is being referred to in the accusative case! For text-critical arguments regarding the non-inclusion of the imperative "receive" (προσλαβοῦ, cf. 17b) in v. 12, see Omanson 2006:450.

8.2 Sonic structure display and commentary 295

ʷThe close relationship between Paul and his spiritual "son" is further accented through strategic pronominal usage in v. 13a—each on one side of the forceful verb ἐβουλόμην (conveying an imperfect "customary" or "continuative" sense here).

ˣPaul again (cf. 11b) strategically utilizes the word order to highlight the close connection between himself ("me") and Philemon ("you"), which will obviously influence how the latter is to perceive and evaluate the former's "appeal" on behalf of Onesimus, the runaway slave who had presumably so wronged and grieved his master, but who was now so valuable to the Apostle Paul. Paul clearly states his preference and desire—that Onesimus could continue to serve him and the Gospel in prison—before removing from the discussion (v. 14), as it were, his authority to request, if not command, this favor from Philemon.

ʸRepetition of the key term "chains/imprisonment" (cf. 9c, 10b) on behalf of "Christ Jesus (9c)–the Gospel" (13c) highlights the price that Paul had to pay for preaching The Message, and thus indirectly, how Philemon might contribute to Paul's ministry and alleviate his situation by means of the "man-in-the-middle," namely, Onesimus! One might argue that lines 13a, b, and c illustrate rhetorical *logos*, *ethos*, and *pathos* respectively—or more accurately, perhaps, a mixture of all three at once.

ᶻThe extensive front-shifted material—οὐδὲν and χωρὶς [δὲ] τῆς σῆς γνώμης— serves to underscore Paul's point that he did not want to pull rank and "force" Philemon to do anything against his will regarding the potentially contentious case of Onesimus, a concern that is further emphasized in the following lines.

ᵃᵃSyntactic parallelism in the pair of κατὰ phrases highlights the contrasting terms "compulsion" and "free will"—with "your (Philemon's!) goodness" sandwiched in-between (which is also situated between the prominent **μὴ**...**ἢ** sounds of the line). How could Philemon refuse or fail to "freely" respond to Paul's request(s) in a positive, Gospel-motivated manner? L&S end their "Period 5" here; it thus extends through verses 10–14, far too long to be encompassed within "the duration of a breath" (ibid., 109).

ᵇᵇThe similarity in sound at the onset of adjacent lines 14d and 15a masks a perceptible semantic as well as a syntactic break, that is between the contrastive certainty of ἀλλὰ and the relative vagueness of τάχα.

ᶜᶜThe word-final *–ον* sequence, including three rhythmic lines of nearly equal syllabic length, first foregrounds the contrastive notion of time ("for a short time/hour/forever"), and then "him" (i.e., Onesimus, perhaps diplomatically left unmentioned by name), who is now much "more than a slave" to Philemon; rather, he is a "beloved brother." Surely, to make this possible would further reflect Philemon's "goodness" (ἀγαθ**όν**—v. 14)! The significance of the concluding **–όν** sound chain probably is intended to reach even further back in the text: Thus, "Onesimus" (Ὀνήσιμ<u>ον</u>, 10c), who was formerly "useless" (ἄχρησ<u>τον</u>, 11a) but is now "useful" (εὔχρησ<u>τον</u>, 11b), must be received by Philemon, not "as a slave" (ὡς δοῦλ<u>ον</u>, 16a), but "more than a slave" (ὑπὲρ δοῦλ<u>ον</u>, 16b), as a "beloved brother" (ἀδελφ<u>ὸν</u> ἀγαπητ<u>όν</u>, 16c).

ddParallel sounds and syntax serve to underscore the corresponding ideas that again link Paul (ἐμοί) and Philemon (σοί) in the fellowship of *faith* and *ministry* (ἐν κυρίῳ can refer to both) by means of their "beloved brother" Onesimus!

eeThe parallel construction of this line suggests that an internal dramatic pause might have been inserted here (underscored by the chiastic arrangement of sounds within the key terms) to highlight the contrastive (i.e., with "in [the] flesh") and climactic (i.e., end stress) concluding phrase, "in the Lord." The subunit comprising vv. 15–16 begins tentatively (τάχα) with human ambiguity but ends with spiritual certainty. L&S comment: "Although the Pauline letters often set these two phrases in contrast, here they are coordinates. Onesimus is to be a beloved brother both in the flesh and in the Lord" (ibid., 233). ἐν κυρίῳ in v. 16f forms an *inclusio* with ἐν Χριστῷ in 8a, thus demarcating the first and principal portion of the letter's medial "body" section. The second and somewhat shorter section (vv. 17–20) begins in 17a with a pair of conditional clauses, marked also by the only "conclusive" οὖν in the letter. The shortest segment of the letter body comprises vv. 21–22.

ffThe front-shifted object **με**, coupled with the clause-final phrase ὡς ἐμέ, with the similar sounding κοινωνόν and αὐτὸν in between, interposes Paul syntactically as it were, as a mediator between Philemon and their new "partner" in common (implied), Onesimus. This usage further supports the assumed truth of the protasis of this conditional sentence. Since there is no doubt about that, Philemon is encouraged to act in accordance with the imperative of the apodosis. Thus, as L&S observe: "Paul does not appeal to apostolic authority, but to the κοινωνόν that Philemon and Paul share" (ibid., 234) when making his personal request on behalf of Onesimus. Paul's indirect intercessory argument reaches its peak in v. 17.

ggA double syntactic front-shift, involving the direct as well as the indirect object, underscores Paul's (ἐμοὶ) promise to pay any debt (τοῦτο—cf. the preceding τι) that Onesimus might owe Philemon.

hhThe reiterated full personal pronouns (ἐγώ, including word-end rhyme in ὼ), emphasized by the phrase τῇ ἐμῇ χειρί, highlight Paul's personal involvement in the case of Onesimus and reinforce the strength of his appeal on his behalf.

The paired forceful ἐγώ assertions function to counteract, as it were, the two previous paralleled εἰ conditional sentences (vv. 17–18; note the assonance in εἰ). L&S argue that "[h]iatus sets apart Paul's emphatic statement, ἐγώ ἀποτίσω (I will pay you back), and also his insistence that he writes the statement with his own hand (ἔγραψα τῇ ἐμῇ χειρί)" (ibid., 235). According to classical Greco-Roman canons, "hiatus" (i.e., the juxtaposition of vowel sounds between two words, marked by * above) "creates disjuncture...[t]he momentary stoppage of breath...slows the pace...lending a grave tone. The shift is sudden and dramatic, signaling a turning point in the letter" (ibid., 234). Such claims are highly impressionistic and debatable with regard to how dramatic or even perceptible such subtle vocalic features actually were. Besides, it assumes that Paul was writing this letter according to current rhetorical principles of the day, which is just as dubious (why not rather in a "Semitic style"?). I do not doubt that a break in the flow of Paul's discourse occurs at v. 17, but would suggest that other stylistic markers operate together to indicate this, e.g., the introduction of the complex syntactic structure initiated by a double conjunction (Εἰ οὖν), coupled with the emphatic pronouns and patterned word order of v. 17 (continued with εἰ δέ in v. 18).

[ii]The B and B' segments (vv. 18b, 19c) manifest a chiastic word order: *ἐμοὶ* ἐλλόγα // λέγω *σοι*, which intertwines the active participants involved in Paul's proposed "transaction."

[jj]A longer chiastic construction serves to emphasize the corresponding situations that Paul compares in vv. 18–19, namely, the *material* debt that Onesimus might owe Philemon with the *spiritual* debt that Philemon owes Paul. The *greater* significance of the latter debt is reflected in the *intensified* corresponding terms in A and A'— that is (σε) with (σεαυτόν) and (ὀφείλει) with (προσοφείλεις).

[kk]Another front-shifted element (σου) puts pronominal references to Philemon in juxtaposition with Paul (ἐγώ), a syntactical reflection of the pragmatic impression that the Apostle wishes to give his addressee concerning their close spiritual and ministerial personal relationship (cf. vv. 11, 13). Note also the sound correspondence with a parallel reference in v. 19.

[ll]Corresponding line endings (sound—sense—syntax), i.e., ἐν κυρίῳ—ἐν Χριστῷ, reinforce Paul's implicit plea regarding Onesimus: release him ("my [*front-shifted*] bowels"—v. 12) unto my service here in prison! (cf. vv. 12–14). Segment two of the letter's "body" ends in 20c with ἐν Χριστῷ, which matches ἐν κυρίῳ at the close of the preceding section in 16f (an instance of structural *epiphora*).

ᵐᵐSound similarity at the beginning and ending of these two lines (21a–b) reflect their content, i.e., Paul's making an implicit request of Philemon regarding a matter that is too delicate, perhaps also controversial, to mention in writing—namely, freeing the slave Onesimus to return to assist the apostolic prisoner Paul.

ⁿⁿThe two καί's (vv. 21b–22a, the second accented within an alternating sound pattern: μα—οί—μα—οί) covertly connect the seemingly unrelated content of these juxtaposed utterances: The "even more" in Paul's implicit request for Onesimus will "also" become an issue—whether confrontational or confirmatory—when Paul comes to make his proposed visit to Colossae.

ᵒᵒThe second person singular pronominals suddenly shift to plurals at the end of adjacent lines (22b–c) as Paul involves the entire congregation at Colossae in his prospective visit in answer to their prayers (front-shifted phrase) that would obviously engage them all in the Onesimus affair as well—as witnesses of how Philemon responded to their beloved, beleaguered apostle's request. This also marks the end of section three of the letter's body. L&S consider line 22c to be part of 22b—hence a colon that "is elongated, signaling closure" (ibid., 236). My reason for breaking this line (colon) is based largely on the placement of the significant 2ⁿᵈ p. pl. pronouns (ὑμῶν...ὑμῖν), and this decision may be regarded as somewhat arbitrary. On the other hand, as noted several times already, the length of L&S's proposed "Period 9," covering verses 21–22, is equally debatable, if, as argued, the extent of a "period" is to be defined by the length of a natural breath span (ibid., 109).

ᵖᵖThe alliteration in sibilant sounds, which continues from verses 21–22 (L&S, 237), seems to vocally highlight this fellowship (συν-) of faith, of which Philemon (σε) is an integral part (cf. v. 2; he must now act accordingly with respect to Onesimus in order to preserve their common bond. L&S conjoin these four lines of vv. 23–24 into two much longer "cola" (ibid., 236), whereas I have broken them on the basis of sonic and syntactic parallelism. Rather strange (to me) is the conclusion that "[s]ound...signals that, although the semantic fields of the two terms [apparently, συνεργός and συναιχμάλωτός] overlap, the words associated by sound function for a single purpose—and ὁ συναιχμάλωτός stands apart from this purpose" (ibid., 237). On the contrary, the term "fellow prisoner" reminds all concerned that their "fellowship" (koinōnia) includes being bound together as co-captives of Christ Jesus, which Paul intimates at the very beginning of this letter by referring to himself as a δέσμιος Χριστοῦ Ἰησοῦ (cf. v. 9c; Col 4:10).

qqThe assonance in -ου catches the ear, and significantly recalls the beginning of this letter (1a, 3c)—one that is founded on the senders' and receivers' common foundation of faith in Christ. It is interesting, and perhaps even significant, to note that a chiastic arrangement of this compound name is formed with the second occurrence of the earlier pairing (3c), i.e., Χριστῷ Ἰησοῦ...Ἰησοῦ Χριστοῦ.

8.3 Hearing and performing Paul for yourself

How do you *hear* Paul's epistle to Philemon? In other words, do you agree with the preceding analysis of the sound-structure of this text? If not, make a list of those passages and points within them where you would propose modifications or changes in what has been documented above and then present these for a critical comparative study and discussion in some exegetical and/or translation group.

On the other hand—and this is rather more challenging—how would you *perform* the letter to Philemon before an actual listening audience (with a specific group of hearers in mind)? Obviously, carrying out such an exercise from memory and in the original Greek would be the ideal. But even reading an English translation aloud several times can give one a feeling for its potential phonic dynamics. For example, where would you increase or decrease the volume, rate of speech, pause breaks, or stress points in response to how you interpret the Apostle's emotions as he penned these words in the initial instance? Furthermore, what sort of facial expressions, hand gestures, and general body motions might accompany passages of special feeling, emphasis, or importance? How would this focus on the phonology of the text in public performance affect its translation into English (or any other language)? Select several examples to illustrate these effects in an effort to produce a more "oratorical" rendition, and again, if possible, critically discuss these in a group of interested colleagues.

When you are ready then, try "performing" (i.e., proclaiming, reciting, rhythmically chanting, intoning, etc.) Philemon for practice in the presence of a cooperative friend or relative (before doing this in public, before a larger group). What constructive criticism does s/he have in response to your oral interpretation of this epistle? Do you agree with her/his evaluation? If not, give reasons. If so, incorporate these modifications when presenting a revised articulation of the text, perhaps now to enrich a communal Bible study session. It would be important now to imagine yourself in Paul's place. How would he have expressed his fervent appeal on behalf of Onesimus before Philemon and in the company of Apphia and Archippus, as well as the Christian congregation who were accustomed to meet for worship in Philemon's home (Phm 2)?

9

An Exercise in Poetic, Oral-Aural Analysis and Translation

9.1 Overview: The purpose of an applied study of 1 Corinthians 13

Thus far in this book, we have considered the results of research into orality as they relate to various literary, rhetorical, poetic, and discourse-oriented analyses of the Scriptures. Selected applications of these exegetical studies have also been made periodically to illustrate the challenge of translating biblical texts meaningfully in another language and cultural setting. Special emphasis has been placed on the actual "sound" of these translations in the target, or "consumer," language—sounds selected to resonate with the many distinct oral-aural features that are manifested in the source document.

As a little practical task to conclude this collection of essays, it may be helpful now to give readers a greater opportunity to exercise their own skills when rendering a well-known pericope, 1 Corinthians 13, in their mother tongue. The aim is to produce a dynamically matching "poetic" and meaning-centered version, one that is based on a prior analysis of the Greek text and that also highlights the sonic dimension of this stirring passage in the TL. I have not presented the results of my own study of this favorite section of Scripture below; readers will have seen enough of my approach to the task in preceding chapters. Rather, I have simply suggested (and in certain cases also briefly exemplified) a number of exploratory "steps" that may be followed during the process of biblical discourse "analysis" and its subsequent "synthesis," or translation, into another language. I have periodically inserted some specific, text-related questions along the way (*marked by italics*) in order to stimulate further thought (and possibly discussion if this is being done as a group project).

The following 16 guidelines, arranged into two sets of eight (moving from *analysis* to *synthesis*), may be followed exactly, or modified as desired (e.g., reordered, reworded, added to, deleted from), or ignored completely during this practical exercise—as long as the ultimate objective is accomplished. That goal would be the production of a TL rendition that proclaims the Word of the Lord in a manner that reproduces in "the tongues of human beings" (ταῖς γλώσσαις τῶν ἀνθρώπων) something of the text's manifold forcefulness, feeling, and esthetic effect in addition to its author-intended meaning (content + intent). In a sense then, you are free to "practice what you preach" in terms of (a) your chosen method of discourse analysis, (b) your style or type of translation, and (c) your preferred manner of publicly vocalizing a given composition of Scripture in a contemporary language.

9.2 *Analysis*: Eight suggested steps for studying a biblical text

An unformatted version of the Greek text of 1 Corinthians 13 (from *Paratext 7.1*) is reproduced below for reference, accompanied by an example of its moderately formal rendering in English, namely, the *New English Translation*.[1]

---

[1] Scripture quoted by permission from the *NET Bible*®, copyright © 2003 by Biblical Studies Press, L.L.C., www.netbible.com, all rights reserved.

9.2 Analysis: Eight suggested steps for studying a biblical text

¹Ἐὰν ταῖς γλώσσαις τῶν ἀνθρώπων λαλῶ καὶ τῶν ἀγγέλων, ἀγάπην δὲ μὴ ἔχω, γέγονα χαλκὸς ἠχῶν ἢ κύμβαλον ἀλαλάζον. ²καὶ ἐὰν ἔχω προφητείαν καὶ εἰδῶ τὰ μυστήρια πάντα καὶ πᾶσαν τὴν γνῶσιν καὶ ἐὰν ἔχω πᾶσαν τὴν πίστιν ὥστε ὄρη μεθιστάναι, ἀγάπην δὲ μὴ ἔχω, οὐθέν εἰμι. ³κἂν ψωμίσω πάντα τὰ ὑπάρχοντά μου καὶ ἐὰν παραδῶ τὸ σῶμά μου ἵνα καυχήσωμαι, ἀγάπην δὲ μὴ ἔχω, οὐδὲν ὠφελοῦμαι. ⁴Ἡ ἀγάπη μακροθυμεῖ, χρηστεύεται ἡ ἀγάπη, οὐ ζηλοῖ, [ἡ ἀγάπη] οὐ περπερεύεται, οὐ φυσιοῦται, ⁵οὐκ ἀσχημονεῖ, οὐ ζητεῖ τὰ ἑαυτῆς, οὐ παροξύνεται, οὐ λογίζεται τὸ κακόν, ⁶οὐ χαίρει ἐπὶ τῇ ἀδικίᾳ, συγχαίρει δὲ τῇ ἀληθείᾳ· ⁷πάντα στέγει, πάντα πιστεύει, πάντα ἐλπίζει, πάντα ὑπομένει. ⁸Ἡ ἀγάπη οὐδέποτε πίπτει· εἴτε δὲ προφητεῖαι, καταργηθήσονται· εἴτε γλῶσσαι, παύσονται· εἴτε γνῶσις, καταργηθήσεται. ⁹ἐκ μέρους γὰρ γινώσκομεν καὶ ἐκ μέρους προφητεύομεν· ¹⁰ὅταν δὲ ἔλθῃ τὸ τέλειον, τὸ ἐκ μέρους καταργηθήσεται. ¹¹ὅτε ἤμην νήπιος, ἐλάλουν ὡς νήπιος, ἐφρόνουν ὡς νήπιος, ἐλογιζόμην ὡς νήπιος· ὅτε γέγονα ἀνήρ, κατήργηκα τὰ τοῦ νηπίου. ¹²βλέπομεν γὰρ ἄρτι δι' ἐσόπτρου ἐν αἰνίγματι, τότε δὲ πρόσωπον πρὸς πρόσωπον· ἄρτι γινώσκω ἐκ μέρους, τότε δὲ ἐπιγνώσομαι καθὼς καὶ ἐπεγνώσθην. ¹³νυνὶ δὲ μένει πίστις, ἐλπίς, ἀγάπη, τὰ τρία ταῦτα· μείζων δὲ τούτων ἡ ἀγάπη.

13:1 If I speak in the tongues of men and of angels, but I do not have love, I am a noisy gong or a clanging cymbal. 13:2 And if I have prophecy, and know all mysteries and all knowledge, and if I have all faith so that I can remove mountains, but do not have love, I am nothing. 13:3 If I give away everything I own, and if I give over my body in order to boast, but do not have love, I receive no benefit. 13:4 Love is patient, love is kind, it is not envious. Love does not brag, it is not puffed up. 13:5 It is not rude, it is not self-serving, it is not easily angered or resentful. 13:6 It is not glad about injustice, but rejoices in the truth. 13:7 It bears all things, believes all things, hopes all things, endures all things. 13:8 Love never ends. But if there are prophecies, they will be set aside; if there are tongues, they will cease; if there is knowledge, it will be set aside. 13:9 For we know in part, and we prophesy in part, 13:10 but when what is perfect comes, the partial will be set aside. 13:11 When I was a child, I talked like a child, I thought like a child, I reasoned like a child. But when I became an adult, I set aside childish ways. 13:12 For now we see in a mirror indirectly, but then we will see face to face. Now I know in part, but then I will know fully, just as I have been fully known. 13:13 And now these three remain: faith, hope, and love. But the greatest of these is love.

Before beginning the little exercise below, one important discourse feature needs to be determined—or at least a hypothesis made that may be either confirmed or corrected by the subsequent analysis. The crucial question is this: what type of a text are we dealing with, or what is its literary "genre"?

❖ We have begun with the assumption that we are dealing with a "poetic" text in the case of 1 Cor 13. Would you agree? If so, what would you call it in terms of genre? Check several commentaries and give your terminological preference, with reasons.

❖ If you agree that the text is "poetic" (if not pure poetry, then poetic prose), there should be some significant literary features to support this conclusion. Mention the most important characteristics, in your opinion. Does the TL that you are working with have a functionally equivalent genre? If so, what are its primary features? If not, how do you plan to translate this chapter, which is so prominent that it is frequently published as a separate portion?

❖ Finally, make a tentative division of the text above into poetic "lines" by inserting a vertical stroke (/) at the end of each line. Do this in pencil so that you can revise your segmentation as you proceed with the following analysis.

The following eight subsections (9.2.1–9.2.8) outline one practical way to carry out a specifically "literary-structural" discourse analysis:[2]

9.2.1 Evaluate the text's "given" external boundaries plus any text-critical issues.

We tend to accept the chapter divisions recorded in our published Bibles without much thought. In certain cases, however, there is appreciable room for doubt. Consider, for example, the comments regarding 12:31, which precedes ch. 13:[3]

> The footnotes on punctuation in the UBS Greek text show that editions and translations differ in the paragraphing of 12.31 and 13.1. The UBS

---

[2] These heuristic steps may be compared with those suggested in Wendland (2004b:ch. 7); cf. Hill et al. (2011:283–284).

[3] Cited from the *Paratext 7.1* version of the Translator's Handbook on 1 Corinthians.

Greek text begins a new paragraph at 12.31b, but not at 13.1. This example is followed by **REB**, **ITCL**, **TNT**, and **AT**. But most CLTs, like **TEV**, begin a new paragraph at 12.31b and a new section at 13.1. **NJB**, on the other hand, begins a new section at 12.31a, and a new paragraph at 13.1. Most translations do not agree with **NJB**'s interpretation.

❖ *Study the preceding note and draw your own conclusion, based on the textual evidence:*
Should a new paragraph begin at 13:1—why or why not?

❖ *Evaluate Kenneth Bailey's opinion on this matter:* "Seeing 12:31 as a hinge verse between the two chapters [12 and 13] appears to be the best option because verse 31 does indeed conclude chapter 12 and at the same time it provides an important introduction to chapter 13. In like manner 14:1 concludes chap. 13 and introduces chap. 14.... A similar hinge appears in 15:58 and joins chapter 15 to chapter 16" (Bailey 2011:355, reordered). *If you agree with this reasoning, how do you propose handling such "hinge" verses in your translation?*

Major text-critical problems, too, are profitably examined at this initial stage so that a more or less "confirmed" source-language document can serve as the basis for the following analysis. Most of these matters do not significantly affect the content of a given passage, but some do, for example, the disputed reading **καυχήσωμαι** ("I might boast") as opposed to **καυθήσομαι** ("I will burn") in 13:3. Then too, there are a number of readings that affect the form rather than the meaning of the text—or, as in the case of 1 Cor 13, its special "poetic" and "oral-aural" character. Evaluate the following comments by Omanson with respect to the variants in v. 4:

> There is good manuscript support for the third occurrence of the words ἡ ἀγάπη. On the other hand, the rhythm and structure (οὐ..., οὐ..., οὐ...) favor understanding ἡ ἀγάπη as a later addition to the text. In order to represent a balance of these considerations, the words ἡ ἀγάπη are kept in the text but are put in brackets. In addition to the textual problem is the difficulty of knowing how Paul structured the words in this verse. According to the punctuation in the text, the second ἀγάπη goes with the verb χρηστεύεται (is kind). But it is possible to take this

noun with the following words οὐ ζηλοῖ, as in the following two translations: "Love is patient and kind. Love envies no one, is never boastful, never conceited" (REB) and "Love is always patient and kind; love is never jealous; love is not boastful or conceited" (NJB). Either way… nothing other than stylistic rhythm is at stake. (Omanson 2006:348)

❖ *While one cannot decide this textual matter at such a preliminary stage, translators who are seeking to produce a poetic rendering in their language will have to come back to this question at the close of their analysis: Should ἡ ἀγάπη be included in v. 4? And which verb should the second ἀγάπη be construed with? (See sample translations below.)*

9.2.2 Locate the chief "break points" within the text—its internal boundaries.

The most important unpunctuated boundaries in biblical discourse are those that indicate new "paragraph" (in poetry, "strophic") units. These may coincide with a larger border, such as a new section or episode (in narrative). Such larger constituents, however, must be established at a later stage of the analysis. One of the clearest markers of the start of a new paragraph is the occurrence of a notable *shift* in form or content from one verse to another, e.g., a change in the topic, speaker, addressees, time or place setting, type of composition (genre), and so forth. At times such a "break" in the text will also be signaled by a certain conjunction or introductory phrase (e.g., "Therefore…"; "Now concerning spiritual gifts…") and/or by some other distinctive form, such as a vocative (e.g., "Brothers…").

❖ *Where would you posit paragraph "breaks" in 1 Cor 13, and what evidence can you provide to support these? As a result of this exercise, what are the provisional paragraph units that comprise this chapter? How do these relate in terms of relative size?*

❖ *Bailey (2011:353, 359) proposes the following chiastic organization for chapter 13 and its surrounding verses. Evaluate this proposal in terms of form, content, and function. In other words, how credible is this suggested structure; how does it affect our understanding of Paul's message; and, if granted, what does this literary arrangement contribute to the Apostle's argument at this point? Finally, if this structure is deemed valid in terms of the original text, what are the implications for translators—how can they convey this significance in their version?*

1. **Continue in zeal** for *the higher gifts* and I will show the way (12:31)
2. **Love and the spiritual gifts** (13:1–3):
   Opens with tongues, prophecy, and knowledge;
   closes with faith, hope, and love.
3.   **Love defined positively** (13:4a)
4.   **Love defined negatively** (13:4b–6):
   In **3:4–7**, Paul begins with an indirect reference to knowledge and closes with a mention of faith, hope, and love.
5.   **Love defined positively** (13:7)
6. **Love and the spiritual gifts** (13:8–13):
   Opens with tongues, prophecy, and knowledge;
   closes with faith, hope, and love.
7. **Continue in zeal** for *the gifts* and run after love (14:1)

9.2.3 Mark areas of key term/phrase repetition and parallelism.

In a poetic text, repetition—whether synonymous or exact, explicit or implicit (e.g., pronominal)—defines instances of adjacent parallelism, which is common, of course, in all genres of Hebrew poetry. The recursion of prominent terms or phrases may also assist in demarcating the larger components of a given passage, for example, the reiteration of ἡ ἀγάπη at the beginning of verses 4 and 8 (i.e., an instance of structural *anaphora*,[4] which signals the onset of a new paragraph). Repetition, of course, also helps to indicate and/or to underscore the central ideas as well as the principal theme of an established pericope.

❖ *Locate all of the significant instances of repetition in ch. 13 and determine their possible structural (formal), semantic (topical), and/or rhetorical (functional) purpose in the text. These areas of recursion may be distinctively marked during the analysis process in different ways, depending on the textual medium, e.g., colored highlights, different font styles, underlines, etc.*

---

[4] For this and similar structural markers, see Wendland (2004b:127).

❖ It is also important to note how a biblical author employed certain key terms in the rest of a given composition, especially in passages that precede the pericope being studied. Consider the references to "love" elsewhere in 1 Corinthians, e.g., 1:10–16; 2:9; 3:3; 4:14; 8:1, 11–12; 10:24, 28–29, 32–33; 12:26. Does such intratextual recursion affect our understanding of ἀγάπη in ch. 13? Explain any significant (possible) resonances that you discover.

9.2.4 Determine places where important literary-rhetorical features converge.

During this step, we attend to the microstructural characteristics of the text, noting in particular where several of these literary-rhetorical devices come together, e.g., striking figurative language, adjacent lexical repetition, rhetorical questions, hyperbole, irony, imperative, vocative, word-order variation, and phonological marking (e.g., assonance, alliteration, rhyme, rhythm, wordplay—see also §9.2.8 below). Such areas of *convergence* often highlight a point of structural, thematic, and/or pragmatic significance, for example, the beginning or ending of a discourse unit, a semantic "peak," or an emotive "climax."

❖ Identify the major areas of stylistic "convergence" in 1 Cor 13 and posit their apparent communicative function(s) within the composition—whether structural, thematic, and/or pragmatic. Note in particular verses 7 and 13. Begin to think of how these points of literary marking may be handled in a corresponding manner in your language.

9.2.5 Do a lexical-semantic study of key terms and figurative expressions.

Such a detailed examination of the principal concepts within a passage is essential for its interpretation as well as in preparation for translation into another language and semantic framework. Obviously, in 1 Cor 13, the central word is "love" (ἡ ἀγάπη), and in this case, it might be tempting for interpreters to simply assume that they already "know" its meaning, particularly in English and other languages where accepted biblical terminology has already become well-established and (overly) familiar.⁵ In other languages, however, the choosing of the correct term here (whether a word or phrase) might be an issue of debate. In such cases, the controversy may best be resolved by an extensive lexical-semantic investigation of the original expressions (use of Bible dictionaries, commentaries, a concordance, etc.) coupled with more intensive local cultural study and a corpus analysis of common usages. In the Tonga language of Zambia, for example, the noun used to render ἀγάπη is *luyando,* which is derived from the verb *kuyanda* that has the sense of "to love," "to like," or "to desire," depending on the context. (In fact, the verbal "infinitive" form may be a more natural way of expressing Paul's intended meaning here.)

❖ *Which other key terms and figures of speech in 1 Cor 13 need further inspection in order to determine their most appropriate expression in English (or some other language)?*

In addition to lexical items that are used in their *literal* sense, the various types of *figurative* language (metaphors, similes, metonyms, etc.) also need to be examined with regard to their contextual meaning and consequent expression in translation. At times, such an investigation can turn out to be more complicated than one anticipated. With respect to the imagery at the beginning of v. 12, for example, even scholars are not agreed on what the Apostle was referring to—that is, the primary basis, or ground, of comparison. The text says literally "For we still see (as) through a mirror ἐν αἰνίγματι." But what does the last Greek phrase mean? The following are two possible explanations:⁶

- Reference to a mirror may suggest to readers a modern mirror made with glass and mercury. Ancient mirrors, however, were made of polished metal and therefore gave a generally less clear reflection, as the contrast shows.

---

⁵ With time and language change, such long-established usages in the case of certain key biblical terms can become misleading or even erroneous—for example, KJV's "charity" for ἡ ἀγάπη in 1 Cor 13.

⁶ The first explanatory note is from the UBS Translator's Handbook, the second from the NET.

- *Greek* "we are seeing through [= using] a mirror by means of a dark image." Corinth was well known in the ancient world for producing some of the finest bronze mirrors available. Paul's point in this analogy, then, is not that our current understanding and relationship with God is distorted (as if the mirror reflected poorly), but rather that it is "indirect," (i.e., the nature of looking in a mirror) compared to the relationship we will enjoy with him in the future when we see him "face to face" (Fee 1987:648). The word "indirectly" translates the Greek phrase ἐν αἰνίγματι ("in an obscure image") which itself may reflect an allusion to Num 12:8 (LXX οὐ δι' αἰνίγματων), where God says that he speaks to Moses "mouth to mouth [= face to face]...and not in dark figures [of speech]." Though this allusion to the OT is not explicitly developed here, it probably did not go unnoticed by the Corinthians who were apparently familiar with OT traditions about Moses (cf. 1 Cor 10:2). Indeed, in 2 Cor 3:13–18 Paul had recourse with the Corinthians to contrast Moses' ministry under the old covenant with the hope afforded through apostolic ministry and the new covenant. Further, it is in this context, specifically in 2 Cor 3:18, that the apostle invokes the use of the mirror analogy again in order to unfold the nature of the Christian's progressive transformation by the Spirit.

❖ *Study the two preceding notes and other commentaries at your disposal and compare the meaning indicated with the renderings found in a number of modern translations, e.g., "Now we see things imperfectly, like puzzling reflections in a mirror" (NLT). Then propose a dynamic way of translating the sense of this imagery in English (or another language).*

9.2.6 Posit a structural-thematic outline for the entire text.

This exercise requires one to organize the main sections of a larger portion of defined biblical document, such as a chapter or more, and to formulate summary *headings*, or titles, for the major units. This can serve as a further check on the discourse analysis that was progressively carried out during steps #1–4 and will result in a final analytical proposal for the pericope as a whole. Titles for the various internal subunits should reflect the overarching heading suggested for the macro-unit as a whole. Such subtitles

9.2 Analysis: Eight suggested steps for studying a biblical text 311

are intended to serve as a guide to readers (and listeners) regarding the *thematic development* of the composition so that they can more easily follow the author's narrative flow, sequence of ideas, line of reasoning, or—in this case—an unfolding descriptive expression of praise. On the other hand, too many proposed subtitles may be a distraction and disrupt the smooth flow of the text. Most modern versions give only a single heading to cover the entire content expressed in ch. 13.

❖ *Is a single section heading sufficient for 1 Cor 13 in your opinion? If not, where do you suggest placing another one—and what is your proposed wording for this? Evaluate the following chapter headings and select which one you feel is best—or make your own suggestion, e.g., "Love Is the Greatest"(NLT), "Love" (GNT), "The Way of Love" (NET), "The Gift of Love" (NRSV).*

❖ *Consider again your evaluation of the proposed chiastic arrangement of this chapter (cf. §9.2.2). To what extent, if any, does this affect your thematic outline? Explain.*

9.2.7 Note the primary "speech acts" (illocutions) and "text act" (genre).

As explained in ch. 2, a "speech act" consists of three elements: the *locution*—the actual text recorded; the *illocution*—the intended communicative function of that segment of text; and the *perlocution*—the particular effect produced in a particular audience by communicating that text. When we investigate the speech acts of a given section, we are primarily interested in its sequence of principal illocutions and how this relates then to the illocutionary progression of the composition as a whole, which normally coincides with the typical discourse functions of its genre. The following is a literary description of 1 Cor 13 (Ryken 1992:474):

> The genre of 1 Corinthians 13 is the *encomium*, a lyric pericope that praises an abstract quality. The subject of this encomium is love. The passage praises its subject by means of the usual formulas of an encomium: the indispensability of the subject (vv. 1–3), a catalogue of praiseworthy acts and attributes (vv. 4–7), the superiority of love

(vv. 8–13), and a concluding command to emulate the subject (14:1, "Make love your aim").

❖ How would you evaluate the preceding text characterization of 1 Cor 13? Is "love" an adequate term to describe the central theme of this chapter? If not, what do you suggest? What about the division of the text—is it accurate? Any corrections?

❖ While "praise" might be adequate to designate the overt illocution (speech act) of 1 Cor 13, is that designation really sufficient to characterize Paul's primary purpose—or might there be an underlying communicative aim, namely, an "exhortation" or "encouragement" to do likewise? In other words, as Paul lauds the theological subject of Christlike love, he simultaneously enjoins his readers/hearers ethically to pattern their lives after this supreme (albeit implicit) divine Model (cf. 12:27). What do you think?

❖ How then does chapter 13 relate both topically and functionally with ch. 12, on the one hand, and ch. 14, on the other?

9.2.8 Identify the major oral-aural characteristics of the text.

Here we again investigate—orally and aurally—the main *phonological* properties of the pericope at hand and note how these relate to the previously analyzed structural and stylistic features of the text (cf. steps 9.2.2–3). In the case of 1 Cor 13, the parallel phrasing is very prominent throughout the discourse. Thus, if this passage is not in fact an instance of Hellenistic poetry, it is most certainly an instance of "poetic prose," and hence ideally suited for public oral articulation. If that is so, the usual prose paragraph block format of Bible publications is not very suitable or helpful in revealing the crucial rhythm of speech and patterns of repetition. The CEV is one modern translation that does format the text by means of a sequence of "utterance units," or poetic "lines." The first three verses are reproduced below for assessment:

1 What if I could speak
all languages of humans
    and even of angels?
If I did not love others,

9.2 Analysis: Eight suggested steps for studying a biblical text

    I would be nothing more
than a noisy gong
    or a clanging cymbal.
2 What if I could prophesy
and understand all mysteries
    and all knowledge?
And what if I had faith
    that moved mountains?
I would be nothing,
    unless I loved others.
3 What if I gave away all
    that I owned
and let myself
    be burned alive?
I would gain nothing,
    unless I loved others.

❖ How helpful do you find this poetic format? Suggest ways in which it might be improved, for example, if there were no restriction on line length (i.e., in a single column text)?

❖ Critically compare the CEV selection above with the following re-formatted section of vv. 1–3 from the NIV. Which do you prefer and why? Can you suggest some improvements to the following proposal? Test the composition and its format by actually reading/reciting it aloud (and if possible by listening to someone else read it):

If I speak in the tongues of men and of angels,   1.
    but have not love,
        I am only a resounding gong or a clanging cymbal.
If I have the gift of prophecy   2.
and can fathom all mysteries and all knowledge,
and if I have a faith that can move mountains,
    but have not love,
        I am nothing.
If I give all I possess to the poor   3.

and surrender my body to the flames,
>   **but have not love,**
>   I gain nothing.

9.3 *Synthesis*: Eight suggested steps for translating a biblical Text

After carrying out the preceding eight steps (+/– other methods) when analyzing a particular text of Scripture, one may turn one's attention either to rendering the original message in another language or to revising/improving an already existing version. However, before any program of translation can be embarked upon, it is necessary to do some research in order to specify the parameters, or job commission (technically termed the "translation brief"), for the project.[7] The following eight subsections will cover some of the issues that such research and sampling will investigate and decide upon.

9.3.1 Identify the intended audience for the translation.

The most important aspect of a translation project brief is to determine *for whom* the version is intended. The day of the "one size fits all" translation has virtually ended, except for those projects that are undertaken for reasons other than adequate and acceptable communication with a specified constituency or group (e.g., an ideological aim, such as the *New World Translation* of the Jehovah's Witnesses). Translators need to be able to *imagine* some actual representatives of their intended target community as they seek to employ wording that will satisfy them in terms of the purpose for which the version is primarily being prepared (point #2). Quite a range of demographic variables or options are relevant here, for example: audience age (children, youth, middle-aged, elderly), church affiliation (Catholic, Protestant, Interconfessional), educational standard (basic, secondary school, college/university), general level of biblical literacy (novice, medium level, mature), economic capacity, and so forth.

---

[7] For more information about a translation brief and related issues, see Wendland 2004b:50–53, 290–291.

9.3 Synthesis: Eight suggested steps for translating a biblical Text

❖ *Specify the primary audience constituency or particular sub-group that you intend to communicate with, generally speaking. Has the Bible version that you normally use been specifically composed and designed with this community in mind? Give several precise reasons supporting your negative or positive response. How might your new translation (or revised version) differ? List some of the most important features, and tell why such modifications or changes are necessary.*

9.3.2 Specify the primary purpose, medium, and principal setting of use.

After the intended audience (readership), the second most important consideration is this: *why* is the version in question being prepared? What is the chief communicative goal that it is intended to achieve? Next, the *how*, the primary medium and mode of communication must be determined—oral/aural, written, video, electronic, dramatic stage, or some combination of these. Also important is the major location of use: *where* will this version be mostly used? Here again, there are a number of potential options, for example: in formal worship and liturgical settings, theological college, Bible school, etc., or in more informal situations—outside of "church" or "school": for home Bible study sessions or to provide Scriptural readings as a stimulus to prayer; simply reading through the Bible in a year or studying particular texts to learn more about them; using the text for the purposes of memorization or to serve as the basis for creating a musical version of the passage.

❖ *How would you specify the purpose and occasion for the Bible translation that you normally use? Assuming that there are a number of possibilities here, do you find that a single version is suitable for them all? If not, which setting and use would seem to require a different translation? Does 1 Cor 13 seem to lend itself to one particular setting and religious purpose? If so, describe what you have in mind.*

❖ *In which ways would a completely oral text, as on a CD recording, differ from a written one in the case of your translation of 1 Cor 13? What are some of the "oral markers" that would be needed, for example, to indicate major text transitions, emphasis or focus, key implications, deictic references, and so forth? Mention three specific items. Would some additional verbal signals be* needed for naturalness in conjunction with hand gestures, facial expressions, and body movements if this text were to be performed dramatically, as in a public stage production?[8]

9.3.3 Determine the type of translation to be prepared.

Many different translations are possible, depending on the primary consumer group envisaged (see #1 above) and the type of use for which the version is mainly intended (see #2). In some cases, there is also a definite ideological factor involved; certain conservative religious constituencies, for example, assert that only an essentially literal ("formal correspondence") version can be "faithful" to the original Word of God. Any other type of translation always distorts or mis-represents the biblical text, or so it is alleged.[9] Depending on the situation then, the type or style of translation desired may range from the very literal to the very free with regard to the linguistic forms used to render the language forms found in the source document, English examples being the *English Standard Version* (ESV) on the one hand, and the *New Living Translation* (NLT) on the other (Wendland 2004b:88–92). Often a compromise must be made between representing significant forms of the SL text and communicating these meaningfully in the TL—thus resulting in a "middle-of-the-road" version. The relative success and ultimate acceptability of any translation must be ascertained through subsequent research and testing procedures (see #7 below).

❖ *In view of your answers to exercises 1–2, what type of translation draft do you propose preparing for 1 Cor 13? Summarize the reasoning that leads to your decision in this case: what are the chief factors of influence involved, e.g., the manifest orality of the original text, its poetic qualities, its rhetorical objectives, other prominent concerns or issues?*

---

[8] For a more detailed discussion of some of these issues pertaining to oral in comparison with written procedural discourse, see Blass 2011.

[9] For example, "The goal of dynamic equivalence translators is to express the primary thought of each verse or passage clearly but they see no need to translate the meaning of every word, and they see nothing wrong with adding some details and expressions that they think will make the primary thought more clear or vivid.... The goal of translation is not being faithful to the original text, but rather the goal is to bring about a proper response from the reader" (Grudem et al. 2005:48, 53).

9.3.4 Outline a text-comparative translation methodology.

It is one thing to select a particular style of translation to pursue; it is quite another to specify the appropriate practical methods and operational procedures to carry this out in a real-life situation. However, without a clearly-defined methodology and set of procedural guidelines, it is doubtful that such an enterprise will produce a successful, or at least a consistent result. This is especially important where a diverse "team" of translators and reviewers must work together. There are a number of published translation approaches from which to choose nowadays,[10] but one needs to pick the one that will most closely approximate the type of version desired (determined in #3 above) that will, in turn, effectively accomplish the goals that have been set out for the project (modeled in #2). Normally, one's methodology will include a prominent *comparative* component. Here a translation draft is first critically and closely compared in various vital respects with the source document. Second, it is compared with other versions of that same passage in the TL if they happen to exist (if not, with a set of different drafts that have been composed by the same translator or team) as well as other language translations that the target community may have access to.

❖ *Draw up a set of general guidelines plus several more specific translation procedures with respect to the translation of 1 Cor 13 that you intend to prepare, given the presuppositions that have been established by means of exercises 1–3. Note that due attention needs to be accorded in this outline to the dimension of orality.*

❖ *Specify the principal translations that your target audience can read with understanding. Which of these are most important, and why? How might they affect your own version?*

9.3.5 Prepare an English draft translation on the basis of the prior analysis.

This is the step where a team might be tempted to begin—that is, simply to sit down and intuitively convert a text from one language

---
[10] For a survey, see Wendland 2004b:42–80; also Munday 2009b and Pym 2010.

to another. But as has been suggested above, working through the preceding steps helps translators (whether an individual translator or a team of three or more members) not only to zero in on their primary target audience and communicative aim, but also to develop an explicit compositional strategy and modus operandi for carrying out this multifaceted interlingual, cross-cultural task. Consider, for the sake of an initial practice exercise, the following "poetic prose" English draft of vv. 4–7 of 1 Cor 13:

Ἡ ἀγάπη μακροθυμεῖ, χρηστεύεται ἡ ἀγάπη,	Love is patient, love is kind.
οὐ ζηλοῖ, ἡ ἀγάπη οὐ περπερεύεται,	Does not envy, never boasts.
οὐ φυσιοῦται, οὐκ ἀσχημονεῖ,	It is not proud, never rude,
οὐ ζητεῖ τὰ ἑαυτῆς, οὐ παροξύνεται,	it seeks not self, nor fires up fast.
οὐ λογίζεται τὸ κακόν,	Love records no wrongs,
οὐ χαίρει ἐπὶ τῇ ἀδικίᾳ,	nor delights at all in evil,
συγχαίρει δὲ τῇ ἀληθείᾳ·	rather rejoices in the truth.
πάντα στέγει, πάντα πιστεύει,	Love always protects and trusts,
πάντα ἐλπίζει, πάντα ὑπομένει.	yes, ever hopes, ever perseveres.

❖ Now prepare your own <u>English</u> draft translation of vv. 4–7 (or indeed, the whole chapter if so desired). Then double-check by comparing your version with the Greek text, if possible, but otherwise with some relatively literal version (e.g., NRSV, ESV), on the one hand, and several more meaning-oriented versions, on the other—for example, the two modern translations below. After your comparative study, summarize your conclusions.

- [4] Love is patient, love is kind, it isn't jealous, it doesn't brag, it isn't arrogant, [5] it isn't rude, it doesn't seek its own advantage, it isn't irritable, it doesn't keep a record of complaints, [6] it isn't happy with injustice, but it is happy with the truth. [7] Love puts up with all things, trusts in all things, hopes for all things, endures all things. *(Common English Bible)*[11]

---

[11] http://www.commonenglishbible.com/Explore/PassageLookup/tabid/210/Default.aspx, accessed on 26/10/2011. The NLT below has been reproduced from Paratext 7.2.

- ⁴Love is patient and kind. Love is not jealous or boastful or proud ⁵or rude. It does not demand its own way. It is not irritable, and it keeps no record of being wronged. ⁶It does not rejoice about injustice but rejoices whenever the truth wins out. ⁷Love never gives up, never loses faith, is always hopeful, and endures through every circumstance. *(New Living Translation)*

9.3.6 Translate the same text in another language.

It is often helpful to try to compose an initial draft translation relatively quickly, especially a poetic one, while one is in a lyric mood and the words are flowing smoothly. Later on then one can take the time to critically compare (once again!) this first attempt with the source text for accuracy with regard to content (no vital semantic components missing or added) and with other translations, if available, with respect to form and function. In other words, other Scripture versions or the translations found in commentaries may suggest alternative terms and expressions that would better fulfill the objectives of the translation at hand. Finding other versions for comparison is quite easy for English and other languages of wider communication, but this may prove more difficult in the case of languages that do not have a long or developed history of publication. In such situations, perhaps it is possible to find a translation in a related language or some other well-known vernacular version which can serve as the basis for the essential comparative and cross-checking operation.

❖ *Prepare a draft translation in a language other than English, giving special attention to the form, content, and function of the text in relation to the translation parameters that were specified in steps 1–4. After a draft has been prepared, check this for possible revision by carefully comparing it with all of the other versions that are available, including the draft that you composed in step #5.*

9.3.7 Check the draft with added attention to its oral-aural dimension.

This step incorporates another review of your translation draft (step #6) with special reference now to its phonological qualities. This property of the discourse normally needs to be checked as a separate feature so that it receives the full attention it deserves. An initial way of doing this is for the translator to actually utter the TL composition aloud—several times—in order to discern how it sounds in one's own ears. Listen in particular for attractive and forceful instances of rhythm, alliteration, and euphony in general, and where such characteristics are missing, then seek to build them into the draft in some way that does not compromise its content. Thereafter, the translation should also be tested in a public "performance"—that is, before an actual listening audience: with fellow translators or project committee members, first of all, and, if possible, also before a gathering of members of the target group. If available, more than one lector should be given the opportunity to articulate the text.

❖ *Review your draft translation of 1 Cor 13 (4–7) aloud as suggested above and make any revisions or improvements that such an exercise may reveal are necessary—namely, for producing an "oratorical" version, a text that virtually calls out to be uttered aloud. Do the same with your sample English translation that was prepared during step #5. Would your drafts need to be modified in any way if they are to be presented orally alone, that is, in the absence of a written text in the hands of the intended audience (cf. 9.3.2)? If so, specify how.*

❖ *1 Cor proclaims the beauty of divine love in a poetic form that is meant to be heard and responded to in a manner that reflects the sublime character of its content. How often do our translations, in turn, reflect the beauty of the biblical text—its verbal concinnity—using the full literary resources of the TL? Organize a discussion of this issue in relation to your rendering of 1 Cor 13 as well as your translation project as a whole with reference to the following quotation (for "Christianity," read "Bible translation"):*

> "But it is this third virtue, the virtue of beauty, that has been most marginalized in the way we understand and evaluate Christianity. As a result, Christianity has suffered a loss of beauty—a loss that needs to be recovered. With an emphasis on truth, we have tried to make Christianity persuasive (as we should). But we also need a corresponding emphasis on beauty to make Christianity

attractive. Christianity should not only persuade with truth, but it should also attract with beauty. Along with Christian apologetics, we need Christian aesthetics. Christianity needs…to be presented as beautiful. Often where truth cannot convince, beauty can entice" (Zahnd 2012; cited in *Christianity Today* 56:50 and at www.christianitytoday.com/ct/2012/february/excerpt-beauty-world.html).

9.3.8 Indicate how the translation will be tested after publication.

This step cannot of course be implemented at the present time, unless an actual translation project is being conducted. The point is that the publication of any translation, whether just a portion like 1 Cor 13 or a complete Bible, is not the end of the story. In one sense, it is only the beginning—that is, the onset of a new project aimed at eventually producing a revised publication of a certain text of Scripture. No translation is perfect, and improvements—great and small—can always be made, sooner or later. A variety of test samples and styles (types of testing) should be prepared (in advance) and a credible assessment procedure devised that is in keeping with the pre-determined translation brief. Individual respondents as well as review committees, informal (ecclesial, lay, non-specialist) and formal (academic, specialist), from among members of the target audience may then be selected, educated, trained (if necessary, depending on the scope of the project), and engaged in this task as soon after publication as feasible. A reliable method must also be developed for accurately compiling and categorizing the results of all these translation testing exercises.

❖ *Make a list of qualified individuals or groups, both professional and lay, who would be in a position to evaluate your translation and to offer critical suggestions for improvement. Again, this should entail not only an examination of the written text but also its oral proclamation before a listening audience comprised of members of the target group. If it is achievable to gain such feedback (even in a preliminary manner), then make the appropriate revisions, as needed, to prepare an official "final corrected copy" of the translation, which should be safely stored both in hard copy and electronically for future reference and possible use.*

❖ If it is achievable to gain such feedback (even in a preliminary manner), then make the appropriate revisions, as needed, to prepare an official "final corrected copy" of the translation, which should be safely stored in both hard copy and an electronic file for future reference and possible use.

❖ Evaluate the following quote, which defines the distinction between an "analytic" and a "synthetic" translation, and comment on whether, in your opinion, the activity of "summarizing"—orally!—might be used to evaluate a draft translation—if not of 1 Cor 13, then a less familiar epistolary passage of Scripture: "The analytical translation enables the 'reader' to tear the text apart, to get at the details, to perform word studies, even to hear the underlying original language.... The synthetic translation enables the reader to process the text's meaning, to follow the flow of the author's thought, to engage in the narrative.... I can't help but think that a good text—that is, a well written one—enables a reader to summarize" (Sangrey 2012)—that is, more readily than an analytic (more formally correspondent) version would.

9.4 A final exercise—1 Cor 13:7

❖ Read through the following interesting and informative blog post and subsequent comments, which deal with the translation of 1 Cor 13:7.[12] Use this as the basis for a further discussion of the various issues that are brought up by the various writers—however, now with reference to your mother tongue or the language into which you are translating.

1 Cor 13:7—the language of love

One of the most famous and beloved passages in the NT is 1 Cor 13. I have been digging into the Greek text of verse 7 recently and thought I might share my thoughts with you.

The Greek words are: πάντα στέγει, πάντα πιστεύει, πάντα ἐλπίζει, πάντα ὑπομένει. RSV provides a fairly literal translation: *Love bears all things, believes all things, hopes all things, endures all things.*

---

[12] The initial entry was written by Iver Larsen, posted on May 15, 2011 at 12:45 pm at this website: http://betterbibles.com/2011/05/15/1-cor-137-the-language-of-love/#comments

9.4 A final exercise—1 Cor 13:7

The verse is poetic in two ways: the rhetorical repetition of πάντα (*panta*)—*all things* or *everything* or *all the way* and a chiasm. Let me explain the chiasm. The Greek word στέγει (*stegei*) is very close in meaning to ὑπομένει (*hupomenei*), so the first and last words are close. Similarly the words for believe and hope are close in meaning, so the two middle words correspond to each other.

στέγω only occurs 4 times in the NT and all in Paul's letters. Let us look at each of these: 1 Cor 9:12—we endure everything (NET), we put up with anything (NIV); 1 Cor 13:7—bears all things (NET), always protects (NIV); 1 Thess 3:1—we could bear it no longer (NET), we could stand it no longer (NIV); 1 Thess 3:5—I could bear it no longer (NET), I could stand it no longer (NIV).

I like the NIV idiom "I cannot stand it." This idiom is mainly used in a negative construction, I believe, so for the positive usage NIV says "we put up with anything." Why NIV did not also say "Love puts up with anything" in v. 7 I do not know. It would be consistent with 9:12 and give the meaning nicely. Why did they use "protect" and why say "always" instead of "everything" or "anything"? Paul commonly used the standard word for always (*pantote*).

I can only guess the reason for the NIV rendering. My guess is that it was to forestall possible misuses of the text. Because we have a long tradition of pretty unreadable Bible translations,[13] Bible readers, including pastors, cannot stand to read many verses at a go before they get tired. Maybe that is one reason for their habit to take one or two verses out of context and meditate or preach on them. The result is often some strange teaching and ideas. Of course, we are not to "put up with everything" in every situation. But this text talks about the characteristics of love. It must be set in the context of a relationship between people, especially the context of a natural and spiritual family. PANTA—*everything/all things* is a rhetorical hyperbole, it does not literally and absolutely mean everything, but it does mean a lot. A loving person puts up with a lot that an unloving person would not put up with. Another reason for the NIV may be that a text is supposed to be read aloud, and "Love bears everything" might possibly be understood when spoken as "Love bares everything." Or maybe "bear" is just too old-fashioned English?

---

[13] In this connection, evaluate the following observations: "We may have to learn many more new things all at the one time when we read the Bible, but that doesn't require weird language. All human languages have the capacity to express the new concepts which the Bible teaches, although for convenience's sake sometimes a few new words, introduced by the language's existing conventions for introducing jargon, can help. Keep your symbols familiar, even if what they reference is not!" (Dannii Willis, http://betterbibles.com/2011/04/30/weird-books-in-normal-language/).

The final word ὑπομένω (*hupomenw*) means to endure something, *to stay put* when others might have left. These words describe love very well, including the relationship between husband and wife. If I have love, I can put up with (almost) everything in my spouse, and I will stay put in the relationship through difficult times.

The two middle words are πιστεύω (*pisteuw*) and ἐλπίζω (*elpizw*). PISTEUW can have a semantic frame with three participants or with two. When pisteuw has three participants, it means that A entrusts P to G....

Quite often the verb is used without any object or prepositional phrases, and in such cases there is no way to know whether it is the tri-valent verb "entrust" or the di-valent verb "accept as true." Context will usually clarify it, but not always.

So, "accept everything as true" shows the attitude of love. You accept that this other person (husband, wife, child, etc.) speaks the truth and can be trusted. It does not mean that we are to accept and believe every wind of doctrine that comes our way. The accusative object "everything" indicates that this is not a matter of believing in God or Jesus, but of accepting as true what the other person is saying.

ἐλπίζω (*elpizw*—hope) can be used with a semantic Goal in the dative case or a preposition like EIS (towards), e.g. John 5:45 "Moses, in whom you have placed your hope."...However, in most cases ἐλπίζω (*elpizw*) has the two semantic participants Agent and Patient (object). This object may be a clause introduced by *hoti* (that) or it may be a noun that stands for something that you can hope and expect will happen...

In 1 Cor 13:7, the two words hope and believe are parallel in the sense that they are both used with an object (Patient). Love accepts everything as true and hopes for everything. A relationship has hopes and aspirations, but these hopes require acceptance and love to be realized.

16 Comments:

1. John Hobbins (Posted May 15, 2011 at 1:42 pm)
Hi Iver,
I think you are right that 1 Corinthians 13 is full of poetry (though it is not poetry in the strict sense).

9.4 A final exercise—1 Cor 13:7

As Suzanne McCarthy recently pointed out, the passage has iconic value for many of us whose native tongue is English. Like you, many of us feel most comfortable with a literal translation like **RSV** as a point of departure in 1 Cor 13:7.

From there we may explicate along the lines you suggest, or some other. Here is a chart of the wording of RSV, where it comes from, and which translations have preserved it:

KJV: Beareth all things,
believeth all things,
hopeth all things,
endureth all things.

HCSB: bears all things,
believes all things,
hopes all things,
endures all things.
So also: **NASB**.

NRSV: It bears all things,
believes all things,
hopes all things,
endures all things.
So also: **NAB**.

RSV: Love bears all things,
believes all things,
hopes all things,
endures all things.
So also: **ESV**.

Innovating translations: NIV, REB, NLT, and NJB.

2. Mike Sangrey (Posted May 15, 2011 at 2:20 pm)
I think I'd unwrap the chiasm and so make it more natural English. Also, Hebrew parallelism, and even non-Hebrew, tends to meld or blend together the two concepts. Unwrapping the chiasm helps to accomplish this in English. Something like:
Love never gives up, enduring through everything. It never drops its trust, hoping in every case.

3. Iver Larsen (Posted May 15, 2011 at 2:28 pm)
Hi, John,
Apart from the poetic aspects, my main interest was a study of the various Greek words. I quoted RSV to help readers who may not be able to understand the Greek directly.

As far as translation goes, I am not comfortable with RSV, and I am not in favor of keeping old familiar phrases just because they are familiar. But then, I am not a traditional guy. I think an innovative translation can be refreshing, but it has to be based on good exegesis and good linguistics. NLT is my favorite English version, but there are places where I disagree with what they have done. Their translation of this verse is: "Love never gives up, never loses faith, is always hopeful, and endures through every circumstance."

4. Iver Larsen (Posted May 15, 2011 at 2:30 pm)
Thanks, Mike, You are quite right, it is often a good idea to break up a chiasm into parallel structure. I really like your translation.

5. John Hobbins (Posted May 15, 2011 at 5:38 pm)
Iver,
That is my experience too, if the goal is to "help readers who may not be able to understand the Greek [or Hebrew] directly," RSV or ESV are better starting points than NIV or NLT.
I also agree that NLT is an excellent translation. I think of it as a paraphrase which unpacks the source text in various ways, very often, though not always, in successful ways.

6. Oun Kwon (Posted May 15, 2011 at 8:03 pm)
As to the English idiom 'put up with', it does not fit in the text. It has a sense of 'tolerate', as in 'put up with something or somebody unpleasant'. The nuance is very different from 'bear up' or 'endure'.
As for the English word 'bear', it is clearer with 'bear up'.

7. Theophrastus (Posted May 15, 2011 at 8:44 pm)
Because we have a long tradition of pretty unreadable Bible translations, Bible readers, including pastors, cannot stand to read many verses at a go before they

9.4 A final exercise—1 Cor 13:7

get tired. Maybe that is one reason for their habit to take one or two verses out of context and meditate or preach on them. The result is often some strange teaching and ideas. Of course, we are not to "put up with everything" in every situation. But this text talks about the characteristics of love. It must be set in the context of a relationship between people, especially the context of a natural and spiritual family.

I'm sorry, I disagree with almost everything you've written in this passage. *Bible readers, including pastors, cannot stand to read many verses at a go.*
first, it is not difficult to read a long Biblical passage at length. On Saturday mornings, in Jewish synagogues 1 or 2 *parhsos* (representing at about 1/50th of the Torah—typically about 7 chapters of text) as well as a *haftarah* portion (typically about a chapter's worth from the prophets or writing) as about 40 psalms. I have not heard any reports of exploding heads from individuals unable to handle this amount of text.

Further, many Evangelical readers desire to the Bible quickly. Thus we have books such as *Read Through Bible in a Year* (ISBN 9780802471673) or *Read the Bible in 90 Days* (ISBN 031093351X) or even the *The Light-Speed Bible* (ISBN 1586400665) (which promises a full Bible experience in 16 hours plus 8 more for review and meditation.)

I don't believe you have any evidence for the claim that Bible translations unduly tire readers.
I suspect the reason why some readers make only little progress in their Bible reading is that they are not given annotated editions that explain the many difficult passages and concepts necessary to read the Hebrew Bible.

But this text talks about the characteristics of love. It must be set in the context of a relationship between people, especially the context of a natural and spiritual family.
You are engaging in eisegesis here.

The text talks about love as a spiritual gift, and how love is a more valuable spiritual gift than others (such as the gift of tongues or prophesy), and how those spiritual gifts are empty without love:

Though I speak with the tongues of men and of angels, and have not charity, I am become as sounding brass, or a tinkling cymbal.

And though I have the gift of prophecy, and understand all mysteries, and all knowledge; and though I have all faith, so that I could remove mountains, and have not charity, I am nothing. In particular, I do not see support for your claim that this must be set in the…context of a natural and spiritual family. The text does not do talk about natural families in this passage (and Paul did not have a wife or children, according to the traditional account).

8. Eric W (Posted May 16, 2011 at 1:04 am)
I wish more translations would bring out the fronting of πάντα in 13:7. ISTM there's an emphasis on "ALL things" that's subdued when the verb is the first word in the English clause.

9. Suzanne McCarthy (Posted May 16, 2011 at 4:38 am)
I remember giving some thought to the chiasms in this post:
http://betterbibles.com/2007/07/27/longanimity/
For the passage in question I wrote
always sustains
always trusts
always hopes
always supports
I tried to use alliteration to indicate the chiasm.

10. Wayne Leman (Posted May 16, 2011 at 5:03 am)
Nicely done, Suzanne. I like alliteration. We could use more of it in English translations of biblical poetry, if we believe in functional equivalence. (Of course, English has many other poetic devices.) I like to think of much of 1 Cor 13 as poetry, or at least prose poetry.

11. Iver Larsen (Posted May 16, 2011 at 5:04 am)
Theo,
Yes, the paragraph you refer to was deliberately provocative and hyperbolic in order to make a point.
I am not disputing that it is possible to read an unnatural and unclear translation. I believe the whole of KJV was recently read in public in the UK. But if you ask the men and women on the street if it was understandable to them, what do you think they would answer? Most would say: Sorry, I wasn't listening. My point is that much of it cannot be read with understanding.

I am not saying that everything must be immediately understandable, but the translation should not add a smoke screen and make it less understandable than the original, but this is what happens quite often in literal translations. One of the reasons for much of our Bible translation tradition is that it was part of the goal to make the translation obscure. This may not be the stated goal, but as long as the translators are theologians (or rabbis) rather than translators, they are acutely aware of all the many and different theological takes on many passages. In order not to offend anybody and allow the theologians, rabbis and pastors who read the translation to interpret the text the way they want to interpret it, it has to be rather obscure, vague and "open."

I have not seen exploding heads in a church congregation – I can see that you appreciate hyperbole – and it is very rare to see people in the congregation raise their hands to interrupt the pulpit authority and say that they did not understand what was being read. However, I do have evidence. I have asked many people about their reaction when they read the bible privately and come to a passage they don't understand. The usual answer is: "This is too deep for me. Maybe one day I will understand it, but for now I will just skip it and forget it." Unfortunately, the more common situation is that they have heard the passage read so many times that they are familiar with it and may even be able to quote it, but if you ask them to express the meaning in their own words or explain the meaning, they are at a loss. Not only did they not know the meaning, but they did not know that they did not know.

Chapter 13 is not about love as a spiritual gift, because love is not a spiritual gift according to the NT. It is a fruit of the Spirit. What you can say and what Paul is saying is that the spiritual gifts must be used in an atmosphere of unselfish love. Yes, I agree that the major context is the spiritual family relationship as Christians interact with one another in their home meetings. But the exercise of love is not restricted to that environment. You think that Paul did not know about having a wife and children? Then I don't see how he could have written chapter 7 and many other parts of his letters. I assume he was married when he met Jesus and his wife did not appreciate his new faith and left him. But I take your point, the text talks about the spiritual family, and the physical family is an application of the text that I used to illustrate it.

12. Iver Larsen (Posted May 16, 2011 at 5:15 am)
Eric,

You are right that there is an emphasis on ALL things. BUT, remember that English does not work like Greek. In many cases in an English sentence, the last position is the position of emphasis, so it is the opposite of Greek. Apart from word order, English usually expresses emphasis by the words chosen or by stress.

If you remember Mike's translation: "Enduring through everything, hoping in every case" would you not agree that the emphasis on ALL/EVERYTHING is expressed?

13. Theophrastus (Posted May 16, 2011 at 6:06 am)
Iver — I agree that often people don't understand Scripture.
These leaves open a question — what is the best way to help understanding? One approach, as you suggest, is translations that do "not add a smoke screen and make it less understandable than the original." Another approach is to make supplementary materials available that help readers interpret the text, such as a commentary or annotations. (Of course, these approaches are complementary, and can be combined.)

I know that in the US, students who are exposed to literature in early modern English (such as Milton or Shakespeare) usually encounter it with annotations, and that seems to work. I know that I studied both Shakespeare and Milton (with annotations) in high school, and I felt that I understood the text well enough.

In fact, I just saw a production by children of Shakespeare's Midsummer's Night Dream — with the actors aged from 5 to 15. Most of them seemed to understand the story quite well, despite the Elizabethan language. Perhaps they missed some of Shakespeare's wordplay and puns, but they certainly got the main gist of the plot.

If 5–15 year-olds can understand Shakespeare, then I believe there is hope that when properly educated, adults can understand literal translations. That is one reason I am so excited about the forthcoming Norton Critical Editions of the KJV (<u>volume 1,</u> <u>volume 2</u>). I think this version will make the KJV and its literary elegance available to a new generation of readers.

As another example, I think that Tom Wright's commentary and translations in his New Testament for Everyone series are relatively easy to follow for a broad audience. Perhaps some might disagree with points in his commentary, but I think he is a master teacher, and prepare his readers to read the material on their own.

I know that when I read the Hebrew Bible in Hebrew, I read a version that has extensive commentary. I'm not sure I would be able to understand it well without that commentary.

To summarize: I'm not arguing that in many cases Biblical translation language can be made better. But I think that education (in the form of commentary or annotations) is also an essential step.

14. Iver Larsen (Posted May 16, 2011 at 7:33 am)
Theophrastus,
I agree with and use a combined method. When we translated the Bible into Danish, we had lots of introductory notes and footnotes. The two of us may not quite agree on the mix between the ingredients. A bishop made a Danish translation one hundred years ago. On most pages, the translation itself, which is very literal, takes up one third of the page or less. The rest of the page is devoted to explaining what the text is supposed to mean plus background information. What you choose depends on your audience. For students, it is fine with an annotated text, but for the average person, I am afraid they might not take the time or have the interest to dig into all those notes to try to understand the text. So, for such an average person, notes should primarily give background information rather than explain an obscure and poorly translated text.

I also think there is a difference between reading a text in your own language, albeit a few hundred years old, like Shakespeare and Milton, as compared to reading a translation. (When I hear or read quotes from these two gentlemen, I quickly give up understanding it and move on. It is not worth the effort to me to try to understand them, but I might have enjoyed reading an understandable version.)

We always end up with this dilemma. Where do the translators want to be on the spectrum from literal to free translations. I don't think there is a simple answer that applies to all situations. It depends on your purpose and your intended audience. When our Danish version was published in a special edition for bikers, all the notes were scrapped, because the publisher was convinced that this clientele do not read footnotes. This is part of the reason for my practice as a translator that the text as much as possible should be understandable without notes, but notes can defend a certain translation choice, give other exegetical options and provide additional background. The notes in our Danish version has proven to be one of the main reasons behind its acceptance, as one person said: If we don't agree with the translation of a disputed passage, we can always refer to the notes.

15. Eric W (Posted May 16, 2011 at 2:03 pm)
iverlarson:

I agree with you in part. But it seems to me that English is constrained in print for emphasis to using italics or boldface or unexpected syntax—like putting "ALL things" first. When reading aloud one can raise one's voice when saying ALL. And I'm not sure I like translating the adjective πάντα as an adverb. There's a difference in my mind between "verbs all things" (or "all things verbs") and "always verbs."

16. Iver Larsen (Posted May 16, 2011 at 2:23 pm)
Eric,

I agree, I would want to avoid "always", but it is not a serious point in my mind. Danish is like English in how we mark emphasis, that is, mainly be intonation, although we have more leeway than English in terms of fronting words and phrases. So, what we did was to mark stress by italics in the translation.

9.5 Implications: Practicing what you preach

In this chapter, we have attempted a "trial run" at producing a translation that is more in tune with the literary (poetic) features, the rhetorical dynamics, and the oral-aural properties of the biblical text. In this case, the pericope under examination—1 Corinthians 13—was an obvious candidate to serve as the basis for such an exercise because all commentators call attention to its lyrical characteristics in the original Greek. However, as the analyses of other chapters in this volume have suggested, there are many other passages in the Scriptures that give abundant evidence of these literary-structural and phonic-rhetorical attributes, which must therefore also be given appropriate attention when seeking to render these texts with corresponding impact and appeal in another language. To fail to take

9.5 Implications: Practicing what you preach

this into account is to neglect a crucial dimension of the total "meaning," including the soundscape, which was encoded in the source composition and hence also intended to be communicated to successive generations of readers and listeners.

Our concluding section's theme of "practicing what you preach" may be applied to the various studies of this book in a twofold sense: In the first place, all those who are convinced of the validity of the claims being made regarding the biblical text can now endeavor to "proclaim" these literary-rhetorical and oratorical aspects of the biblical message by means of their translations (or revisions of existing ones). Such versions will therefore be carefully attuned also to the phonological level of discourse so that the vernacular creation resonates accordingly in that language. Second, all students and proclaimers of Scripture realize that this work is not merely an analytical-translational-transmissional exercise. Rather, there is an ethical need also to apply what these passages—first Corinthians 13 in particular—declare in a corresponding biblical life-style, one that seriously reflects ἡ ἀγάπη of Christ in action.

שִׁמְעוּ מוּסָר וַחֲכָמוּ וְאַל־תִּפְרָעוּ׃
אַשְׁרֵי אָדָם שֹׁמֵעַ לִי

(Proverbs 8:33–34a)

μακάριοι οἱ ἀκούοντες τὸν λόγον τοῦ θεοῦ καὶ φυλάσσοντες. (Luke 11:28)

10

Giving "Voice" to the Ancient Orality of the Scriptures Today

10.1 The challenge

In the preceding chapters we have had occasion to listen to voices both from within the text of Scripture (e.g., the different "speakers" represented in Song of Songs 8, Isaiah 66, 1 Corinthians 13, Philippians, Philemon, and Revelation 5) and also from without—that is, various scholars who have written about the composition and transmission of the source-language text as well as how to re-present it nowadays in a manner that specifically reflects its inscribed oral-aural qualities and respects the fact that "[t]wo-thirds of people worldwide are oral learners" (Eshleman 2010:11). As for the major implications of my study for Bible translation principles and procedures today, in short, I have argued in favor of a more stable and conservative process of biblical text transmission with respect to both the Hebrew and also the Greek Testament traditions. Such an approach would generally adhere to a firm preservation of essential content and communicative function, including our methods of textual criticism in relation to the various Scriptures that we translate.

On the other hand, I have also proposed a *freer and more creative* methodology in relation to the stylistic form of our contemporary translations, that is, along with rendering the text meaningfully in a modern target language, and then also transmitting it via one of the diverse media currently available. Thus, the crucial functional questions of effective Scripture perception/reception and audience engagement, or relevant use, remains a pressing challenge. In particular, what can be done to encourage and promote more orality-oriented applications in Bible translation and its contemporary presentation via disparate media? We may all be convinced of the importance of this issue, yet feel rather powerless or out-of-position in terms of feasibility to do much about it. My question does not mean to imply that little or nothing has been accomplished in the field to highlight the auditory element (the many references cited in this book would attest to that). But I think that even more might be undertaken in order to give this acoustic component its due, especially on the concrete, "performance" (or production) side of the communication process.[1]

10.2 Seven suggestions

To further develop some of the practical implications of my ongoing investigation, I have listed seven suggestions below (not necessarily in order of importance), which are intended to initiate a discussion that might well continue beyond the context and confines of the present study:

---

[1] For example, in a newly launched journal that promises to devote "much needed space for a new kind of analysis of translation," one that is "characterized by its transdisciplinary approach," we read about the need to explore crucial topics like "the hybrid nature of languages, cultures, identities in our deterritorialized world of difference...," "our globalized and localized world," "differential power relations and ideologies," "new media scenarios," and even "war and conflict" (Arduini and Nergaard 2001:15). There is a concern expressed for attending to "epistemologically relevant themes that clearly connect to translation," such as "memory... space...conflict...and economics" (ibid., 14). But nothing in this proposed "new paradigm" searching for "a missing epistemology" (ibid., 9) is mentioned about such a fundamental feature as "orality" (or "aurality") and how this vital phenomenon influences and affects all types of translation (even its metaphorical applications) and communication in general.

10.2.1 Analysis

Bible translators should be (trained so as to be) able to conduct a systematic, sound-sensitive analysis of the source composition, with at least a minimal degree of competence.[2] To begin with, they might pay special attention to all types of phonic correspondence, since even such a fundamental feature is often ignored in exegetical study.[3] An examination of biblical texts with the ear tuned to their oral potential adds another important dimension in the task of interpretation. As Brickle points out:

> [M]any texts await further exploration of their multi-media character, including probing their written nature, aural profiles and memory dynamics, and reconstruction of their original performances.... [T]he study of ancient media culture promises innovative means to explore texts in ways that enhance conventional modes of exegesis. (2011:28)

Investigating biblical texts with the ears as well as the eyes will undoubtedly reveal new discourse features of literary and exegetical significance.[4] The strongly antiphonal character of Psalm 114, for example, is clearly revealed—and heard(!)—when adopting such a combined methodology.[5]

---

[2] As illustrated, for example, in Wendland 2008d:192–193, however, with greater attention paid also to sound similarities (or dissonances!) on the *syllabic* level of text organization.

[3] The two-volume *Dictionary of Biblical Interpretation* (Hayes 1999), for example, does not include an entry on "orality" or any related subject, and the same absence may be noted in an otherwise well-rounded introduction to *New Testament Exegesis* (Erickson 2005). Works that pertain to secular "translation studies" fare no better in this regard (e.g., Baker and Saldanha 2008; Munday 2009a; Pym 2010).

[4] As for the biblical exegete, commentator, or translator, so also for the pastor, preparing a sermon to preach, or a teacher, seeking to coax a class to conceptually and physically "embody" some pericope (Ruge-Jones 2010:289), a performance-oriented approach, especially when actually orally performing the Scripture at hand, will frequently have this hermeneutical result: "old understandings are shattered, old unities are broken, old texts are cracked open" (Swanson 2010:319).

[5] "The redundancy between vv. 3, 4 and 5, 6 of Ps 114 requires us to ask if it was written to be performed by two choirs singing antiphonally.... Setting Ps 114 in such a canonic response fashion yields a highly integrated structure..." (Amzallag and Avriel 2011:303, from the Abstract). The authors' analysis is interesting and insightful, but for reasons that I cannot go into here, I would dissent from their interpretation of this psalm's poetic structure and theological theme.

Translators should then ensure that, whenever possible (it may not always be *achievable*), similar *oral-aural cues* for signaling critical aspects of discourse structure, text-sequencing and transitioning, stylistic shading, pragmatic implications, and rhetorical dynamics are carefully built into their vernacular versions.[6] This presupposes that a thorough, discourse-oriented analysis of the TL has already been completed and the results absorbed by the translators.[7] The vernacular compositional exercise needs to be carried out as a normal procedure in a relevant, functionally equivalent manner. This might be accomplished, for example, by employing appropriate and natural target language *correspondents* (e.g., rhythmic utterances, rhymes, parallelisms and other structures of repetition, word-order variations, conjunctive and disjunctive transitions, ideophones, exclamations, etc.),[8] which

---

[6] In this endeavor, the insights of specialists engaged in the mission of "Chronological Bible Storying" and related fields may prove helpful, for example (with modifications as necessary, depending on the language/culture concerned), "regarding character dialog I found it helpful always to include who was speaking to whom by using proper names and not pronouns" (Terry 2009b).

[7] Such research into the oral (including musical) and written (if available) verbal art forms of the TL cannot be taken for granted, and additional time, talent, and expense must be factored into any translation program in order to adequately cater for this type of study. In some cases, it may be the first time that translators have been encouraged to investigate and write about the stylistic artistry, structural diversity, and rhetorical forms that are available in their mother tongue. But without such a foundational background in the verbal resources extant in the TL, no Bible translation can expect to attain a widely recognized level of excellence via any medium of textual transmission.

[8] It is important to note that a single TL correspondent (word or phrase) is not always sufficient to fully convey the intended semantic and pragmatic significance of the biblical text, especially where poetry is concerned. In such cases, the additional meaning—as much as practical—will need to be expressed by some other appropriate means, e.g., an explanatory footnote, a parenthetical "aside" (in the case of an oral translation). For example, in a recent study of the Hebrew text of Job, Seow observes that "the conservative orthography proves in many instances to serve a poetic function. This orthography allows homographic wordplays [i.e., based on orthographic correspondences and patterns] in addition to the numerous homophonic ones that scholars have long noticed. Poetry in Job, it seems, is written not only for the ear. It is written as well for the eye. It is 'visual poetry.'…A further implication of this claim of visuality in Joban poetry, which is not to deny its aurality but to highlight the frequent need for rearticulation of the words and retrospective adjustment of understanding as one reads along, is that the persistent claim of Job as a drama—whether a tragedy or a comedy—will not hold, if by 'dramA' one means a script composed for public performance. Moreover, visual poetry in Job constantly demands interpretive decisions on the part of the reader—decisions that, once made, may yet be questioned again and revised. Translations [even literal ones!]

are both readily perceptible to, and easily understood by the primary consumer audience.[9] Furthermore, Scripture texts intended for some form of audio transmission will usually need to have additional *redundancy* built into them, whether through exact or partial repetition, paraphrase, or grammatical "de-concentration" (e.g., fewer event nouns, fewer complex, top-heavy constructions, less syntactic embedding, etc.). Such additional redundancy can help to reduce the average rate, or density of information flow—hence at the same time to facilitate the aural decoding process.[10]

10.2.2 Testing

As emphasized throughout this study, translation drafts must be also thoroughly "tested" (and revised) with the ultimate *performance dimension* in mind—that is, orally, aurally, individually, and communally, involving

---

inevitably limit the expression of such poetry, for every translation commits one to a single interpretation, usually at the expense of whatever ambiguities may indeed be part and parcel of poetry. Translations do not accommodate retrospective adjustments" (Seow 2011:84; material in brackets added).

[9] Thus, an oral-aural investigation of the biblical text is one important component of a complete examination of the discourse, and the results of such study should be manifested also in a *LiFE* translation. As Schart observes (2010:5): "The awareness [of] the soundscape can furnish important insights within the analysis of the form of the text, certainly not only in the Book of the Twelve, but in ancient texts in general. It seems to be a worthy enterprise to listen with open ears to the sound impressions a text conveys, to undertake, so to speak, a virtual 'listening walk' through the world of the text (cf. Schafer, *The Soundscape*, 212). The interpreter of the ancient text should be aware that part of his or her task is to act as a 'soundscape historian,' that is 'to determine in what significant ways individuals and societies of various historical eras listen differently' (Schafer 1994:151)."

In my studies of various books and genres of Scripture, I have not found that sound-based textual "subdivisions...discovered by means of aural structures...often conflict with...literary subdivisions"—though this may be true in the case of "traditional" segmentations (Maxey 2009:120, with reference to the work of Scott and Dean 1993:672–725).

[10] How should we handle the non-verbal aspects of "performing the text" (e.g., gestures, facial expressions, paralinguistic modulation, body positioning, etc.)? These "dramatic" dimensions of the discourse are perhaps best left to the intuition of the coached, or technically "informed," proclaimer, in keeping with the genre of the biblical text at hand, the functional nature of the pericope, the audience, and the setting. Thus, any communal proclamation of Scripture needs to be carefully contextualized to suit the circumstances of its immediate and momentary public declamation, whether read "interpretively," recited, chanted, or sung to the tune of an appropriate melody (cf. Maxey 2009:183–191).

as many different speakers and audience sub-groups of the host community as possible. How *readily* and *correctly* is a given rendition both *articulated* publicly as well as *interpreted* aurally by those who are listening while it is being proclaimed in their hearing?[11] Where difficulties of any type are encountered with respect to either performance or text processing,[12] what are the apparent reasons and how might they be counteracted or compensated for?[13] This evaluation would thus pertain to the quantity and quality of communication with regard to variables such as speed, fluency, accuracy, sustainability, repeatability, and so forth.[14] Furthermore, how *aesthetically* or *emotively* do most people respond as they actually hear the Scriptures being read in their mother tongue? On the one hand, the testing team must assess the extent to which the plain printed text, whether rendered more or less idiomatically, is potentially subject to certain errors of interpretation or simple ambiguity due to the lack of sufficient phonological (plus facial, gestural, etc.) representation. On the other hand, in the case of audio and AV productions, where more information must be made explicit due to the nature of the medium of transmission, any probable instances of

---

[11] For example, "[t]hrough performances, we may be able to identify which interpretations [of the biblical text] have a consensus, which interpretations are controversial but permitted, and which interpretations constitute a fundamental misconstrual of the possibilities of the text.... In this way, performance may be an important way to test the limits of viable interpretations and provide criteria for making critical judgments in adjudications over interpretation" (Rhoads 2010:101).

[12] Such difficulties may be conceptual as well as lexical and semantic. Thus, from a frames of reference perspective, the task of a translator/textual mediator is "to produce a text which would create a comparable...set of interpretation frames to be accessed in the target reader's mind.... A successful mediator must be consciously aware of both text and context, which means both the words and the implied frames" (Katan 2004:171).

[13] There are indications, for example, that a new idiomatic translation in a particular language (whether a small vernacular or a widely spoken lingua franca) will not necessarily be read more fluently than a long-established literal version simply because people are more familiar with the older version and have probably memorized portions of it. As David Ker has recently observed (2011): "In considering the fluency and comprehension levels of readers of Scripture, several factors come into play. First, there is the ability of the reader and existing knowledge of the passage. A fluent reader with familiarity with the Bible is going to read faster than a less fluent reader with little Bible knowledge.... A 'difficult' translation is going to be read at a slower rate. I put difficult in quotes because based on the first criterion a more idiomatic translation can actually be more difficult since it renders a passage in unfamiliar ways forcing the reader to slow down and increasing the error rate."

[14] For further details, see Wendland 2011:406–441.

interpretive "eisegesis" (reading too much into the text), misrepresentations of the intended sense and purpose of the source text, or misleading "transculturations" (overly favoring the target sociocultural setting) need to be identified, discussed, and resolved where necessary—in accordance with the project *brief*.[15]

10.2.3 Publishing

Target language communities and church "special interest" groups (e.g., those that focus on Scripture reading and teaching) must put more pressure on Bible publishers to adopt a format of printing that does more to encourage and facilitate a reader's *visual perception* and subsequent *vocal expression* of the orality of the text, e.g., a single print column, ragged right margins (not justified, or worse, hyphenated!), larger more legible type faces, meaningful paragraphing, and the use of strategic space on the page to indicate prominence, semantic parallels or contrasts, structural designs, etc. This would include the tactic of punctuating the text more according to its oral phonology, rather than its written grammar, e.g., by the use of commas at natural "pause points" within a longer utterance (sentence) and dashes to signal deliberately broken or truncated segments of speech. Of course, this will probably cost more in terms of production, but the host constituency ought to be afforded the opportunity at least to evaluate the cost implications versus potential comprehension benefits of such reader- and hearer-friendly Scriptures. This will undoubtedly require a substantial amount of initial accompanying instruction regarding how to visually interpret any new format designed to increase people's understanding of the text and then how to orally express it with greater impact and appeal in public discourse. Such basic aspects of interpreting the layout features

---

[15] Such evaluative text-testing may be effectively organized according to the four "maxims" that comprise Grice's "cooperative principle"—adapted for translation in the threefold light of skopos theory, speech-act theory, and relevance theory: (1) *Quality*: with reference to comparative literary/oral excellence in the vernacular; (2) *Quantity*: with reference to information structure and positioning (in the text or in the paratext); (3) *Relevance*: with reference to the processing "cost" versus conceptual "gain" parameters of RT; (4) *Manner*: with reference to all aspects of perspicuity and clarity in view of the target audience (see Stenning et al. 2006:434–439, 461–467).

and typographic "signs" of a printed text may be helpfully introduced in literacy programs in the language.

10.2.4 Research

The present momentum towards encouraging more widespread and effective use of oral-aural Bible products in diverse media must be maintained. In some cases, these developments in the field need to be made a more explicit and prominent aspect of translator training programs, especially in secular educational institutions.[16] Ongoing performance-centered research into time-honored traditional,[17] as well as modern verbal art forms is of great importance as part of a wide-ranging,[18] coordinated program of Scripture communication for a given society.[19] This is obviously critical when

---

[16] Very little is said about investigating the potential influence of oral-aural factors on the translation process itself or on the products of translation, for example, in the otherwise valuable guides of Williams and Chesterman (2002) or Baker (2011). In contrast, the importance of orality has been recognized and documented for a considerable time in the field of Bible translation, for example: "To understand something about the style of oral literature in a language, it is essential to make thorough studies of the literary forms of legends, myths, and stories from candidly recorded texts.... One of the best tests of a translation is to get several different people to read a text aloud" (Nida and Taber 1969:158, 172).

[17] In my opinion, serious research in the target language must *precede* translation into it. I began my various investigations into Bantu-language vernacular oral performances with research into *traditional oral* art forms as well as *professional radio* broadcasts in order to discover the most excellent models to follow in Bible translation. I then worked with national colleagues in order to identify and describe the main structural and stylistic features of various genres of Chewa verbal discourse in order to teach these principles to MT translators, mainly through the use of positive and negative comparative examples. I feel that a Scripture translation (in most situations) is very much like a *radio script*—a written text that is ultimately intended to be articulated orally and aurally apprehended (see Wendland 2004a).

[18] "Adequate ethnographic field methods are needed if the documentation of a representative corpus of oral verbal arts is to be collected. The collection and transcription of 'natural oral events,' however, is time-consuming, but indispensible. Ironically, the study of living oral traditions is probably the ideal preparation for recognizing the oral dimensions of biblical texts" (D. Fitzgerald—personal correspondence, 2012).

[19] In support of his thesis that "we need to study the writings of the New Testament as (trans)scripts of performances in an oral culture," David Rhoads proposes "that we can experiment with twenty-first-century performances as a way to explore the first-century performance event. Here are some reasons to employ performance as a tool of research:

10.2 Seven suggestions

preparing some of the newer, *non-print media* transmissions of biblical texts, e.g., in diverse audio formats (cassette [still called for in parts of Africa!], CD, MP3), FM radio broadcasts, video/TV productions, electronic platforms (including the ubiquitous and multipurpose cell phone!), as well as customary public performing media (e.g., oral narrative, praise poetry, songs, dramatic plays, etc.).[20] The creative combination of *poetry* and *music* (involving culture-specific melodies and instrumentation) seems to be an especially fruitful field for experimentation with a view towards new models and methods of textual transmission.[21] The researchers and the producers must then be encouraged to meet together regularly in order to discuss how best to transform (via the *multimodal* process of "transmediazation") specific audience needs/desires and current media resources into Scripture

---

• Performance may help us to investigate the range of meaning potential for a given composition;
• Performance may help us to explore the potential rhetorical impacts upon ancient audiences;
• Performance may help us to recover oral features of the text and performance dynamics to which we might not otherwise have access;
• Performance may help us to restore the emotive dimensions to the text." (2010:157, 168–169).

[20] For example, what are the manifest (demonstrated) oral/aural qualities of different versions in a given language, and how do these relate "to the possibilities of various oralities/new oralities introduced by the move to electronically mediated communications" (Bulkeley 2011).

[21] Carr notes this in his broadly comparative study of "the origins of Scripture and literature" in ANE societies: "I have taken space to discuss the role of what might be termed 'elevated language' in the incising of traditions on the mind—especially the role of singing or canting the tradition and of patterned language that might be broadly termed 'poetic.' Multiple cultures appear to have found that the use of 'poetic' and 'musical' modes in the performance of tradition more indelibly impressed it on the mind than mere rote reading." So also contemporary Bible translators "must reckon with the immense power of joined music and text (along with image) to shape the hearts of the young and old. It is as if music and poetry (or poeticized, canted prose) is the indelible marker for writing word on the heart, while silent reading is pencil" (2005:289, 296).

Dan Fitzgerald adds: "'poetry is performed more commonly as *sung* rather than spoken discourse in *all* oral traditions' (citing Banti and Giannattasio 2004:297, emphasis added). Even within literate traditions worldwide, *sung* poetic discourse—song—is no less ubiquitous. Yet, while most of the world's poetic discourse is *sung*, it is most often *translated to be read*. Surely, then, 'something is lost in the translation'. What is that something? How can it be regained?" (personal correspondence, 2012; cf. Fitzgerald 2011).

products that more successfully serve the particular socio-religious constituency for whom they are intended.[22]

10.2.5 Scripting

Another practical suggestion concerns the preparation of performance aids. Detailed written scripts based on a careful orality-attuned analysis of the biblical text can help to keep the non-print media productions referred to above more "faithful" to the original communication setting and also more effective in attracting new, non-traditional (perhaps "a-literate") audiences to the message of Scripture today.[23] It is important to provide a sufficient number of these performance-related *background* notes and *production* guidelines, for example, "scripting" for variants in the oral interpretation of key passages, such as the pertinent "illocutionary force" in Pilate's "what is truth?" query of Christ, or Paul's "who has bewitched you?" in Galatians. Other supplementary aids may also be helpful as cues for the reader/audience, e.g., headings to indicate the different possible "speakers" in a complex composition, such as the Song and many of the Psalms. This information might be desirable to a certain extent in printed versions of the Bible, but it would pertain especially to audio and visual productions, for example, in the form of oral "asides" and "bridge material," or "sidebars" and "windows" on a video screen. Thus, not only the *voice,* but also the *mind* (thoughts, emotions, etc.) needs to be taken into account and engaged in all translation publications—that is, by adopting a versatile and adaptable strategy aimed at evoking a suitable as well as a sufficient cognitive context for perceiving, interpreting, and perhaps even memorizing the text, no matter what the medium whereby it is transmitted.

---

[22] For some early seminal thinking on the challenges of "transmediazation," see the following articles in Hodgson and Soukup 1997: Hodgson, "An Urgent Need," 7–10; Goethals, "Multimedia Images," 237–247; Roschke, "From One Medium to Another," 340–343.

[23] See, for example, Maxey 2009:186–188, for a sample display of Mark 2:1–12; see ibid., 89–90 for a summary of Dennis Tedlock's suggestions for transcribing an oral performance. An "a-literate" person is someone who is able to read and write, but prefers to communicate via other media. Mathews provides a set of notes concerning "script, actors, audience, scene, and improvisation" (2012:88) to accompany her performance-oriented, formal correspondence ("iconic") translation of Habakkuk (ibid., chs. 5–7).

10.2.6 Training

Communication theories and functional methodologies that focus on *direct speech* and *conversational analysis* should be integrated and applied in practical training programs as well as exegetical-hermeneutical studies when teaching translators about the dynamics of orality within the various biblical compositions and genres as well as those in the TL.[24] This would include approaches that investigate issues such as situational relevance, sociolinguistic registers, conceptual frames of reference, speech acts within speech events, ambiguity in discourse, and extended dialogue processing. Appropriately contextualized vernacular instruction material is then necessary in both written and non-written (audio +/- visual, electronic, musical, etc.) formats. Computer-assisted translation techniques can also be explored in this effort (Wendland 2009:360). Exercise workbooks as well as easy-access reference texts are needed, prepared from a multidisciplinary, culture-conscious perspective and encompassing several levels of difficulty and detail. Thus, the aim is also to *educate* prospective audience-consumer groups with regard to the various *options* as well as the *benefits* of an oral-aurality-oriented,[25] multi-media approach to contemporary communication.

---

[24] Strange as it may seem, translators too sometimes need to be "educated" (or "enculturated") with respect to the *artistic* and *rhetorical* resources of their own language and its oral and (possibly also) written tradition, including its principal verbal genres and associated works of the "masters," past and present. This may be a special problem in highly educated societies, where the electronic and video age has dulled the ability of many people to discern and appreciate excellent written texts and oral discourses. This may affect Scripture proclaimers as well. Thus, T. David Gordon calls for a renewal of "literary literacy" among ministers (in America) as a way of increasing their communication sensibilities and skills, for example, "Reading poetry cultivates both our sensibility of the significant and our instinctive appreciation and use of the aural properties of our language, since poets devote themselves to that very thing" (2010:75). Systematic TL genre research and analysis is crucial, for "discerning genre is basic to communication...[and] appropriately discerning the genre helps us negotiate the form, entertain proper expectations, and discern the purpose of the [communicative] exchange" (DeSilva 2009:9). Thus, the ability to determine and creatively manipulate functionally equivalent genres across language-cultures is an essential capacity of competent Bible translators.

[25] It is rather strange that an approach to translation which takes orality into serious consideration, both in composition or draft testing, does not seem to feature strongly in modern secular theory and practice. For example, in Mossop's training manual, his "revision parameters" and "summary of revision principles" make no mention of the oral/aural features of texts and their importance in qualitative

They must also learn how the diverse available resources, whether printed versions or different media productions, might be utilized together (not one in opposition to another) in an *integrated* program of teaching, learning, (re)telling (or *singing!*),[26] and living the messages of Scripture.

10.2.7 Networking

Finally, but no less important (on the global scene), it would seem expedient to implement more coordinated group networking in order to *support* current programs, *initiate* new developments, and *facilitate* ongoing interdisciplinary and inter-agency cooperation in this expanding field of orality in biblical studies with special reference to Bible translation. This need has long been recognized in the secular field: "Both cultural studies and translation studies have tended to move in the direction of the collaborative approach, with the establishment of research teams and groups, and with more international networks and increased communication" (Bassnett 2011:78–79). Such networking would involve engaging, encouraging, and empowering mutual interest sections within translation agencies (UBS, SIL, LBT, Nida Institute, etc.), the "Performance Criticism" school, traditional performing arts (ethnomusicology, ethnopoetics, SIL), "interpreter-mediated" Scriptures,[27] and other closely related SBL research groups (e.g., Ancient and Modern

---

evaluation (2001:99, 149; cf. also Kelly's *Handbook* in the "Translation Practices Explained" series of coursebooks, which is "designed to help self-learners and teachers of translation" (2005:i).

[26] A good method and model of how research, testing, training, and educating the constituency may be carried out together with respect to the musical genres of a traditional society is available from the ethnomusicology department of SIL International (formerly Summer Institute of Linguistics), who offer such workshops around the world. For example, the following is a summary of one that was recently held in Burundi: "The primary objectives of the workshop were to (a) produce traditional songs with key messages on good nutrition practices and child protection, (b) train Burundian musicians how to produce songs in the traditional style with new messages, and (c) train project staff how to use the songs for sensitizing the community to the songs' themes" (Boswell 2010). This type of workshop could lay the foundation for producing songs based on biblical texts, perhaps even close oral translations. (For more information, see http://www.sil.org/arts/ethnomusicology.htm; http://www.sil.org/sil/news/2010/burundi-song-composition-workshop.htm.)

[27] For example, see Karlik 2010.

Media).²⁸ An "internet forum" of topical articles and books pertaining to issues of orality and the field of Bible translation already exists, i.e., *www.biblicalperformancecriticism.org*, and this website has been recently enlarged and hyper-linked with additional sites in order to cater for the needs and interests of this varied company of Scripture researchers, translators, educators, facilitators, producers, publishers, performers, promoters, and proclaimers.

Orality studies represent an exciting, rapidly developing area of research and application, one that is not just the "new kid on the block" in the interrelated macro-fields of Bible interpretation, translation, transmission, and reception. On the contrary, as I have endeavored to underscore in this book, the original Hebrew and Greek Scriptures were first generated in a vibrant

---

²⁸ For example, initiatives such as the following (by David Rhoads, personal correspondence, 2011) might be encouraged—this, in view of the annual SBL meeting in San Francisco (November, 2011): "Those of us representing organizations listed below have joined forces to support each other and to explore cooperative and co-ordinated efforts in orality studies, performance criticism, and related disciplines in biblical studies. We are planning a kind of 'summit' of different groups, programs, organizations, and individuals working to further our understanding of the predominantly oral cultures of the ancient world and the dynamics of performance in biblical times. Our goal is to see in what ways we can encourage one another, promote each other's efforts, cooperate together on common projects, and contribute to the work being done. We are not seeking to establish a new group. Rather, we are simply seeking to initiate a network of individuals and groups to work together and to support each other."

The Bible in Ancient and Modern Media (BAMM), SBL Seminar: Holly Hearon, Tom Thatcher

Performance Criticism of Biblical and Other Ancient Texts, SBL section: Glenn Holland

The Network of Biblical Storytellers (www.nbs.org): Tom Boomershine, Phil Ruge-Jones

Nida Institute of the American Bible Society: James Maxey

GoTell Communications: (http://gotell.org): Tom Boomershine

Provoking the Gospel (http://provokingthegospel.ocom): Richard Swanson

Ancient Israelite Drama (http://home.nwciowa.edu/barkerplays/): Jeff Barker

Biblical Performance Criticism Web site, www.biblicalperformancecriticism.org: Peter Perry

Biblical Performance Criticism Series with Wipf and Stock Publishers: Dave Rhoads

Memory Perspectives on Early Christianity and its Greco-Roman Context: SBL Section

Orality, Textuality, and the Formation of the Hebrew Bible: SBL Section

Speech and Talk: Discourses and Social Practices in the Ancient Mediterranean World: SBL Section.

oral-aural world, and despite the great advances in electronic and visual technology today, it is still largely a voice-saturated environment in which we are seeking to communicate the same Word of God in distinct and diverse media, languages, cultures, and settings all over the globe.[29]

> Making a translation particularly for oral presentation requires special attention to the needs of listeners.... While it is true that signals for some sound qualities are rarely recoverable from anything written (e.g., volume), others are strongly signaled through the written text (e.g., repetition, rhythm) and still others are indicated by context (e.g., tone of voice).... Effective oral communication is also highly structured. The hearer needs to be able to remember what is said through what has been heard. The structure that provides the framework for memorability need not be simple and is often highly complex.... Beauty of language is a characteristic of good oral presentations. It is this quality that lends classic appeal to such Bible translations as the King James Version in English or the Luther Bible in German, which remain favorites for public reading. (Thomas and Thomas 2006:71)

My hope is that the various text studies of this book have convinced readers of the accuracy of the claim that the Scriptures are literature—*excellently* composed literature, intended for the ears as well as the eyes. The diverse books of this sacred corpus thus deserve also to be re-presented as such in translation—that is, verbally fashioned *faithfully* (accurately), but also *oratorically* (artistically, rhetorically) in appealing speech cadences with listeners, and potential memorizers too, in mind.

---

[29] "Oral communication continues to be predominant throughout much of the world—even when literacy is available" (Maxey 2009:47). Indeed, already by the close of the last century a "paradigm shift" was taking place in the communications media, namely, "a shift from a literate culture to an aural visual culture. People read less and are entertained more. Sight and sound dominate popular culture. This is the age of the satellite dish and the hand-held television" (Harvey 1998:302). Therefore, Bible translators and project administrators alike must take this dynamic, ever-changing dimension of message transmission into serious consideration when carrying out all phases of their daily work in the text of ultimate reference, the *written* Word of the Lord.

> Blessed is the one who reads the words of this prophecy, and blessed are those who hear it and take to heart what is written in it, because the time is near.... I, John, am the one who heard and saw these things And when I had heard and seen them, I fell down to worship at the feet of the angel who had been showing them to me. But he said to me, "Do not do it! I am a fellow servant with you and with your brothers the prophets and of all who keep the words of this book. Worship God! (Revelation 1:3; 22: 8-9)

10.3 Orality—beyond the written Word

In a fascinating study of the "oral aspects of Scripture in the history of religion," William Graham documents the importance of the *oral use* of the sacred writings in religions around the world, including not only the Hebrew and Christian "holy books," but also corresponding hallowed texts in the Hindu, Buddhist, Islamic, and Chinese cultures (Graham 1987). He points out that this oral-aural dimension not only is a vital factor of influence in the composition, transmission, and translation of these texts (as has been the focus of my preceding studies), but also plays a crucial role in comprehending their full spiritual function and significance when the faithful carry out various religious practices. The perspective of orality also helps us to understand the Scriptures' continued relevance and appeal as the "proclamation" of God and of his people in some societies contrast to its current obvious decline in others.

In this section I will present several pertinent quotes from Graham's concluding chapter that highlight some of these often "unexplored but enduring oral dimensions of Scripture, which, however closely tied they may be to it, always extend well beyond the written word alone" (ibid., 171).[30] Readers are encouraged to carefully consider and critically evaluate these statements in order to determine their accuracy and contemporary relevance with respect to the "living and active" character of the Word of

---

[30] All the citations that follow come from this book, with the page numbers given in parentheses.

God.³¹ I have included some questions (in *italics*) to stimulate further critical reflection after each quote:

- Implicit in the loss of the fundamental orality of the written word is also the loss of an important perspective on the functional aspect of Scripture. The relationship of the spoken word of the text is inherently dynamic and personal in a way that the relationship to the printed word alone is not, or is only rarely and with difficulty, at least in the present day. (155) *What is meant by "the fundamental orality of the written word"? In which ways have the preceding studies of this book tried to demonstrate this feature?*

- The oral dimension is, however, the one most intimately bound up with the major personal and communal roles of Scripture in religious life, especially those that move not only in the intellectual or ideational realm, but also in that of the senses—as, for example, in ritual or devotional use. (155) *How does a "ritual or devotional use" of the Scriptures activate more of a person's "senses"? Give some examples, if possible.*

- [T]o understand the phenomenon of Scripture in any fashion that is remotely faithful to historical realities, we must look to its function as a text that has above all been read and recited aloud, repeated and memorized, chanted and sung, quoted and alluded to in the oral and aural round of daily life. (156) *Why should "historical realities" be a factor of some importance with regard to "faithfulness" where Bible translations are concerned? Can you list any other ways in which Scripture is used in the "oral and aural round of daily life" within a specific religious community?*

- Thus, the vocal word conveys with peculiar force a sense of spontaneity, participation, or personal involvement for the individual and the group through the emotional, sensual impact of hymnody and prayer, litany and praise, formulaic chant, ritual dicta, and

---

³¹ Ζῶν γὰρ ὁ λόγος τοῦ θεοῦ καὶ ἐνεργής...(Heb 4:12).

10.3 Orality—beyond the written Word

texts read or recited aloud. Such *engagement* is characteristic of religious sensibilities at the oral end of the spectrum. (157) *Can you mention another significant quality of the "vocal word" (in addition to "a sense of spontaneity, participation, or personal involvement") when "texts are read or recited aloud" during worship?*

- I have sought to explore those cases in particular in which strong orality coexists with a strong tradition of holy writ—a state of affairs that I am convinced is characteristic of every scriptural tradition with few exceptions—these being, most prominently, certain Christian and, to a lesser degree, Jewish communities in very recent times in the modern West, where the oral presence of Scripture has greatly dwindled.[32] Writtenness and orality are not finally antithetical, but complementary; the absence or loss of either is significant. (159) *Can you name any other contemporary society in which "the oral presence of Scripture has greatly dwindled"? On the other hand, can you name one in which such oral presence has increased significantly? What have been the respective results in each case?*

- At the most obvious level, the dominance of oral/aural interaction with sacred texts has been the rule rather than the exception for the vast majority of persons and communities throughout history. A treatment of Scripture that ignores or slights this fact is historically anachronistic, culturally biased, or both. (159) *In what sense is any "treatment of Scripture" that "ignores or slights" the fact of "the dominance of oral/aural interaction with sacred texts" open to the charge of being "historically anachronistic"? "Culturally biased"?*

---

[32] On the gradual (or should it be characterized as rapid?) shift in media orientation and development that is taking place in the world today, Graham notes: "It would be hard to deny that the spread of at least minimal literacy among the majority of the population and a high degree of reliance upon the printed word have been hallmarks of Western 'modernity'.... This significance is not diminished even if we are now in the process of passing beyond the high-print-literacy, typographic culture of the last one hundred years into a new age of electronic communications—one in which visual images and audiovisual media are beginning to replace visual texts, and visual literacy skills are being superseded by oral/aural skills quite different from those of preliterate oral culture" (1987:166).

- The very act of learning a text "by heart" internalizes the text in a way that familiarity with even an often-read book does not. Memorization is a particularly intimate appropriation of a text, and the capacity to quote or cite a text from memory is a spiritual resource that is tapped automatically in every act of reflection, worship, prayer, or moral deliberation, as well as in times of personal or communal decision or crisis. It is hard to conceive of a highly oral relationship to a scriptural text that does not greatly reinforce spiritual piety. (160) *Is the memorization of Scripture a faculty that is encouraged in your church tradition—specifically, in recent years? If so, how is this done? If not, why—and how has this negatively impacted communal "spiritual piety" within the group?*

- A shared text—one that can be chanted in unison and constantly referred to as a proof text common to an entire community—is a powerful binding factor in any group, and especially a minority group at odds with and bent on reforming or converting the larger society around it. (161)*In which ways does a corporately "shared text"— or, more accurately, a shared corpus of texts ("canon")*[33]*—serve as a*

---

[33] Mention of the "canon," both Jewish and Christian, raises the important literary issue of "intertextuality" and its influence in composing, transmitting, interpreting, and indeed, translating the Scriptures. The old hermeneutical maxim "the Scriptures interpret themselves" was/is not just a trite saying; rather, it is a vital factor in our understanding of the nature of the Bible as a text that has been carefully woven together from many other texts—one passage serving to exposit, expand upon, substantiate, reflect on (and so forth) another passage that has preceded it in the history of divine revelation and proclamation. A "canonical approach" to the interprestion of the Bible has been especially helpful in revealing these varied structural and thematic ties and threads that bind the constituent books together in many meaningful ways. For example, in the Hebrew Bible a focus on the supreme importance of the Torah is found at its conclusion (Deut 34:10–12), the beginning and ending of the Prophets (Josh 1:8–9; Mal 4:5), and at the beginning of the Writings (Ps 1:2–3) (Dempster 2006:294). All of the chapters in Bartholomew et al. (2006) substantiate this fact in various insightful ways, as well as promoting a certain hermeneutical respect for the (implied) author of a given book, that is, in relation to his text on the one hand, and his implied readers and their circumstantial context on the other. Contemporary readers, including translators, must first try to understand this original communicative setting before attempting to convey the biblical text within their own (for "implied readers" see Parry 2006:394).

For example, "Lamentations is widely regarded as reflecting knowledge of several of Israel's holy books. There seems, for instance, to be a knowledge of the

10.3 Orality—beyond the written Word   353

> "powerful binding factor" within a reform-minded "minority group"?
> What other function(s) does such a communal sacred text serve? Give
> some specific examples.

- Perhaps the most important result of attention to the oral dimension of Scripture is to make more vivid the intensely personal engagement of a community with its sacred text. Sacred books are not just authoritative documents or sources of doctrinal formulas; they are living words that produce a variety of responses—emotional and physical as well as intellectual and spiritual. Moreover, at no point in the life of a sacred book is it likely to elicit more varied responses than when it is being chanted, sung, or recited in some meaningful context such as that of worship or meditation. (162–63)
  Why are the oral-aurally-evoked "emotional and physical responses" important (in addition to "intellectual and spiritual" ones) in the life of a religious community? Do you agree with Graham's conclusions concerning these issues that involve "the oral dimension of Scripture"? Give reasons in either case.

In short, as the preceding insights and reflections clearly suggest, the dimension of orality is a vital element in all facets of proclaiming as well as appropriating the Scriptures today. It must therefore be taken into serious consideration during the initial planning stages of any Bible translation project as well as for the duration of its ongoing implementation during the overlapping stages of composing, testing, transmitting, and audience-engaging the new vernacular text.

---

theology of Exodus, Deuteronomy, parts of the text of Jeremiah, and especially of the Psalmic traditions in general and some Psalms in particular. These inter-textual connections come out both at the level of underlying theology and at the level of linguistic parallels. Lamentations could be considered as a carpet that has been woven from numerous threads that include previous texts, religious traditions, and the actual experience of the destruction of Jerusalem. The upshot of this is that seeking to read (or hear!) Lamentations against its original horizon will require reading (hearing) it alongside certain other biblical texts because the implied readers (audience) would be expecting to recognize the quotations and allusions as they engage in meaning-making" (Parry 2006:397–398, material in parentheses added).

10.4 Conclusion—a meditation: "In Defense of Listening"[34]

"I like to listen," said Ernest Hemingway. "I have learned a great deal from listening carefully." Hemingway speaks of a significant virtue, lamenting accurately, "Most people never listen." But I wonder if he would feel differently if it were his books to which people were listening.

The popularity of audio books is redefining the notion of reading, and some authors—and readers—are unhappy about it. "Deep reading really demands the inner ear as well as the outer ear," says literary critic Harold Bloom. "You need the whole cognitive process, that part of you which is open to wisdom. You need the text in front of you." Others who doggedly defend the entire experience of reading—the feel of a book in their hands, the smell of its pages, the single-minded escape of delving into a story—find listening to a book something akin to cheating. "You didn't read it," they contest; "you only listened to it"—as if this somehow means they took in a different story. For those who love the written word and printed page, for those who are elated at the sight of a bookstore, not only is listening to *Hamlet* or *The Count of Monte Cristo* something like picking up the cliff notes, e-books are equally offensive. There is no substitute for books, no surrogate for reading.

I mostly agree. I find myself responding to the question, "Have you read such and such?" with a similar admittance of guilt: "Well, I listened to it" (usually accompanied with a comment about Atlanta traffic). And yet, I am becoming more and more convinced that audio books definitely have their place in learning—with or without traffic. Auditory processing is essential to any learning. Hemingway is right; listening carefully is a vital skill to keep sharp.

I find that I pick up different facets when I listen to a paragraph than I might have gleaned from reading that same paragraph. C. S. Lewis's *Mere Christianity* is a book I have read many times. When I bought the book on CD, however, I found listening to the work an entirely different, altogether helpful experience. Interestingly, *Mere Christianity* began as a series

---

[34] "In Defense of Listening," by Jill Carattini, *A Slice of Infinity*, No. 2387, originally published 31 January 2011 (www.rzim.org). Used by permission of Ravi Zacharias International Ministries. Final italics added.

10.4 Conclusion—a meditation: "In Defense of Listening"

of lectures for the radio, perhaps amplifying its effectiveness as an audio book. And yet some words are simply powerful whether heard internally or aloud.

Of course, much of the Bible has a similar origin, resonating powerfully in both oral and written traditions. The importance of memorization and oral tradition in Israelite culture played a significant role in bringing the collected works of Scripture into being. Listening to narratives, songs, and the Torah read aloud was an integral part of keeping the name of God and the history of God's presence before them. Throughout the Old Testament, the people of Israel are charged with the command to remember, to hear, and to keep before them: "Hear O Israel the LORD our God, the LORD is one" (Deuteronomy 6:4). Listening carefully was imperative to living before the God among them.

And it still is. In homes where Christians are not violently punished for owning a Bible, in countries where it is not a crime to read these sacred texts, it is easy to dismiss the wonder of a God who speaks. As countless translations continue to emerge and divide its readers, it is easy to overlook the authority of words that are strikingly reliable as historical documents, words which continue to come into new generations and change cultures with new influence. Read aloud or studied silently, God is still speaking, crying out for ears to hear and hearts to search. And Christ himself, the living Word, rises from the pages, revealing that it is always far more than a book.

As Ezra read the words of the Law before a generation who had forgotten, the people wept in the presence of the LORD and immediately fell down in worship. When the apostle Paul's letter was read aloud to the Roman church, the words resounded similarly among the crowd: "Consequently, faith comes from hearing the message, and the message is heard through the word of Christ" (Romans 10:17). If the voice of God is still speaking, if the kingdom is among us: *Who among us will listen?*

References

Achtemeier, P. 1990. *Omni verbum sonat*: The New Testament and the environment of Late Western Antiquity. *Journal of Biblical Literature* 109:3–27.

Agourides, S. 1968. The "high priestly prayer" of Jesus. *Studia Evangelica* 4:137–145.

Allison, D. C. 2010. *Constructing Jesus: Memory, imagination, and history*. Grand Rapids: Baker Academic.

Amzallag, N. and M. Avriel. 2011. The canonic response reading of Psalm 114 and its theological significance. *Old Testament Essays* 24:303–323.

Arduini, S. and S. Nergaard. 2011. Translation: A new paradigm. *Translation*, Inaugural Issue:9–15.

Arrojo, R. 2011. Writing, interpreting, and the struggle for control of meaning. *Translation*, Inaugural Issue:34–35.

Assmann, J. 2006. Memory as a mnemonic device: Cultural texts and cultural memory. In Horsley et al., 67–82.

Aune, D. E. Jesus tradition and the Pauline letters. In Kelber and Byrskog, 63–86.

Austin, J. L. (1962) 1975. *How to do things with words*. Cambridge Mass.: Harvard University Press. Second edition, Cambridge Mass.: Harvard University Press.

Bailey, K.E. 2011. *Paul through Mediterranean eyes: Cultural studies in 1 Corinthians*. Downers Grove: IVP Academic.

Baker, M. 2006. Contextualization in translator- and interpreter-related events. *Journal of Pragmatics* 38:325–328.

Baker, M. 2011. *In other words: A coursebook on translation*, Second edition. London and New York: Routledge.
Baker, M. and G. Saldanha, eds. 2008. *Routledge encyclopedia of translation studies*. London and New York: Routledge.
Banker, J. 1997. *A semantic and structural analysis of Philippians*. Dallas: Summer Institute of Linguistics.
Banti, G. and F. Giannattasio. 2004. Poetry. In A. Duranti (ed.), *A companion to linguistic anthropology*, 290–319. Malden, Mass.: Blackwell.
Barnett, P. 2005. *The birth of Christianity: The first twenty years*. Grand Rapids: Eerdmans.
Bartholomew, G. L. 1987. Feed my lambs: John 21:15–19 as oral gospel. *Semeia* 39:69–96.
Bartholomew, C., S. Hahn, R. Parry, C. Seitz, and A. Wolters, eds. 2006. *Canon and biblical interprtetation*. Grand Rapids: Zondervan.
Bascom, R. 2010. Review of *Contextual frames of reference in translation*, by E. Wendland, *The Bible Translator* 61:51–53.
Basevi C., and J. Chapa. Philippians 2:6–11: The rhetorical function of a Pauline "hymn." In Porter and Olbricht, 338–356.
BasisBibel. 2010. http://www.basisbibel.de/basisbibel-nt/bibeltext/basisbibel/bibeltext/lesen/stelle/76/50001/59999/ (accessed September 1, 2010).
Bassnett, S. 2011. The translation turn in cultural studies (excerpt from the article in S. Bassnett and A. Lefevre, eds., *Constructing cultures: Essays in literary translation*. Clevedon: Multilingual Matters, 1998). *Translation* (inaugural issue):78–79.
Bauckham, R. 2006. *Jesus and the eyewitnesses: The gospels as eyewitness testimony*. Grand Rapids and Cambridge: Eerdmans.
Bauman, R. 1984. *Verbal art as performance*. Prospect Heights, Ill.: Waveland.
Bauman, R. 1992. Performance. In R. Bauman (ed.), *Folklore, cultural performances, and popular entertainments: A communications-centered handbook*, 41–49. New York: Oxford UP.
Beasley-Murray, G. R. 1987. *John*. Waco: Word Books.
Bellos, D. 2011. *Is that a fish in your ear?: Translation and the meaning of everything*. New York: Faber and Faber.
Ben Zvi, E., and M. H. Floyd, eds. 2000. *Writings and speech in Israelite and Ancient Near Eastern prophecy*. Atlanta: Society of Biblical Literature.
Berg, T. F. 1989. Reading in/to Mark. *Semeia* 48:187–206.
Biblesocieties. 2010. http://intranet2.biblesocieties.org/intranet/news/view.php?id=1253 (accessed February 6, 2010).
Biddle, M. E. 2004. Hebrew Bible redactions criticism. In D. A. Knight (ed.), *Methods of biblical interpretation*, 135–139. Nashville: Abingdon Press.
Biven, D. 2007. *New light on the difficult words of Jesus: Insights from his Jewish context*. Holland: En-Gedi Resource Center.

Black, D. A. 1985. Paul and Christian unity: A formal analysis of Philippians 2:1–4. *Journal of Evangelical Theological Society* 28:299–308.

Blass, R. 2011. How orality affects the use of pragmatic particles, and how it is relevant for translation. In S. E. Runge (ed.), *Discourse studies and biblical interpretation: A Festscrift in honor of Stephen H. Levinsohn*, 57–66. Bellingham, Wash.: Logos Software version.

Boda, M. J. and J. G. McConville, eds. 2012. *Dictionary of the Old Testament: Prophets*. Downers Grove: IVP Academic.

Booth, W. 1961. *The rhetoric of fiction*. Chicago: Chicago University Press.

Boswell, F. 2010. Update. http://www.sil.org/sil/annualreport/2010-sil-update.pdf (accessed July 30, 2011).

Botha, P. J. J. 1990. Mute manuscripts: Analyzing a neglected aspect of ancient communication. *Theologia Evangelica* 23:35–47.

Brant, J. A. 2004. *Dialogue and drama: Elements of Greek tragedy in the Fourth Gospel*. Peabody, Mass.: Hendrickson.

Breck, J. 1994. *The shape of biblical language: Chiasmus in the Scriptures and beyond*. Crestwood, N.Y.: St. Vladimir's Seminary Press.

Brickle, J. E. 2011. Seeing, hearing, declaring, writing: Media dynamics in the letters of John. In Le Donne and Thatcher, 11–28.

Briggs, R. S. 2008. Speech-act theory. In Firth and Grant, 75–110.

Brown, J. K. 2007. *Scripture as communication: Introducing biblical hermeneutics*. Grand Rapids: Baker.

Bulkeley, T. 2010. Oral/aural qualities of the KJV/AV. http://bigbible.org/sansblogue/bible/auraloral-qualities-of-the-kjvav/ (accessed June 10, 2011).

Byrskog, S. 2009. Introduction. In Kelber and Byrskog, 1–20.

Campbell, A. F. 1989. The reported story. *Semeia* 46:77–85.

Campbell, A. F. 2002. *Story as history: History as story*. Leiden: Brill.

Carattini, J. 2011. In defense of listening. http://www.rzim.org/a-slice-of-infinity/in-defense-of-listening/ (accessed August 30, 2012).

Carlson, M. 2003. *Performance: A critical introduction*. New York: Routledge.

Carr, D. M. 2005. *Writing on the tablet of the heart: Origins of Scripture and literature*. Oxford: Oxford University Press.

Carr, D. M. 2010. Torah on the heart: Literary Jewish textuality within its ancient Near Eastern context. *Oral Tradition* 25:17–40.

Carr, D. M. 2011. *The formation of the Hebrew Bible: A new reconstruction*. Oxford: Oxford University Press.

Carson, D. A. 1991. *The Gospel according to John*. Grand Rapids: Eerdmans.

Carter, W. 2006. *John: Storyteller, interpreter, evangelist*. Peabody, Mass.: Hendrickson.

Chiaro. D. 2009. Issues in audiovisual translation. In Munday, 141–165.

Clark, D. K. 1993. *Dialogical apologetics: A person-centered approach to Christian defense*. Grand Rapids: Baker.

Coleman, J. 1992. *Ancient and medieval memories: Studies in reconstruction of the past.* Cambridge: Cambridge University Press.

Cowan, N. 2001. The magical number 4 in short-term memory: A reconsideration of mental storage capacity. *Behavioral and Brain Sciences* 24:97–185.

Culley, R. C. 2000. Orality and writtenness in the prophetic texts. In Ben Zvi and Floyd, 45–64.

Davies, P. 1998. *Scribes and schools: The canonization of the Hebrew Scriptures.* Louisville: Westminster John Knox.

Davis, C. W. 1999. *Oral biblical criticism: The influence of the principles of orality on the literary structure of Paul's Epistle to the Philippians.* Sheffield: Sheffield Academic Press.

Dempster, S. G. 2006. The prophets, the canon and a canonical approach: No empty word. In Bartholomew et al., 293–329.

De Regt, L. J., J. De Waard, and J. P. Fokkelman, eds. 1996. *Literary structure and rhetorical strategies in the Hebrew Bible.* Assen: Van Gorcum.

DeSilva, D. A. 2009. *Seeing things John's way: The rhetoric of the book of Revelation.* Louisville: Westminster John Knox.

De Vries, L. 2008. Bible translation and primary orality. In Wendland 2008d:297–310.

De Waard J., and E. A. Nida. 1986. *From one language to another: Functional equivalence in Bible translating.* Nashville: Thomas Nelson.

Dewey, J., ed. 1994. *Orality and textuality in early Christian literature (Semeia 65).* Atlanta: Scholars Press.

Doan, Wm. J., and T. Giles. 2005. *Prophets, performance, and power: Performance criticism of the Hebrew Bible.* New York: T&T Clark.

Doane, A. N. 1994. The ethnography of scribal writing and Anglo Saxon poetry: Scribe as performer. *Oral Tradition* 9:420–439.

Dudrey, R. 2003. 1 John and the public reading of Scripture. *Stone Campbell Journal* 6:235–255.

Dunn, J. D. G. 2003. *Jesus remembered: Christianity in the making*, Vol. 1. Grand Rapids: Eerdmans.

Dunn, J. D. G. 2011. John's gospel and the oral gospel tradition. In Le Donne and Thatcher, 157–185.

Edelman, D. V., and Ehud Ben Zvi, eds. 2009. *The production of prophecy: Constructing prophecy and prophets in Yehud.* Oakville, Conn.: Equinox.

Engle, D. 2010. Review of *A literary Bible: An original translation*, by David Rosenberg, http://www.bookreviews.org/pdf/7446_8120.pdf (accessed April 11, 2010).

Erickson, R. J. 2005. *A beginner's guide to New Testament exegesis: Taking the fear out of the critical method.* Downers Grove: InterVarsity Press.

Eshleman, P. 2010. The state of the unfinished task. *Mission Frontiers* 32(4):10–11.

Fauconnier G., and M. Turner. 2006. Conceptual integration networks. In D. Geeraerts (ed.), *Cognitive linguistics: Basic readings*, 303–371. Berlin/New York: Mouton de Gruyter.

Fee, G. D. 1995. *Paul's letter to the Philippians*. Grand Rapids: Eerdmans.

Fee, G. D. 1997. *Paul's first Epistle to the Corinthians*. Grand Rapids: Eerdmans.

Firth, D. G., and J. A. Grant, eds. 2008. *Words & the word: Explorations in biblical interpretation & literary theory*. Downers Grove, Ill.: InterVarsity Press.

Fishbane, M. 1985. *Biblical interpretation in ancient Israel*. Oxford: Oxford University Press.

Fitzgerald, D. 2011. Why Kùnda sings: Narrative discourse and the multifunctionality of Baka song in Baka story. Ph.D. dissertation, University of Florida, Gainesville.

Floyd, M. H. 2000. "Write the revelation!" (Hab 2:2): Re-imagining the cultural history of prophecy. In Ben Zvi and Floyd, 103–43.

Foley, J. M. 1991. *Immanent art: From structure to meaning in traditional oral epic*. Bloomington: Indiana University Press.

Folger, T. 2008. "Science's alternative to an intelligent Creator: The multiverse theory. http://discovermagazine.com/2008/dec/10-sciences-alternative-to-an-intelligent-creator (accessed June 29, 2012).

Fowl, S. E. 2005. *Philippians*. Grand Rapids: Eerdmans.

Fowler, R. 1991. *Let the reader understand: Reader-response criticism and the Gospel of Mark*. Minneapolis: Fortress.

Fowler, R. 2009. Why everything we know about the Bible is wrong. In Hearon and Ruge-Jones, 3–18.

Frank, D. 2009. Do we translate the original author's intended meaning? Paper presented at the Bible Translation Conference, Dallas, October 2009.

Frendo, J. 2011. *Pre-exilic Israel, the Hebrew Bible, and archaeology: Integrating text and artefact*. New York: T&T Clark.

Friedman, M. D. 2002. In defense of authenticity. *Studies in Philology* 99:33–56.

Gamble, H. 1995. *Books and readers in the early church: A history of early Christian texts*. New Haven and London: Yale UP.

Garland, D. E. Philippians. In T. Longman and D. E. Garland, eds. *The Expositor's Bible commentary*, Second edition, 175–261. Grand Rapids: Zondervan.

Gentry, P. J. 2012. The Septuagint. In Grudem et al., 157–165.

Gerhardsson, B. 1961. *Memory and manuscript: Oral tradition and written transmission in rabbinic Judaism and early Christianity*, ASNU 22. Lund: Gleerup.

Gerhardsson, B. 1964. *Tradition and transmission in early Christianity*, Coniectanea Neotestamentica 20. Lund: Gleerup.

Gerhardsson, B. 1998. *Memory and manuscript: Oral tradition and written transmission in rabbinic Judaism and early Christianity*, with *Tradition and transmission in early Christianity*. Grand Rapids: Eerdmans.

Gerhardsson, B. 2001. *The reliability of the gospel tradition*. Peabody, Mass.: Hendrickson.

Gerhardsson, B. 2005. The secret of the transmission of the unwritten Jesus tradition. *New Testament Studies* 51:1–18.

Giles, T. 2012. Performance criticism. In Boda and McConville, 578–583.

Giles, T., and William J. Doan. 2009. *Twice used songs: Performance criticism of the songs of ancient Israel*. Peabody Mass.: Hendrikson.

Gitay, Y. 1991. *Isaiah and his audience: The structure and meaning of Isaiah 1–12*. Assen: Van Gorcum.

Gitay, Y. 2009. History, literature and memory. *Journal of Semitics* 18:275–300.

Goethals, G. 1997. Multimedia images: Plato's cave revisited. In Hodgson and Soukup, 229–248.

Gordon, T. D. 2010. A literate ministry. *Tabletalk* May:75–76.

Graham, Wm. A. 1987. *Beyond the written word: Oral aspects of Scripture in the history of religion*. Cambridge: Cambridge UP.

Graham, Wm. A. 2010. Summation. *Oral Tradition* 25:231–238.

Greenlee, J. H. 1992. *An exegetical summary of Philippians*. Dallas: Summer Institute of Linguistics.

Grice, P. 1975. Logic and conversation. In P. Cole and J. Morgan (eds.), *Syntax and semantics 3: Speech acts*, 41–58. New York: Academic Press.

Grudem, W., C. J. Collins, and T. R. Schreiner, eds. 2012. *Understanding Scripture: An overview of the Bible's origin, reliability, and meaning*. Wheaton: Crossway.

Grudem, W., L. Ryken, C. J. Collins, V. S. Poythress, and B. Winter. 2005. *Translating truth: The case for essentially literal Bible translation*. Wheaton: Crossway.

Guthrie, G. H. 1995. Cohesion shifts and stitches in Philippians. In Porter and Carson, 36–59.

Gutt, E-A. 1992. *Relevance theory: A guide to successful communication in translation*. Dallas: Summer Institute of Linguistics.

Habel, N. 1985. *The book of Job*. Philadelphia: The Westminster Press.

Haenchen, E. 1984. *John 2*. Philadelphia: Fortress Press.

Haines-Eitzen, K. 2000. *Guardians of letters: Literacy, power, and the transmitters of early Christian literature*. Oxford: Oxford University Press.

Hansford, K. L. 1992. The underlying poetic structure of 1 John. *Journal of Translation and Textlinguistics* 5:126–174.

Harvey, J. D. 1998. *Listening to the text: Oral patterning in Paul's letters*. Grand Rapids: Baker.

Hatim, B., and I. Mason. 1990. *Discourse and the translator*. London: Longman.

Hatim, B., and J. Munday. 2004. *Translation: Advanced resource book*. London and New York: Routledge.

Hawkins, R. K. 2012. Review of *Pre-exilic Israel, the Hebrew Bible, and archaeology: Integrating text and artefact*, by Anthony J. Frendo, *Review of Biblical Literature*. http://www.bookreviews.org (accessed February 10, 2012).

Hawthorne, G. F. 1983. *Philippians*. Waco: Word Books.

Hayes, J. H., ed. 1999. *Dictionary of biblical criticism* (two volumes). Nashville: Abingdon Press.

Hearon, H. E. 2010. The interplay between written and spoken word in the Second Testament as background to the emergence of written gospels. *Oral Tradition* 25:57–74

Hearon, H. E., and P. Ruge-Jones, eds. 2009. *The Bible in ancient and modern media: Story and performance*. Eugene Ore.: Cascade Books.

Heil, J. P. 2010. *Philippians: Let us rejoice in being conformed to Christ*. Atlanta: Society of Biblical Literature.

Heim, K. M. 2010. Solving the riddle of 'Amon: Wordplay in Proverbs 8:30. Paper presented at the Annual Meeting of the Society of Biblical Literature, Atlanta, November 2010.

Herington, C. J. 1993. Greek poetry—The Hellenistic age. In A. Preminger and T. V. F. Brogan (eds.), *The new Princeton encyclopedia of poetry and poetics*, 486–488. Princeton: Princeton University Press.

Hess, R. S. 2008. Scribes. In T. Longman III and P. Enns (eds.), *Dictionary of the Old Testament: Wisdom, poetry & writings*, 717–720. Downers Grove, IL: IVP Academic.

Hezser, C. 2010. Oral and written communication and transmission of knowledge in ancient Judaism and Christianity. *Oral Tradition* 25:75–92.

Hill, H. 2009. Adjusting contextual mismatches: Do study Bibles provide a good model? Paper presented at the Bible Translation Conference, Dallas, October 2009.

Hill, H., E-A. Gutt, M. Hill, C. Unger, and R. Floyd. 2011. *Bible translation basics: Communicating Scripture in a relevant way*. Dallas: SIL International.

Hirsch, E. D, Jr. 1976. *The aims of interpretation*. Chicago: University of Chicago Press.

Hobbins, J. 2010 Retaining and transcending the classical description of ancient Hebrew verse. http://ancienthebrewpoetry.typepad.com/ancient_hebrew_poetry /2005/04/retaining_the_s.html (accessed July 3, 2010).

Hock, R. F. and E. N. O'Neill. 1986. *The chreia in ancient rhetoric*, Vol. 1: *The Progymnasmata*. Atlanta: Scholars Press.

Hodgson, R. 1997. An urgent need: God's Word in a post-literate world. In Hodgson and Soukup, 3–13.

Hodgson, R., and P. A. Soukup, eds. 1997. *From one medium to another: Basic issues for communicating the Scriptures in new media*. New York: American Bible Society.

Holland, G. S. 2007. Playing to the groundlings: Shakespeare performance criticism and performance criticism of the biblical texts. *Neotestamentica* 41:317–340.

Hooker, M. D. 2000. The letter to the Philippians. In L. E. Keck (ed.), *The new interpreter's Bible*, Vol. XI, 469–549. Nashville: Abingdon Press.

Horsley, R. A. 2006. Introduction. In Horsley et al., vii–xvi.

Horsley, R. A. 2010. Oral and written aspects of the emergence of the Gospel of Mark as Scripture. *Oral Tradition* 25:93–114.

Horsley, R. A., J. A. Draper, and J. M. Foley, eds. 2006. *Performing the gospel: Orality, memory, and Mark*. Minneapolis: Fortress Press.

House, P. R. 1989. *Zephaniah: A prophetic drama*. Sheffield: Almond Press.

Huang, Y. 2007. *Pragmatics*. Oxford: Oxford University Press.

Huttar, G. 2010. Review of *Introduction to cognition and communication*, by K. Stenning, A. Lascarides, and Jo Calder, http://www.sil.org:8090/silebr/2010/silebr2010-011 (accessed March 3, 2010).

Jaffee, M. 2001. *Torah of the mouth: Writing and oral tradition in Palestinian Judaism, 200 BCE–400 CE*. Oxford: Oxford UP.

Jakobson, R. 1960. Linguistics and poetics. In T. Sebeok (ed.), *Style in language*, 18–51. Cambridge: MIT Press.

Jenny, H. 1967. *Kymatik: Wellen und Schwingungen mit ihrer Struktur und Dynamik* [Cymatics: The structure and dynamics of waves and vibrations]. Basel: Basilius Press.

Jerusalem School of Synoptic Research. 2010. http://www.jerusalemschool.org/Methodology/index.htm (accessed January 8, 2010).

Karlik, J. 2010. Interpreter-mediated Scriptures: Expectation and performance. *Interpreting* 12:160–185.

Katan, D. 2004. *Translating cultures: An introduction for translators, interpreters, and mediators*, Second edition. Manchester: St. Jerome.

Katz, M., and G, Schwartz. 1998. *Swimming in the sea of Talmud*. Philadelphia: Jewish Publication Society.

Keener, C. S. 2003. *The Gospel of John*, Vol. 2. Peabody: Hendrickson.

Keesmaat, S. C. 2006. In the face of the empire: Paul's use of Scripture in the shorter epistles. In S. E. Porter (ed.), *Hearing the Old Testament in the New Testament*, 182–212. Grand Rapids: Eerdmans.

Kelber, W. 1983. *The oral and written gospel: The hermeneutics of speaking and writing in the synoptic tradition*. Philadelphia: Fortress.

Kelber, W. 1987. Biblical hermeneutics and the ancient art of communication: A response. *Semeia* 39:107–133.

Kelber, W. 1994. Jesus and tradition: Words in time, words in space. In J. Dewey (ed.), *Orality and textuality in early Christian literature*, 139–167. Atlanta: Scholars Press.

Kelber, W. 2007. Orality and biblical studies: A review essay. In J. G. van der Watt (ed.), *2007 Review of Biblical Literature*, 1–24. Atlanta: Society of Biblical Literature.

Kelber, W. 2008. The oral-scribal memorial arts of communication in early Christianity. In Thatcher, 235–262.

Kelber, W. 2009. The work of Birger Gerhardsson in perspective. In Kelber and Byrskog, 173–206.

Kelber, W. 2010. The history of the closure of biblical texts. *Oral Tradition*, 25:115–140.

Kelber, W., and S. Byrskog, eds. 2009. *Jesus in memory: Traditions in oral and scribal perspectives*. Waco: Baylor University Press.

Kelly, D. A. 2005. *Handbook for translator trainers*. Manchester: St. Jerome.

Kennedy, G. A. 1984. *New Testament interpretation through rhetorical criticism*. Chapel Hill: University of North Carolina Press.

Ker, D. 2011. Reading speed of Scripture. http://futurebible.org/2011/reading-speed-of-scripture/ (accessed August 21, 2011).

Kessler, M. 1982. A methodological setting for rhetorical criticism. In D. Clines, D. Gunn, and A. Hauser (eds.), *Art and meaning: Rhetoric in biblical literature*, 1–19. Sheffield: Sheffield Academic Press.

King James Bible Trust. 2011. http://www.kingjamesbibletrust.org/ (accessed March 4, 2011).

Kirk, A. 2008. Manuscript tradition as a *tertium quid*: Orality and memory in scribal practices. In Thatcher, 215–234.

Kirk, A. 2009. Memory. In Kelber and Byrskog, 155–172.

Kitchen, K. A. 2003. *On the reliability of the Old Testament*. Grand Rapids and Cambridge: Eerdmans.

Köstenberger, A. J., and R. D. Patterson. 2011. *Invitation to biblical interpretation: Exploring the hermeneutical triad of history, literature, and theology*. Grand Rapids: Kregel.

Kotze, P. P. 1985. John and reader's response. *Neotestamentica* 19:50–63.

Labahn, M. 2011. Scripture talks because Jesus talks: The narrative rhetoric of persuading in John's use of Scripture. In Le Donne and Thatcher, 133–156.

Landers, C. E. 2001. *Literary translation: A practical guide*. Clevedon and Toronto: Multilingual Matters.

Le Donne, A., and T. Thatcher, eds. 2011a. *The Fourth Gospel in first-century media culture*. New York: T&T Clark.

Le Donne, A., and T. Thatcher. 2011b. Introducing media culture to Johannine studies: Orality, performance and memory. In Le Donne and Thatcher, 1–8.

Lee, M. E., and B. B. Scott. 2009. *Sound mapping the New Testament*. Salem Ore.: Polebridge Press.

Lévi-Strawss, C. (1955) 1974. The structural study of myth. In T. A. Sebeok (ed.), *A symposium*, 81–106. Bloomington: Indiana University Press.

Levý, Jiří (Z. Jettmarová, ed.; P. Corness, trans.). (1963) 2011. *The art of translation*. Amsterdam: John Benjamins.

Loh, I-Jin., and E. A. Nida. 1977. *A Translator's handbook on Paul's Letter to the Philippians*. New York: United Bible Societies.

Lohmeyer, E. 1928. *Kyrios Jesus: Eine Untersuchung zu Phil 2,5–11*. Heidelberg: Winter.

Loubser, J. A. 2004. How do you report something that was said with a smile?—Can we overcome the loss of meaning when oral-manuscript texts of the Bible are represented in modern print media? *Scriptura* 87:296–314.

Loubser, J. A. 2007. *Oral and manuscript culture in the Bible: Studies on the media texture of the New Testament*. Stellenbosch: SUN Press.

Luter A. B., and M. V. Lee. 1995. Philippians as chiasmus: Key to the structure, unity and theme questions. *New Testament Studies* 41:89–101.

Luz, S., S. Malmatidou, and S. Marshall. 2010. *Corpus building with TEC tools: Tutorial*. http://www.llc.manchester.ac.uk/ctis/research/english-corpus/ (accessed June 10, 2010).

Malatesta, E. 1971. The literary structure of John 17. *Biblica* 52:190–214.

Malina, B. J. 1981. *The New Testament world: Insights from cultural anthropology*. Atlanta: John Knox.

Malina, B. J., and J. H. Neyrey. 1991. First-century personality: Dyadic, not individual. In Neyrey, 67–96.

Malina, B. J., and J. J. Pilch. 2006. *Social-science commentary on the letters of Paul*. Minneapolis: Fortress Press.

Malina B. J., and R. L. Rohrbaugh. 1998. *Social-science commentary on the Gospel of John*. Minneapolis: Fortress Press.

Marshall, J. W. 1993. Paul's ethical appeal in Philippians. In Porter and Olbricht, 357–374.

Martin, G. D. 2010. *Multiple originals: New approaches to Hebrew Bible textual criticism*. Atlanta: Society of Biblical Literature.

Mathews, J. 2012. *Performing Habakkuk: Faithful re-enactment in the midst of crisis*. Eugene, Ore.: Pickwick Publications.

Matthews, V. 2008. *More than meets the ear: Discovering the hidden contexts of Old Testament conversations*. Grand Rapids: Eerdmans.

Maxey, J. A. 2009. *From orality to orality: A new paradigm for contextual translation of the Bible*. Eugene: Cascade Books.

Maxwell, K. 2010. *Hearing between the lines: The audience as fellow-worker in Luke-Acts and its literary milieu*. New York: T&T Clark International.

Mazor, Y. 2009. *Who wrought the Bible? Unveiling the Bible's aesthetic secrets.* Madison: University of Wisconsin Press.

Metzger, B. M. 1994. *A textual commentary on the Greek New Testament,* Second edition. Stuttgart: German Bible Society.

Millard, A. R. 2000. *Reading and writing in the time of Jesus.* New York: New York University Press.

Millard, A. R. 2012a. Writing and prophecy. In Boda and McConville, 883–885.

Millard, A. R. 2012b. Review of *Writing and literacy in the world of ancient Israel,* by Christopher A. Rollston. *Biblical Archaeological Review.* http://www.biblicalarchaeology.org/reviews/writing-and-literacy-in-the-world-of-ancient-israel/ (accessed July 22, 2012).

Miller, G. A. 1956. The magical number seven, plus or minus two: Some limits on our capacity for processing information. *Psychological Review* 63:81–97.

Miller, R. D., II. 2011. *Oral tradition in ancient Israel.* Eugene, Ore.: Cascade Books.

Mitternacht, D. 2007. A structure of persuasion in Galatians: Epistolary and rhetorical appeal in an aural setting. In D. F. Tolmie (ed.), *Exploring new rhetorical approaches to Galatians,* 53–98. Bloemfontein: University of the Free State.

Morris, L. 1995. *The Gospel according to John,* Revised edition. Grand Rapids: Eerdmans.

Morrison, C. D. 1965. Mission and ethic: An interpretation of John 17. *Interpretation* 19:259–273.

Mossop, B. 2001. *Revising and editing for translators.* Manchester: St. Jerome.

Motyer, A. 1999. *Isaiah.* Downers Grove: InterVarsity Press.

Mournet, T. C. 2009. The Jesus tradition as oral tradition. In Kelber and Byrskog, 39–61.

Munday, J., ed. 2009a. *The Routledge companion to translation studies.* London and New York: Routledge.

Munday, J. 2009b. Key concepts. In Munday, 166–240.

Murphy, N. C. 1994. *Reasoning and rhetoric in religion.* Valley Forge: Trinity Press International.

Naudé, J. A., and C. H. J. van der Merwe, eds. 2002. *Contemporary translation studies: A South African perspective* (Acta Theologica, Supplementum 2). Bloemfontein: University of the Free State.

Neufeld, D. 1994. *Reconceiving texts as speech acts: An analysis of 1 John.* Leiden: Brill.

Neufeld, D., ed. 2008. *The Social sciences and Bible translation.* Atlanta: Society of Biblical Literature.

Neyrey, J. H. 1991a. *The social world of Luke-Acts: Models for interpretation.* Peabody, Mass.: Hendrickson.

Neyrey, J. H. 1991b. The symbolic universe of Luke-Acts: "They turn the world upside down." In Neyrey, 271–304.

Neyrey, J. H. 2009. *The Gospel of John in cultural and rhetorical perspective.* Grand Rapids: Eerdmans.

Nida, E. A., and C. Taber. 1969. *The theory and practice of translation.* Leiden: E. J. Brill.

Niditch, S. 1996. *Oral world and written word.* Louisville: Westminster John Knox.

Nord, C. 1997. *Translating as a purposeful activity: Functionalist approaches explained.* Manchester, UK: St. Jerome.

Norton D. 2011. *The King James Bible: A short history from Tyndale to today.* Cambridge: Cambridge University Press.

Noss, P. A. 2001. Ideas, phones, and Gbaya verbal art. In F. K. Erhard Voeltz and Christa Kilian-Hatz (eds.), *Ideophones,* 259–270. Amsterdam: John Benjamins.

O'Brien, P. T. 1991. *Commentary on Philippians.* Grand Rapids: Eerdmans.

Oesterreicher, W. 1997. Types of orality in text. In E. Bakker and A. Kahane (eds.). *Written voices, spoken signs,* 190–214. Cambridge, Mass.: Harvard University Press.

Omanson, R. A. 2006. *A textual guide to the Greek New Testament.* Stuttgart: Deutsche Bibelgesellschaft.

Ong, W. J. 1982. *Orality and literacy: The technologizing of the word.* London and New York: Methuen.

Osborne, G. R. 2006. *The hermeneutical spiral: A comprehensive introduction to biblical interpretation,* Second edition. Downers Grove: IVP Academic.

Parry, R. 2006. Prolegomena to Christian theological interpretations of Lamentations. In Bartholomew et al., 393–418.

Parunak, H. Van Dyke. 1981. Oral typesetting: Some uses of biblical structure. *Biblia* 62:153–168.

Patte, D. 1988. Speech act theory and biblical exegesis. *Semeia* 41:85–102.

Patterson, R. D. 1993. Old Testament prophecy. In L. Ryken and T. Longman III (eds.), *A complete literary guide to the Bible,* 296–309. Grand Rapids: Zondervan.

Persen, R. F. Jr. 2010. *The deuteronomic history and the book of Chronicles: Scribal works in an oral world.* Atlanta: Society of Biblical Literature.

Petersen, N. R. 1984. The reader in the gospel. *Neotestamentica* 18:38–51.

Phillips, P. 2008. Rhetoric. In Firth and Grant, 226–65.

Pieper A. 1979. *Isaiah II* (E. E. Kowalke, trans.). Milwaukee: Northwestern Publishing House.

Pilch J. J., and B. J. Malina, eds. 1993. *Biblical social values and their meaning.* Peabody, Mass.: Hendrickson.

Polak, F. H. 1998. The oral and the written: Syntax, stylistics, and the development of biblical prose narrative. *Journal of the Ancient Near Eastern Society* 26:59–105

Porter, S. E. 1993. The theoretical justification for application of rhetorical categories to Pauline epistolary literature. In Porter and Olbricht, 100–122.

Porter, S. E. and D. A. Carson, eds. 1995. *Discourse analysis and other topics in biblical Greek*. Sheffield: Sheffield Academic Press.

Porter, S. E. and T. H. Olbricht, eds. 1993. *Rhetoric and the New Testament: Essays from the 1992 Heidelberg conference*. Sheffield: Sheffield Academic Press.

Porter, S. E. and J. T. Reed, eds. 1999. *Discourse analysis and the New Testament: Approaches and results*. Sheffield: Sheffield Academic Press.

Pratt, M. L. 1977. *Towards a speech act theory of literary discourse*. Bloomington: Indiana University Press.

Pretorius, M. 2011. Sound: Conceivably the creative language of God, holding all of creation in concert. *Verbum et Ecclesia* 32:[7 pp]. doi:10.4102/ve.v32i1.485 (accessed July 17, 2012).

Pym, A. 2010. *Exploring translation theories*. London and New York: Routledge.

Rainey, A. F. 2010. Queries and comments. *Biblical Archaeology Review* 36(3):79–80.

Reed, J. T. 1993. Using ancient rhetorical categories to interpret Paul's letters: A question of genre. In Porter and Olbricht, 292–324.

Reed, J. T. 1995. Identifying theme in the New Testament: Insights from discourse analysis. In Porter and Carson, 75–101.

Reed, J. T. 1997. *A discourse analysis of Philippians: Method and rhetoric in the debate over literary integrity*. Sheffield: Sheffield Academic Press.

Reiss, K., and H. Vermeer. 1984. *Grundlegung einer allgemeinen Translationstheorie*. Tübingen: Niemeyer.

Rhoads, D. 2006a. Performance criticism: An emerging methodology in Second Testament studies—Part I. *Biblical Theology Bulletin* 36:1–16.

Rhoads, D. 2006b. Performance criticism: An emerging methodology in Second Testament studies—Part II. *Biblical Theology Bulletin* 36:164–184.

Rhoads, D. 2009. The memory arts of the Letter of James. Paper presented at the Annual Meeting of the Society of Biblical Literature, New Orleans, November 2009.

Rhoads, D. 2010. Biblical performance criticism: Performance as research. *Oral tradition* 25:157–198.

Rhoads, D. Forthcoming. The art of translating for oral performance. In J. Maxey and E. Wendland (eds.), *Translating sound and performance of the Bible*, ch. 2. Eugene, Ore.: Cascade Books.

Richards, E. R. 2004. *Paul and first-century letter writing: Secretaries, composition and collection*. Downers Grove, IL: InterVarsity.

Robbins, V. K. 1996. *Exploring the texture of texts: A guide to socio-rhetorical interpretation*. Valley Forge, PA: Trinity Press.

Robbins, V. K. 2006. Interfaces of orality and literature in the Gospel of Mark. In Horsley et al., 125–146.

Robbins, V. K. 2009. *The invention of Christian discourse*, Vol. 1. Dorset UK: Blandford Forum, Deo.

Rollston, C. 2010. *Writing and literacy in the world of ancient Israel: Epigraphic evidence from the Iron Age.* Atlanta: Society of Biblical Literature.

Roschke, R. W. 1997. From one medium to another. In Hodgson and Soukup, 337–344.

Rosenberg, D. 2009. *A literary Bible: An original translation.* Berkeley: Counterpoint.

Rothenberg, J., and D. Rothenberg. 1983. *Symposium of the whole: A range of discourse toward an ethnopoetics.* Berkeley: University of California Press.

Ruge-Jones, P. 2010. Performance criticism as critical pedagogy. *Currents in Theology and Mission* 37:288–295.

Runge, S. 2010. *Discourse grammar of the Greek New Testament.* Peabody, Mass.: Hendrickson.

Ryken, L. 1992. *Words of delight: A literary introduction to the Bible,* Second edition. Grand Rapids: Baker.

Ryken, L. 2012. Reading the Bible as literature. In Grudem, Collins, and Schreiner, 37–43.

Safrai, S. 1976. Education and the study of Torah. In S. Safrai and M. Stern (eds.), *The Jewish people in the first century,* 945–970. Amsterdam: Van Gorcum.

Safrai, S. 2009. The value of rabbinic literature as an historical source. http://www.jerusalemperspective.com/default.aspx?tabid=27&ArticleID=1969 (accessed October 3, 2009).

Sangrey, M. 2012. When summarizing is too hard. http://betterbibles.com/2012/03/07 (accessed November 3, 2012).

Schafer, R. M. 1994. *The soundscape: Our sonic environment and the tuning of the world.* Rochester, Vt.: Destiny Books.

Schart, A. 2010. Deathly silence and apocalyptic noise: Observations on the soundscape of the Book of the Twelve. *Verbum et Ecclesia* 31:1–5.

Schneidau, H. 1987. Let the reader understand. *Semeia* 39:135–145.

Schniedewind, Wm. 2004. *How the Bible became a book.* Cambridge: Cambridge UP.

Schrag, B. E. 1992. Translating song texts as oral compositions. *Notes on Translation* 6(1):44–62.

Schrag, B. E. 2007. Why local arts are central to mission. *International Journal of Frontier Missiology* 24:199–202.

Schröter, J. 2006. Jesus and the canon: The early Jesus traditions in the context of the origins of the New Testament canon. In Horsley et al., 104–122.

Scott, B. B., and M. Dean. 1993. A sound map of the Sermon on the Mount. In E. H. Lovering (ed.), 672–725. *Society of Biblical Lterature Seminar Papers.* Atlanta: Scholars Press.

Seow, C. L. 2011. Orthography, textual criticism, and the poetry of Job. *Journal of Biblical Literature* 130:63–85.

Shils, E. 1971. Tradition. *Comparative Studies in Society and History* 13:122–159.

Shiner, W. 2003. *Proclaiming the gospel: First-century performance of Mark.* Harrisburg, Penn.: Trinity Press international.

Shiner, W. 2006. Memory technology and the composition of Mark. In Horsley et al., 147–165.

Shklovsky, V. 1965. Art as technique. In L. T. Lemon and M. J. Reis (eds.), *Russian formalist criticism*, 3–57. Lincoln: University of Nebraska Press.

Silberman, L. 1987. Introduction: Reflections on orality, aurality, and perhaps more. *Semeia* 39:1–6.

Silva, M. 2005. *Philippians*, Second edition. Grand Rapids: Baker Books.

Simon, H. 1983. *Reason in human affairs.* Stanford: Stanford University Press.

Soanes, C., and A. Stevenson, eds. 2006. *Concise Oxford English dictionary*, Eleventh edition. Oxford: Oxford UP.

Soulen R. N., and R. K. Soulen. 2001. *Handbook of biblical criticism*, Third edition. Louisville amd London: Westminster John Knox.

Snyman, A. H. 1993. Persuasion in Philippians 4:1–20. In Porter and Olbricht, 325–337.

Sparks, K. L. 2008. *God's word in human words.* Grand Rapids: Baker Academic.

Stenning, K., A. Lascarides, and J. Calder. 2006. *Introduction to cognition and communication.* Cambridge, Mass.: MIT Press.

Sternberg, M. 1987. *The poetics of biblical narrative: Ideological literature and the drama of reading.* Bloomington: Indiana UP.

Sterner, R. H. 1998. *A semantic and structural analysis of 1 Thessalonians.* Dallas: Summer Institute of Linguistics.

Swanson, R. W. 2010. Truth, method, and multiplicity: Performance as a mode of interpretation. *Currents in Theology and Mission* 37:312–319.

Talmon, S. 2010. *Text and canon of the Hebrew Bible.* Winona Lake: Eisenbrauns.

Tate, W. R. 1991. *Biblical interpretation: An integrated approach.* Peabody, Mass.: Hendrickson, 1991.

Terry, J. O. 2009a. Scripture passage to story. http://www.churchstarting.net/biblestorying/scriptostory.htm (accessed April 11, 2009).

Terry, J. O. 2009b. Oralizing Bible stories for telling. http://www.churchstarting.net/biblestorying/oralizing.htm (accessed April 11, 2009).

Thatcher, T., ed. 2008. *Jesus, the voice, and the text: Beyond the oral and written gospel.* Waco: Baylor University Press.

Thatcher, T. 2011a. The riddle of the Baptist and the genesis of the prologue: John 1:1–18 in oral/aural media culture. In Le Donne and Thatcher, 29–48.

Thatcher, T. 2011b. John's memory theatre: A study of composition in performance. In Le Donne and Thatcher, 73–91.

Thiselton, A. C. 1992. *New horizons in hermeneutics: The theory and practice of transforming Bible reading.* Grand Rapids: Zondervan.

Thiselton, A. C. 1999. Communicative action and promise in hermeneutics. In R. Lundin, C. Walhout, and A. Thiselton (eds.), *The promise of hermeneutics*, 133–239. Grand Rapids: Eerdmans.

Thiselton, A.C. 2006. Canon, community, and theological construction. In Bartholomew et al., 1–30.

Thomas, K. J. 1990. Seeking a methodology for exegetical checking of audio Scriptures. *The Bible Translator* 41:301–311.

Thomas K. J., and M. O. Thomas. 2006. *Structure and orality in 1 Peter: A guide for translators.* New York: United Bible Societies.

Thompson, I. H. 1995. *Chiasmus in the Pauline letters.* Sheffield: Sheffield Academic Press.

Thuren, L. 1993. On studying ethical argumentation and persuasion in the New Testament. In Porter and Olbricht, 464–478.

Toorn, K., van der. 2007. *Scribal culture and the making of the Hebrew Bible.* Cambridge Mass.: Harvard University Press.

Toulmin, S. E. 1958. *The uses of argument.* Cambridge: Cambridge University Press.

Tov, E. 1992. *Textual criticism of the Hebrew Bible.* Minneapolis: Fortress Press.

Tov, E. 2008. *Scribal practices and approaches reflected in the texts found in the Judean desert.* http://www.emanueltov.info (accessed July 10, 2008).

Translating Multimodalities. http://www.port.ac.uk/translationconference (accessed March 3, 2010).

Tuckett, C. 2009. Form criticism. In Kelber and Byrskog, 21–38.

Ukpong, J. S. 1989. Jesus' prayer for his followers (Jn 17) in mission perspective. *Africa Theological Journal* 18:49–60.

Ulrich, E. 1999. *The Dead Sea scrolls and the origins of the Bible.* Grand Rapids, MI: Eerdmans.

Van der Merwe, C. 2009. Another look at the Hebrew focus particle גַּם. *Journal of Semitic Studies* 54:313–332.

Van Wolde, E. 2009. *Reframing biblical studies: When language and text meet culture, cognition, and context.* Winona Lake, Ind.: Eisenbrauns.

Vanhoozer, K. J. 1986. The semantics of biblical literature. In D. A. Carson and J. T. Woodbridge (eds.), *Hermeneutics, authority, and canon*, 49–104. Grand Rapids: Zondervan.

Vanhoozer, K. J. 1998. *Is there a meaning in this text? The Bible, the reader, and the morality of literary knowledge.* Grand Rapids: Zondervan.

Verheyden, J. 2008. Oral performance, popular tradition, and hidden transcripts in Q. In J. G. van der Watt (ed.), *2008 Review of Biblical Literature*, 349–351. Atlanta: Society of Biblical Literature.

Wallace, D. B. 2011. Lost in transmission: How badly did the scribes corrupt the New Testament text? In D. B. Wallace (ed.), *Revisiting the corruption of the New Testament: Manuscript, patristic, and apocryphal evidence*, 19–55. Grand Rapids: Kregel.

Wallace, D. B. 2012. The reliability of the New Testament manuscripts. In Grudem, Collins, and Schreiner, 111–117.

Ward, R. F. 1994. Pauline voice and presence and strategic communication. In J. Dewey (ed.), *Orality and textuality in early Christian literature* (Semeia 65), 95–107. Atlanta: Society of Biblical Literature.

Watson, D. F. 1988. A rhetorical analysis of Philippians and its implications for the unity question. *Novum Testamentum* 30:57–88.

Watson, D. F. 1992. Chreia/aphorism. In J. B. Green and S. McKnight (eds.), *Dictionary of Jesus and the gospels*, 104–106. Downers Grove: InterVarsity.

Watson, D. F. 1997. The integration of epistolary and rhetorical analysis of Philippians. In Porter and Olbricht, 398–426.

Watson, D. F., and A. J. Hauser. 1994. *Rhetorical criticism of the Bible: A comprehensive bibliography with notes on history and method*. Leiden: Brill.

Watts, J. D. W. 1987. *Isaiah 34–66*. Waco: Word Books.

Webb, B. 1996. *The message of Isaiah*. Downers Grove: InterVarsity.

Wegner, P. D. 1999. *The journey from texts to translations: The origin and development of the Bible*. Grand Rapids: Baker.

Wegner, P. D. 2006. *A student's guide to textual criticism of the Bible: Its history, methods & results*. Downers Grove: IVP Academic.

Wegner, P. D. 2012. The reliability of the Old Testament manuscripts. In Grudem, Collins, and Schreiner, 101–109.

Weissenberg, H. von, J. Pakkala, and M. Marttila, eds. 2011. *Changes in Scripture: Rewriting and interpreting authoritative traditions in the Second Temple period* (Beihefte zur Zeitschrift für die alttestamentliche Wissenschaft 419). Berlin: de Gruyter.

Wendland, E. R. 1976. *Nthano za kwa Kawaza* ("Folktales from Kawazaland"). Lusaka: Zambia Language Group and UNESCO.

Wendland, E. R. 1979. Stylistic form and communicative function in the Nyanja radio narratives of Julius Chongo. Ph.D. dissertation, University of Wisconsin, Madison.

Wendland, E. R. 1990. What is truth? Semantic density and the language of the Johannine epistles, with special reference to 2 John. *Neotestamentica* 24:301–333.

Wendland, E. R. 1992. Rhetoric of the Word: An interactional discourse analysis of the Lord's Prayer of John 17 and its communicative implications. *Neotestamentica* 26:59–88.

Wendland, E. R. 1993. *Comparative discourse analysis and the translation of Psalm 22 in Chichewa*. Lewiston, N.Y.: Edwin Mellen Press.

Wendland, E. R. 1994. Oral-aural dynamics of the Word with special reference to John 17. *Notes on Translation* 8(1):19–43.

Wendland, E. R. 1998. *Buku Loyera: An introduction to the New Chichewa Bible translation.* Blantyre, Malawi: Christian Literature Association in Malawi, 1998.

Wendland, E. R. 2002a. Aspects of rhetorical analysis applied to New Testament texts. In A. J. Blasi, J. Duhaime, P. A. Turcotte (eds.), *Handbook of early Christianity: Social science approaches*, 169–195. Lanham, Md.: AltaMira Press.

Wendland, E. R. 2002b. *Analyzing the Psalms: With exercises for Bible students and translators*, Second edition. Dallas: SIL International.

Wendland, E. R. 2003. Responses to Colin Yallop lectures. *The Bible Translator* 54:225–228.

Wendland, E. R. 2004a. *Poceza m'madzulo: Some Chinyanja radio plays of Julius Chongo, with English translations.* Lusaka: University of Zambia Press.

Wendland, E. R. 2004b. *Translating the literature of Scripture: A literary-rhetorical approach to Bible translation.* Publications in Translation and Textlinguistics 1. Dallas: SIL International.

Wendland, E. R. 2005. *Sewero! Christian drama and the drama of Christianity in Africa.* Zomba, Malawi: Kachere Series.

Wendland, E. R. 2008a. Performance criticism: A summary of assumptions, applications, assessments, and implications for Bible translation. *Tic Talk* 65:1–9 (see also http://www.ubs-translations.org/tt/past_issues/tic_talk_65_2008/).

Wendland, E. R. 2008b. *Finding and translating the oral-aural elements of written language: The case of the New Testament epistles.* Lewiston, N.Y. and Lampeter, UK: The Edwin Mellen Press.

Wendland, E. R. 2008c. Modeling the message: The christological core of Philippians (2:5–11) and its communicative implications. *Acta Patristica et Byzantina* 19:350–378.

Wendland, E. R. 2008d. *Contextual frames of reference in translation: A coursebook for Bible translators and teachers.* Manchester: St. Jerome.

Wendland, E. R. 2009. *Prophetic rhetoric: Case studies in text analysis and translation.* Longwood: Xulon Press, 2009 (second, revised and expanded edition in press, Dallas: SIL International).

Wendland, E. R. 2010 (published in 2011). Framing the frames: A theoretical framework for the cognitive notion of "frames of reference." *Journal of Translation* 6:27–50.

Wendland, E. R. 2011. *LiFE-Style translating: A workbook for Bible translators*, Second edition. Publications in Translation and Textlinguistics 2. Dallas: SIL International.

Wendland, E. R. 2013. *Lovely, lively lyrics: Selected studies in biblical Hebrew verse.* Dallas: SIL International.

Wendland, E. R. and S. Hachibamba. 2007. *Galu wamkota: Missiological reflections from South-Central Africa.* Zomba, Malawi: Kachere Series.

Wendland, E. R. and J. P. Louw. 1993. *Graphic design and Bible reading.* Cape Town: Bible Society of South Africa.

Westenholtz, J. G. 2010. Historical events and the process of their transformation in Akkadian heroic traditions. In D. Konstan and K. A. Raaflaub (eds.), *The ancient world: Comparative histories 4*, 26–50. Chichester, UK: Wiley-Blackwell.

Williams, J. and A. Chesterman. 2002. *The map: A beginner's guide to doing research in translation studies.* Manchester: St. Jerome.

Williams, P. 2010. Old Testament history—Is the playing field level. http://www.theologynetwork.org/biblical-studies/getting-stuck-in/old-testament-history-is-the-playing-field-level.htm (accessed March 15, 2010).

Wilson, J. R. 2008. Canon and theology: What is at stake? In C. A. Evans and E. Tov (eds.), *Exploring the origins of the Bible: Canon formation in historical, literary, and theological perspective*, 241–253. Grand Rapids: Baker Books.

Wilt, T. L., ed. 2003. *Bible translation: Frames of reference.* Manchester: St. Jerome.

Wilt, T. L., and E. R. Wendland. 2008. *Scripture frames and framing: A workbook for Bible translators.* Stellenbosch, South Africa: SUN Media Press.

Wire, A. C. 2011. *The case for Mark composed in performance.* Eugene, Ore.: Cascade Books.

Witherington, B., III. 2009a. *What's in the word: Rethinking the socio-rhetorical character of the New Testament.* Waco: Baylor UP.

Witherington, B., III. 2009b. *New Testament rhetoric: An introductory guide to the art of persuasion in and of the New Testament.* Eugene: Cascade Books.

Zahnd, Brian. 2012. *Beauty will save the world: Rediscovering the allure and mystery of Christianity.* Lake Mary, Fla.: Casa Creacion.

Zogbo, L., and E. Wendland. 2000. *Hebrew poetry in the Bible: A guide for understanding and for translating.* New York: United Bible Societies.

Index

A

acceptability 156
   translation 59, 72
accuracy 156n
aesthetic factor 320, 340
alliteration 129, 197, 210
   Phlm 293, 298
allusions 138
Amos 82n
anadiplosis, structural 182
analysis
   conversational 57–58
   methodology 302
   textual 2, 73, 302–314
analytical audition 287
anaphora 128, 131
   Phil 229
   structural 136, 137, 182, 307

Ancient Near Eastern norms 255
anthropomorphism 139
antithesis. *See also under* thematic
   John 17 172
aperture 272. *See also under*
   discourse
appositional doublets 210
argumentation 251n
argument peak, Phlm 296
argument-structure analysis 61–62
argument theory 62n
art 32
artistry 24n. *See also under* literary
ascribed honor 256
assonance, Phlm 293, 299
asyndeton 127
audience 30, 35, 45, 116, 250. *See*
   also under significance
education 158, 341, 345

377

engagement 285
identification 314
implied 167, 352n
intended 149
research 51
secondary 170
target 150, 315
tertiary 173
audio. *See also under* translation
features 148
"voices" 274, 281
audiovisual
complementation 141
structure, Phil 2:5–11 219–223
aural interpretation 340
author. *See also* sense: authorial
anonymity 89
implied 55n, 167, 352n
intention 55n, 98n, 108n, 190n, 215n, 274n
scribal 24
authority, Scripture 99
authorship 24, 45
individual 111
Scripture 46, 54n, 80, 85, 90n
autopsy factor 98n

B

Baruch 96n
base-amplification, John 17 179
BasisBibel 279n
beauty of translation 320
BetterBibles 322
Bible translation. *See* translation: Bible

biosphere 88n
body imagery, Phlm 294
break points, 1 Cor 13 306
breath span 209
brief (job commission), translation 64, 149, 204, 285, 314
Buku Lopatulika (Sacred Book) 145n
Buku Loyera (Holy Book) 146n, 260n

C

canon 46n
of Scripture 55n, 106, 352
canonical approach 352n
canonicity 102n
canonization 78n, 105n
Chewa language 145n
Phil 2:5–11 260
chiasmus 127, 128, 153, 197, 233, 291
1 Cor 13 306, 311
John 17 199
Phil 222, 231
Phlm 297
chirographic texts 88
chreiai 14n, 34n
Christ as model, Phil 225, 230, 236, 252, 255
christological
confession, Phil 263
core, Phil 230
texts, Phil 229
chronological Bible storying 338n

Index

chunking 100n
ciyabilo 209
  poetic devices 212
climactic pronouncement, John 17 191
closet drama 273n
closure 272
cola 292
commata 292
Common English Bible 318
Common English Version (CEV) 312
communication, communicative. *See also under* media
  effects 61
  event 166, 176
  functions 73, 121, 204, 253n
  goal. *See Skopos* (communicative goal)
  intention 61
  significance 162
  strategies 13
comparative approach 317
compensation 340
computers in translation 345
concentric structure, Phil 222, 233
contextual effects 59
contrast, Phil 226
cooperative principle 341
core values, Phil 234
cotext, Phil 224
creative. *See under* translation
crowded stage 279
cultural bias 100n
cymatics 1n

D

day of the LORD 140
Dead Sea Scrolls 105n
de-concentration of grammar 339
defamiliarization 186
demographic variables 314
diction 280. *See also under* rhythmic
direct speech 138
  John 17 177
discourse
  analysis 116, 166, 302
  aperture 128
  constituents, John 17 178
  didactic 171
  display chart 124
  markers 148
    Phil 238, 240
  structure 41
    John 17 175–184
    Rev 5 277
    Song 8 271
divine
  declaration formulas 130, 135
  name 133
    John 17 179n
  oracle 135
doxologies, Phil 228, 229
draft translation. *See* translation: draft
dramatic
  discourse 137
  poetry, Song 273
  readings 283n
dualistic language, John 17 172
dyadic personality 256

E

education 93n
eisegesis 341
electronic communication 351n
elocution 34, 36
   public 162
emotive
   climax 308
   element 340
   translation, Song 273
emphasis 124n
encomium. *See* praise poem
   (encomium)
engagement, contextual 299
English Standard Version (ESV)
   193n
enigma 129
enjambment 131
epiphora 130, 133
   Phil 229, 240
   structural 136, 137, 182, 240
epistolary
   dialogue 238n
   formulas 240n
   genre, Phil 250n
   orality 241n
   outline, Phil 228
   structure, Phil 239
equivalence 65n
   literary 201
eschatological oracle 134
eschatology, John 17 180
essential indeterminacy 89
ethnomusicology 346n
ethnopoetics 268n
ethos-logos-pathos 251
euphony 138
exclusio 182
exegesis 161
eyewitness testimony 49, 103

F

farewell address 169
feedback encouragement 322
felicity conditions 57
field methods 342n
figurative language
   1 Cor 13 309
   John 17 200
figurative linkage 141
fluency of reading 340n
focalization 123
focus 123
   constituent 127
   particle 128, 130
      visualizing 131
form. *See under* literary
format 50, 262n, 341
   design 341
   functional 214
   interpretive 280
   literary 214
   meaning 273
   Rev 5 280
   translation 146, 267
form-functional
   analysis, target language 144
   equivalents 143
   inventory, target language 145
   profile 204

resources 142
frame-fillers 69
frames, conceptual 68n
frames of reference 18n, 66–69
   topical 124n
framework
   conceptual 68
front-shifting 123
   Phlm 295, 297
function 64
   literary 25n
functional equivalence 65, 145
functionalist theory 64–66

G

gatekeepers. *See under* scribal
genre 26n, 64
   1 Cor 13 311
   factor 345n
gobbets 86
Good News Translation (GNT) 277
Gospel tradition 87
Gricean maxims 57–58

H

hearing the Word 355
Hebrews 189n
hermeneutical tradition 55n
hiatus 294, 297
high-context cultures 20n
higher criticism 21n
high-value text 6
hinge verse
   1 Cor 12:31 305

Phil 246
holiness code 256
honor-shame 255, 256
hortatory discourse, Phil 230
humiliation-exaltation of Christ 222

I

ideology 67n, 316
ideophone 13n, 144
idiomatic expressions, Tonga 211
illocution 60, 253, 311
illocutionary
   force, John 17 173
   goals, Phil 253–254
   intent 167
imagery 132, 133, 137. *See also under* body; sound
   mythic 140
implicatures 57–58
inclusio 128, 132, 134, 136, 182
   Phil 248
   Phlm 296
indentation marking 277
inference 59
information structure 122
inspiration 55n, 167
intensification 124
intercessory illocutions, John 17 171
interjective comments 210
internet forum 347
intertextuality 46n, 138, 148n, 352n
   John 17 168, 169
   Phil 237n, 257

intonational features 54n
intratextual
  linkage, John 17 184
  recursion, 1 Cor 13 308
intratextuality 139
inverted structure, Phil 221
irony 129
Isaiah 117n, 163
  Isa 61–66 119
  Isa 66 118
  Isa 66:1–16 117–142
  Isa 66:17–24 119n
isomorphic equivalent 213

J

James 238n
Jeremiah 80n
Jerusalem School of Synoptic Research 101n
Jesus as Lord, Phil 235
Jewish motifs, John 17 177n
Job 87n
  drama 338n
  poetry 338n
job description. *See* brief (job commission), translation
John, Apostle 102
John, Gospel
  John 17 165–216
joy, Phil 227n

K

key
  concepts, Phil 236
  terms. *See also under* repetition 307
    Phil 230
King James Version (KJV) 162
knowledge, John 17 174

L

Lamentations 352n
lexical balance 223
listening 354–355
literacy 99n, 351n. *See also under* literary
  ANE 42
literary. *See also under* equivalence; format; function; translation
  artistry 141
  evaluation 25
  form 24
  functional equivalence (LiFE) 65, 203, 258
  literacy 345n
  marking 225
  quality 204
  structure 135n
    John 17 182–183
  studies 65n
literary-rhetorical
  analysis 120–124, 218n
  features, John 17 198
literary-structural
  analysis 304
  devices 240n
  markers, Phil 229
  overview, Phil 238
literature 24–26. *See also under* oral; poetic

of Scripture 25, 70, 86n
liturgical version 66
locution 60, 253, 311
locutionary form 167
logotactics, John 17 185
Lord's prayer 187
Luke-Theophilus 108n
lyric
  lament 69
  poetry
    1 Cor 13 301–335
  prose 218

M

macrochiastic structure, Phil 232n
macro-illocution, John 168
macro-structural comparison, Phil 4 248
macro-structure 66n
manuscript evidence 95n
marked features 121
Mark, Gospel 43n, 95n
Masoretic
  segmentation 122n
  Text 105n, 107n, 110n, 190n
meaning
  connotative 203
  denotative 203
  formal 202
  manifold 176
  multimodal 50n
media
  of communication 315
  of transmission 51, 343
medium shift 205
memorability 162

memorial processes 103
memorializing activities 104
memorizability 44, 162, 262
memorization 39, 44, 48, 92, 93, 94n, 97
  of Scripture 350, 352
  Phil 234
memory 34, 38–44
  aids 14n
    Phil 235
  collective 39n, 40
  communicative 39
  cultural 39
  sites of 102n
  structure, Phil 248
  technologies 43
  variants 94
merismus 126
message. *See also under* modeling
  mismatches 52
micro-frames 68
middle-of-the-road version 316
minimax principle 59
mnemonic
  devices 13, 39n, 41, 102
  structure, Phil 233
model. *See* Christ as model, Phil
modeling 227
  message 217–264, 263
    in translation 259
  Phil 237
motivational topics, Phil 233
motivation for an appeal 63
mouvance 89
multimodality 49–52. *See also under* meaning

musical
  mode 343n
  rendition 338n
  transposition 212
music in translation 343

N

ndakatulo 160, 206n, 260
networking in translation 346–349
New English Translation (NET) 268, 302
New Living Translation (NLT) 149, 277, 319
non-print. *See under* translation
non-verbal
  devices 36
  dimension 339n
  features 72, 276
nthano (Chewa) 19

O

Onesimus 294. *See also* Philemon-Onesimus
opponents, Phil 252n
oracles of salvation 118
oral
  assessment 161
  communication 175
  composition 16, 54
  elocution, Phil 248
  history 98, 102n
  interpretation 190, 340
    Rev 5 281
  learners 335
  literature 27
  performance 29
  potential 37
  proclamation 219
  Scripture 355
  style 43n
  stylistics 154
  tradition 47, 49, 88, 98, 107
  transmission 102, 103
  typesetting 188–189
oral-aural. *See also under* translation
  adjustments, Rev 5 281
  aids to memory 262
  analysis 287, 337
  approach 74
  "asides" 275
  checking 320
  clues 162
  cues 338
  dimension 319, 349
  dynamics 267
  emphasis 275
  envelope 259
  evaluative criteria 157
  factor 115, 336n
  features 22
    1 Cor 13 312
    poetic 275
  markers, 1 Cor 13 315
  medium 3
  methodology 120
  organization, Phil 241
  paratext 52
  potential 175

Index

signals, Phil 238
style 19
text "breaks" 275
training 345
translation, 1 Cor 13 315
translation techniques 344
oral-elocutionary
  analysis 176
  structure, John 17 192
orality 1, 3, 12, 18–21, 98, 160. *See also under* epistolary
  amplifying 163
  and writing 351
  essential 274
  factor 337n
  in translation 262
  in translation studies 342n, 345n
  markers 116, 117, 188–191
  model 104
  of Scripture 350
  persistent 14
  primary 19n
  studies 17, 101n, 347
  target language 142
orality-oriented version 148
  Song 8 269
oralized version 147
orally-modified version 150
oral-rhetorical approach 250
oral-written. *See also under* stylistic
  continuum 28
  interaction 110
  interface 48n, 97
  style 136
  transmission 94
oratorical 65
  style 99
  translation 142, 156, 176, 204n, 218, 348
  version 74
    Phil 258
oratory 27
orature 26–28
original text 87, 88, 90n, 106n
  multiple 47n, 106n
  Scripture 78, 107
  virtual 108n

P

Papias 104
Paraclete 187
paradigmatic-topical analysis 176
paradigm shift 348n
paraenetic
  discourse 63
  thesis, Phil 229
parallel 199
  pericopes, Phil 230
  phrasing, Phlm 296
  structures, John 17 182
parallelism 137, 149
  poetic, Phil 4 249
  syntactic, Phlm 295
Paratext 7.1 304n
paratextual
  features 71
  tools 51
pause points 341
peak. *See also* argument peak, Phil

emotive, Song 8 272n
of discourse, Phil 234n
semantic 308
thematic, Song 8 272n
performance 29–32, 97n. *See also under* oral; scribal; scripting for performance; translation
   criticism 5, 37, 56, 69–73, 97n
      biblical 31, 347
   dimension 339
   directions 13
   event 29n
   features 20
   interpretation 340n
   mode 19n
   notes 344
   perspective 175
   "script" 276
   style 18
performative approach 56
performing Scripture 268
   Phlm 299
periods, Greco-Roman 292
perlocution 60, 253, 311
perlocutionary effects 167
   John 17 172
persuasion 32. *See also under* rhetorical
petitions, John 17 179–180
Philemon-Onesimus 295, 296
Philippians 1:14 1
phonic
   correspondents 338
   dimension 259
   factor 12, 54

phonological
   devices, James 238n
   equivalence 216
   factor, John 17 201n
   features 268
   phrase 123n
   properties 312
poetic. *See also under* ciyabilo; parallelism
   devices, John 17 197
   format 155
      1 Cor 13 313
      John 17 202
   function of literature 201
   genres, target language 205
   lineation 148
   lines. *See* cola
   marking 220
   prose
      1 Cor 13 312, 318
      John 17 181, 185, 192
   re-creation 205
   redundancy 211
   structure, Song 8 272
   style, John 17 202
   syntax, Tonga 211
poetically organized discourse 218
poetic-architectonic analysis 181–184
poetry 161, 343. *See also* dramatic; Job; *ndakatulo*
   sung 343n
polysyndeton, John 17 200
post-colonialism 109
postmodernism 109n

Index

power and solidarity, John 17 174
pragmatic
  analysis 254
  intent 176
pragmatics 57
praise poem *(encomium)* 261, 311
prayer 165–175. *See also* Lord's prayer
  didactic 170
  Jesus 174
predictive. *See under* prophecy
pre-texts, Isa 139–140
principle of relevance 58, 66n
production guidelines 344
pronominal
  emphasis, Phlm 296
  forms, John 17 199
pronunciatio 36
prophecy 116n
  predictive 138n
prophetic. *See also* transmission
  characters 83
  genres 118
  performer 81
  proclamation formula 128n, 131
prosaic style 134
prose. *See under* lyric; poetic
prosodic
  features 54
  word 123n
proverbs 211
Psalm 114 337
published Bible format 213
publishing factors 341
punning 82n

Q

qualitative assessment 215
Qumran 43n
quote margins 190

R

rabbinic. *See also* scribal/rabbinic model; transmission: rabbinic
  techniques 93
radio 143
  script 342n
reader-response criticism 190n
redundancy. *See under* poetic features 339
re-familiarization, John 17 187
refrains, Song 272
reinforcement, John 17 174
reiteration, John 17 199
rejoicing, Phil 235
relevance theory 58–60, 341n. *See also* principle of relevance
re-oralizing Scripture 116, 268, 284
  Isa 66:1–3 145–156
repetition 137
  1 Cor 13 307
  key terms 307–308
research factors 342
Revelation 5 277–284
rhetoric 24n, 32–36, 175, 202, 251
  deliberative 33, 252
  epideictic 33, 252
  Greco-Roman 33, 34, 250, 292
  judicial 33, 252

rhetorical. *See also under* target
language (TL)
  analysis 250
  argument 178
    Phil 251
  argumentation 33
  canons 33
  criticism 32
  culture 43, 95, 173
  dynamics 191
  exigence 254–255
  functions 191, 213
  logic, John 17 185
  persuasion, Phil 257
  processes 191n
  questions 56, 129, 130
    Tonga 211
  species 252
  strategy, Isa 134n
  structure, Phil 228
  theory 35n
  triangle 251
rhyme 130
  internal, Phlm 293
rhythmic
  diction, Phlm 295
  envelope, John 17 188–191
  pronunciation 148
  sequence 127
ring constructions, John 17 182, 183n

S

salience 69
SBL (Society of Biblical Literature) 53n, 347n

schemata 68
scribal. *See also under* author; tradents
  additions 81n
  composition 85, 87
  features 22n
  gatekeepers 79
  manipulation 77
  performance 84
  performer 79
  pluriformity 107n
  power dynamics 82, 83n
scribality 21–24
scribal/rabbinic model 100
scribes 21, 80, 100n, 110n
  hyperactive 23
  passive 22
  proactive 23
scripting for performance 344
Scripture 11, 47, 77, 78n, 99n. *See also under* authority, Scripture; authorship; canon; literature; memorization; oral; theology of Scripture; transmission
  composition 101
  engagement 353
  use 350
  vocal articulation 350
scrolls 15, 38, 42n
semantic. *See also under* peak
  analysis 308
  density 224n
    John 17 180, 186
  network, John 17 185
sense
  authorial 174n

textual 55n
service ideal 256
setumah 128
Shema 171n
shift, significant 306
significance. *See also under* communication, communicative; sonic
  audience 174n
  textual 55n
sites of memory. *See under* memory
Skopos (communicative goal) 36, 64–65, 149, 285
social-scientific
  approach, Phil 255
  criticism 62n
sociolinguistics 57n
socio-rhetorical functions 205
Song of Songs 268–276
songs, biblical 71n
sonic. *See also under* translation
  background 281
  dimension 26
  medium 12
  methodology 299
  significance 54
  structure, Phlm 287–300
sound
  effects 163
  imagery 136
  mapping 121, 188n
  sequences, John 17 198
  similarity 130, 132
  symmetry 131
    Phil 226
    Phlm 297

sound-responsive analysis 161, 337
soundscape 6, 339n
source language (SL) 26n
spatialization of discourse 120
speech acts 60–61, 73, 204, 253, 311
  analysis 166
  approach 253
  theory 60–61, 166n
speech events 61
spoken-written word 110
stanzas, Song 8 271
status 256
strophes 135, 220
  1 Cor 13 306
strophic
  aperture 135
  boundaries 306
  units 148
strophic structure
  Isa 66:1–16 133–136
  Phil 2:1–4 248
structural
  design 100
  evaluation 249
  form 41
  markers
    Isa 66:1–16 135
    John 17 199
    Phil 241
  variation 198
structural-thematic
  outline 310
  summary, Isa 66: 1–16 135–136
study notes 262n

stylistic
  convergence, 1 Cor 13 308
  devices 191
  distribution 144
  mixing, oral-written 27
supplication 171
synagogue 43n, 105
Synoptic Gospels 101n
syntactic analysis 122
syntactic clues 120n
syntagmatic-propositional analysis 178–181
synthetic translation. *See* translation: synthetic

T

target language (TL) 26n, 258. *See also* orality; poetic: genres, target language
  artistic resources 345n
  research 143, 162, 342
  rhetorical resources 345n
technique 32. *See also* oral-aural: translation
testing a translation. *See* translation: testing
text 40n. *See also* analysis: textul; sense: textual; significance: textual; transmission: text; written text; *See also under* textual
  acts 167, 311
  Scripture 3n
  synthesis 314
textual

criticism 106, 108, 304
  flexibility hypothesis 90
  mobility 89
  re-creation 89
  variation 109
textuality 47n
thematic. *See also under* peak
  antithesis 132
  cluster, Phil 235
  headings, 1 Cor 13 310
  recycling, Phil 237
  reversal, John 17 181
  themes, John 17 169, 178
theology of Scripture 79
thesis statement, Phil 224n
The Voice 283
throne room vision, Rev 4–5 277n
Tonga
  language 206
  stylistic devices 210–212
topical
  interweaving, John 17 184
  sequence, Phil 241
topicalization 123
topics 123. *See also* motivational topics, Phil
  John 17 176–177
tradents 94
  scribal 79
tradition 45–49. *See also under* oral
  eyewitness 92n
traditional
  performing arts 31n
  verbal art forms 342, 342n

Index

training. *See also under* oral-aural
  translators 345
  workshop 346n
transcription 143
transculturation 273, 341
transdisciplinary approach 336n
translation 2, 73. *See also under* acceptability; emotive; format; modeling; message; music in translation; oral-aural; orality; oratorical; performance
  analytical 322
  articulation 74
  audio 273n
  audiovisual 52, 276, 282, 351n
  Bible 106–111, 115
  challenge 335
  comparison 319
  creative 336
  draft 317–319
  evaluation 157
  genre-matching 261
  genre-oriented 206
  guidelines, 1 Cor 13 317
  literary 161
    1 Cor 13 332
  matching 259n
  methodology 206, 215, 314, 317
  missionary 146
  multimedia 50, 345
  non-print 343
  performance 320
  phonic-poetic 216
  polemics 316n
  popular-language 146
  quality 156
  setting of use 315
  sonic 215
  studies 160–163
  synthetic 322
  team 317
  testing 4, 157, 159, 321, 339–341
    instructions 158
    methods 158
    oral-aural 63
    performance 156–160, 343n
    procedures 321
    stylistic 144
  type 316
translator as mediator 340n
transmediazation 344n
transmission. *See also under* media; oral; oral-written
  prophetic 96
  rabbinic 97, 103, 106
  Scripture 2–3, 78, 83n, 100n, 335
  text 15
    fluidity 88n
    models 103
    pluriform model 110n
    restrained 92
typographical layout 213, 288n
typography 50, 63n, 280, 341

U

unity, Christian 225
Urtext 82n
utterance

markers, John 17 197
units 192, 292, 312

V

valorization 91
variation. *See under* memory; structural; textual; word order
verbless utterance 129, 133
visual pun. *See* punning
vocal articulation. *See under* Scripture
vocal characterization, Rev 5 282
vocatives, John 17 198, 210
voiceprints 19
voice-typing 281

W

word of the LORD 142
word order
   Hebrew 123
   variations, John 17 200
wordplay 82n, 127, 133
   Phlm 294
workshop training, *See under* training
worldview 67n
writing 15, 96. *See also* orality: and writing
written text 95, 101

SIL International Publications
Additional Releases in the
Publications in Translation and Textlinguistics Series

5. **Lovely, lively lyrics; selected studies in biblical Hebrew verse,** by Ernst R. Wendland, 2013, 461 pp., ISBN 978-1-55671-327-9
4. **The development of textlinguistics in the writings of Robert Longacre,** by Shin Ja Hwang, 2010, 423 pp., ISBN 978-1-55671-246-3
3. **Artistic and rhetorical patterns in Quechua legendary texts,** by Ågot Bergli, 2010, 304 pp., ISBN 978-1-55671-244-9
2. **LiFE-style translating: A workbook for translators,** by Ernst R. Wendland, 2006, 347 pp., ISBN 978-1-55671-167-1
1. **Translating the literature of scripture: A literary-rhetorical approach to Bible translation,** by Ernst R. Wendland, 2004, 509 pp., ISBN 978-1-55671-152-7

SIL International Publications
7500 W. Camp Wisdom Road
Dallas, TX 75236-5629

Voice: 972-708-7404
Fax: 972-708-7363
publications_intl@sil.org
http://www.sil.org/resources/publications

www.ingramcontent.com/pod-product-compliance
Lightning Source LLC
Chambersburg PA
CBHW052139300426
44115CB00011B/1441